Martin Short is the author of the bestselling *Inside the Brotherhood: Furthe~~~~~~~~~~~~~~~~~~~~~~~~~~~~ime Inc.: A History o~~~~~~~~~~~~~~~~~~~~~~~~~~~~lso co-authored (in ~~~~~~~~~~~~~~~~~~~~~~~~~~~ut police corruption~~~~~~~~~~~~~~~~~

After reading h~~~~~~~~~~~~~~~~~~~~~~~~~~tin Short worked – fro~~~~~~~~~~~~~~~~~~~~~~~~~~~irs programmes for th~~~~~~~~~~~~~~~~~~~~~~~~~~nd London Weekend. ~~~~~~~~~~~~~, produced and narrated the prize-winning ITV documentary series on the Mafia in America, *Crime Incorporated*, and in 1989 completed a TV series based on his book *Inside the Brotherhood* for the ITV network with Twenty Twenty Television and Granada. He is now an independent producer.

MARTIN SHORT

Lundy

The Destruction of
Scotland Yard's Finest Detective

Grafton
An Imprint of HarperCollins*Publishers*

Grafton
An Imprint of HarperCollins*Publishers*
77–85 Fulham Palace Road,
Hammersmith, London W6 8JB

Published by Grafton 1992
9 8 7 6 5 4 3 2 1

First published in Great Britain by
GraftonBooks 1991

Copyright © Martin Short 1991

The Author asserts the moral right to
be identified as the author of this work

ISBN 0 586 20964 6

Set in Times

Printed in Great Britain by
HarperCollinsManufacturing Glasgow

Contents

Acknowledgements

I owe my thanks to very many people. They include dozens of detectives serving in the Metropolitan Police and other forces. For obvious reasons, they cannot be named. Many former officers have also helped me, as is evident from the text. I thank all those I have quoted by name, but most of the rest prefer to remain anonymous.

I must also thank many members of North London's underworld, but again they need to keep their heads down and do not wish to be identified. Certain non-criminal residents of Finchley have also been most considerate. Some Customs officers too deserve my gratitude.

I owe a vast debt to other journalists, not only those named in the text but hundreds more whose pieces I have gutted in order to summarize crimes, court cases and other relevant events. It would be invidious to thank some by name but not others. The only exceptions I make are Graeme McLagan, whose past work on this affair was as valuable to me as his enduring neutrality, and Brian Hilliard.

I have long respected the work of Paul Lashmar, Andrew Jennings and Vyv Simson, so it is with regret that I have come to disagree with them over Tony Lundy. We do not see eye-to-eye but I must say that their articles, programmes and book have been very useful to me in writing this book. No doubt the controversy will continue.

I may openly thank Craig Lovato of America's Drug Enforcement Administration and Charles Scott. My wife deserves the usual medal for her patience, endurance and stamina during yet another painful act of creation.

Finally, I owe the title of Chapter 13 to the headline for an article in *Time Out*.

Prologue
Straight Cop

This is the story of Tony Lundy, Britain's most successful and most controversial detective, a policeman who solved more serious crimes and put more major criminals in jail than any other officer in the 160-year history of Scotland Yard. In a meteoric career this blunt, working-class Lancastrian became London's outstanding thief-taker, leading a team which greatly contributed to the biggest fall during the past twenty years in the capital's otherwise soaring armed robbery rate. He went on to spearhead multi-national investigations that tracked down some two hundred million pounds of illicit profits in the world's dirty-money machines. He is still the only senior British detective whose results show he understood and could combat the late-twentieth-century revolution in organized crime activity: from armed robbery, to narcotics, to washing drug proceeds and other bent billions through the international banking system. He matched the gangsters move for move, and his crime-fighting skills drove one leading English crook, stuck in a cell 4,000 miles away fighting extradition, to beg Scotland Yard, 'take Lundy off my case!'

His skills were formidable. He was successful and forceful. He clearly had many detractors. He achieved what he set out to do and sometimes annoyed other officers by his single-minded approach to the task in hand. He did not take to either 'time servers' or those who, for one reason or another, were unsuccessful. His record as a murder investigator was excellent. His manner was of a man who got results but he did not care who knew it.

That is how Detective Superintendent (now Commander) John Grieve described Lundy in 1987 in a statement to a police corruption inquiry. As staff officer to the chief of all Metropolitan detectives in the mid-1980s, Grieve was privy to much sensitive inside knowledge of the 'Lundy affair' when it threatened to split Scotland Yard wide open. For as well as being a superb thief-taker, Lundy became the most investigated copper in British police history. Through the 1980s he was subjected to unrelenting inquiries by anti-corruption squads who, despite limitless resources, came up with no evidence to justify criminal charges.

Instead, Lundy was subject to a decade of trial by press and television. Several investigative reporters concluded he was 'bent' – corrupt – but they never produced any direct evidence. In 1990 there appeared a book which implied he was the inside man on a £100 million drug-smuggling conspiracy – nothing less than *Scotland Yard's Cocaine Connection* – yet even this publication, the fruit of many years' research, failed to prove anything of the sort. Instead the three authors blended a little circumstantial evidence with layers of coincidence and innuendo and the views of a few retired detectives, to mount a superficially persuasive case that Lundy must have been a crook in cop's clothing all along.

It was only in 1986 that I began to look deeply into the 'Lundy affair', despite the fact that I had reported on Metropolitan Police corruption for the previous thirteen years: on television, in newspapers and in a book, *The Fall of Scotland Yard*, which I co-authored. From 1978 I had closely monitored the calamitous saga of Operation Countryman (the provincial investigation into alleged corruption among London detectives) but from the start of 1981 until autumn 1984 I was wholly involved in preparing a television history of organized crime in America, *Crime*

Inc., which I originated, co-produced, wrote and narrated. For much of this period I was living in America, and it took me more than a year to regain some grasp of Metropolitan Police affairs. By then the alleged crimes of Tony Lundy had long been an urgent topic of conversation among London journalists with an interest in the seedier side of Scotland Yard. My inclination was to believe the worst, on the grounds that in the 1960s and 1970s the truth about London's CID had almost always turned out to be far worse than even the most shocking rumour, but then it dawned on me that none of these journalists had managed to question Tony Lundy about the allegations. Some had tried but apparently he had always referred them to Scotland Yard's press bureau which ritually rejected such approaches.

In 1985 I became deeply concerned at the Yard's fierce, sustained and ultimately successful campaign to prevent the BBC broadcasting a *Brass Tacks* programme, in principle because it offended my belief that no vested interest should be allowed to block any programme, but specifically because this move deprived me of seeing at last what I thought would be the conclusive proof that Lundy was indisputably corrupt.

Half-way through 1986 my curiosity finally got the better of me and I approached Tony Lundy direct. It was only after many weeks, and the emergence of much of the suppressed *Brass Tacks* research in an edition of ITV's *World in Action*, that I first met the man. There was nothing surreptitious about the encounter (later I found out that he had told his commanding officer of my approach before seeing me) but I soon became aware that behind his bald, full-moon face and his piercing blue eyes was a seething sense of injustice about his treatment by one faction of the media and an extreme caution about someone like me who might be regarded as belonging to that same hostile fraternity. Yet the mere fact that he had agreed to see me was itself a pointer to the possibility that he might after all be a straight copper with nothing to hide.

In occasional meetings during the next two years (including a seventeen-month period of suspension) Lundy told me enough to refute the most damning allegations published against him and to convince me that straight he probably was. It was only in 1989 when he was out of the force that he was free to tell me much more, not only proving beyond infinitesimal doubt that he was straight but showing that his downfall had been achieved largely by a combination of avenging criminals and fellow London detectives, of whom some may genuinely have believed Lundy was 'bent', but others seem to have been bitter at what, they felt, were the machinations of successive Scotland Yard hierarchies against them during the previous twenty years. Some of his detractors believed Lundy was the creature of those power structures, a thief-taking myth invented by men far more cunning than he for their own devious purposes. Ironically, Lundy saw himself to be a victim of those same forces but on entirely different grounds: they had aggrandized themselves on the back of his achievements but distanced themselves from him as soon as the going got rough.

This book is based partly on long interviews which I conducted with Tony Lundy. In the course of cross-examining him at mutually exhaustive length on every single allegation of which I am aware, I feel I have come to know him pretty well. He lacks the easy charm, bluff chumminess and hail-fellow-well-met style affected by many London detectives (including a number of officers whom I had met in earlier years only to find out later that they were deeply corrupt and destined for jail). In contrast Lundy has an ascetic air which must have rubbed many of his one-time colleagues up the wrong way: part mean

Northerner among flash Cockneys ridiculing his contorted vowels, part Catholic outsider in a largely masonic culture, part workaholic achiever out of step with many men accustomed to a less-than-demanding workload. Such officers could not have felt comfortable with his near-obsession about physical fitness and long-distance running. Occasionally I have seen the flash of horror in his gaze at my vast girth and gross lack of fitness. He is about the same height as I, yet I am 100 pounds heavier than he is. I guessed that such a man must have been difficult for less self-disciplined mortals to work with. I later discovered this was indeed true. One still-serving detective chief superintendent put it this way:

Tony used to upset many people because he never stopped working. At the end of the day most officers like to put their feet up and take it easy. Not Tony. He'd be driving everyone on, dreaming up new ways to gather evidence, develop informers and discover who did what crime. That ferocious commitment didn't go down well with a lot of his colleagues. It made him a lot of great cases, but a lot of enemies too.

Some of those former colleagues resent the suggestion that his staggering thief-taking statistics were achieved by his own hard work and ability. One told me that in his early career Lundy had been a constable with neither personality nor talent and that his subsequent successes could be put down entirely to the fact that he had been 'bag-carrier' to an older generation of corrupt detectives, who had initiated him in the crooked old ways of dealing with informants. When I pointed out that Lundy had never worked with any of the officers whom this person had named, I was told that the corrupting process had taken place outside working hours, through meetings in north London pubs, arranged by means of telephone calls overheard by my source. When I confronted Lundy with this allegation, he said he could recall no occasion on which he had ever received any calls from those far more senior officers, whom he had met only socially at charity amateur boxing shows. He was adamant that they had never discussed detective work with him or introduced him to any informants. My source's claim was yet another lie, he said. Some twenty years on it is impossible to prove or disprove. An objective investigator can only try to look at the man from all angles and arrive at a dispassionate judgement, but dispassion is the rarest quality when people talk of Tony Lundy. It seems you either hated him or you idolized him. One serving chief inspector volunteered this tribute:

I worked with Tony Lundy very closely and I've got the greatest admiration for him and I think he was very badly done by. Among 27,000 serving Metropolitan officers there might be some who disagree but I found him a very good man to work for and a great asset to the force.

Retired Detective Chief Superintendent Dave Little was his superior:

I've got the highest regard for Tony Lundy and I've never once doubted his integrity. He must have been *the* most successful detective certainly during the period I served in the force. I can't think of anybody else who achieved anything like what he achieved and certainly there would be a lot of professional jealousy. Not that I was ever jealous of the fellow. He was a hard-working good detective and I was very pleased to think he was one of my staff.

A serving senior officer justifies his dislike for Lundy this way:

I think he was driven by a lot of ambition and a lot of people were pushed aside by him. We were colleagues from way back, we were aids to CID together, so we know each other well. I've got no reason to consider him corrupt but I would query his motivation on certain things. I'll say no more than that.

Most past and present police with direct knowledge of Tony Lundy do not hold that view, Commander John Grieve for example.

His conduct with me was always amiable and professional. Many of my colleagues seem to share a view of him which I would describe as a man whose comments were always positive. Sometimes unpalatable, tactlessly and forcibly expressed, but never negative. He was a useful, valuable tool.[1]

A tool is all a detective really is: a tool of his bosses in the force, a tool of their political masters and – ultimately – a tool of the public, honed to protect property, catch criminals, recover stolen goods and more or less keep the peace. And no matter how 'big' a cop becomes or how glamorous his image, he is always dispensable. Clean or corrupt, bent or brilliant, any detective may find he has become a liability to the force and his talents are no longer required. Once his edge is seriously blunted, another 'tool' – however poorly made – can always be found to replace him.

Detectives are only one tool in the law enforcement kit. Another is the informer, the criminal insider who betrays underworld comrades out of revenge, to eliminate rivals, sometimes just for the thrill of it, but usually for rewards. The best 'snouts', like the best detectives, are vital weapons in the credibility battle which police chiefs perpetually fight with both public and politicians. As one senior officer allegedly told a remarkably productive informer, 'Get back out on the streets again and get a few more bodies in. Results, statistics, that's all people think about. Get back out there and help us!'[2]

It was Lundy's connection with a particularly high-grade informer, Roy Garner, that eventually caused the detective's downfall. Garner was a substantial criminal whose double role became public when confidential documents were leaked by other detectives, and Lundy's one-time chief, former Deputy Assistant Commissioner David Powis, succeeded in a libel action against the *Observer* newspaper. This had the unforeseen consequence (deeply deplored by Powis himself) that further documents were published which confirmed that Garner was an informant and Lundy was his 'handler'.

Many media exposés have harped on the fact that while Garner was collecting large rewards for informing on major crimes he was himself an active criminal. The two roles are not incompatible. Indeed, they complement each other and may be mutually essential. So observed Daniel Defoe in 1725 when considering the rise of an even more notorious informer, Jonathan Wild. 'All just governments discover a disposition to bring offenders to justice,' said Defoe, and that is why they 'receive and accept informations of the worst of crimes from the worst of criminals'.[3]

To quote John Grieve again, Roy Garner 'was an outstanding informer, who cost the public purse little. He was dangerous and undoubtedly deeply criminal. So are nearly all the top informers.'

Lundy has always acknowledged knowing Garner but will still not discuss the specific role or contribution of any particular informer, on the grounds that any such discussion would breach the trust which must exist between a detective and his sources. In this book, therefore, all references to Garner's informant role are based on official documentation to which I have gained unprecedented access (through various confidential sources of which I as a journalist must be as protective as if I were a detective) or on material previously published elsewhere. It is a stark reality that if Britain's police were to become known for betraying the identity of informers, most sources of information would soon dry up, and the service's dismal rate of solving serious crimes would plunge even lower.

The irony is that while by definition an informer is a creature whose trade is treachery, he must be handled with the utmost loyalty. Indeed, the more he betrays his criminal kind, the more he must be protected by the police. This does not mean giving him a free pass to commit crime, only protecting his identity as an informer. According to Lundy, that is all he ever sought to do for his informers. Contrary to the worst interpretation, he never shielded any of them from investigation and often told them he would be the first to arrest them if he found out they were actively involved in crime. If Roy Garner really was 'The Untouchable' or Mr 'Not To Be Proceeded With', as some officers who targeted him from 1980 came to believe, that was not due to any power of Lundy's. For years dozens of detectives had the task of nailing Garner. When they failed some blamed Lundy as if he was the Godfather's Godfather. Yet if he had ever been given the job of investigating Garner himself, there should be little doubt that he would have made a better job of it than his critics.

As it happens, Scotland Yard's CID hierarchy operated a policy of not letting the left hand know what the right hand was doing. Lundy was Garner's authorized handler. He had the job of encouraging him to 'shop' the under-world. Other officers had the job of investigating Garner and putting him in jail, without (it seems) being formally told he was an informer. For some months neither 'side' knew of the other's existence, but there was nothing sinister in this. Indeed, it would seem important that they did not know. At deputy assistant commissioner level both lots of information could be considered and compared. A relatively lowly officer like Lundy would have no power to insulate Garner from the due process of law. If Garner was *untouchable*, rather than *uncatchable*, the responsibility lies higher up Scotland Yard's greasy pole.

In this book I endeavour to tell, for the first time, the true story of the Lundy–Garner relationship. Although one can rarely prove a negative, I also feel it is justifiable to assert that Lundy is not guilty of any of these offences:

Knowing Garner was an active criminal and not taking action against him.

Shielding Garner from other detectives' investigations.

Supporting Garner in bogus reward claims.

Authenticating information from Garner on crimes which Garner had set up in order to claim rewards.

Having a corrupt relationship with Garner, by taking a share of his rewards.

Being a co-conspirator with Garner in Britain's biggest-ever detected cocaine importation.

Tipping off Garner or any other alleged participant in that cocaine importation that they were being investigated.

Living a lifestyle above his police income, indicating that some of his wealth must have come from corrupt activities.

It has also been claimed that Lundy built his career on information from Garner. That is untrue. Only a small portion of his triumphs stemmed from their relationship. Lundy had many underworld informers and he persuaded many more crooks to go public as 'supergrasses'. Their testimony sent hundreds of criminals to jail for thousands of years. Yet despite his remarkable ability to 'turn' villains, it was through his mastery of other skills, and sheer hard work, that he rapidly climbed the CID ladder and in

1980 stood on the verge of achieving a glittering career in Scotland Yard's highest ranks.

His very success brought bitter consequences. The more he succeeded the more he was reviled: by criminals he put away, by lawyers who defended them, and by press and TV reporters who sniffed a mega-conspiracy led by Britain's most brilliantly crooked cop. Yet despite ten years under the microscope, none of their claims against him has been found worthy of submitting to an English jury. After spending millions of pounds of tax-payers' money, all his final police investigators could muster were six minor discipline charges. These were either baseless or merely procedural, but to fight them would have cost him £30,000 which he could never have recovered.

Even if Lundy had spent that much to clear his name, he was a 'busted flush'. By 1988 the media had branded him so corrupt that he was being seen as a liability by the very force he had served with such distinction for so long. He retired from the Metropolitan Police on ill-health grounds after twenty-seven years' service. Yet, he says, he had never been corrupt. Indeed, it seems it was the arrogant way he wore his integrity which had aroused anger and jealousy in other men, and ultimately caused his downfall. He was also naive. He really believed that virtue has its own reward, and his name would surely be cleared on the simple grounds that he had done nothing wrong.

Let not your peace depend on the tongues of men. For whether they put a good or a bad construction on what you do, you are still what you are.
                    Thomas à Kempis, 'Against the Tongues of Slanderers'

Rather than trust to the solace of a saint, Tony Lundy would have done better to adopt the stoicism far better suited to the high politics of Scotland Yard:

Begin each day by telling yourself today I shall be meeting with interference, ingratitude, insolence, disloyalty, ill-will and selfishness – all of them due to the offenders' ignorance of what is good or evil.

Marcus Aurelius

1

Rain Man

Belgrave Close, Oakwood, is a drab dead end of lock-up garages built next to a railway line in outer North London. Only the most pressing business could have dragged dozens of police to this back alley late at night on 3 June 1980: the search for nearly three and a half million pounds' worth of silver, stolen ten weeks earlier in Britain's biggest-ever robbery.

At £340,000 the standard ten per cent reward should have provoked a torrent of tip-offs from London's ever-treacherous underworld. Yet two months after the robbery there was still no hint of the bullion's whereabouts or who had stolen it. Not a whisper. Until out of the blue a trusted informant called a meeting with Detective Chief Inspector Anthony Lundy and named some of the robbers. Lundy, head of Finchley Robbery Squad, had already caused the arrest of one of the men, Micky Gervaise, over a series of major burglaries. Now police rounded up four of the others, including Lennie Gibson whom Lundy soon persuaded to hand back the loot. At eleven that Tuesday night Gibson led Lundy and other senior detectives to Belgrave Close and pointed to garage 17. He had no key so Chief Superintendent Taylor used a jemmy to prise open the door. At first all that could be seen was a heap of wooden pallets and a motor bike. Then Eureka! The detectives spotted piles of silver bars neatly stacked at the back of the garage.

A squad of coppers was given the job of moving the bars to a safe place but they had to wait while police photographers turned up and recorded the scene, forensic scientists searched for clues, and a convoy of lorries came to carry off the load. It was going to be a long night so some officers went to a pub and brought back crates of beer. As everyone had a drink it began to rain. The downpour did not please men about to spend three hours shifting ten tonnes of metal by hand but Chief Inspector Lundy and his boss, Mike Taylor were untroubled. They were still in the garage, discussing the next phase of the operation, when they heard a shout. It was Lundy's deputy, Inspector Pat Fleming: 'Hey T.L.! Get yourself out here and stop this rain falling!'

The view that Lundy had the power to make Heaven open – or close – had long been widespread at Finchley Police Station. In two and a half years his squad had solved hundreds of robberies, put scores of major criminals in jail and brought London's robbery rate tumbling down. This astonishing achievement owed much to Lundy's remarkable knack of convincing top robbers to confess. Even more extraordinary, he talked many into 'grassing' on all their accomplices, past and present, in open court.

The bullion breakthrough was the climax to three weeks of outstanding investigation at Finchley during which three crooks had turned 'supergrass' and obliged sixty more to confess to hundreds of crimes. First-division villains were tumbling like dominoes. Dozens more arrests followed, hundreds of interviews were conducted, and the inevitable price of detective success – endless paperwork and daily court appearances – had all but exhausted the man behind it all, Tony Lundy. If a detective's success is to be judged on the number of professional criminals convicted through his efforts, then by 1980 and aged only thirty-eight Lundy was already the most successful detective in the history of the Metropolitan Police.

There was nothing in his background to indicate he would become any sort of copper. He was a Lancashire lad born into what used to be called humble circumstances on 14 April 1942 in New Springs, a coal-mining village just outside Wigan. His earliest memories are of his father, John, coming home covered in black dust from the coal face. John's parents had migrated from Ireland, like thousands who worked in Lancashire's booming coal industry at the turn of the century. Most were Roman Catholics and staunch church-goers, including the Lundy family.

John waited until he was thirty before he married Frances, an English girl from Top Lock, two miles down the road. In twelve years they had seven children: four boys and three girls, one of whom died soon after birth. Tony was the second son. The family home, a terraced house in a typical North of England cobbled street, had just two bedrooms. Life was hard, there was little money but the kids were always well-fed. They wore mostly hand-me-down clothes, and clogs – not shoes – on their feet. Against his mother's wishes Tony always told the local 'clogger' to put irons, not rubbers, on the soles. Like most village boys, he insisted on irons so he could skate down the streets.

This was the start of a very sporting life. Indeed, young Tony would become 'sport-mad'. In what now sounds like a Southern caricature of Northern existence, he, his brother and his 'old man' used to race miling pigeons and go fishing on the canal. In the summer Tony would swim in the canal, but his mother went 'potty' if she found out because the canal usually had dead dogs in it and kids used to catch jaundice. The big local team sport was rugby league. Tony's father was a devoted supporter of the legendary Wigan club. His greatest shame came when he discovered his fourth son, Bernard, had fallen for the rival rugby union code and was joining an obscure club named Orrell. For a whole year John would not speak to Bernard because this defection went against the grain.

Bernard later became Orrell's captain and coach, and
helped make it one of England's top union clubs. By
then John was talking to him again and even watched a
few of his games. Family honour was only fully redeemed
when John's daughter Margaret married Colin Clarke who
went on to play rugby league for Wigan and Great Britain,
and then became Wigan coach. Their son, Phillip, now also
plays for Wigan and has made the Great Britain team.

Years earlier Tony had also 'defected': to soccer, the
game played at the grammar school which he entered on
passing the eleven-plus. This was a rare achievement in
New Springs and the cost of the uniform strained the family
budget. There was no Catholic grammar in Wigan so every
day Tony travelled two hours to and from Thornleigh
Salesian College in Bolton, fifteen miles away. Here he
became a soccer fanatic. He played for Lancashire at
under-fifteen level and so convinced himself he was going
to join Bolton FC as a professional that he put little effort
into his studies. He left school at seventeen with five
'O' levels and went to work for an insurance firm in
Manchester. This bored him stiff but his football ambitions
were waning, so he did what many bored provincial lads
have done before and since: he joined the Metropolitan
Police.

London was unknown territory. Tony's only previous
visits to the capital had been to cheer for Wigan in rugby
league cup finals at Wembley. He began his career on 22
January 1962 with the standard three months' training at
Hendon College. He was then posted to a place he had
never heard of: Stoke Newington. When the police bus
dropped him outside the section house where he would live
for three years, he was shocked. The area was run-down
and depressed. It made even Wigan with its dying coal
mines and shut-down cotton mills seem prosperous.

Stoke Newington was where nineteen-year-old PC Lundy

did his beat training, learned how courts worked, and was ribbed mercilessly for his broad Lancashire accent. The best thing about the posting was Beresford Paul, the chief superintendent in command, who wanted his 'N' Division to be best at sports in the entire force. Paul's great love was boxing and every year he set his sights on winning the force-wide Lafone Cup, so much so that all his boxers would be spared normal duties for a straight three months so they could concentrate on training. Lundy had boxed a bit at school so he joined the team and became in effect a full-time professional sportsman, fitting in days of football between fights.

When obliged to serve the public, young Lundy showed a precocious aptitude for arrests. 'It was the usual run of offences: from burglars, to drunks to offensive weapons. When I was working I was busy, but when I didn't have to work and had to play sport, even better.' Whether for sporting ability or thief-taking flair, in 1965 he was asked if he wanted to become an 'aid to CID', the first step for anyone wanting to join Scotland Yard's prestigious Criminal Investigation Department. He leapt at the chance and soon made impressive arrests. He also learned that in 'the job' success is often soured by rebukes which seem designed to bring cocky cops crashing back to earth.

In 1965 Lundy was on duty in his private car with a Scots colleague, Jock Gardner. They were watching for burglars in Stoke Newington's back streets. If there were no burglars they would try and spot thieves stripping roof lead from derelict houses. On this day there were no burglars or thieves, so at the end of the shift Lundy started driving back to the station. Suddenly a minivan roared past from the opposite direction, with a damaged front end hanging off. Lundy had no idea why it was going so fast but he gave chase. He lost it but, as he drove round trying to spot it again, two smartly-dressed men came sauntering coolly out of a block of flats. Lundy slowed so he and Gardner could get a look at them but the men panicked and started running through the flats. The coppers jumped out and sped after them. They were at peak physical fitness and were unlikely to be outrun, but when they rounded a corner into a long straight street they could see no fugitives, only the tiny, ten-foot front gardens of the terraced houses on each side.

Lundy and Gardner figured the men had not had time to reach the far end so they proceeded up either side of the street, looking in every garden. Suddenly on Lundy's side a man hared off, hurdling the garden fences. Lundy caught up and brought him down, but the man put up a violent fight, nutting Lundy in the face and wrestling to get his hand inside his overcoat. Jock Gardner ran to Lundy's aid and the two detectives held the man down. In his overcoat they found a loaded automatic pistol. By now people had come out on the street and called for more police. The other man was found, still hiding in one of the gardens.

Lundy and Gardner had no idea what crimes went with the loaded gun as they dragged the captives into Stoke Newington 'nick', but there they ran into 'Sailor' Wright, a long-serving local PC and celebrated thief-taker. A little earlier in the day, when he was on patrol, he had seen these same characters outside an estate agents' office with a safe in the back of their van. He was not convinced when they explained 'we're just delivering it for somebody', so he stuck his arm through the driver's window to take the ignition key. At this point the van drove off with Wright half-way in, trying to grab the key, steer the car and duck the whacks which the passenger was inflicting. The van hit another vehicle, Wright was thrown on to the road and was lucky not to get killed.

When police later found the van, the safe was still inside.

It had come from a burglary in Southgate and the men had been in the estate agents trying to rent a garage where they could crack it open. It turned out they were two prisoners on the run, called Hobbs and Napier, who were later convicted and put back in jail. For Lundy it was 'a good job' and he felt he had earned a day on the sick list to nurse his injuries.

His satisfaction was short-lived. He was immediately summoned back to the station for a reprimand: he had used his private car on duty without authority. At the time this perquisite was granted only to senior officers. As an aid Lundy had no chance, even though many aids and junior detectives regularly used their cars on work. London's CID could barely have functioned without them, yet by officially banning their use Scotland Yard avoided paying mileage allowances and the high insurance costs which go with high-risk use. This was the first of Lundy's many run-ins with rule-makers in his police career, but both he and Jock Gardner were awarded a Commendation. For Lundy it was the first of thirteen from commissioners, and thirty in total from judges, the Director of Public Prosecutions and other authorities.

In May 1966, after little more than a year as an aid and temporary detective constable, Lundy was promoted to full DC and posted to West Hampstead. The same month he married Violet Moore, a bank clerk he had met at a party, given by some nurses who were friends of hers, in Bethnal Green. The couple spent all their savings on a honeymoon in the Canary Isles (Tony's first trip abroad), then moved into a furnished flat in Enfield, North London. Vi was working in the City, and by 1967 the couple had saved enough money to buy the furniture they needed to move into an unfurnished police flat in a less distant suburb, East Finchley. Almost immediately Vi gave birth to Karen, the first of the Lundys' three daughters.

West Hampstead put Lundy's thief-taking talent to the
test. When he arrived almost all the station CID officers
were investigating the murder of Patricia Langan, a society
hairdresser. This left the investigation of every fresh crime
to just two officers, novice DC Lundy and 'a tremendous old boy' named Detective Sergeant Les Smith, who
together took on ten men's work. 'We turned up in the
morning and went out looking into everything that had
been reported: motor vehicles, gas meters, burglaries,
you name it. For months we were working like slaves,
up to twenty hours a day. Later I became a workaholic
but as I hadn't suffered a nervous breakdown as a DC at
West Hampstead, I felt I was never going to have one.'

Eventually the Langan murder squad returned to general CID duties, but by then Lundy was well dug into
one of London's liveliest areas: Finchley Road with its
gambling clubs, Kilburn with its Irish community and busy
pubs, and the lush avenues of St John's Wood promising
rich pickings for burglars. Already Lundy was learning
how to use his powers of deduction in solving crimes,
rather than leaping to the easiest and laziest conclusion,
and also how to develop informers. His mentor was Les
Smith. Lundy soon put his teachings to good use in the
half-dozen local casinos which had sprung up since 1962
when gaming was legalized.

One night in November 1967 a violent shoot-out occurred
on Finchley Road and left eight big pimples protruding
from the outer steel-plated door of the El Toro casino.
Uniformed police arrested two people on the word of the
doorman, Fred Rondel, who had blamed outsiders coming
into the club, having a row and firing shots. This version
was becoming accepted as the truth but it did not ring
true to Lundy. For months past he had made it his job
to pop into the casinos and find out what was happening.
That was how he came to know Fred Rondel who was no

mere bouncer but a famous wrestler, 'the Polish White Eagle': a greatly-feared individual who had once been an enforcer for the notorious racketeer, Peter Rachman, and had served several jail sentences for crimes of extreme violence.

Rondel, a big man with a big beard, seems to have looked on Lundy with an amused eye, as a gullible upstart who would believe any yarn, but Lundy knew from informers that a rival mob of Greeks had been threatening to kill Rondel for some time. He therefore suspected that on this night the Greeks had finally come for Rondel who, fearing his end was near, had loosed off eight shots from a handgun. No gun had yet been found so Lundy deduced that Rondel must have hidden it.

Rondel had a string of witnesses supporting his account but the terrier-like Lundy, with his quaint Lancastrian way of speaking, kept nagging the chief inspector: 'It's not right, this story we're getting. I'm telling you, Fred fired that gun and it's hidden somewhere in that club!' In the end the chief's resistance snapped and he told Lundy, 'Well, nick him and bring him in.'

This was easier said than done. Nobody in their right minds would nick Fred, who had once bitten a man's ear off, but this was where Lundy's North Country simpleton act came in handy. He went back to the club and told him, 'We need some witness statements, Fred, and we can't take them here.' As meek as a lamb Rondel set off for the station, convinced that the raw detective believed he was just a witness to other folks' crimes but, as soon as he arrived, he was slammed in a cell. Now all hell broke loose as the caged 'White Eagle' screeched he had been duped. Yet, sure enough, the police found his gun, a Walther pistol, and proved it was the weapon from which the shots had been fired, while a rival gang of gambling club racketeers were trying to break in. Lundy was right. Fred Rondel went to court screaming blue murder, he was convicted and sent to jail for three months for illegal possession of the gun. In 1975 he was charged with supplying guns to the robbers in the 'Spaghetti House Siege' and conspiracy, but was acquitted.[1]

Lundy had another success in Finchley Road's clubland. To cater for the gambling clientele two entrepreneurs dreamed up the Georgia Brown Movie Restaurant which offered a new concept in entertainment: watching film classics while you dined. There was a grand opening with much publicity, but contractors and suppliers were soon claiming they had not been paid. West Hampstead CID started a fraud inquiry but the sergeant in charge was transferred and no one else wanted to take on the job, so it was passed to lowly Lundy. He turned it into a big case and proved that the owners had been systematically bilking suppliers of their due monies and of threatening them at gunpoint not to complain. The case went to the Central Criminal Court at the Old Bailey, everyone was convicted and Lundy was again 'highly commended'.

In October 1968 he was promoted to detective sergeant and posted eight miles north, to Finchley. In terms of crime Finchley was not a busy station. It had just four CID officers, two sergeants and two constables, and there was no risk of anyone collapsing from overwork. The trouble with Lundy was that he was not prepared to sit around waiting for crimes to be reported. He went out searching for information about crime in progress. Although few serious offences were committed in Finchley, he soon found out it was home to a surprisingly large number of full-time criminals or 'villains' as London detectives habitually call them. Lundy turned several into informers, and in future years they would give him spectacular leads.

Lundy soon found out which crooks drank in which pubs, but Finchley detectives used the Torrington Arms.

It was quiet (except on band nights) and had a function
room ideal for gatherings like retirement dinners. It was
owned and run by Alan and Pamela Bartlett who were
liked by police and well-known locally for their role in
many charities and clubs. They were patrons of Finchley
Amateur Boxing Club where some hundred local youths
and schoolboys learned to box. Through the Torrington a
couple of Finchley CID men became involved, attending
the club's twice-weekly sessions at Christ's College, the
local Catholic grammar school. Sport-mad, fitness-fanatic
Lundy joined in almost as soon as he moved to Finchley.
He would spend each Tuesday and Thursday helping to
erect the boxing rings in the gymnasium, then take them
down again and put them in store. He also used to take the
boys on training runs round the streets. Within months he
was on the committee and the club became a focal point
of his life, along with home and work. Vi Lundy also
contributed, spending many nights making dressing-gowns
for the boxers.

In later years Lundy's links with the club would become
the subject of intense scrutiny and hostile comment but in
the 1960s Scotland Yard actively encouraged officers to get
stuck into voluntary social work.

At the time the Commissioner's policy of greater involvement
in the community was being hammered home to everybody. They
were screaming, 'Youths are in trouble! Juvenile crime!', so we
were told to get involved in our spare time with youth clubs and
the like. In those days the main community activity in Finchley
was the boxing club. We had stacks of youngsters. Many were
'yobbos'. By teaching them to box, taking them on training
runs and physically exhausting them, we were doing our bit
to stop them hanging round street corners and causing trouble.
I dealt with a lot of juveniles when they had street fights, got
arrested and had to go to court. I'd say, 'You want to get
down to the boxing club. Get in the ring down there and
take a few smacks on the nose, then you won't think you're

Jack the Lad any more.' It was an old-fashioned approach but
it worked.

There was a dark side to the club. Lundy found out
that several boys' fathers had criminal records. There
was Stevie Salter, who had convictions for handling stolen
goods. There was Lennie Gibson, also convicted of handling, shop-breaking and going equipped to steal, but he
seemed to have gone straight in recent years. Another
father with a moderately respectable air was Roy Garner who had been a meat porter and glazier but was
now a pub-owner and businessman. Lundy suspected that
some of these characters might still be involved in crime,
to a greater or lesser degree but, he says, he had no
evidence.

Lundy was the sort of copper who is never off duty.
He was always thinking up new ways to solve crimes and
gather information, so the boxing club became another
way of making contacts he would later exploit for the
benefit of police and public. Such contacts were not made
at the club itself. All the fathers did there was drop their
boys off. 'There everything was Go! People were either
sparring in the ring, changing over or out for a run
but afterwards parents, trainers and committee members
would all go back to the Torrington for a drink.'

Whenever Lundy was tipped off that a boxer's father
had a criminal past he would check his record and draw
his intelligence file from Scotland Yard. Lundy had several
motives. If he learned anything fresh about the man's
activities or lifestyle, he would update the file. If he discovered anything that conflicted with the existing contents,
he would make a correction. If the file said the man was
believed to be still active, Lundy vowed to catch him. And
whether he was or was not 'at it', Lundy hoped to turn him
into an informant.

We'd go back in the Torrington, for a committee meeting or whatever, and then everyone would break up into their own crowds and buy a drink. I'd be with a detective constable from Finchley, or I'd be chatting with the landlord Alan Bartlett, but then I'd also make a point of chatting to the likes of Lennie Gibson. And these kind of people would also want to talk to me.

Now, bear in mind, in those days I was a nobody. I was just a sergeant. I had no power to do these men any favours, not that I wanted to. But they wanted to talk to any officer anywhere. Look at it from their side of the fence. Whatever league they're in, they think that the more detectives they know the better. They're that type of high-level criminal. To all outward appearances Lennie Gibson and co. were respectable property dealers or whatever, but there would come a point in the evening when I would start winding them up. I'd say to one of them, 'I reckon you're still at it. And if you are still at it, then one day I'll have you.' Then he'd say, 'Leave off! That's all in the past!' So the conversation progresses. I used to say to Gibson time and again, 'Come on, Len, it's time you gave us a little whisper or two. What's going on out there? You're still among it, even if you're *not* at it. You must have some idea!' And Len would say, 'Aah, that's not my game.' But with others I had more success.

It wasn't only the boxing club that brought Lundy into the Torrington or gave him the excuse to talk to villains. 'We'd often be doing "late turn" at Finchley with no particular job to investigate. So we'd get round the pubs trying to find things out, as we were encouraged to do.'

By now Lundy had noticed that in some pubs, including the Torrington, there would often be a burst of activity around nine or ten o'clock, as characters like Gibson would come in wearing dark suits and black ties, and carrying little briefcases. He learned that on such occasions the gentlemen had just returned from an evening at a Masonic temple. What puzzled him was that sometimes the villains would turn up with a cluster of police who had attended the same lodge meeting. Much later in his career the issue of Freemasonry would crop up time and again, as he struggled to comprehend the forces behind his downfall. Yet even at this early stage he drew a distinction between his community work at the boxing club, which brought him into social contact with criminals coincidentally, and the secret society of Freemasonry where criminals and police officers seemed to meet systematically, as a matter of course. Worse still, they had all bound themselves together 'in a column of mutual defence and support', through solemn oaths of brotherhood and mutual aid.[2]

During his police service Lundy was often asked to become a mason, to go 'on the square'. He had a good excuse for refusing: 'I'd say, "It's not my game. I'm a Catholic, Popes have banned us from joining Freemasonry for centuries, and I don't want to know about it."' Later he would be forced to take a rather greater interest in 'The Craft'.

In benign contrast, the Torrington Arms and the boxing club also brought Lundy into contact with the comedian Eric Morecambe. Eric was married to Joan, the sister of Torrington landlord Alan Bartlett, and occasionally he would appear at functions to raise money for the club and other boxing charities. Once when he was photographed handing over a fund-raising cheque, who should pop into the frame but the delinquent Roy Garner and his business partner, the equally delinquent Kenny Ross! In later years as Garner grew notorious, that photo was published in the tabloid press. The implication was that Eric habitually associated with gangsters, when all he had done was help a cause close to his brother-in-law's heart. In Lundy's view that was 'atrocious reporting'.

Eric Morecambe was sport-mad, like Lundy, and the two men became close friends. Eric was a director of Luton Town Football Club, and from 1973 to 1975 when Lundy was lecturing at detective training school and worked regular hours, the pair went to most of the club's home games together in the comedian's chauffeur-driven car. For several years Tony, Vi and their daughters spent Easter holidays together with Joan and her family in the Morecambes' villa on the Algarve in Portugal – with the Lundys paying their way. In the late 1970s, when the detective's workload became all-consuming, he saw far less of Eric but when he died in 1984 from a heart attack Tony felt a great personal loss. Today that feeling is coupled with anger that Eric's memory has been tainted in the media's ferocious search for any mud to sling at Roy Garner and Tony himself. 'Eric didn't deserve it. He was one of the nicest people I have ever met.'

The Rise of the Supergrass,
The Fall of Scotland Yard

At the end of 1969 Lundy left Finchley CID to join
the Flying Squad, then considered Scotland Yard's elite
crime-fighting formation. He was immediately put on the
inquiry into the grotesque kidnap of Muriel Mackay, the
wife of the deputy chairman of the *News of the World*.
This was Britain's first big extortion kidnap – the ransom
demand was for one million pounds – so the methods
used to catch the kidnappers had to be improvised. Lundy
was in a team tracking the Mackays' Rolls-Royce as it
travelled to tortuous meeting-points with the unknown
extortioners. At one rendezvous where police had left
a bag of ransom money the team spotted a car number
which led back to the Hosein brothers. By the time they
were arrested, however, Mrs Mackay was nowhere to
be found. It was believed she had been killed at the
Hoseins' Hertfordshire farm and her body fed to pigs.
Arthur and Nizamodeen Hosein were tried for murder as
well as kidnapping and the case became another macabre
'first': the first modern murder trial in which a conviction
was secured without a body. The brothers were jailed
for life.

Although poor Mrs Mackay was dead and, even worse,
a victim of mistaken identity (it seems the intended victim
was the wife of *News of the World* chairman, Rupert
Murdoch), the case was a fair success for Number 7
squad within the Flying Squad, especially for Lundy's
lean and wiry inspector, John Bland, who bravely secreted

himself in the boot of the Rolls-Royce as it was driven to rendezvous dictated by the Hoseins.

Another bittersweet achievement was the inquiry into the murder of Police Superintendent Gerald Richardson, shot dead in Blackpool on 23 August 1971 by jewel thieves from London. Lundy was on a team of Lancashire and London officers trying to find Freddie Sewell, who had fired the shots. They were also after his sidekick, Charlie Haynes, who had gentlemanly pretensions. He was with the horsey set, watching his daughter compete at a pony show in Warwickshire, when he had the indignity of being arrested by Lundy and his colleagues.

Lundy was also involved in the arrest of the two Lee brothers who shot a security guard near Earls Court station in 1970, while they were still in their teens. They were jailed for eight and ten years, but when they came out they went straight back 'on the pavement' only to be captured in 1977 after robbing a bank in Brentford. Still only twenty-eight and twenty-six, they were sentenced to a further seventeen years.

After a year and a half on the Flying Squad Lundy was promoted to first-class sergeant and transferred to West End Central, the station policing London's vibrant West End. This is also 'clubland' and Lundy had to investigate the shooting of a gorilla-sized doorman named Ian Hales, who had had six bullets pumped into him but miraculously survived. He identified a villain named Micky Morris as the gunman but at the pre-trial committal hearing Hales suddenly backed off. He claimed he could identify no one and Morris walked out a free man. This riled Lundy who monitored Morris's future criminal career and would eventually restore him to the care of Her Majesty's prison service.

Lundy disliked the West End, preferring the homelier pleasures of North London's outer suburbs. By now he and Vi had three infant daughters so it was convenient when after just six months at West End Central he was moved back to Finchley, seven miles from home in Potters Bar. Since his last Finchley spell, the station's CID had been upgraded and was now capable of major inquiries. Almost immediately Lundy made a breakthrough which would start him on a career-boosting but controversial course: he cracked his first 'supergrass'.[1]

The term 'supergrass' was coined only in the 1970s but the principle, of pardoning criminals for informing on confederates, stretches back almost 400 years under the judicial tradition known as Queen's (or King's) Evidence. Since the 1600s courts have ruled that accomplices are competent witnesses in criminal proceedings. In 1650 Chief Justice Hale described the 'plea of approvement', which Sir James Stephen reiterated in his *History of the Criminal Law of England* (1883).

If a person accused of any crime, but especially of robbery, chose to plead guilty and to offer up his accomplices he was handed over to the Coroner, before whom he confessed his guilt, and accused other persons. The King might 'grant him life and limb', if he would deliver the country from a certain number of malefactors either by his body (by killing them upon battle waged) or by the country (convicting them before a jury). If he failed to fulfil the conditions imposed on him, he was hanged on his own confession.

No doubt hanging concentrates the mind wonderfully, even to the point where, to save his own skin, the condemned person may be driven to accuse the innocent. In modern times the supergrass emerged to avoid not capital punishment but up to twenty-five years in jail. The first supergrass, Derek 'Bertie' Smalls, was arrested in December 1972, over a £138,000 bank raid in Wembley, by a squad set up especially to combat the alarming increase in armed robberies since 1968. Smalls volunteered to testify in court against his accomplices provided he was given total immunity from prosecution. Amazingly, this is what the Director of Public Prosecutions gave him. Despite admitting twenty robberies, often as the leader of the gang, he was never sentenced to a single day in jail for any of these crimes.

In contrast, 150 people were arrested on his evidence. He went on to testify against twenty-seven former henchmen. They were jailed for a total of 315 years (excluding concurrent sentences) but nineteen appealed. In 1975 the Court of Appeal released three men and reduced the sentences of a further twelve, but otherwise confirmed the original verdicts. Even so, Lord Justice Lawton uttered this swingeing criticism: 'The spectacle of the Director of Public Prosecutions recording in writing, at the behest of a criminal like Smalls, his undertaking to give immunity from further prosecutions is one which we find distasteful. Nothing of a similar kind must ever happen again.'

When the unsuccessful appellants took their case to the House of Lords, Lawton was himself rebuked by Lord Dilhorne, a lord of appeal in ordinary: 'I am wondering to what extent it is right for any court to give directions to the Director of Public Prosecutions as to how he should conduct his business . . . He may be condemned for what he has done but he must not be told what he has got to do in the future.'

Despite this support, the DPP would never again grant supergrasses immunity. In future they would have to be sentenced by the courts before or after giving evidence. In 1974 an arrested robber named Maurice O'Mahoney offered to tell the Flying Squad about other criminals. After Smalls no prior deal was possible, but when O'Mahoney appeared at the Old Bailey charged with robbery, burglary and attempted robbery (with ninety-two other offences taken into consideration) the judge said that, although he deserved twenty years for 'grave and terrible crimes', he was 'entitled to credit for his courage and determination in bringing other evil men to the attention of police'.

O'Mahoney was sentenced to just five years in jail, even though he had still not testified in court against his accomplices. This arrangement persuaded two of them to do the same. In return they also received five years. In 1976 this unofficial tariff came unstuck when Charlie Lowe was dealt with at Chelmsford Crown Court. Despite Lowe's readiness to step in the witness box against other criminals, Justice Stocker gave him eleven and a half years. Not surprisingly Lowe appealed. In 1977 Lord Justice Roskill cut his sentence for these reasons:

> It must be in the public interest that persons who have become involved in gang activities of this kind should be encouraged to give information to the police in order that others may be brought to justice . . . unless credit is given in such cases there is no encouragement for others to come forward and give information of invaluable assistance to society and the police, which enables these criminals . . . to be brought to book . . . we think that the Appellant is entitled to greater credit than that which the learned judge allowed . . . in these circumstances we think justice will be done if we reduce the sentence to five years.

So, in the 1970s when Tony Lundy developed his own enhanced supergrass system, five years had become the norm almost irrespective of the crimes of the individual supergrass. It was not Lundy's fault if such leniency stuck in the craw of judges, journalists or defence lawyers, but five years was certainly a tempting carrot he used to the full.

In recent years the Metropolitan Police has redrawn its map of London but in 1972 Finchley formed part of 'S' Division and came under Golders Green. On 20 March

that year Lundy was at Golders Green, deputizing for
his divisional inspector, when an armed robbery occurred
four miles away at a bakery in East Finchley. The robbers
had fired shots at a security guard and escaped with a bag
of money. Lundy went to the scene and took charge. He
learned that a major criminal called Ronnie Clare might
have been involved. Lundy arrested him and then talked
him into testifying against his partners, Georgie Jones and
Jack Drury. At that time it was very rare for a professional
criminal openly to implicate others so Lundy's cynical
colleagues kept ribbing him, 'You'll never get Ronnie
Clare in the witness box.' Lundy, keen to prove them
wrong, replied, 'Wait and see.'

On his recommendation Clare was allowed home on
bail, an act of faith which other detectives swore he would
abuse by 'legging it' and disappearing. Yet he did give
evidence and helped send Jones and Drury to jail for
ten years. Clare received only a suspended sentence in
recognition of his help to the police. Georgie Jones was
undone as much by his vanity as by Clare. On the robbery
he had worn a hairpiece. Some hairs from it were found
in the boot of a car where the gunman had hidden while
waiting for the security van to arrive. The hairs had the
same dyes as the hairpiece. They matched as surely as
fingerprints.

Already Lundy was aware that some colleagues felt he
was over-zealous:

I was always encouraging people to talk and tell. I wasn't
one of those detectives who simply got hold of the villains,
charged 'em and left 'em. I always talked to them and tried
to elicit everything. Most officers don't bother, but all the
blokes who ever worked with me will tell you, they all got
the bit between their teeth in the same way in the end.
So, you might waste a day talking to the guy and get nothing, but more often than not you get something, just like

Ronnie Clare. He was my first supergrass, pre-dating even Bertie Smalls.

In 1973 Lundy was promoted to detective inspector and posted to Hampstead. There was plenty of crime to investigate, including murders, and Lundy was content until he was told to return to detective training school: as an instructor. He protested that by nature he was not a teacher but an operational cop, and he had only just completed the same six-week course he was now expected to teach. He threw in every excuse to avoid going but he had no choice. As it turned out, he greatly enjoyed his two years at the school: 'It was local to where we lived, and it was an easy life compared to what I'd been used to. I was still at the boxing club, running with the boys and training them, and I was as fit as a fiddle.'

Most detectives who become instructors find the school a rest-cure from the stresses and strains of CID work, and Lundy could now have slipped into a cosy existence, but he did not want a quiet life and was still making work for himself.

Even at training school I was meeting informants and getting news from criminal sources. I would put it on paper and pass it to the appropriate office to ring it through. If the information led to 'a result' – convictions or the recovery of stolen cash or goods – I would have to deal with any reward claim because I was usually the only copper who knew the informer. The old chief superintendent who dealt with me used to say, 'That's the first time we've ever had informants' reports submitted through training school!'

Later, when I was being investigated, my interrogators tried to claim I had no right getting involved in submitting reward claims while I was at training school because I was 'non-operational'. I went mad and said, 'What about all the villains arrested and convicted because of the information I supplied at that time? Are you also telling me that, because I was non-operational, those weren't to happen either?'

In December 1975 Lundy completed two years at the school and moved on to Willesden Green. His eighteen months were dominated by three investigations. The first concerned Steven 'Cramble' (a pseudonym necessary in order to conceal the identity of his offspring).

Cramble was the most horrid, objectionable bastard I have ever met in my life. He was very clever. When we first arrested him for a series of burglaries we had no idea what a monster he was. He used to take his children out on burglary trips all over the country. He even taught his youngest boy, who was only five or six, how to burgle. That was only the start. He also stole sheep and would bring them home and lock them in a dog kennel. Then he would teach the little 'uns blood lust: he'd have 'em cutting up these live sheep, attacking them with knives and killing them.

We then found out he had buggered his son and raped his own daughters. What's more, he was involved with another family and had slept with all the daughters in that household. One of the girls had even had two kids by him when she was thirteen or fourteen. Nobody had ever reported these crimes until I nicked him and his burglar offspring. To instil fear and stop them talking he used to break their arms and legs. Despite a serious criminal record, he had recently been working as a security guard. He was a dog-handler and patrolled a big industrial estate while it was still being built. For some reason he had been sacked. In revenge he burned the estate to the ground, so I did him for arson too.

At the Old Bailey Lundy had all the abused youngsters testifying against Cramble but, before then, his eldest son was bailed over his own offences, provided that he lived with his grandparents. While free he sexually assaulted two women, then robbed and beat up a fourteen-year-old boy who died. He was given fifteen years for manslaughter, cut to ten because of his appalling upbringing. He still testified against his father who was given life for rape. The Court of Appeal quashed that sentence but he still served four years

for indecent assault on two girls. Meantime his son told
Lundy that Cramble had falsely accused another man of
sexually assaulting the son. The framed man had already
served an eighteen-month term but Lundy ensured his case
went to the Court of Appeal where he was cleared. By then
Cramble had been jailed for four more years for perverting
justice.

Lundy's second big inquiry at Willesden was into a gang
who had stolen millions of pounds of property from guests
at the smartest West End hotels. The gang included two
small teenagers named Tyrell Glover and Steven John.
Of mixed race, they had light brown skins and could be
mistaken for Arabs. The gang leaders used to dress them
in £1,000 suits so they looked like rich Arab princes. They
then wandered in and out of hotels like the Dorchester and
the Grosvenor House without any staff daring to question
their right to be there.

What they did was known as 'loiding' – using bits of celluloid
to open hotel room doors. They knew which bedrooms held
the best pickings because they worked in league with white
prostitutes who had serviced the occupants and would tip them
off. These boys were so clever. Just in case they *were* stopped
going past reception they would not carry celluloid on them.
Instead, once they were safely inside the hotels and had reached
the guest floors, they would go to a fire extinguisher, unscrew
the instruction case and remove the transparent cover. They
then used it to 'loid' the doors of rich guests. They did the
same with the celluloid on instruction boxes in public telephone
cubicles within the hotels. They peeled it off and slipped it in
door-locks.

Some of the ring were violent robbers. They did one nasty
job in a hotel by Heathrow Airport. Two elderly women came
into their room and caught them going through their belongings.
They beat the women unmercifully and even stole the rings off
their fingers.

Lundy turned the 'Arab princes' into mini-supergrasses

and used their evidence to win convictions against twenty-seven gang members.

The irony was that we managed to clear up all these crimes committed in plush Mayfair hotels from dear old Willesden Green where there wasn't a decent hotel in sight. That was because our original informant lived nearby, and we arrested a local couple who talked. That led us to the West Indian ringleader and the main white prostitute who also lived round Willesden Green. We had a lot of help from the Flying Squad but it was very much a local job.

When caught, many of the thieves co-operated and remembered enough details to identify their victims, most of whom had reported their losses at the time – even though the prostitution angle might have been embarrassing. One item recovered by Lundy's team was a watch worth £25,000 stolen from a princely member of the Saudi Arabian royal family who had reported the loss at the time. The Director of Public Prosecutions gave Lundy authority to visit the prince in Riyadh but, despite several requests, the Saudi authorities never granted him permission to enter Saudi Arabia. He never took a statement from the Prince, and the Prince never claimed the watch. So, like all valuables whose owners cannot be formally traced, the watch was sold as prisoners' property and the proceeds went to various charities.

Lundy's third big inquiry while at Willesden was not into the underworld but into corruption among police colleagues. Despite fourteen years in the Metropolitan Police this was his first direct encounter with an issue which had publicly dogged the force since 1969 when *The Times* newspaper ran a story about three South London detectives extorting money from a petty crook. In the next seven years a series of press revelations disclosed systemic corruption, particularly among Scotland Yard's specialist units such as the Drug Squad, Obscene Publications Squad and Flying Squad. On 27 February 1972 for example, the *Sunday People* revealed that Commander Ken Drury, head of the Flying Squad, had holidayed in Cyprus with one of London's leading pornographers, Jimmy Humphreys, along with both men's wives. Even worse, Humphreys was claiming he had paid for the Drurys' trip.

The scandal coincided with Sir Robert Mark's accession as Metropolitan Commissioner on an anti-corruption ticket. He is credited with coining the saying, 'A good police force is one which catches more criminals than it employs', and set up a special anti-corruption squad known as A10 to investigate the growing number of complaints against his 27,000 officers and his 3,000 detectives in particular. In his five years as commissioner (1972–77) over 400 detectives retired early or were dismissed in circumstances casting doubt on their integrity, but as early as 1974 the credibility of his entire campaign depended on what was done about Drury and thirty-seven other detectives named by Humphreys after he had been jailed for eight years for causing grievous bodily harm. If Drury and his far more corrupt colleagues were to get off scot-free, then Mark and the senior officers spearheading his anti-corruption purge would have egg not just on their epaulettes but all over their faces.

None of this affected Detective Inspector Tony Lundy, who says he had nothing to fear from the anti-corruption drive. However, he was forced to take an interest in January 1976 when he assisted his chief superintendent, Stan Sayers, on an internal inquiry which he had been asked to conduct. In an era of now legendary corruption Sayers was a fish out of water, says Lundy. 'He was a real gentleman who had spent most of his career inside a laboratory and places like that. He was a real nice man and destined to go even higher, especially in those days when detective chief superintendents were falling like flies, departing without warning and retiring before their time.'

Sayers had to investigate a complaint which had its origins in the arrest, some five years earlier, of an American hard-core pornographer named Charles Marandola for passing forged US dollars. Marandola (also known as Charlie Julian) was acquainted with Jimmy Humphreys, and when Humphreys turned witness against the many detectives he had bribed himself, he threw in an allegation that Marandola had bribed a Flying Squad officer so Marandola could get bail and flee abroad. He then failed to show up for his trial, but after a warrant was issued for his arrest he came back voluntarily from Amsterdam. He was convicted and given a fine but fled again without paying it. Years later anti-corruption detectives tracked down Marandola in the USA only to hear him say he had never bribed the officer in question. This meant there was no evidence to justify criminal charges, but in November 1975 that same officer and a colleague faced a discipline hearing for failing to investigate the Marandola case properly.

The prosecution called Detective Sergeant Ted Domachowski to testify about nothing more than a warrant issued for Marandola's arrest after he had failed to turn up for his original trial. However, the officer defending the detectives then started asking him about his role on the day Marandola had first been arrested. Domachowski readily explained how he had accompanied the two accused officers to the Playboy Club where a man had tried to change a forged $100 bill. It turned out that he was the friend of a high-class call girl whom Marandola had paid off with the counterfeit note. In that regard, the couple were innocent but they would now be witnesses against Marandola. Domachowski took the man to West End

Central police station while his colleagues went to arrest
Marandola at an address which the girl identified. She
too was then brought to the station, where Domachowski
remained with both witnesses and recorded their details.

While Domachowski was recounting this to the discipline board, the prosecuting officer became agitated.
Immediately after the hearing he demanded to know why
Domachowski had not volunteered this evidence when he
had been interviewed by anti-corruption officers a year
before. He replied that he would willingly have done so
but they had asked him only about the warrant, as was
clear from the statement they had taken from him which
was less than a page long. He had assumed they already
knew of his role on the day of Marandola's arrest but had
decided not to question him about something as minor as
escorting witnesses.

Next day he was called back into the hearing, to be confronted by accusations of untruthfulness and colluding with
one of the accused. It turned out that overnight the officers, who had originally interviewed him, had made fresh
statements claiming his evidence contradicted what he had
told them a year earlier outside the formal interview. They
said he had then failed to disclose his full role, by falsely
claiming that he did not know why Marandola had first
been arrested and that he had not been involved in the
original inquiry. They also claimed he falsely denied being
the third officer present when Marandola was brought into
the station. Domachowski learned of these allegations
only when Deputy Assistant Commissioner Ray Anning
summoned him three weeks after the hearing. Anning said
that, because he had lied at the hearing, he was going to be
returned to uniform. This punishment amounted to demotion. An outraged Domachowski told Anning that it was
his accusers who had lied. He then slammed in a complaint
saying he had told the truth and requesting an inquiry.

That was where Chief Superintendent Stan Sayers came in. He reviewed the case papers and on 5 January 1976 interviewed Domachowski, with Lundy present. Domachowski said that nothing he had told the hearing contradicted his original short statement, and that if what his accusers said was true (about his denying any knowledge or involvement) they must have written down these additional questions and his answers in their official pocketbooks, which they should then have shown him and asked him to sign. They did not do this, he said, but had concocted their latest statements to cover up the inadequacy of their original investigation. In a written statement he told Sayers: 'Throughout my career I have been straightforward and honest in all I have done and have always felt the need of truth and justice. I find it hard to believe that police officers deputed to carry out investigations of other officers, and who should above all be beyond reproach, do not share my ideals.'

Sayers then questioned Domachowski's accusers and asked for the notes of the interview which had occurred one year earlier. Sayers told them they would not have been able to compose their recent statement in such detail without referring to such notes. Again Lundy was present and recalls that this question 'dropped like a bombshell'. Sayers insisted on seeing the men's pocket-books but, when they told him these were not available, he ended the interview by saying he intended to resume it when they were found. In the next few days he requested the pocketbooks repeatedly but they never turned up. He then wrote an interim report saying he believed Domachowski was telling the truth, that his complaint appeared to have merit and that it was the conduct of his accusers which required investigation. He also wrote that he needed to interview them again.

The day after sending this report, Sayers called Lundy

into his office and said: 'We've got to go to the Yard. Commander Steventon wants to see us.' Ronald Steventon was then head of the A10 anti-corruption branch, but Lundy had scarcely heard of him. It was Steventon who had taken Humphreys's mammoth statement and had spent the best part of two years investigating the pornographer's allegations against Flying Squad detectives in particular. When Sayers and Lundy arrived at Steventon's office Lundy was excluded, but he says Sayers was 'absolutely livid' when he came out. He told Lundy how Steventon had stressed that an inquiry into these two officers could have serious consequences. Presumably, what Steventon meant was that, with so many Flying and 'Porn' squad detectives on the verge of arrest, their lawyers might exaggerate the significance of any inquiry into these men who would be prosecution witnesses in the trials to come. The result might be that the juries would acquit detectives who were manifestly guilty of appalling corruption. Sayers told Lundy he appreciated these considerations but they were 'beside the point'. Making no attempt to suppress his outrage, he said his main concern was that Ted Domachowski was being crucified. He said he would write his final report as he saw fit, then the hierarchy could do whatever they wanted with it. According to Lundy:

The next thing we hear, Ted Domachowski has been sent for and told he'll be staying in the CID! He's over the moon and very grateful to Stan Sayers for clearing his name. That ended the inquiry, but the inquiry ended Stan's career. He had had enough. He had already served long enough to retire on full pension, so he 'put in his papers' and quit.

Domachowski meantime had been called in to see Deputy Commissioner Colin Woods and told he would not be returned to uniform after all. Woods also said he was sorry that sometimes people run around with heavy boots and tread on people inadvertently. He then asked what action Domachowski now wanted taken against his two accusers. The detective replied that as Woods was in charge of discipline for the entire Metropolitan Police, that was a matter for Woods. Domachowski was not a vindictive person and had already got what he wanted: the chance to stay in the CID, which he did for the rest of his service. If he had not stuck up for himself and complained, however, he would certainly have been put into uniform, and suffered all the stigma which such a transfer would have inflicted.

On 28 February 1976 a dozen 'Porn' and Flying Squad detectives were arrested. In 1977 a total of fifteen appeared at the Old Bailey in three separate trials. Thirteen were convicted and sentenced to between three and twelve years in jail (ninety-six years in all). They included two commanders (Drury and Wally Virgo, who was later cleared on appeal), a chief superintendent (Bill Moody), a chief inspector and five inspectors. The press hailed the verdicts as proof that Scotland Yard really did have the will to punish the crooks in its ranks. This author was one of three journalists who wrote *The Fall of Scotland Yard*, a book which praised Sir Robert Mark and his anti-corruption team.[2] Little did we know how near their crusade had come to disaster, for, just as the Yard hierarchy had feared, several of the defendants had heard about Domachowski's complaint well before the trials. Hoping to discredit the prosecution, they approached him through intermediaries to ask if he would testify on their behalf. He let it be known that he was prepared to stand up and talk about his complaint, but this might be no help to them because he would have to add that he was never told what became of it.

In the end he did not give evidence. The defendants probably realized that nothing he could say would have countered the shocking evidence stacked up against them.

Yet there is no doubt that if his story had come out during the trial, it would have dented A10's whiter-than-white image which was so important to the Yard at the time. Certainly, had the trials failed, then politicians, press and public would have believed that the Yard was incapable of getting rid of its 'rotten apples' because the entire CID barrel was putrefied.

As for Tony Lundy, this was his first taste of the high politics of policing. The affair also showed him how easily an innocent officer could have his reputation damaged by unjust allegations. It was an experience he himself would suffer many times in years to come.

3

Meet Mr Smith

In March 1977 Detective Inspector Lundy flew to Canada to collect a man named Robinson who was wanted in Britain for several robberies. He had fled to Montreal only to carry out more robberies, habitually firing a gun. When arrested prior to extradition, he told the local police nothing about the crimes but confessed them to Lundy on the flight to Heathrow. Lundy promptly sent a report back to Montreal where detectives were pleased to clear up these unsolved shootings. Lundy too was pleased to do his buddies this service, for what he had seen of policing in their city changed his entire view of how to combat armed crime in London.

In Montreal Lundy had been stunned to learn there were 6,500 armed robberies in 1976, or nearly seventeen a day. In London, three times as large, there were just twenty-eight in which gangs used firearms in the whole year, although there were 1,700 robberies in all. During Lundy's one weekend in Montreal there were thirteen murders: more than half London's homicide total throughout 1976. At that time armed robberies in London were dealt with by the CID inspector in whichever district they happened to occur. This meant that no inspector had any interest in solving robberies in other districts, even though they might be committed by the same gang. Co-operation between districts was patchy and haphazard, so many robberies went unsolved, even though the combined knowledge of all districts might have cracked them.

Lundy was impressed by Montreal's central homicide and robbery squad which followed up all robberies. They

collated and broke down every piece of information –
whether it came from eye-witnesses, or was related to
method, weapon used or other forensic evidence. The
result of this highly co-ordinated approach was a ferocious
workload but a very high clear-up rate. It was never likely
to bring Montreal's robbery rate down to UK levels, but
it struck Lundy as a method long overdue and well worth
applying in London.

Within two months of this trip, Lundy was promoted
to chief inspector and left Willesden to rejoin the Flying
Squad. This coincided with a rapid increase in armed
robberies which no one at the Yard seemed to know how
to combat. Lundy repeatedly pestered his commander
saying, 'We're playing games over here, we've got to bring
in this robbery squad system they have in Montreal.' His
words seemed to fall on deaf ears, even though London's
robbery rate had doubled in just three years. Divisional
CID offices were overwhelmed yet at the same time many
Flying Squad officers were under-employed. 'We should
be investigating these robberies ourselves, systematically,'
said Lundy. By July 1978 Scotland Yard's chiefs felt the
same way. They decided to restructure the Flying Squad
so that 110 of its officers (some eighty per cent of its entire
strength) would now form the Central Robbery Squad.
This would itself be divided into four local branches,
covering the entire Metropolitan Police district.

Lundy would very soon become the leading exponent
of the robbery squad system, but for the moment he
continued to work on the old Flying Squad, which was
itself split into ten smaller squads. He was in charge of
5 and 7 squads, based at Scotland Yard. They achieved
'good successes' as he puts it, but he upset some officers
by banning lunchtime drinking. He was no Puritan. He
was simply applying his own and most people's experience:
if you drink during the day your work usually suffers.

He knew that some Flying Squad men drank as if they believed alcohol increased their efficiency, while others did not accept that work should be their priority. Such officers regarded Lundy as a grinding task-master against whom they would store up animosity. On the other hand, his approach earned him the ferocious loyalty of many officers who would thrive following his example.

Even when Lundy's efforts went farcically wrong they ended up right. On the Flying Squad he inherited the task of cracking the 'Circle Team', so-called because they carried out all their robberies near Underground stations on the Circle Line. There was reason to suspect (wrongly as it turned out) that their leader was a man called Kendrick, so one day he tailed Kendrick and two associates in a car. There were several vans and a motor bike in Lundy's surveillance squad but they were taken by surprise when Kendrick's car suddenly headed up the M1 motorway. Instead of doing a convenient raid in North London, the team either had plans up North or were having a day out with no criminal act in mind. Lundy was crestfallen. If he had known this was going to happen, he would have had a communications van on the job. Instead he rapidly lost half his squad as he roared out of radio range up the motorway. Only a motor-cyclist managed to stick with him, but a couple of surveillance vans eventually caught up. On Kendrick's tail they all drove over a hundred miles to Nottingham, a city which no member of Lundy's squad knew in any detail.

We're steaming round this strange place, not knowing where we are, when our radio calls start coming up on local broadcasting. We're getting demands, 'Who are you? Identify yourselves! What's going on?', when we don't know ourselves what's going on. Kendrick's crew keep going to different places, stopping, then taking off again. We have no idea what they're going to do or where. Then all of a sudden, we're in a street, waiting for the 'off' again, when I see our sergeant in his little van going out to a junction ahead. And coming across this junction is a motor-cyclist and a passenger – and they hit, bang! Side on into his van. I can see them now, going across the end of the street, doing somersaults in the air. Oh God! And I have to leave them there, while I'm off in pursuit again.

Fortunately they weren't badly hurt, but that caused a big problem because we were driving round another police force's patch unannounced when we're always supposed to warn them what we're doing. Anyway, at last Kendrick and his mates stop at a big store on the city's outskirts. One stays out while the other two disappear inside. We think, 'They must be doing a robbery here' so I say, 'When they come out this time, let's have 'em and just end it or mend it, here and now.' So there am I, with armed officers ready to fire, not having told the local force anything, and out come these blokes in this little quiet place on the outskirts of Nottingham – and all our heavies jump out with guns and arrest them. And just across the road is a police station!

Then it turned out they weren't armed robbers after all. They were doing what they called 'the Creep'. They used to go in these big stores, a couple would distract attention while Kendrick would creep into the offices and nick the takings. A lot of these places used to leave their safes open and cash lying around, so these thieves often picked up three or four thousand pounds. We brought them back to London on suspicion of the 'Circle' jobs. They hadn't done any of them, but they admitted hundreds of 'Creep' offences all over the country, going back years. Kendrick was brilliant. In all he'd stolen hundreds of thousands. So although we didn't get our armed robbers, we cleared up a massive number of offences, so even Nottingham forgave us. We were in hot pursuit, off they went, so what could we do? You can't plan for every possibility.

In September 1977 a reliable informer told Lundy about a gang of robbers including Dave Smith, George Williams and Alf Berkeley who all had heavy criminal records. Lundy could not pursue them because he was working on general operations at the time, so he gave the tip-off to Number 5 Regional Crime Squad (5 RCS) which pursues criminals operating across police force boundaries north

of London. 5 RCS had an interest because Williams lived
in Hertfordshire. Its inquiries were still continuing in
October when Lundy joined the robbery squad section
of the Flying Squad and could take a direct role. He
was both impressed and dismayed by the gang's counter-
surveillance skills.

They were brilliant. They had their own observation van which
was better than ours, with chairs and a bed in the back and little
holes drilled in the side. They would park it up to keep watch on
security vehicles delivering and collecting cash. One man would
drive the van to the 'plot' of a robbery while another would be
lying in the back, making notes. We were keeping observation on
them, but they were keeping observation on security vehicles.

Not even this sophistication could explain how the gang
knew the police were waiting to ambush them on Thursday
13 October 1977 as they were on the point of robbing a
Security Express van at the Schweppes bottling factory in
Colindale, North London. Lundy had surrounded the site
with an armed response group and was ready to pounce.

The entire gang had been in shoot-outs before, so we were
ready for the worst. Imagine all the adrenalin in our team,
everybody's ready for it, we know where they were, and where
they've left stolen cars ready for the getaway. The next thing
we hear, two of them have left their meeting place, a café
in Bounds Green, and are heading in their own private car
towards the Schweppes plot! Sure enough, we see them come
driving through, they go straight back to the café, and then they
all go home. What a let-down!

There could only be one explanation. Instantly Lundy realized his operation had been 'blown out' – betrayed from
within. His suspicions were confirmed in the following days
as surveillance teams reported that gang members were
lying low at home, barely moving outside their front doors.

They even stopped talking on their telephones, which were being tapped legally on a Home Secretary's warrant. These had been yielding much information but, after the tip-off, they all went dead.

Lundy was furious. He was sure his own team were above suspicion, so the leak must have come from some detective on the fringes of the inquiry. Whoever he might be, Lundy resigned himself to the probability that for the next few months the gang would play safe and give up the robbery game. He could now write off the entire job, but that was not his style. Instead he mounted another operation in total secrecy. Only his deputy, Inspector John Robertson, knew why he was ordering so many men to parade at Finchley at four o'clock on the morning of 8 November. Only then did he tell each unit to drive to a separate location, and wait for his radio signal to open a sealed envelope containing instructions to go to an address and make an arrest. After these security precautions, Lundy was relieved to learn all the suspects had been picked up without trouble and were being held at various local police stations.

He calculated that, although he had been sabotaged in catching the gang in the act, he had enough evidence of a conspiracy to rob. He had surveillance reports of the robbers' various meetings and their several trips around the Schweppes premises. He could also prove they had travelled there in their surveillance van which they would have difficulty explaining away, especially now it was in police custody.

Lundy also knew of other robberies the gang had recently committed. His underworld informant had identified three or four jobs, including an appalling attack near the Thatched Barn Restaurant at Boreham Wood in Hertfordshire. Every week two elderly men used a private car to collect £7,600 for company wages from a local bank. Their regular route took them on a flyover over the A1 trunk road. On Friday 23 September 1977 two cars overhauled them on the flyover, an ideal place for an ambush. The robbers jumped out, smashed the wages-car windscreen with a crowbar, thrust a sawn-off shotgun at the men and demanded the wages bag. The men complied immediately but one robber (Alf Berkeley) grabbed the glasses of the driver, Mr Pate, who was in his seventies, and threw ammonia straight in his eyes. As a result Mr Pate permanently lost most of his sight. There was no need for the attack. The robbers already had the money and Pate was offering no resistance. He was a victim of violence for the sake of violence.

If the men Lundy now held really were the 'Thatched Barn' gang, he had the motive and the method to prise a confession from at least one of them. He concentrated on thirty-five-year-old Dave Smith about whom he knew most, but Smith – big, bearded and six feet tall – admitted nothing. All Lundy had on him at this stage was some stolen cigarettes found in his garage. This was not enough to make a hard man like Smith blink, even after two days' interrogation. Around the chief inspector were faint-hearts. 'Everyone was saying, "When are you letting 'em go? We're getting nowhere!" I just told 'em, "Keep at it!", while I kept telling Smith, "One of the others is going to go and when he does . . ."'

Then Keith Warne weakened. He was not a robber but a con-man known to be mixed up with Smith. Lundy suspected Warne because he lived in Ashford in Kent, not far from Erith where an armed robbery had been carried out in June 1977 in exactly the style used by Smith and the gang elsewhere, including ammonia in victims' eyes. 'Fortunately,' says Lundy, 'Warne's bottle went. He started to crack a bit, and he let on that they'd used his house as a flop, to hide in, after that robbery.'

This enabled Lundy to go back into Smith with added zest. From his early years in approved schools, Smith had never been free for more than a few months. His last sentence had been fifteen years for armed robbery, reduced to ten on appeal. Lundy now applied the clinical pressure – legal blackmail, some might call it – which society requires of detectives.

He knew that if we got him for armed robbery this time he was going to get at least twenty years. On the other hand, if he turned supergrass, he would probably get no more than five. That was the carrot I was dangling in front of him, but at the same time I was waving the stick of saying, 'You realize somebody's going to roll, and when he goes, you're in dead, so you'd better help.'

Sure enough, another robber did start to 'bottle' (lose his nerve). George Williams told Lundy's team about a lock-up garage which he and Smith had rented in Hertfordshire near his home. Squad officers went there and found a stolen car, and crash helmets of the same colour as those worn at Erith and a crowbar matching the one used to smash the windscreen on the 'Thatched Barn' job. Even better, the woman who had rented out the lock-up identified Williams as the person who rented it. Armed with this evidence, Lundy says that he again went in to Smith: 'Now we're getting somewhere, because we can put you on for that nasty one at the Thatched Barn.'

Since the Police and Criminal Evidence Act (PACE) was applied in 1986 there have been strict limits on the time suspects may be held without charge before being released, but back in 1977 there were no such limits. It was a matter for police officers' judgement, provided that eventually they could satisfy a court they had not acted oppressively. Here, for example, were professional criminals believed to be actively involved in serious crime.

In such circumstances magistrates' courts would invariably give the police what they wanted. That was how Lundy was able to keep going at Smith for three or four days. His persistence succeeded.

According to Lundy, Smith started to crack and said, 'Right, that's it. You've got me. I'll tell you everything', but the detective told Smith he was unimpressed and insisted he come up with one piece of wholly original evidence which would prove beyond doubt that he really was going to 'roll over' and give evidence. Smith obliged by telling him where all the weapons were hidden: in George Williams's home. Lundy told him that this must be nonsense because his detectives had already searched the house and found nothing, but Smith insisted that the weapons really were there, having been shifted from the lock-up a week or so before and hidden under the floor. He said that police should be able to spot one floorboard in particular where the nails had recently been removed and then put back in again.

The first time Lundy's squad had searched the house, they had no reason to tear the place apart. Even when they returned and jemmied up the suspect floorboard, they found nothing. 'He's had us over,' said the detectives at first, but they kept searching the channels under the floor and eventually found seven sawn-off shotguns, hundreds of rounds of ammunition, several handguns, some teargas and some masks.

It was absolute dynamite [says Lundy]. Fantastic! Then Smith's dead, isn't he? There's no way back, now he's giving us that sort of stuff, so he starts to talk.

The beauty of the situation is that we could now go in to the other villains – Williams, Berkeley and co. – and say, 'You've been on this job and that job' and increase the pressure. Some still wouldn't give us the time of day, so our next strategy – to make sure Smith would have absolutely no way back – was to bring his accomplices into my offices, one by one, and confront them with Smith. I told them which jobs they were on, and if they denied it, Smith chipped in to say, 'I'm sorry but you were on it.' I would ask, 'What armed robberies did this man take part in?' and Smith replied, 'He was on the Thatched Barn' or whichever.

Now Smith had become a supergrass, his partner George Williams tried to follow and begged Lundy to be given the same deal. It was Williams who had supplied the initial information about the garage which helped crack Smith. Williams had also admitted a minor role on one robbery but he had failed to own up to other crimes, even though from the start Lundy had given him the same lecture as Smith: 'If you've been telling lies, concealing crimes, don't expect any mercy.' That warning drew no further admissions from Williams about robberies or the weapons still hidden in his home at that time.

When Smith named him as taking part in dozens of robberies, Williams suddenly found his tongue: 'OK, I'll admit everything, I'll help.' Lundy refused the offer, 'No, I don't want you. Too bad, mate. You had your chance, you didn't take it.' He packed Williams off to Brixton prison to await trial. This put Williams in a tricky position because the other gang members, now also in Brixton, half-suspected he had already done some talking and might go the whole way like Smith.

'By now it was chaos. We were breathless because Smith was rattling off admissions to sixty-nine or seventy armed robberies: not just ones he'd done since coming out of prison, but many he had committed earlier in his career. Then came the bombshell!' Once Smith started talking freely, Lundy told him he must admit every crime he had committed: 'If you miss anything out, somebody else will bring it up later and they'll use it to discredit you. Then your credibility's gone, you're no good to us, and you're going to end up getting your twenty years.' Smith's confession went on for at least two days with Lundy repeating the same question: 'Are you sure you've told us *everything*?'

One morning he came into the office to be told that Smith wanted to see him urgently. Lundy brought him up to his office and asked, 'What's the matter, Dave?' Smith came out with it. According to Lundy, the conversation went something like this: 'I've gotta tell you. I've been thinking for the past two or three days about what you keep saying, so I'm gonna have to tell you.' 'What? What's the worry?' 'Well, I don't know what's going to happen to me now, but I thought I'd tell you. A few years ago I killed a bloke on an armed robbery.'

There was a silence as Lundy wondered if he had mis-heard the prisoner, then he blurted an inadequate response: 'Pardon?' 'Well, we did one a few years ago. We didn't intend to kill anyone – we only had sticks – but I gave this bloke a smack on the head and he died.'

Smith went into the details: 'We went to rob him of a bag, he started to fight back, we gave him a whack with this little stick and blow me! Next day we pick up the papers and the geezer's died!'

He explained that the victim was a handbag manufacturer, Kurt Hess, but Smith only found that out – and that he was dead – as he sat at home watching *Police Five* on television. Hess had been attacked in August 1971 in Nile Street, Hackney, and died a month later – for a 'take' of just £782. The inquiry into that crime had got nowhere and without Smith's present confession – six years after the event – his killer would probably never have been identified.

Smith named the other Nile Street robbers as his old gang from Finchley. Lundy promptly had them all arrested and charged Smith with murder. This was later reduced to manslaughter, partly because the post mortem on Hess had shown his skull was so thin that any tap would probably have killed him. This matched what Smith was saying: 'I can't believe the bloke died, cos all I did was give him a light smack.' Later some prisoners whom Smith had 'grassed' – and some journalists – would scream that the manslaughter switch was a Lundy cover-up, to prop Smith up as a credible witness. His admission had certainly dismayed Lundy but the switch was made by the Director of Public Prosecutions over whom Lundy had no influence. 'You can't rig those sort of things. That decision is way up above the police. And even if it had stuck at murder, Smith would still have got a reduced sentence and parole because, if he hadn't told us, nobody would ever have known.' Smith's one-time Finchley mates – Arthur Geeves, Terry Leonard and Alan Keech – all pleaded guilty to robbery and received reduced sentences.

Another mystery which Smith cleared up was the 'blow-out' at Colindale. Lundy asked him why the Schweppes job was abandoned.

Because we had a tip-off. Alf Berkeley turned up at the meet and said, 'It's off! They're on to us. They're waiting for us!' We laughed at first. We thought he was joking. So two of the others decided to drive through the plot and see if there was anything suspicious. They saw two vehicles they reckoned were police undercover, so we believed what Alf was saying.

Smith then told Lundy that Alf had been in the Bluecoat Boy, a now-demolished pub in the City of London which was a meeting-place for criminals and City police. There he heard about a 'ready-eye' (police ambush) set up for a robbery in Colindale. At the time Smith knew only that the source was a copper well-known to the pub landlords, Alf and Jenny Walker. He later found out that Alf Walker had it from a City detective on the Regional Crime Squad.

When Smith named the officer, Lundy realized he knew
him·and that he would indeed have had prior knowledge
of the Colindale ambush. Lundy reported the matter but
it was not up to him to investigate – he was too busy
on all the robbers named by Smith. However, he was
perturbed by the response of senior officers to the fact
that he had pursued the matter even this far. They told
him to concentrate on the villains and to forget about the
corruption side of Smith's allegations.

'I can't do that,' Lundy retorted, 'not when we've
insisted Smith tell us everything so he can't be discredited.
He's told us about this man so he must be investigated.'
With some reluctance, a senior officer was appointed to
inquire but little happened until a wide-ranging probe
into Metropolitan and City police corruption was set up
in August 1978. Staffed by provincial officers and dubbed
Operation Countryman, this took over the Colindale
inquiry. Even so, the suspect was still not prosecuted
because there was no direct evidence. For a start, his identity would have had to be confirmed by Alf Berkeley, but
as he was denying all Smith's allegations against Berkeley
himself, he certainly was not going to support Smith on
any other matter. Anyway, the offending detective had
been transferred off the RCS, and left the City police
soon after.

One bent cop may have escaped Lundy's vengeance but
overall the Dave Smith job was a remarkable success. Even
so, there were problems at Finchley which caused Lundy to
argue that the Metropolitan Police needed special offices
and facilities for 'supergrass' operations.

In the past the force had only had two real supergrasses: Bertie
Smalls and Maurice O'Mahoney. The Smalls inquiry had caused
a big squad to be set up at Wembley police station, specially
equipped for the purpose. O'Mahoney had received similar
treatment at Chiswick. Both operations had been prepared in

advance, but our Dave Smith job snowballed from nothing. Uniformed officers of all ranks co-operated to give us excellent facilities at Finchley: extra cell space for Smith and extra office space for us and our massive workload.

Lundy had been particularly concerned about Smith's physical safety so he went to see Len Chalkwright, deputy clerk at Highgate Court, and explained his worries about having to bring Smith there every three days to keep him in custody. This routine became increasingly dangerous as more and more people were arrested on his evidence, and they all knew he had to be brought to Highgate every three days. An ambush or assassination attempt could not be ruled out.

Lundy suggested an imaginative solution: why not give him bail on condition that he resided at a police station? Chalkwright saw no reason why not, but the chief clerk balked lest this would conflict with the principle behind the Bail Act. Chalkwright asked if this was what Smith wanted. 'Of course it is,' said Lundy. 'He doesn't want to go on Rule 43 in Brixton prison. He wants to stay in a police station. It's the safest place.'[1] Chalkwright said, if it was what Smith really wanted, it was not against the spirit of the act: he could be remanded on bail for a month on that condition.

Lundy would use this formula many times with future supergrasses, but with Smith the immediate consequence was that hardly any other prisoners could be kept in Finchley's cells. For fifteen months they were kept free for him, like a hotel suite. He needed the space because detectives were working with him twelve hours a day, taking statements. The place also had to be fit for visits from his wife, Rita.

She was a lovely woman, but Smithie didn't make life easy for her. For most of their marriage he was either away in prison or he had just come out of jail and was off elsewhere with other birds. Now he was a supergrass, her safety was threatened too. There was nothing to stop a villain, fingered by Smith, inciting some mates to harm Rita and the kids. So we physically moved house for them all. We had to ask the local council to liaise with the county to house them as far away as possible. Imagine! Between all our official work – making arrests, doing interviews, taking statements, going to court – our lads had to pick up the entire house contents and do the removal. It was the least we could do for a woman who put up with a hell of a lot from Smithie – and from us. It drove her to the verge of suicide.

One evening about 9.30 or 10.00 I was working late, talking to people at Finchley when they said, 'Rita's downstairs. She wants to see you.' I said, 'Bring her up' so she walked into my office on the first floor and she's got the two kids with her, and she says, 'It's all your fault!' or something similar, 'You've caused all these problems, Dave's having a good time, getting all he wants in here, so you can have 'em and look after 'em!' She turns and storms off out of the nick leaving me with the two girls! That was it. She was gone! By the time I react and look out the window, she's jumped in her car and driven off. So now it's about ten at night and we've got two girls of ten and twelve sitting there. We had to go and see the in-laws and ask them if they would look after 'em. And all I got was a bollocking off *them*, that it was my fault. So while I thought I was doing a terrific job, achieving successes from the police point of view, all I was getting from the other side of the fence was a lot of flak for causing them hassle.

As a result of Smith's confessions sixty-nine people were charged, mostly with robbery, conspiracy to rob, burglary, firearms offences or handling stolen goods. Over ninety per cent pleaded guilty, a rate repeated throughout Lundy's supergrass years,[2] but six who pleaded not guilty were convicted in jury trials and sentenced to terms ranging from fourteen to twenty-five years. One trial lasted half a year. Crimes yielding three-quarters of a million pounds had been solved. Had various proven 'conspiracies to rob' gone ahead, the robbers would have taken a further

five million. Smith himself formally pleaded guilty to eight
robberies, five conspiracies and a burglary but he admitted
over eighty robberies in all. He was sentenced to five
years in jail which by then was the 'supergrass' tariff.
Two of his partners also turned supergrass, including
George Williams whom Lundy had originally blocked.
When he was later allowed to turn prosecution witness
by the Director of Public Prosecutions he was able, like
Smith, to get just five years despite admitting more than
eighty robberies.

Some of Smith's spin-offs were bizarre; for instance, he
revealed that, shortly before his arrest, he had carried out a
fake robbery in Finchley. A Jewish couple named Newman
had been tied up in their own home, while their jewellery
and fine china was stolen. They then put in an insurance
claim for £29,000, but the truth was that they had arranged
the whole thing.

They picked the cream of first-division villains to do the fake.
Smith and Berkeley went to the house, tied them up and cleared
the place out. The Newmans actually gave them a lot of the
property and promised them a share of the pay-out. When we
dragged them in, they admitted the whole thing and were jailed
for five years. What a come-down for a respectable couple in
their fifties, but if it hadn't been for Smith they would have got
away with it.

The Dave Smith operation was a mighty achievement
for Lundy, his Finchley squad and their Hertfordshire
colleagues. It was slightly dented in 1981 when the Court
of Appeal cleared Danny Gowan, who was serving twenty-
five years for three robberies and the Schweppes conspiracy. He had been implicated in all four crimes by both
Smith and Williams, but the evidence of accomplices is
almost worthless unless corroborated. Police sightings of
Gowan spying out Schweppes were not enough; the only

corroboration took the form of verbal admissions which he was said to have made in police interviews. The Court of Appeal found that these 'verbals' had been involuntary, made under duress, and the judge should have excluded them as evidence. Gowan had been taken into custody without being formally told he was being arrested or why. He was then held without access to a solicitor for eight days before being charged (his solicitor was about to issue a writ for *habeas corpus*). His admission to one robbery took place when he was on hunger strike in protest at his detention and lack of access to a solicitor. He also fainted, and it was argued his judgement may have been impaired. He himself denied making any confession but, if he did confess, the appeal judges found he should have been charged immediately, not five days later. They made no personal criticism of Lundy but felt overall that Gowan had been handled oppressively. As a result he walked out of jail.

Lundy took comfort in the Court of Appeal's view of Gowan as a 'dedicated, mature, professional criminal' (he had recently served seven years of an eleven-year prison term for robbery) and that for 'serious and experienced criminals . . . long and repeated questioning will not necessarily amount to oppression . . . The individual circumstances of the defendant are of very great importance.'

Convicted with Gowan had been another career criminal, Bernard 'Podger' Rees from Cardiff, who was also cleared on appeal of two robberies in the Midlands. The appeal judges were highly critical of the original judge, Michael Argyle, for allowing inadmissible evidence and making a shoddy summing-up. Rees certainly had the form. He had already served a six-year term for conspiracy to rob, and had been given six and a half years for squirting ammonia in a policeman's face during questioning. The officer's eye had to be removed.

It is not always the innocent who suffer. During a 1977 raid on a crowded department store in Birmingham, Rees's co-defendant had shot himself so badly in the leg that it had to be amputated. This occurred just before Christmas, and he suffered the indignity of being arrested by Santa Claus who sat on him until police arrived. A witness of such impeccable character is rarely on hand.

Losing Gowan and Rees was a blow, but they were the only two people cleared on appeal out of hundreds imprisoned through the efforts of Lundy and his Finchley squad, a remarkably low rate of 'failure'. On all other occasions the Court of Appeal backed Lundy, as when it had to judge a bizarre case which came his way through Keith Warne. Having agreed to give evidence against Berkeley and others on one robbery, Warne was treated as a semi-supergrass. Like Dave Smith, therefore, he was kept in police custody and entrusted to the care of two Regional Crime Squad officers from county forces.

Blow me! One day they took him for a home visit and let him see his wife, but while they're sitting waiting, he's gone out the back window and escaped. All hell broke loose! I went absolutely mad and we transferred the officers off the squad. He was adrift for about a month before we re-captured him, but even from this disaster came a good result. When we caught him and were ready to hang, draw and quarter him for running away, he said, 'Hang on a minute. I think you ought to listen to what I've got to say.'

Warne then told us that, while on the run, he had met someone he knew from prison who was now committing robberies to raise funds for the IRA. We passed Warne on to the Anti-Terrorist Squad, but we arrested the robbers he had named, including a man called Turner. This man refused to speak at all! From his arrest onwards nobody ever heard him say a word. So while our witness Warne – a self-confessed con-man and liar – was saying Turner had told him all about a robbery he'd done, Turner never spoke a word to us. No name, no address, nothing. He also refused to go on i.d. parades, but witnesses identified him during

confrontations instead. Throughout my interviews he still said
nothing, but he did nod or shake his head to various questions, so
when I gave evidence against him, my evidence consisted entirely
of me saying that he had nodded or shook his head. The defence
argued that this evidence should not be admitted because he'd
never spoken, but the judge allowed it. Turner was convicted,
he went to appeal but stayed convicted: ten years.

This vindication only intensified the dislike which defence lawyers felt towards Lundy. One of them joked that
Lundy had now created the 'non-verbal verbal'. Some
solicitors claimed that what had happened to Danny
Gowan was Lundy's normal *modus operandi*: that officers
under his command often invented 'verbals' and pushed
the rules governing detention without charge to their limit.
This allegation Lundy fiercely denies. To top it all, some
defendants who had denied all charges in the past, and
fought long and expensive trials, were now admitting their
crimes. ('Perhaps these solicitors thought I was doing them
out of business by getting their customers to plead guilty,
and so wiping out their fat fees.') But whichever way you
looked at Lundy, in less than five years he had sprung from
the CID's unknown ranks to become the most prominent
detective at the world's most famous criminal court. With
up to six Old Bailey trials running simultaneously, he was
Scotland Yard's equivalent to Andrew Lloyd Webber,
packing them in at several West End theatres at a time.

Ironically, some of Lundy's star performers rose and fell
just like show-business entertainers. One year Dave Smith
was informing on so many violent robbers that, almost
single-handed, he caused the fall in attacks on banks,
security vans and cash delivery vehicles in London which
occurred in the late 1970s. Yet for Smith himself life did
not get any better. After spending fifteen months in police
custody, he had to go to prison, where he suffered hepatitis
and a slipped disc. When he testified against Berkeley and

Gowan in 1979 he had to be brought from hospital where two armed policemen guarded him twenty-four hours a day. Later his marriage broke up.

The prosecutor at Smith's own trial had said Smith 'wanted to wipe the slate clean and start afresh', but when he was freed in 1980 he returned to the only life he knew: crime. On 29 September 1986 he was arrested after raiding a Securicor vehicle in Golders Green, and charged with conspiracy to rob under his new identity, 'Edwards'. Many supergrasses return to crime. More surprisingly, they often do so close to their old neighbourhoods where they might run into vengeful friends of people they have grassed. Golders Green was only a mile from Smith's old stamping ground of Finchley and three miles from his former home in Southgate. In the local police station it all proved too much for him. On Monday 13 October he was found in his cell dying in a pool of blood. He had cut his throat with a razor blade.

Newspapers speculated that he killed himself because he feared going to jail once more as a supergrass. At the inquest it emerged he had again confessed and turned 'grass'. Officers with him the day before he died said he had been in a jovial mood. His two daughters, who had also seen him that day, said in written statements that he had been happy, confident and was well-treated by the police. His only complaint was about drunks in other cells. On 8 October his own cell was festooned with balloons. It was his birthday.

Despite the celebrations, he knew there could not be another five-year supergrass deal for him. This time he was sure to get over twenty years. Janet Clark, his common-law wife, said he could not face it. After his death she told police he had tried to kill himself once before. Within the station he was treated as a 'high-risk' prisoner but this had not stopped him acquiring the lethal razor.

Throughout this time Tony Lundy had seen nothing of Smith. By October 1986 he was investigating a wholly different area of crime, yet back in 1977 the Dave Smith operation was just the first in an extraordinary series which the rising star of London's CID would conduct into organized crime in Britain.

Fury 'Cross the Mersey

Dave Smith was more significant than either Bertie Smalls or Maurice O'Mahoney, his two predecessors in Scotland Yard's supergrass 'Hall of Fame'. They had never served a long term of imprisonment. He had. More important, he had spent most of that term in Gartree maximum security prison in Leicestershire, which meant that his knowledge of professional criminals spread nationwide.

In earlier years, no matter how 'big' convicted criminals may have been, they tended to be sent to local or regional jails. Thus London villains were usually incarcerated alongside other Londoners, and so on throughout the country. But after the 1966 Mountbatten Inquiry into prison escapes and security, it was decided to concentrate England and Wales's most dangerous criminals in a few maximum security jails because not all prisons could be made fully secure. This reform was well-intentioned but it had a disastrous side-effect: it created what Tony Lundy calls 'a national league of first-division criminals'. By bringing together gangsters from all over the country, maximum security jails can be regarded as a leading cause of the rapid increase in sophisticated armed robberies in Britain in the 1970s.

Dave Smith had been in Gartree for many years as a Category A prisoner (meaning highly dangerous and likely to try to escape). When he came out, he had top-level associates in every part of Britain. The significance of this emerged only when he started talking. At the time each police force tended to investigate major robberies on its 'patch' from the starting point that the robbers were probably local men. At best forces worked regionally, through the RCSs. Now, on Smith's information, Lundy's team was arresting people from Scotland, Newcastle, the Midlands and the South for crimes they had committed together all over the country.

One day when Lundy was busy hauling suspects from the provinces into various North London stations, Dave Smith tossed him a suggestion. 'Another bloke will help you, if you do it right.' 'Who's that?' 'Billy Amies.' Lundy had never heard of him but Smith revealed that Amies was in Walton prison in Liverpool, facing trial for a series of violent armed robberies. 'Billy and me were in Gartree together,' Lundy recalls Smith saying. 'He could open up more areas than me 'cos he's worked all over the country, and with South London people as well. He's been well at it. If you get into him you could really clear up some stuff.'

Smith said he had recently visited Amies in Walton where the prisoner had confided that he was in a terrible position. 'He's nicked with a couple of Liverpool villains, including one called John Tremarco, but there's a bent old bill [corrupt policeman] up there who's trying to do favours for Tremarco. He's trying to shove everything onto Billy, to lighten the load on Tremarco.' Amies had also told Smith that recently some London detectives had gone to see him about another crime, but a Liverpool sergeant had insisted on going with them to the prison. Smith told Lundy: 'They won't let anybody near him unless they go too.' Smith said Amies was also claiming that one Merseyside officer had suggested he 'do a nutter' – pretend to be mad – and plead guilty to everything, then he and his colleagues would try to get him a lightish sentence. 'He's so sick that they're pushing it all on him,' said Smith, 'but he feels there's no way out. He doesn't know what to do.'

Drawing on later knowledge, Lundy says:

In some ways Billy was a nutter. He was also known as Billy the Queer because he's a raving homosexual. A big hard man, over six foot, a real animal, a compulsive armed robber who was really feared, but clever too. In Gartree the best place to be is in the prison hospital, so now and again Billy would do his nutty turn: he'd go a bit off his rocker. It was just a big act to get himself better facilities, but they called his bluff. He kept saying he was hearing voices in his brain, so one day they took him to the hospital for tests and started to shave his head, so they could put things on it – or even inside. That cured Billy all right. He came back absolutely gutted! He didn't do any more pretending about voices in his head!

Now, in 1977, it seemed at least one wayward Liverpool cop was telling Amies to put on a similar show in court, or so Smith said. If Lundy was to check it out – and also persuade Amies to turn 'supergrass' – he had to by-pass the Merseyside Police and see him alone. Lundy faced a huge formal obstacle. 'It is normal practice to tell the force that's already dealing with a remand prisoner that you want to see him. As these were extraordinary circumstances I had to adopt another course of action.'

Lundy called the prison liaison office at the Home Office and explained that he wanted two of his officers to see Amies but did not want any Liverpool police to know. He asked for a visit to be arranged through Prison Security. The ploy worked. He managed to get two sergeants into Walton unaccompanied. When Amies saw them he expressed amazement and asked what had happened to his Liverpool guardians. The London detectives told him to forget them and to concentrate on the fact that Dave Smith had become a supergrass. At first Amies did not believe them but when he read Smith's statements naming him on robberies he rapidly decided to admit everything and give evidence, but he implored the London men to get him out of Walton jail straight away.

To show good faith he instantly gave them a brief

summary of what he could say about his own and other people's crimes. He also revealed his own dealings with a sergeant on Liverpool's Serious Crimes Squad named John Keating. As soon as his own sergeants reported back, Lundy set about getting Amies transferred to London. This was far from easy, as Amies had been remanded to Walton because he was awaiting trial in Liverpool. Merseyside Police were bound to find out what was going on, as Lundy recalls:

> Out of the blue all hell breaks loose. Liverpool chief super-intendents are on the phone saying, 'How dare you go and see our prisoners without our permission. What's it all about?' We responded, 'We can't tell you at this stage. It's confidential. We had to interview him about armed robberies.' They came back saying, 'You've no right to do this. He's coming up for trial here.' But bang! Suddenly we move him down to Brixton prison, into a secure Rule 43 wing, and make a special application through the Home Office to put him in a police station. We get everything approved. Out he comes and by 16 December 1977 we put him in Acton Police Station. But, oh boy! Are they going potty up in Liverpool! No wonder, as we find out later.

Secure in Lundy's supergrass set-up, Amies told the story of his nationwide life of crime. This sent Finchley detectives off again all over England on another round-up of dozens of accomplices. He also confessed to the robberies he had committed on Merseyside and made detailed statements against his co-defendants in the forth-coming trial. Lundy assumed that this would please the Merseyside detectives, for they were now almost certain to win convictions against the other two accused including John Tremarco. 'We think, Magic! They must be over the moon! But instead of being overjoyed, all they're giving us is hassle and aggravation, so it was obvious that what he was telling us was true.'

By now Amies had gone further, claiming that the

crooked Liverpool cop, John Keating, had asked him
for money but he had refused to pay. In view of current
difficulties Lundy was inclined to believe him. The story
also heightened his worries for Amies's safety in October
1978 when he was to return to Liverpool, plead guilty
and testify. The night before this court appearance Lundy
sent him north escorted by Finchley officers. To Lundy's
relief it now seemed all inter-force arguments had been
put aside as Merseyside agreed to provide Amies with
secure overnight accommodation in a local police station
– clearly he could not stay in Walton jail from which he had
so recently been spirited. With great relief Lundy's men
duly deposited him in the station, which happened to be
the base of the squad which had handled his original arrest.
The London detectives then checked into a local hotel.

When they returned to the police station next morning
to take Amies to court, the custody officer told them
he had been moved to the 'main bridewell'. This was
Liverpool's central police station where overnight prisoners were usually lodged.[1] Off went Lundy's men to collect
Amies, only to discover the other inmates had been told
that he was the supergrass they had recently read about
in the newspapers. Amies told his minders of a terrifying
night, throughout which the other prisoners had expressed
their contempt by banging on cell walls, shouting and
doing everything to stop him getting to sleep.

By now Tony Lundy had arrived in Liverpool to watch
the trial and look after Amies. He fumed when he found
out about the overnight goings-on – that was just the kind
of thing he had taken precautions to avoid – but the show
had to go on. Amies went into court and pleaded guilty.
The other defendants denied the charges. The prosecution
solicitors now said that as Amies had made all his previous
statements as a defendant, he must now make a fresh
statement as a witness. Meanwhile the trial began with

a recital of the gang's crimes, including the nasty detail that one villain had sunk his teeth into a victim's private parts to frighten him into opening a safe. Was that Amies, as the defence were to allege, or someone else, as Billy claimed?

On the first Friday of the trial Amies stepped into the witness box. As soon as he said he was prepared to testify against the other defendants their lawyers asked for an adjournment. It was granted. Half an hour later they returned and the defendants changed their pleas to guilty. There was uproar in the public gallery, as relatives and friends screamed revenge at Amies. 'So he never had to give evidence,' recalls Lundy. 'They never believed he'd do it, but as soon as he set foot in the box, they had no choice but to change pleas.'

The judge adjourned the case till the following Monday when he would sentence everyone including Amies. Lundy refused to stay for the weekend: he wanted to take Amies to Finchley and bring him back again on Sunday. Even so, he was worried about further surprise developments so he rang his commander, Don Neesham, and requested 'a bit more fire power'. Neesham took the point and suggested the Flying Squad's new chief superintendent, Jimmy Sewell, should also go to Liverpool. Sewell agreed, made some helpful suggestions, and concurred with Lundy's arrangements to take Amies north and lodge him overnight in the same police station where they had left him last time – only this time he must stay there all night. An official message to this effect was sent to Merseyside Police.

Lundy and Sewell agreed to meet in Liverpool early on Sunday evening at their hotel. Once they were sure Amies was safely lodged, they were going to spend the rest of the evening at Orrell rugby club nearby where Lundy's brother Bernard was at the height of his playing career.

When Sunday night came that arrangement was 'blown out'. Sewell and Lundy had arrived at the hotel on time but then they waited for hours with no sign of sergeants Brian O'Rourke and Bernie Craven who were taking care of Billy. At last O'Rourke rang up to say they were having difficulty lodging Amies. When they finally turned up they still had Billy with them.

The sergeants then explained how they had taken Amies to the very same police station, only to be told by the custody officer that he had no notification that Amies was to be lodged there. All attempts to raise local Serious Crime Squad officers failed, so O'Rourke and Craven tried to lodge Amies in other bridewells but without success. Chief Superintendent Sewell was outraged but even his calls to Merseyside Police failed to secure an overnight cell. He then voiced the only solution: Amies must be booked into the hotel. One of the sergeants had to stay in a double room with him, the other one had to sleep next door.

But *which* sergeant was to sleep with Amies? This was no pleasant prospect, so Brian O'Rourke and Bernie Craven tossed a coin. Craven lost. Somewhat later than ten o'clock he took Amies to their room. Now at last the others could relax, even if Craven could not. Jimmy Sewell decided to go to bed. Lundy and O'Rourke fancied a drink in a bar next to the hotel.

When they returned an hour later they found Sewell 'in orbit' in the foyer. Amies had escaped and Craven was in hospital, dangerously ill. Lundy could not believe his ears. As the senior detectives paced round, trying to work out how the pair could have left their room – let alone got into this mess – the hotel doors burst open and in ran Billy Amies, with his clothes torn and tattered and blood streaming down his face. O'Rourke marched him back to the bedroom which he should never have left.

Sewell and Lundy headed for the hospital, where they found Craven in intensive care.

At first he looks like he's dead. His head seemed to be swollen to twice its size [recalls Lundy with a shudder], then he flickered into life and explained how Amies had told him about a dockland pub called the Crows Nest where they could get a late-night drink. Unfortunately, it was also the pub used by Liverpool's top villains – including mates of John Tremarco whom Amies has just given evidence against, and who was going to be sentenced with him the very next day!

Typical of the fearless animal he is, off goes Amies with Craven into the lions' den. But as soon as they walk in, they're set upon! Amies, big strong beast, fights his way out and escapes, but Bernie Craven gets an almighty kicking. He's almost kicked to death but he manages to stagger out of the pub, he's found in the front garden of a nearby house and he's rushed to hospital. In the meantime Amies has run all across Liverpool. So while we were thinking he had escaped from us, in fact he's running back *to* us!

Next morning when we go to court, Billy Amies has plasters all over his face and a broken arm in a sling. The public gallery is jam-packed full of villains and defendants' relatives screaming abuse, especially when the judge tells Tremarco he's going away for fifteen years. Then Amies has to stand up in the box, all battered and torn, while I make an application that he is not sentenced at this court but remanded into our custody to the Old Bailey, to be sentenced at one time for everything he is admitting: another fifty armed robberies.

Naturally the judge has noticed Amies's condition so he says something like, 'There appears to have been some problems overnight, officer' – he knew what had happened because I had told the prosecutor – 'What is going to be his security position in future?' 'He's being kept in strict security M'Lord . . .', I lamely reply. 'Well, I hope it turns out to be better than it seems to have been last night.'

The judge agreed to remand Amies back into the care of the London detectives. In the meantime Jimmy Sewell had been on the phone, involving the Metropolitan commissioner and Merseyside's chief constable. They agreed on a high level inquiry into what had gone wrong. By now Lundy was thanking his lucky stars he had asked for a senior officer to go with him to Liverpool, otherwise he would have been in deep trouble.

In due course the inquiry decided the London officers had not been at fault. Merseyside Police arrested several men for attempting to murder Craven and Amies and causing grievous bodily harm but they were acquitted for lack of evidence. Bernie Craven had suffered severe concussion, a broken nose and a fractured cheekbone. He did not recover enough to remain an operational detective and was invalided out of the force. Lundy was appalled by what happened to him; nevertheless, Craven had allowed Amies to talk him out of strict orders that they both stay in their room throughout the night.

Looking back, we realized it was a mistake to let supergrasses and their protectors get too close. At first we used to leave whoever had the best rapport with the villain to look after him for months on end, but then the 'Stockholm syndrome' applies: the policeman starts being manipulated. After this fiasco I changed the 'guards' every week.

Amies's allegations against Liverpool detectives were investigated in yet another inquiry. This failed to prove or disprove them, but in March 1979 they gained credibility when Detective Sergeant John Keating, who was the subject of Amies's most serious complaints, was convicted of attempting to extort half the reward which insurers had paid to a police informer. The informer had 'squealed' and Keating was sent to jail for two and a half years. One Liverpool defence lawyer says that Keating's corrupt activities had been well-known to the city's underworld for years.

Amies also told Lundy about corruption among London police. He confessed to taking part in a violent robbery

in Rotherhithe in which a Greek hairdresser had been
attacked in the street, seriously beaten and robbed of
£10,000 in takings. The victim claimed he had been set
up by a man working in one of his salons. Mixed up in
the middle was an officer on Rotherhithe Robbery Squad.
He was a good amateur footballer and used to play in
a local team with strong criminal connections. He was
suspended partly on the basis of Amies's allegations, but
there was insufficient evidence to prosecute him. Lundy
gave evidence against him at a discipline hearing, after
which he was dismissed.

Amies admitted a total of twenty-seven robberies, four
conspiracies to rob and eight burglaries. As a result of his
information thirty other criminals were charged. When
Dave Smith had first named him he also revealed Amies
had worked with Micky Morris, whom Lundy had charged
in 1971 for shooting a Soho doorman but who walked free
when the victim suffered lightning amnesia (see Chapter
2). Amies confirmed he had worked with Morris on several
jobs, including a grotesque domestic robbery in Surrey.
One evening in October 1976 Morris, Amies and another
criminal named Richie Smith burst into the Blackwater,
Surrey, home of a forty-five-year-old scrap metal dealer,
David Melbourne, as he and his seven children were
watching *Starsky and Hutch* on television. The real-life
gang were wearing masks and carrying coshes, hammers,
a sawn-off shotgun and a pistol. In a bizarre twist Amies
was dressed as a policeman.

The gang tied Melbourne and his elder children up.
To force him to say where any money might be, they
hit him with a mallet, smashed a bottle in his face and
threatened to cut off his sexual organs and burn him with
cigarettes. Dissatisfied with takings of £1,300 in cash, they
grabbed Melbourne's sixteen-year-old daughter, took her
into the kitchen and threatened her with a knife. When

she screamed that she did not know of any other money, they ordered her to strip. When she was down to her bra and pants they paraded her in front of her father, while one of the gang (Amies says it was Morris) asked, 'How would you like to see your daughter raped?' Eventually the gang accepted there was no more money around so they took £1,700 worth of jewellery, threatened to burn down the house and left.

When Amies first named Morris as a partner-in-crime he was nowhere to be found. Then Dave Smith told Lundy that almost certainly Morris would be sunning himself in Benidorm on Spain's Costa Blanca. Smith knew all about Morris because, in a way, they belonged to the same family. Smith was emotionally involved with Jenny Walker, landlady of the notorious Bluecoat Boy, and Micky was married to Jenny's daughter Sandra. The Walkers owned several apartments in Benidorm, so Lundy decided he should fly there and contact the Alicante branch of the *Comisaria de Policia*, Spain's national CID.

To make this trip Lundy had to get permission. He also had to put up with jibes that all he would get was a holiday because the Spanish police would not help him find Morris. This view was held even in the Yard department responsible for overseas liaison where Lundy was told to be very careful in Spain and to expect no co-operation whatever. As it happened, he struck up excellent relations with two detectives whom he came to know as Vicente, the superintendent, and Felipe, the inspector.

Lundy and his sergeant arrived at two in the morning, but Vicente insisted on immediately spending two hours talking the matter through. The Englishman had little for him to go on, only a photograph and the information that Morris was somewhere in Benidorm on a false passport in a name they did not know. Off went Vicente. Within six hours he had found the man boozing in a bar. When Morris left and walked to his car, uniformed police accused him of being drunk. They demanded his passport and drove him home to get it. Vicente thus discovered Morris's false name and his address. He reported these to Lundy who checked with London and was told the passport was stolen. That was the easy part. Now came the difficult bit. At the time Britain had no extradition treaty with Spain. If Morris was merely told to leave the country, he could slip across the border into France or Portugal and still be out of Scotland Yard's reach. The problem was, how to get him to go straight back to England without suspecting the Yard was involved. The last thing the Spaniards could do, therefore, was disclose they knew his passport was false, or that Lundy was in Benidorm.

They kept him under observation but as he was lazing around with his wife and some friends they had no excuse to arrest him. Instead, after a couple of days they searched his house in the hope of finding any excuse to expel him. Luckily Vicente found a marriage certificate in the couple's true name, so he could now point openly to the false passport. He then told Morris he was arresting him for murder. 'What murder?' said Morris. Vicente responded with the tale of a German who had been found dead in his Mercedes not far from where Morris was living. Vicente knew full well that the German had committed suicide by feeding a pipe from the exhaust back into the car, but he told Morris he thought it was murder. He even took Morris to the police garage and demonstrated how the man had been found. Morris protested it wasn't murder, but suicide. 'What's suicide?' said Vicente, giving a passable imitation of Manuel in *Fawlty Towers*. Morris patiently explained how in England people kill themselves this way all the time. He even demonstrated how it had happened, getting in the Merc. Vicente pretended that the truth had finally dawned on him and said, 'Ah. Si. Ah. Suicide!'

By this time Morris may have thought that Vicente was the biggest fool of all time, but although he was off the murder rap he still faced charges over his passport, for which Vicente was keeping him in a police cell. He therefore concocted a story for the gullible Vicente about using the passport some time back when he was having domestic trouble with his wife. He said he had come to Spain not wanting her to know where he was, but now things were all right between them. She had flown out to be with him, and he no longer had any need to be in Spain on false papers. How would it be, he asked, if he went back to England and returned on his true passport?

This would have suited Vicente and Lundy fine but they doubted he would actually do it, so Vicente kept up the pretence of having to take him to court and order his deportation. Morris begged him to change his mind until Vicente relented. He said that if Morris went back to England voluntarily, he would risk his job by not charging him – provided that his wife booked him on an immediate flight. Morris agreed and he explained the situation to Sandra when she next came in, but he did not know that Felipe, the inspector in the room with them, spoke fluent English. Felipe had deliberately concealed this fact throughout their encounters. Now he heard Micky's uncensored view as he told Sandra that his luck was in. He had 'a right pair of wallies' dealing with him who had obviously not checked him out with Scotland Yard. He said that these dumb Spaniards had agreed to let him go back to England and then return to Spain on the right passport. He told Sandra to ring up her mother, tell her to get his genuine passport ready and to have somebody at the airport waiting to give it to him. Then he would jump on another plane and come straight back to Benidorm.

Sandra went off and tried her best. Alas! there were no

seats for days. Under Spanish law Vicente now had either
to charge Morris (which he did not want to do) or set
him free. He set him free but ordered him to book the
first flight home, then to come to his office so he could
be escorted to the airport. Two days went by but still
Morris had not booked his flight. Vicente visited him
and told him to get on with it. Morris reported that he
was due to fly out a day or two hence, on 22 February
1978. When the day came, Vicente and Felipe turned up
early at the Morris apartment, got Micky out of bed and
stayed there until he was ready to go to Valencia airport.
But just in case Morris suspected anything other than the
false passport lay behind his VIP treatment, Vicente asked
him to perform a special favour: to take a present to his
Spanish girlfriend in London. This seemed to put Morris
at his ease, for Vicente must be genuine if he was asking
him to perform this delicate task.

Half-way to the airport, however, Vicente exclaimed he
had forgotten the present and demanded that Felipe drive
them back to Benidorm to get it. In Spanish Felipe said
if they did that, they would miss the plane. Ever helpful,
Micky consoled Vicente by offering to buy the girl a
substitute present himself in London and delivering it to
her. When he came back in a few days' time, they would
have a drink together and 'call it a deal'. 'Aah, Micky,'
said Vicente in a show of grovelling Hispanic gratitude,
'thank you very much!' and gave him the imaginary girl's
imaginary address.

Morris boarded the plane, flew into Heathrow and,
before he could walk off, Lundy's men came on board
uttering some corny line such as 'Come on, Micky! You're
nicked!' And so he was. When the case came to the Old
Bailey in July 1979, he was convicted and sent to prison
for fourteen years. By now newspapers had given the star
witness, Billy Amies, a suitably treacherous nickname,

'Billy the Snake'. Morris still did not know that other snakes had been his undoing in Spain.

Another person missing when Amies named names on the Melbourne family job was Richie Smith, but finding him was scarcely Lundy's priority. His team was fully stretched, after arresting an average of ten criminals a week for three months. One Saturday he was enjoying a rare night at home when the phone rang to tell him of a robbery ten miles away at Kentish Town. This time the robbers had stolen not just money but an entire Mint Security van. He grovelled an apology to his long-suffering wife Vi and went to the scene. Sure enough, the van had disappeared, a lot of money was missing and the driver had been tied up and dumped. Lundy listened to his story, felt it did not ring true and started to question him in a disbelieving manner. 'He was elderly, he had no form, but I held him in the station overnight and kept on at him. In the end he broke and admitted he had been approached to give the load away.'

The robbery was a fake, a set-up, but it was still a robbery because force had been used on the other guard who knew nothing of the scheme. The driver revealed that among the robbers was none other than Richie Smith and that later he would be celebrating in a certain pub. Off went Lundy's team and arrested him. It was an exhausting day-and-night job lasting forty-eight hours, but all the robbers were captured. In due course Richie Smith was jailed for fifteen years. The triumph was acknowledged when Deputy Assistant Commissioner David Powis, chief of all London's operational detectives, went to Kentish Town police station and thanked the entire team for what he acclaimed as another outstanding success. In previous months Assistant Commissioner (Crime) Gilbert Kelland and even the Metropolitan Commissioner, Sir

David McNee, had offered their congratulations during personal visits.

Another 'Amies' job concerned a gang which specialized in hi-jacking entire lorryloads of goods. In February 1978 Lundy arrested the suspects who were taken to Acton where Inspector Des Lewis was running the Amies operation. After some hours two detectives interviewing a suspect named Edward McGovern reported he was offering them a bribe to 'get a result', meaning, to get the case dropped. Lundy and Lewis decided to talk to him directly. 'We understand you want a bit of help,' they said. McGovern repeated his offer but did not get the 'result' he wanted. Instead, Lundy promptly told him he would be charged not only for the lorryloads but also for attempted bribery. When the case came to court he pleaded guilty and was given eighteen months for that offence.

Despite this robust action, Lundy would later suffer from a stream of claims that he was 'bent': a crooked and corrupt cop. Such claims have never been substantiated but equally they are almost impossible to obliterate because it is impossible to prove a negative. A detective cannot prove he is not corrupt. All he can do is assert his innocence, but the louder he shouts the guiltier he may sound. Yet the McGovern case, along with many other incidents in which Lundy exposed crooked colleagues, show he was second to none in combating graft and corruption. The trouble was that such zeal made him many enemies in both the police and the underworld. There is such a thing as a cop who is too clean.

5

Grasses Not So Green

When Judge Argyle jailed Alf Berkeley and other members of the 'Thatched Barn' and 'Schweppes' gang at the Old Bailey in 1979, he was driven to comment on Dave Smith and George Williams: 'Nobody, I think, listening to these supergrasses giving evidence could doubt the truth of what they had said. In any event, their evidence was corroborated, but it was nauseating to hear these hypocrites and reflect, as a matter of policy, that they have each been sentenced to five years only.'

If a 'hanging judge' like Argyle could say that, the sense of revulsion against supergrass deals must have been widespread among the judiciary. In this respect if no other, Argyle was on the same side as Patrick 'Cowley' (a pseudonym, for legal reasons) whom he had just sentenced to twenty years for four robberies. Cowley gave no evidence but he made an articulate statement from the dock in which he lambasted Chief Inspector Lundy's use of grasses. He attacked the fact that Dave Smith could get a deal even though he had killed one man and permanently injured another. He also slammed Billy Amies (who had not given evidence against him but came into his sights as another Lundy supergrass) for the rape threat on a young girl and for allegedly biting a young man's penis during another robbery.[1] Cowley claimed he was simply a scapegoat to justify Lundy's deals with these awful people.

It is unlikely that the widow of Kurt Hess was satisfied with the five-year sentence imposed on her husband's killer, Dave Smith. Equally, when Amies went down for just five years after being one of a gang who inflicted physical and psychological damage on the entire Melbourne family, Mr David Melbourne must have felt repelled. 'There is a lot of talk about the poor criminal,' he said, 'but it is the victim who really pays.'

Smith and Amies certainly rank high as manifestations of evil, but they were no worse than the criminals they 'grassed', most of whom would have gone unpunished if it had not been for Lundy. It should be appreciated that, if he had not 'turned' these supergrasses, the gangs who killed Hess and violated the Melbourne family would have been free to continue their activities unimpeded for many more years.

Lundy's own family paid a price for his detective success and the controversy it provoked. In the 1980s their home was violated by burglars, and by other criminals attempting to plant drugs. His wife and daughters were subjected to repeated harassment. Yet Lundy has never regretted using controversial weapons such as supergrasses or, as Scotland Yard prefers to call them, 'resident informants' in his war on organized crime. Not only did over ninety per cent of all defendants charged on his supergrasses' evidence plead guilty; of those who pleaded not guilty, very few were acquitted. As for any allegations of 'verbals' and fit-ups, one supergrass case indicates that once Lundy had evidence of an accused man's innocence he did not hesitate to drop charges.

The suspect was a criminal known as Bob 'the Dog' whom Dave Smith had originally named in a conspiracy to blast open a security van. The evidence was too flimsy to justify an arrest but Smith claimed Bob 'the Dog' was 'at it again'. With his record this seemed likely. A compulsive armed robber, he had served three long sentences with barely three months at liberty in between. Now in his late forties, he had walked with a distinctive limp ever since one of his legs was crushed in a getaway crash. Even so, he was a fitness fanatic and played squash every day at a North London club. Big, powerful, swarthy, with dark-dyed hair, Bob 'the Dog' was marked down at Finchley as a definite target for the future.

The squad did not have to wait long. Soon a man with a sawn-off shotgun ambushed a security guard and ordered him to drop the bag of money he was delivering to Wembley Park Underground station. The guard complied, the robber grabbed the bag and ran to a getaway car. Finchley officers went to the scene and talked to witnesses who described him as swarthy and middle-aged. They guessed he was Bob 'the Dog' who lived not far away, but there was no evidence to justify arresting him. Two weeks later at the same place the same guard was challenged in the same way but this time he managed to run into the station offices where an employee tried to slam the door shut. The robber crashed through the door, the shotgun went off and part of the employee's hand was blown away. The robber fled, leaving the bag behind. Witnesses said he ran with a marked limp, wore no mask and described him in terms which, says Lundy, 'fitted Bob "the Dog" to a tee'.

This time Lundy ordered his arrest. Predictably Bob 'the Dog' denied committing any robberies, even though he had paid £5,000 cash into a building society days after the first Wembley Park job. He said that since Lundy had 'turned' Dave Smith and arrested scores of other robbers, he hadn't touched anything. Unconvinced, Lundy put him on an identification parade where witnesses to both robberies, including the security guard, picked him out. Lundy now had game, set and match: identification, the building society money – which Bob 'the Dog' could not explain – *plus* the gammy leg. Yet 'the Dog' still protested his innocence. 'Well, Bob,' Lundy remembers saying, 'if it wasn't you all I can say is, without a doubt, you are going to get convicted: hung, drawn and quartered. If you're innocent, I'm sure one day we'll prove it but, on the evidence, you're going to prison for a very long time.'

Bob 'the Dog' was remanded to Brixton and committed for trial. He had languished inside for six months when an informant named two robbers who were going to rob a Sainsbury's supermarket in the north-west London suburb of Burnt Oak. At the appointed hour Lundy's squad were lying in wait when news came through that a robbery had just been committed at another Sainsbury's. The informant had identified the right street but the wrong branch. Both shops were in Edgware Road, but at opposite ends some eight miles apart.

Despite the confusion Lundy arrested the suspects, Jimmy Gallant and Sammy Samuels. Soon Gallant turned supergrass. He confessed to the Sainsbury's job, then started telling his interviewer, Sergeant Jack Snodgrass, about many other robberies. Lundy was overjoyed, and basked in the glory of this latest triumph until Snodgrass came into his office and told him that Gallant had admitted to the two robberies at Wembley Park Underground. Gallant was the driver and Sammy Samuels did the job.

Lundy was disbelieving; Samuels was only in his early twenties and the witnesses had said the robber was middle-aged like Bob 'the Dog'. Snodgrass explained that on the second robbery, when the shotgun had blown part of the employee's hand away, Samuels was himself hit in the leg so he limped back to the getaway car, his thigh full of shotgun pellets. When the story was put to Samuels he admitted everything.

Lundy promptly phoned the office of the Director of Public Prosecutions and next day Bob 'the Dog' appeared at the Old Bailey. Lundy stood up and produced the confessions of Gallant and Samuels and Bob was discharged.

Despite spending six months in Brixton over a crime he did not commit, Bob 'the Dog' did not sue or ask for costs because, evidentially, the police had done everything by the book. 'But that job never gets publicized,' says Lundy. 'When you've proved a man innocent! All that sticks are the allegations that you're going around all the time fitting people up.'

Much later Lundy bumped into Bob 'the Dog' at a professional boxing match. The detective was apprehensive lest he was going to have a hard time but Bob shook his hand and gushed his thanks without a hint of animosity. In these friendly moments Lundy could not resist asking where that building society money had come from. Bob 'the Dog' volunteered what he could not reveal when arrested, for fear of being charged with another offence. The money had come from a little racket at Heathrow Airport, so maybe he felt there was an element of rough justice about his months on remand in Brixton.

Jimmy Gallant became a very useful supergrass, securing many other robbers' convictions. Not every supergrass operation was so successful. One might have disrupted Lundy's career – not because of any dishonesty on his part but because senior officers did not always approve of his robust approach to combating armed robbery.

On 10 August 1978 Tony Lundy arrested a South London criminal named Ray Fowles on suspicion of robbery. After a few days' interrogation he too decided to 'roll over' and become a supergrass. At that point Lundy and his squad were so busy with work generated by earlier supergrasses that they could not take on the Fowles inquiries. Lundy rang his Flying Squad commander, Don Neesham, and told him there was a big package of work to be done by somebody else. This move became one of Lundy's lasting regrets: 'By this time I had virtually cleared up North London. We had left nothing unturned. We'd cleared up virtually every robbery committed over many years. The beauty of Ray Fowles – and what sickened me about not doing him – was that he was capable of clearing up South London too.'

To house Fowles, and a special squad set up to pursue his allegations, some huts were cleared at Whetstone police station just up the road from Finchley. The man chosen to lead the inquiry was a superintendent who had just joined the Flying Squad, Phil Corbett. In the future Lundy would develop immense respect for Corbett and they would become good friends, but at this time Lundy's instinct to react at speed to hot supergrass information contrasted starkly with Corbett's calmer, orthodox approach. This difference was crucial because, one week after turning supergrass, Fowles suddenly announced that a £300,000 robbery was going to take place the very next day, on 16 August, across the river at Lambeth Town Hall. Even better, the gang included the cream of South London robbers.

Lundy had little time to test Fowles's story, but he promptly sent out surveillance teams who spotted getaway cars parked exactly where Fowles said they would be. Lundy now had to calculate how best to apprehend the robbers. If they were seized before they reached 'the plot' they would doubtless concoct all sorts of defences including tales of fit-ups and fabricated confessions which might convince a cynical inner London jury to acquit them. Instead, experience told Lundy he should try and catch them red-handed in an ambush outside the Town Hall.

The evening before the robbery was to take place Corbett came to see Lundy at Finchley. It was their first-ever meeting. Lundy recalls rattling off the job details to Corbett in this excited fashion:

Guess what's happening: it's terrific! Fowles has stuck up a job going off tomorrow. He says they'll do it even though he's been in custody for a week, because they won't believe he'll have talked. It's worth £300,000 – all the staff wages – and it's the last day they can do it because after tomorrow the staff are going to be paid by cheque instead of cash. The gang's got an inside man at the Town Hall, they've got access at night and they've already cut the alarms. Everything's set up! Fowles says it's definitely going to go. What a team! Freddie Sinfield, John Reid, Kenny Baker, Peter Rose, Tony Colson and Micky Sewell who's fixed the alarms. They've all been at it for years, real bad 'uns. Fabulous!

On Lundy babbled, oblivious to the impact he was having on the stone-faced superintendent.

Anyway, we ambush 'em on the pavement! I've started to put an operation together. This is how we'll do it: I've sent officers to the scene, there's a place above a shop which we could use as an operations post. Three or four of the robbers are meeting at a flat, the others will be outside the Town Hall. They'll have their own shooters, but the other guns and masks are all in a happy bag in Peter Rose's flat. Gonna have a nice ambush. Magic!

'Hang on a minute,' said Corbett, 'I'm in charge of this now.' Lundy steamed on, 'Yeh, that's OK. I've been getting it all organized.' Corbett came to the point: 'But we won't be doing it that way. The way you're planning it, there could be a shoot-out.' Lundy bounced back: 'Yeh, but they won't be expecting us. We'll be ready. They'll be given the chance to surrender. Obviously we'll try and take 'em clean at the scene, but if there's going to be a shoot-out it's not going to be us who'll be shot. It'll be them, 'cos we'll be waiting for them. I've had other jobs where we've done ambushes and we've never shot anybody.'

Corbett was not impressed and told Lundy his scheme was too dangerous: 'Innocent people could get hurt. Instead we'll arrest them at the flat or at the stolen cars, and do them for conspiracy.' He had good reason to be cautious, for as soon as Lundy had mentioned Peter Rose, he remembered the acid-throwing brutality of Rose's last crime (for which he had been jailed for fourteen years). Corbett personally knew the officer, Philip Williams, who had won a George Medal for disarming Rose. 'This was the factor', says Corbett today, 'which above all others persuaded me we could not afford a street confrontation, but there was no point in telling that to Tony because he was so sure his approach was right. I simply said that there would be no ambush.'

This only angered Lundy, who told Corbett: 'Do you know what you're saying? Do you know how hard it is to convict these people even when you catch them on the plot with guns in their hands? They still fight it at the Old Bailey and accuse you of fitting them up. I'm telling you, if you just nick these men by a stolen car, they'll have all the top barristers, they'll fight the case tooth and nail and they'll walk out. But here you've got a heaven-sent opportunity to take 'em bang to rights.' 'That's not how it's going to happen,' insisted Corbett; 'I'll deal with this my way.'

'Right!' steamed Lundy. 'If that's how you want it, you do it your way and I'm off!' Corbett temporized: 'There's no need for that,' but Lundy boiled over. 'If you want to do it your way, you know where all the troops are. I'm away,' and off he roared to the Torrington Arms.

Just as he was calming down over a pint, the pub phone rang: 'Get back to the station, Mr Corbett wants to see you.' 'Tell him, bollocks!' snapped Lundy but the voice on the other end told him: 'You've got to come back because you've got the key to the safe containing the firearms we need for tomorrow.' 'Well, send the driver up for the key, I'm not coming back!' Up came the driver for the key, Corbett took out the firearms and at four in the morning he mustered the squad, held a briefing and did it his way.

It was with a mixture of sadness and satisfaction that Lundy later learned not all had gone well with the Lambeth Town Hall operation. At one flat where some of the robbers had been due to meet, the squad made no arrests because they did not realize the robbers had arrived much earlier and were already indoors. Two or three others were arrested standing by a stolen car, but they had no guns or tools because the 'happy bag' containing the weapons had not yet been given to them. It would have been dropped off a few minutes later but the police had stepped in too soon. So instead of bagging a team of robbers, complete with weapons, all they could do was charge the same men with possessing a stolen car. When they went on to search Peter Rose's flat they found neither the guns nor the happy bag.

Meantime, claims Lundy, the most important robber, Fred Sinfield, was waiting for the others outside the Town Hall but was not recognized by detectives assigned to arrest him. When his colleagues failed to arrive on time, he realized something had gone wrong and cleared off. 'So', says Lundy, 'they ended up with the biggest fiasco of all time.' Yet even he admits that Corbett's 'softly softly' approach brought some good results. For instance, when Rose was arrested and told that Ray Fowles had named him on many robberies, he too turned supergrass and revealed that the happy bag was at his sister-in-law's flat. This enabled the police to mount a conspiracy charge. Even so, just as Lundy had predicted, all the robbers who pleaded not guilty walked out of the Old Bailey free men. They included Fred Sinfield who could not be found until one day he rang the investigators offering to give himself up. Although he was acquitted on the Lambeth Town Hall job he would turn supergrass himself in 1980 (see Chapter 23). He would then make a wholly unsubstantiated hearsay allegation of corruption against Tony Lundy: revenge, maybe, on the man who would have had him jailed a full two years earlier if he had been in sole charge at Lambeth.

Despite its somewhat comical failures, the Ray Fowles inquiry as a whole won good headlines for Scotland Yard. Fowles, Rose and Norman Jones (another gang member named by Fowles) confessed to a total of 315 offences and were all awarded supergrass status after naming another 198 criminals for committing 640 major crimes. On their evidence some sixty-two were charged and many pleaded guilty, admitting 150 offences in all. However, as witnesses in contested trials, this trio would have severe limitations, as Corbett had foreseen from the start. That was why he had methodically gathered statements from other witnesses in support. Inevitably this took months, so, when the time came to make arrests, says Lundy, 'the whole of south London knew what the supergrasses were saying. Now the suspects were ready for any level of interrogation and denied everything. Corroboration was minimal, and no matter how good Fowles was as a witness, juries were almost bound to acquit.' Worse than that: despite frequent appearances in the witness box, none of them persuaded any jury to convict any other robbers.

Not that Fowles was a bad witness – Lundy thought him 'terrific' – but it was all a matter of police technique. Lundy believes his way of doing things had the supreme advantage of surprise.

As soon as I got a bloke talking and he was prepared to tell me all, I always hit hard and quickly. You get as much detail as you can, as quickly as you can, and you go straight out and drag them all in. If you then confront them with their accuser, most men will crumble. If they don't, and you haven't any corroboration, and you have to release them, you haven't lost anything. You can still go looking for corroboration, and if you get it, you drag 'em in again. I'm positive that if Phil Corbett had dragged in the thirty or forty people at the core of Fowles's allegations *before they knew what was happening* he would have had the same results I'd had. They would all have collapsed and pleaded guilty in return for a lighter sentence.

Irrespective of the lack of results, Tony Lundy felt Fowles and Jones deserved their supergrass status – they each received just five years in prison – but not Rose who had been caught 'bang to rights' with guns in his flat. He had emerged from a fourteen-year prison sentence only a year before, so his value – in terms of direct knowledge of recent crime – was bound to be limited. Also, legally, one supergrass does not corroborate another: although Rose might have nudged a jury into giving a little extra weight to evidence from Fowles or Jones, his word could not constitute proof of anything. Lundy thought he deserved twenty years but Rose was outraged when he received seven, especially when he found out that the seventeen months he and Fowles had already spent in police custody would not be deducted. He thought he should have got a 'five'. Alongside another grass, Anthony Sapiano, he protested to the Court of Appeal which now decided there should be no automatic five-year tariff for supergrasses. Each case must be treated on its merits, although judges had to consider the public interest in encouraging other accomplices to come forward. Rose won no reduction, nor did Sapiano whose sentence stayed at five.

Ungrateful grasses were not the only problem to hit the Whetstone squad handling Rose and co. Their station was only a mile from Finchley and Lundy's officers reported seeing Whetstone detectives drinking in pubs with Ray Fowles. Lundy shuddered every time he thought of the Billy Amies fiasco in Liverpool, but that had been an unauthorized exception to his strict application of prison rules and 'no fraternization'. When he found out one detective had breached those rules at Finchley he instantly kicked him off the squad. Just up the road at Whetstone, boozing with supergrasses in public seemed to have become the unauthorized norm for some officers.

Worse was to come. On information from Fowles the Whetstone squad had arrested two people and seized £15,000 worth of jewellery allegedly stolen from hotel display cases. When the Old Bailey trial began the prosecution said, 'it was a matter of regret that the jewellery could not be produced'. It had disappeared from the Whetstone safe in April 1979 and was presumed stolen! Fowles then gave evidence without the missing exhibits. Whether the jury believed him or not, they must have seen the irony in trying two people for stealing jewels which had just been stolen a second time – almost certainly by a copper! Inevitably they were acquitted. Soon afterwards Fowles's supergrass career came to an end.

All in all it was a rum do, but the problems at Whetstone had nothing to do with Tony Lundy who was busy cracking more successful supergrasses. He was also solving spectacular 'one-off' cases which prove his skills went far wider than persuading robbers to 'shop' each other.

6

Country Matters

Some 'Lundy-hunters' say that, even if he was straight, he achieved his spectacular record entirely through exploiting underworld sources: either his one special bounty-hunting informer or supergrasses who handed him dozens of criminals at a time on a plate. His astonishing statistics were achieved through serial convictions – mostly guilty pleas – not individual case-solving. Finchley Police Station was not 221B Baker Street and Lundy was no modern-day Sherlock Holmes. He simply ran a factory whose best-selling product was 'results'.

Even if this were true it would be no discredit to him, for no innocent person pleaded guilty to crimes he had not done, and no one pleading not guilty was tried on supergrass evidence without some corroboration. Yet as it happens, Lundy's 'one-off' successes – scored without using regular informers or supergrasses – more than match the entire career results of his most vocal police critics, whether *they* worked off informers, supergrasses or pure deduction.

In 1978 a series of robberies were perpetrated in north-west London with needless and extreme violence. On each occasion witnesses spoke of two robbers, one tall and one very short. This odd couple had first attracted attention by sneaking into plush West End cinemas at closing time and robbing managers of the night's takings. Using a handgun and a sawn-off, 'Tall and Short' then switched to banks. One sleepy August lunchtime they walked into a National Westminster branch in St John's Wood. The little one – just 5 feet 2 inches – strode to the grille, waved a gun at an elderly staff member and told her to open up the door. Sitting a yard back, the woman told him not to be such a silly young man. Angered by her dismissive attitude, the not-so-young man fired directly at her through the glass. Part of the bullet lodged in her head but she was not badly hurt and her coolness saved the day, for the robbers fled empty-handed. A few months later, in January 1979, they had more success at a supermarket near Balcombe Street but were even more violent. Having already got the takings, the short one turned on the manager and fired dum-dum bullets into his stomach, nearly killing him. The forensic laboratory proved that bullets fired on all these raids came from the same gun, so presumably they had been carried out by the same pair. Catching them – especially the little one – became an urgent priority. As Lundy puts it, 'We had a maniac on our hands but we didn't know who he was.'

At this point Detective Sergeant Jack Snodgrass brought news from the underworld: the Tall and Short were probably George Wilkinson, who was not long out of prison, and someone known as Joe the Greek whom he had met inside. Wilkinson's Scotland Yard file confirmed he was a robber, well over 6 feet tall. It also emerged that the pair had rented a flat right next to the robbed supermarket but, after the crime, they had shot off on holiday (to Greece as the police found out later). It then emerged that they were back in London and had committed another robbery. A few days later, one Saturday at the end of January, Snodgrass called Lundy at home to say that he understood Wilkinson's brother was going that night to the Crown Hotel, Cricklewood, where he might be meeting George and also Joe the Greek.

Lundy called all available officers back on duty, so by the evening the Crown was under close watch. Sure enough, George arrived but there was no sign of anyone

small and Greek-looking. The squad had just given up
hope and decided to arrest Wilkinson anyway, when Joe
arrived and saw what was happening. Unnoticed by the
police, he retreated and went straight to the nearby flat
of Wilkinson's grandmother where the pair had left their
cases. The squad knew about this flat and one officer had
been assigned to sit in an unmarked car outside the block.
Suddenly a man came out of the block and asked the driver
if the car was a minicab. Realizing the man had mistaken
his police radio for a minicab radio, the driver had the
presence of mind to say he was a minicab but was waiting
for a booking. He did not realize the enquirer was Joe the
Greek.

Lundy says:

It was a bloody good job the copper didn't recognize him:
if he'd tried to make an arrest by himself the Greek would
have killed him. He'd zoomed round to the flat and taken
his briefcase with his handguns, ammunition, false passport,
everything inside. So now he's gone. Fortunately we do various
searches, and we find another passport which gives us a photo
but still not his true identity. We eventually found out his true
name through prison records: Iordanis Vratsides.

Lundy went to see the head of all Scotland Yard detectives, Deputy Assistant Commissioner David Powis, to
explain that Vratsides was very violent, 'a lunatic' who
had recently all but killed four people. His use of dum-dum
bullets was pure sadism: when he shot people he would
do them more damage. While in jail he had cut another
prisoner's throat. He then went back to Greece, was jailed
there but escaped and returned to England. He had made
his latest trip home on a false passport, one of several false
passports acquired exactly as in *The Day of the Jackal*: he
had provided birth certificates of dead people who, had
they lived, would have been approximately his age.

Lundy now requested that the Yard appeal through the media for help in catching Joe the Greek. Powis agreed and the national press proved most compliant. On 31 January 1979 the Greek's photo was plastered across the tabloids. He was branded 'Public Enemy Number 1', 'top of the Yard's wanted list'. 'No one is safe from this man,' said one headline, while another paper said that his violence had made him an outcast even in the underworld.[1] This publicity seemed over the top, but, so long as he was free, 'Joe' certainly had the potential to kill.

In fact he had already left the country but the publicity worked. A British diplomat in Italy had seen the pictures in the papers and realized Joe was someone who had just been arrested in Rome under another name, for possession of cannabis and a gun. He had been caught trying to fly from Fiumicino airport to Athens with the gun in his baggage, at a time of intensive anti-terrorist checks. He was now seeking bail on the grounds that he had no convictions. This was true inasmuch as he had no record under the false British identity he was now using. The Italian authorities were about to release him when Lundy requested they hold him until he could do ballistics tests on the gun. Lundy flew to Rome, but he was there for two weeks before getting authority to fire the gun and collect the bullets. The wait was worth it, for tests proved this was the gun fired on the London robberies. The Italians gave Joe two and a half years' prison for carrying the gun; when he was eventually extradited back to England in 1981 he was given twenty-two more years for robberies and attempted murders. His former partner Wilkinson had already been jailed for fifteen years. Even at the Old Bailey Joe almost escaped by sawing through cell bars, and when he was back in an English jail he clouted a prison officer so badly that he needed forty-seven stitches. He was later sentenced to 'life' for attempted murder in prison.

Lundy's squad went after another violent gang who tried to rob a NatWest branch in Burnt Oak. In an attempt to force staff to open a door, they had shot a customer, whose leg later had to be amputated, but got away with nothing. They succeeded on other raids but at one bank they were snapped by a security camera. Two were well-disguised but the third had only a false moustache and sunglasses. Lundy's squad took copies of the photos to every North London police station, making sure that not just detectives but all uniformed constables looked at them as they paraded for duty. The method paid off. A constable in Kilburn recognized him as a man named Kelly who lived nearby. He had been called to Kelly's home not long before over 'a punch-up at a party'. Sure enough, Kelly was one of the robbers and the others were two known associates named Shrimpton and Speed. All three were convicted and jailed for up to eighteen years.

Another 'one-off' involved a robber who had acquired a law degree while in jail. He had just been given parole to start another course at Brunel University, but old habits die hard and he committed a robbery when he should have been on campus. After another robbery the Finchley squad received information that he was the robber, so he was arrested. For a down-to-earth character like Lundy, this man was too clever by half: 'a big-headed, conceited little bastard, no youngster, who had gone all intelligent and spoke very posh. He'd done a lot of long sentences.' Lundy's squad then found out that he had an accomplice whom he had met in jail. This second man had murdered his wife but was not a professional criminal. He soon broke down under questioning and admitted his role. Meantime the 'graduate' was playing it clever.

Every few hours two sergeants used to take him for exercise, walk him round the yard handcuffed. While they were doing this, the clever little bastard used to chat away about the jobs and admit them, saying, 'You know I've done 'em, I know I've done 'em. Of course, you've got your jobs to do, but I've got to fight it and that's why I won't admit them. You can't blame me, can you?'

So I tell my commander I want permission to use a tape-recorder on the officers when they're exercising the prisoner. He objected, saying it wasn't in the rules, so I appealed over his head to Powis: 'This is to protect my officers. That man's going to be charged with armed robberies and be tried at the Old Bailey. My men are making notes of these conversations as soon as they'd put him back in the cell, but what will happen at court? He'll scream verbals. He'll say we've made it all up.' So Powis gave me authority and one sergeant wore the tape-recorder. They took him out on exercise, and sure enough, he did the same thing again. Now we had it all on tape.

So we charged him but we didn't reveal the tape's existence until the committal hearing. The defence went mad. They claimed it was illegal and should not be allowed in evidence, but the Old Bailey judge allowed it in. Loud-speakers were placed in court and the jury heard his arrogant confessions. He got twenty years. And for once we heard nothing of the defence cry, 'Verbal, verbal, verbal'!

I was always being accused of 'verbals' – making up confessions. That's why I was in favour of tape-recording interviews long before the legal reformers. For years defence lawyers were claiming I'd verballed their clients so I responded by saying, 'Well let's tape-record the interviews, then we'll see who's telling lies.' You see, during interviews these big robbers used to sit there saying: 'You're right! I was on this robbery, I was on that raid.' But when the detective goes into the witness box, the barrister always says, 'Well, why didn't he sign the statement?' The answer was: 'Of course, he *won't* bloody sign it because he knows he can destroy it in court and try and discredit the entire prosecution case!'[2]

In the late 1970s one of the most vigorous campaigners against 'verbals' was Henry MacKenney. In December 1976 Flying Squad officers, acting on a tip-off, had arrested him over two robberies on branches of Barclays Bank at Romford and Woodford, east of London. He was placed on eight identification parades but, despite the fact that no witnesses picked him out, he was detained on the basis of general witness remarks about a 'big man'. He was certainly big. Indeed he was widely known as 'Big H' and was the biggest associate of Terry Pinfold who was picked out. Anyway, claimed detectives, he had made verbal admissions that he was on the robberies. MacKenney denied making any admissions, and instead wrote a detailed statement of alibi. Even so, he was charged and locked up in custody. His case was then investigated by JAIL, a group campaigning for 'Justice Against Identification Laws'. In July 1977 at the Old Bailey all charges against him were dropped, after which he roared abuse at Inspector John Treen who was handling the case. Big H seemed particularly upset because his friend Terry Pinfold was not released. Indeed, he was jailed for ten years. MacKenney carried his campaign to the media. He approached newspapers and television programmes specializing in miscarriages of justice, but at least one reporter found his manner strangely menacing.

Tony Lundy had nothing to do with that prosecution, but two years later he intervened to play the crucial role in uncovering an appalling murder conspiracy. Indeed, if it had not been for his excessive zeal, the killers might still be killing to this day. In June 1979 he was assisting Detective Superintendent Neil Dickens of Hertfordshire police in the investigation of a robbery in which a Security Express van had been hi-jacked and £500,000 was stolen. The robbers had held one guard at gun-point while forcing the driver to continue on his round of various banks collecting money. The robbers then tied up both guards, dumped them in a public toilet and cleared off with the cash.

Dickens suspected that it was an inside job and that the driver was involved. This was confirmed after a set of traceable BMW keys were found in a pair of overalls dumped alongside the security guards. They belonged to a car owned by an East London greengrocer. He was arrested, he admitted his role and decided to co-operate fully with the police to get a relatively light sentence. All the money had been left in his charge, so now he gave it back. The driver also admitted his part, and all the gang were arrested with one massive exception: Henry 'Big H' MacKenney. Yet even his capture was considered only a matter of time.

In such circumstances it would be normal for detectives to rest on their laurels and ask no questions about other criminal activities, but Lundy deduced there was no way such a big robbery could have been the gang's first. They must have done others. He decided to go to Dickens's headquarters in Hertfordshire and question each member of the team. He got more than he bargained for.

This individual starts to say, 'Look, I can't tell you about other robberies – and I'm in a very difficult situation because these are very dangerous people – but I can tell you about all the murders they've been doing.' I just sniffed 'Huh!', but this bloke starts to tell me that MacKenney and Bruce Childs, who was already in custody for this same robbery, and Terry Pinfold (who was doing his ten years) had all been committing contract murders. It sounded just like 'Murder Incorporated'.

At first I laughed. He said, 'You can laugh but I'm telling you . . .' and he named three or four people who had disappeared. One was the husband of the woman that MacKenney was then living with, Ronald Andrews. Another was George Brett who had disappeared with his ten-year-old son back in 1975. Mentioning Brett didn't increase my belief in the story because over the previous four years, informers had accused dozens of underworld figures of killing the Bretts. So again I laughed, and he said, 'No. MacKenney did Brett and his son.' Then he talked about three other blokes I'd never heard of: a man down in Kent; someone called Eve who used to run a Teddy Bear factory – of all things – with

MacKenney himself; and another man who had worked at the Teddy Bear factory.

He said, 'You've already got Bruce Childs. Now he's a bit of a nutter, but if you could get in to him, you might get something. But they've all got to have protection from the worst man of the lot, Big H.'

Childs and MacKenney were both nutters, if Lundy were to believe what the man was saying. They had disposed of the bodies by chopping them up and putting them through an industrial mincing machine which, the source said, used to be in the Teddy Bear factory. Presumably, they then burned the remains and could have scattered them anywhere.

What finally made me believe him was when he said, 'There's going to be another murder shortly – and you know the victim.' 'What are you talking about?' 'Do you know a police officer called Treen?' I said 'yeh' because John Treen had been one of my inspectors on the Flying Squad in 1977, so I knew him well. Treen had arrested MacKenney and Terry Pinfold in December 1976 but then the Director of Public Prosecutions dropped the case against MacKenney.

He said, 'MacKenney is going to murder Treen and Butcher', who was the sergeant on the same case. When he said this, I thought, 'Blimey, this rings true!' because I was at the Old Bailey when MacKenney was allowed out and screamed at Treen across the public part of the courts. This man said, 'They've been plotting Treen up where he lives', so can you imagine what was going to happen? Treen would just disappear! Nobody would have known anything. They would have minced him up just like they did all the others. So that was what prompted me to believe the man.

Lundy talked the whole story over with Neil Dickens. Then he checked if the names he had been given (other than the Bretts) really did belong to missing people. Sure enough: Terry 'Teddy Bear' Eve had not been seen since

October 1974, Robert Brown who worked at the same factory had evaporated in December 1975, and Ron Andrews had disappeared in October 1978. (The unnamed Kent man, Frederick Sherwood, had also been reported missing in July 1978.) All this gave the ring of truth to the overall story. The next question was, who was going to follow it all up? Dickens and his squad had enough on their plate dealing with the Security Express job. Lundy was also up to his eyes in his supergrass inquiries so, overnight, he also decided to pass.

Next morning I see David Powis and I tell him this story about six or seven murders which these people had committed on contract. 'Really?' he said, as unbelieving as I had been at first, 'what do you think?' I said, 'I've thought about it overnight and it does seem genuine.' He then calls up Commander Arthur Howard of C1, in charge of all murder squads, who seemed more than disbelieving. Anyhow I sit there while they decide that the only officer suitable to take charge was Frank Cater who would have to be pulled off a South London shooting inquiry. I then went down to Howard's office and dictated all I knew into a tape-recorder, to be transcribed and handed to Cater, a chief superintendent with a top reputation.

At Finchley later that day Lundy took a call from the Yard: Frank Cater wanted to see him. Lundy was snowed under with work but Cater had to be seen, even though his chosen meeting-place struck Lundy as unfit for such a discussion, the Kings Arms, Chingford, near where Cater lived. Lundy vividly recalls the meeting:

So I'm told to report to this pub in bloomin' Chingford – to see a man I've never met in my life before – to talk about these horrible killings! So I find Cater and his inspector, and he says, 'Right, tell me all about this.' I said, 'I can't tell you any more than I've already put on tape.' 'Go on, tell us a bit more.' And it's as if I was wasting his time, dragging him off a serious job to be given this load of rubbish. I was fuming, though I did remember my own original doubts. So I sat in this pub and told him why the thing had to be done in a hurry: 'Because at this moment, with Bruce Childs in custody for a heavy armed robbery, he would probably crack if you go into him armed with this knowledge. That's it, for what it is! You get out there, see Neil Dickens and he'll give you all the help you need.'

Cater then says, 'Right, I need two or three officers from your squad to do some running around.' I was livid. We were absolutely up to the eyeballs with work, and if I had known I would have to man Mr Cater's investigation, I would have handled the whole thing myself. So off he goes.

For a couple of weeks I hear nothing. Then I hear he's suddenly got a bit serious, and he's set up an office somewhere. Do you know, the man never spoke to me again for months! By then I knew it was successful, because Childs had rolled over and given evidence against MacKenney, whom they eventually captured. Childs must have been the first serial murderer in modern times to admit his role and give evidence against somebody else. Then, one day when I'm up at the Old Bailey running several supergrass trials, I come back to Finchley to find a witness summons for me to appear at MacKenney's committal hearing. I know nothing about this so, bloody hell, I get hold of Cater and he says, 'Oh yeh, right. Better have a chat with you. See me at Chingford in the Kings Arms tonight.' Fuming I was, so I had to troop over to Chingford again. And he told me he had already been in the witness box and been asked about the original source. But instead of sticking to the stock answer – 'We don't discuss sources of information' – he lets himself be drawn out by the usual pack of defence barristers to the point where in the end he says, 'The information came from Mr Lundy.'

That was a red rag to the defence, so that's why a solicitor serves this summons on me! So I said to Cater, 'Why didn't you just refuse to answer, and not discuss sources? That's all I'm going to say when I get to court. Anything else would endanger the source's life.' So I go to Lambeth and I get up and say, 'I refuse to discuss sources of information.' The defence had a right go at me, but the magistrate backed me up – as normal. They'll always support you on that. Later I was fully bound to appear at the trial, but they never called me because the source had no bearing on the case. But Frank Cater had put me right bang in the middle.

Although Cater later rose to the prestigious job of Flying Squad commander, the Big H case was perhaps his finest hour, but much of the credit lay with Lundy who had coaxed most of the story out of the original source. Cater carried out a first-class inquiry. Lundy would surely have done so too, if only he had been able to spare the time. The key factor, as Lundy had predicted, was that Childs, confronted with a certain fifteen to twenty years on the armed robbery, was just ripe and ready to talk – and he did, confirming every murder which Lundy's source had originally disclosed. Even the detail of the mincing machine proved to be true. Terry Pinfold had bought it for £25 through *Exchange and Mart*! It was eventually moved to a room in Childs's flat, where the murderers covered the floor and walls with large rolls of polythene, to catch the blood of their future victims. Childs then burned the remains in the household grate.

In December 1979 Childs pleaded guilty and was jailed for life. In 1980 he gave evidence at the Old Bailey against Henry MacKenney who was convicted and given six life sentences. From time to time Lundy popped in to see how the trial was progressing, and to be greeted by Frank Cater's laconic 'Oh hello, Tone.' Even today Lundy still smarts from what he considers a lack of recognition of his role in the downfall of Henry MacKenney.

It was only my determination to explore further offences that made me take the trouble to go and speak to these people. Nobody else would have done. Without that effort, this story would never have come out. Even then, I had to virtually force Scotland Yard to do anything. All that initial 'What a load of cobblers!' reaction I got, and never a word of thanks when I should have got a commendation.[3]

Big H had once told Childs that he was fed up with working 'on the pavement' (doing robberies) because he

was so tall he was always being picked out by witnesses.
He turned to murder because killing someone on contract
was a far safer way for him to earn £2,000. Perhaps that
was why he had been so upset in 1976 when, for once,
he was not picked out by witnesses but was then charged
on a 'verbal'. 'Justice Against Identification Laws' used to
boast that those charges had been dropped 'as a result of
JAIL's bringing this case to the attention of the DPP'.[4] Yet
if they had not been dropped and MacKenney had been
jailed, he would not have been free to murder Frederick
Sherwood and Ron Andrews in 1978. This is not to say
JAIL had blood on its hands, only that criminals who
offer tales of fit-ups and verbals to pressure groups, the
press and even police corruption inquiries, are not always
telling the truth. The consequences of believing them can
be disastrous.

One inquiry which took time learning this lesson was
Operation Countryman, the most famously ill-fated anti-
corruption probe in British police history. Set up in August
1978 to investigate widespread hearsay allegations against
Metropolitan and City of London detectives, it was composed entirely of officers from provincial forces, hence its
self-deprecating title. Contemptuous yard detectives soon
gave it another name, 'The Swedey' (because of the Worzel
Gummidge image of the West Country cops at its head),
but their attitude became less mocking when it rapidly
expanded to ninety-two investigators and began probing
the claims of criminals who would never have said anything
to an 'in-house' inquiry staffed by Scotland Yard. They
were ready to speak to Countryman because they trusted
in its independence, integrity and determination to clean
out the 'rotten apples in the barrel'. They also believed
neither their identities nor their statements would ever be
leaked back to the two London forces against whom they
were making allegations – as Countryman had promised.

These promises were breached as Countryman was by turns emasculated, decapitated and shrunk, until in May 1980 it was taken over by the Chief Constable of Surrey, and later by Scotland Yard. All its files and computer records then fell into the hands of the very force which many of its informers had always refused to talk to. At the end of the operation, which cost more than three million pounds, only two police officers were convicted of corruption: Chief Inspector Phil Cuthbert and Sergeant John Golbourn of the City of London Police, who were jailed for three and two years in 1982. Countryman's only other successes were two criminals jailed for inciting lesser villains to commit robberies in order to pocket rewards (see Chapter 10). Nine more detectives (one from the City and eight from the Metropolitan Police) were also tried but acquitted.

At the time Countryman's failure to nail more crooked cops was blamed on sabotage by those cops or on obstruction by an over-protective Scotland Yard hierarchy. Countryman's chiefs should have been ready for sabotage (such as the burglary of its original London offices or the re-arrest of criminals known to be helping the 'Swedes') but they were taken aback by the increasingly hostile attitude of Yard officers. At first the Yard men had to accept Home Secretary Merlyn Rees's decision that provincial officers should look into allegations which, in any case, mostly related to another force, the City Police, in whose bailiwick three highly suspect robberies yielding £600,000 had occurred between May 1976 and May 1978. Yet when they discovered Countryman was going into different areas, mostly involving the Metropolitan Police, up went the shutters. On one occasion DAC Powis told a meeting of all junior Flying Squad detectives that they should be aware that Countryman officers were apt to believe the word of almost any London criminal making allegations against Metropolitan detectives. One officer sums up the message he took away from the meeting as simply this: Countryman is out to get you, so watch your backs!

In adopting this stance, Powis was trying to protect not guilty detectives but innocent ones, because he had been made aware of actions by Countryman which, he felt, called into question its competence and judgement. At the same time, says one Flying Squad veteran, 'another Yard boss formally instructed us, that if Countryman came in demanding documentation, case papers, diaries or pocket-books, we were to decline to co-operate. Instead we were to inform him and he would deal with the matter.'

Ten years on, while the conduct of some Yard officers still evokes suspicions of a 'cover-up', it is difficult not to feel that Countryman helped cause its own downfall. Its bosses spread their net too wide too early and placed too much credence in some criminals who were very cunning liars. They invested too much manpower following self-serving allegations, and failed to concentrate on cementing cases against some detectives whose conduct even now cries out for the verdict of an Old Bailey jury.

Tony Lundy was one officer whose attitude towards Countryman went from willing co-operation to disillusion. At no time was he the subject of any Countryman investigation. By mid-summer 1979 its chiefs had drawn up a list of seventy-nine Metropolitan and eighteen City officers against whom it had received allegations. He was not on that list nor, according to my information, was he ever added to it. Indeed, from the start he was one of Countryman's strongest supporters. It has been said that 'Lundy's grasses could reel off the names of criminals but were quite ignorant of police corruption'.[5] This is untrue. Indeed, according to former Assistant Commissioner Gilbert Kelland, it was one of Lundy's own supergrasses at Finchley whose allegations against City detectives launched Countryman in August 1978.[6] Dave Smith talked freely to Countryman about the corrupt City cop who had forewarned his gang about the Schweppes ambush in 1977. So did Billy Amies who made statements against a Metropolitan sergeant on the Rotherhithe Robbery Squad and against Liverpool detectives. Over at Whetstone another Lundy 'turn', Ray Fowles, talked to Countryman, as did Rose and Jones. These three had only hearsay evidence of corruption but Fowles also named David Shaw who, while he never turned supergrass, told Countryman a stream of stories about his direct experience of crooked detectives and caused at least one Yard man to be suspended.

Lundy gave Countryman investigators full access to his 'resident informants' and left them to it: 'It was no business of mine what they talked about and I never asked either side how their discussions went, but my supergrasses helped Countryman with my full encouragement.' At the time Countryman was investigating several Flying and Robbery Squad detectives whom Lundy had worked with in the past, but none was on his present squad. His relationship with Neil Dickens of Hertfordshire must have reassured Countryman that he was straight, for it may have been Dickens's supergrass, Leroy Davies, rather than one of Lundy's sources, who had kicked off the Countryman inquiry.[7] Davies had been arrested early in 1978 but he later made hearsay allegations of City police corruption surrounding the *Daily Express* robbery of May 1976 and the Williams and Glyns job of September 1977. When a third City robbery occurred in May 1978 at the *Daily Mirror*, and a security guard was shot dead, fresh allegations made the pressure for some kind of corruption inquiry overwhelming.

By February 1979, however, Countryman officers had managed to upset one of their most helpful allies by attending the Berkeley-Gowan trial (over the 'Schweppes', 'Thatched Barn' and other robberies) at the Old Bailey (see Chapter 3). Normally Lundy would not have objected but on this occasion the officers had come to see his witness, Keith Warne, give evidence. Warne had already talked to these men about corruption. None of his allegations was against Lundy or any member of his Finchley squad. What now worried Lundy was that Warne was a difficult witness who might be put off or react unpredictably if he saw the Countryman officers in court. He might even mention them in his evidence, which would give the jury the false impression that the Berkeley-Gowan case which they were judging itself involved corruption. At the time Countryman was attracting so many sensational headlines that the jury might throw the case out because of a wholly mistaken view that the prosecution was 'bent'.[8]

Lundy explained his anxieties to Yard chiefs and within hours a top-level call asked Countryman's leaders to keep their men out of court. Next day the Deputy Director of Public Prosecutions made the same request, apparently at the instigation of a senior Yard officer. The incident was instantly perceived by Countryman as a severe case of obstruction by the Yard in league with the DPP. It was nothing of the sort, merely the outgrowth of a working detective's legitimate concerns for a case on which he had worked long and hard to get to court.

Lundy's next run-in with Countryman occurred in July 1979 during the very same trial. By now the defence stage had been reached, and one witness called in Gowan's defence was a criminal called Stephen Raymond, whose exploits are worth a book in themselves.[9] In his evidence Raymond made outrageously untrue statements, including a claim that the Deputy DPP had given him immunity from prosecution for offences less than armed robbery, in return for helping Countryman. Raymond certainly was telling them a lot of extraordinary tales but he had not been given any immunity. Lundy now sought Countryman's help.

It was vital to destroy Raymond's credibility, so a request was made to Countryman to come forward with whatever information we needed to prove he was lying. This was rejected. It got to the point where the Director of Public Prosecutions sent his Deputy to court, and there was an almighty stink between Counsel, the DPP and Countryman, which flatly refused to give evidence discrediting Raymond, even though some of its officers had the proof to destroy his story. He had wrapped them round his little finger, and now they were prepared to jeopardize this trial which had lasted nearly six months, rather than upset him.

Lundy's worst row with 'the Swedey' followed a spectacular piece of work which he and his squad performed in December 1979 at the Sheraton Park Tower Hotel in Knightsbridge. Finchley had kept surveillance for many weeks (on flimsy information) and as a result suspected that the hotel casino was to be robbed of £200,000 expected takings before it could be collected by a security van. Lundy set up an ambush but the robbery went off faster than anticipated. The gang burst into the casino, one man firing a shotgun and another named Joey Maybur waving an iron bar with which he struck a receptionist and two cashiers. They grabbed just £16,000 but missed a further £100,000 when one cashier slammed the safe shut.

They fired shots but we ambushed them right outside. Unfortunately, our main strike force, in a large Post Office van, couldn't get to the scene quickly enough because of the speed at which the robbery occurred. I was controlling the job from a taxicab. I had two women detective constables on board but we rammed the robbers in their stolen car, with all the guns and money. The getaway driver, Roger McKenzie, was a freelance crime reporter! He was mixed up with a woman, and it was their flat the gang was using as a flop. They recruited him as the change-over driver. He later got two and a half years.

But the real bad man on the team was Joseph Maybur who was in the car we rammed. He'd just come out of jail after doing an eleven-year stretch. On this raid he'd used superglue to distort his face, so any witness would insist he was a man with a horrible scar. Anyway, he was bang to rights and bound to go down for far more than eleven this time. But when they were in custody awaiting trial, Countryman got in touch about Maybur. He'd sent for them while he's in prison, and told them he's got evidence of corruption. It was nothing to do with us, but over some other job years before. Then suddenly he applies for bail at the Old Bailey! A man who's just come out from eleven years, who's fired shots, who's laid three people out and split their heads open with an iron bar, on an armed robbery, we've got him in custody, and he's making a bail application! And a letter from Countryman turns up, which goes on about how this man is assisting them, and supporting Maybur's bail application! Unbelievable!

I'm absolutely bonkers. I wasn't at court, but somebody rings me and I steam down there. I say, 'How dare they? Bloody hell!' I went mad and so did the judge, and so Maybur stays in custody. But that wasn't all. When they come up for trial Maybur pleads guilty, but all the rest plead not guilty. This was ridiculous, because they had all been caught on the job and were certain to be convicted. I smelled a rat: 'What's going on? This is crazy!'

Then it came out. The others are put back for trial but Maybur's defence asks the judge to sentence their client now. This isn't normal practice. Judges always put back guilty pleas until the end of a trial for sentencing alongside the rest. Naturally the judge asks why he should make an exception. The defence says this man is assisting Operation Countryman over very serious matters. Why that should make any difference escapes me, but anyway the judge agrees. Maybur pleads guilty – using the name Macey – and bugger me! The bloke from Countryman gets in the witness box to speak on his behalf: how he's helping them over this corruption thing. (So what!) The judge listens to all this and then he only gives him eleven years. The same as he'd already done!

We were going mad, the DPP was going mad, but the following week the others asked to be re-arraigned and they all plead guilty. Maybur had a long criminal record – sixteen convictions – so they now say, 'We're minnows compared to that man you've already given eleven years.' This forces the judge to give them only eight- and six-year terms for a job they would all have got eighteens and sixteens on!

Then we find out through the grapevine, the following week, that Maybur tells Countryman to go and get stuffed! Because he's got what he wants! They were being manipulated left, right and centre, which was a great pity because I wanted them to succeed. You see, we all had to work alongside some of the genuinely bent bastards they were trying to lock up. Their targets were men who had screwed up my jobs, like Schweppes, so Countryman's failure knocked back on me. My collaboration with them was held against me in some quarters and by some individuals who later took every opportunity to put the boot in.

7

The Wren That Sang Like a Canary

In the late 1970s there was a series of raids on post offices, post office vans and building societies across North London. The nastiest assault was on a post office in Neasden where, rather than walk in the front, the gang crashed a stolen car through the side door to get direct access behind the counter. Although the door was part-steel, it buckled enough to allow the team's strong man to squeeze under and lever it up so his confederates could 'steam in with shotguns and ammonia'.

Finchley Robbery Squad became involved when Tony Lundy received information that certain robbers had done the Neasden job. Lundy had them arrested, including Colin Francis from Kentish Town. He agreed to become a supergrass. Soon afterwards his wife and mother were brought in to supply moral support, as Lundy recalls.

Normally a robber's family are relieved when he says he's pleading guilty and giving up crime. And they really think he means it if he becomes a supergrass because they realize that he should then never rejoin his criminal mates, for at least two reasons: some will want to kill him – and none will trust him enough to work with him again. He's also unlikely to take up crime elsewhere because if he gets caught, he knows he'll go back to prison for the full stretch and get no favours. We now know that some of the 1970s supergrasses (including Dave Smith) did go back to crime but most didn't, and at the time their wives usually supported them when they said they were co-operating with us.

But with Colin Francis – Jesus! – the family went spare! They ordered him not to do it! They were totally against him grassing. They went mad: 'Don't you dare do it! We'll never speak to you again if you do.' This leaves Colin in a terrible position. He's made his mind up he's going to be a supergrass and give evidence against his mates. He's already started telling us the details, so he's got no way back. He's admitted these bad jobs, and that he was the main man up front, but now all of a sudden his wife is saying, 'I'll divorce you! I'll have nothing more to do with you!' Same with his mother. I couldn't believe it! I'm trying to talk to them sensibly on my own, and for my pains I'm getting abused as a 'no good bastard for getting him to do this'. Anyway, in the end Colin Francis went ahead and did it. And blow me! They *didn't* have any more to do with him. The family *did* cut him off! But from our point of view he became a very valuable supergrass.

One robber who always eluded Lundy was Kenny Baker, named by Francis as the main man on the Neasden job, 'The Heavy'. For several days Lundy interrogated him in the hope he too would become a supergrass.

I was desperate to get Kenny to turn because he could have blown the whole of South London apart. He'd worked with all of 'em! He'd done everything for years but he kept getting off. After Francis turned, Baker admitted Neasden. Then another villain called Tony Azzopardi turned supergrass and he also grassed Baker, so we had quite a lot of evidence against him. When we arrested Baker he had a lot of cash, including some notes with markings from Neasden post office. We even had forensic evidence. It was a stone bonker case against Baker, the best I'd ever had against robbers, other than when we caught them on the pavement. But he pleaded not guilty at the Old Bailey and fought it, and the jury acquitted him! Judge Argyle went mad because it was unbelievable he could have been cleared. There were strong rumours that the jury had been bribed. Baker was acquitted in half a dozen successive robbery trials at the Bailey. Only one was mine but that was bad enough. He was eventually convicted by another squad and went to prison for a long stretch.

In November 1990 Baker was ambushed on a security van raid by robbery squad officers and the crack 'Blue

Berets' firearms unit. He was shot dead – an action
which perhaps vindicates Lundy's thwarted approach to
the Lambeth Town Hall job, in which Baker was also
involved back in 1978.

Another man grassed by Colin Francis was John Yianni
whom Lundy remembers as

> . . . a tiny bloke, about 5 foot 3 or 4. A most insignificant
> little fellow – looked like a schoolboy. Not long out from serving
> a sentence for robbery. Francis had named him on only two
> jobs but when we got him in, he eventually started to talk
> and admitted that in just nine months since he'd come out of
> prison, he'd robbed thirty-six building societies. He did four
> building societies in one day: two in the morning and two in the
> afternoon! Compulsive! He used to work all round the outskirts
> of London. He had a couple of Greek lads in tow. He'd say,
> 'You want to drive me today?' They'd say, 'Yeh, OK', they'd
> nick a car and off they'd go. Some days they'd even use their own
> cars. They would drive him round, he'd say, 'Pull up here at this
> building society' and in he'd go, pull out his sawn-off shotgun,
> shout 'Hand over the money!', walk out, go down the road and
> do another one. Then he'd blow it all on booze and drugs.

Yianni admitted only his own offences, but within
months of Colin Francis turning supergrass a stream
of villains followed his example. The dominoes started
tumbling when Francis and Tony Azzopardi both named
Paddy Flanagan in a conspiracy to rob. Flanagan certainly
had the right record but the evidence was slim. Rather than
arrest him immediately, Lundy resolved to deal with him
'on a quietish day'. When that day came early in 1980
Lundy's squad questioned him over an allegation that
he had supplied a gun. He had previously been jailed
for shooting people on robberies so he was worried about
being convicted for the same offence. That would send
him back inside for a very long time. He panicked and
started to talk, naming two men who, he said, were active

armed robbers. To his relief he was then released without charge, while Lundy and co. looked at the two men he had fingered. One bore the illustrious name Christopher Wren. Lundy had never heard of him, even though Wren lived only a mile from Finchley Police Station. The other was John Hammond who'd just finished a prison sentence for armed robbery. Now they were both put under surveillance, and seen associating with each other and with a big man called John Kennedy.

They were looking round scenes in a way which made it obvious they were plotting a robbery. They visited various addresses, including a flat in the Guinness Trust Buildings, Stamford Hill. On the morning of 12 May 1980 our surveillance boys tried to find and follow them, but they got in touch and said, 'They're all out. Can't find any of the cars. They're missing.' I was going to court that morning when it came up over the air: 'Security Guard shot in East Finchley.' He'd been shot through the stomach at point-blank range, and the bag taken off him. We had seen Wren and Hammond around that area on previous days, so I got on the air and said to my deputy Pat Fleming: 'It's got to be them, they're missing, get round to all their addresses quick! Urgent!' One of our surveillance photographers was over in Stamford Hill at the time, so he says, 'I'll have a look at the Guinness Trust Buildings.' We didn't know why the gang had ever been there – it turned out Wren had a relative living there – we still didn't know which flat they'd been to, but on this day the photographer came on air saying, 'All three have just driven in to the Buildings – two in Wren's Mercedes and Hammond in his little Datsun – they've disappeared into the flats.'

All this time I'm stuck in a car park at court, I can't move, waiting for a committal or remands. So Pat Fleming, my deputy through all the Finchley days, says, 'Right, everybody over to Stamford Hill urgently.' Pat was nearest the scene in a black cab, a standard London taxi which we always kept for such purposes, and as he's getting that way, the photographer reports, 'They've just come out, got in their cars and they're going to drive out of the flats shortly.' So as Pat arrives in the taxi he blocks the exit, which in those old charity dwellings is one gateway, 'in' and 'out', for three or four entire blocks. Pat tells the driver to pull the black cab across the gateway, gets out and pretends he's paying the fare. And on the air I could hear other units saying: 'Arriving in half a minute' or 'a minute', while at the scene the Merc and Datsun are waiting to come out. Pat's still blocking them, delaying and deliberating, pretending to argue with the taxi driver. The robbers have obviously sussed him by now [worked out he's police] but they've nowhere to go.

Then up comes Gordon Reynolds – a fantastic police driver – with a couple of our authorized shots on board, all armed, and they come steaming. By now the robbers have reversed and are off round the other side of the flats. In comes Reynolds in his Fiat and starts a Keystone Kops chase all round these flats. Then more units arrive, one of our men jumps out and slings his stick at the windscreen of the Mercedes, which drives on over his foot and breaks it. This crash-bang job carries on for minutes until Reynolds rams the Mercedes into fencing behind the flats where they back on to a railway line. The Merc's out of action now, Wren is taken, but out from the other side of the car comes big fat Kennedy, 25 stone of him. He jumps on to the Merc roof and up on the fence, with pistols in his pockets.

Two of our boys start firing shots when Kennedy's on the fence but they miss him. He's got wrapped up in the barbed wire on top, but he manages to fall off on the other side. The barbed wire has torn his jacket off him and in it are these two loaded handguns. He runs off down the railway cutting, pursued by Fleming and co. They catch him, all 25 stone, and have a right rollover on the railway line – only now there's a train coming down. Pat's screaming, 'Get 'em off the line!' The train bears on down, hooter blowing, but the driver manages to pull up just yards away. Then out jump two or three of our lads who had the sense to scoot up to Stamford Hill station, commandeer a train standing there and bring it down the line. Kennedy's captured, along with Wren and Hammond. The stolen monies are in their cars, so are the loaded handguns that they'd fired at the guard. Money, guns, attempted murder. In they come.

Lundy had missed all this fun, but when he came back from court he quickly focused on the subject of who could be persuaded to turn supergrass. It turned out to be Chrissie Wren. This sealed the fate of Hammond and

Kennedy, who admitted not only this job but many other robberies. They pleaded guilty and received fifteen-year sentences. Hammond also admitted shooting the security guard through the stomach but claimed the gun went off by accident. The guard survived, but only just.

When Lundy debriefed Wren he soon realized that, although the man had almost no criminal record and appeared to be a nonentity, he had not only committed armed robberies, he had also been on major burglaries over many years. The men he claimed were his partners-in-crime – Michael Gervaise, Tony Fiori, John Goodwin – were believed to be among Britain's leading burglars. Nobody had betrayed such top-grade burglars and safe-blowers before: they had allegedly cut open dozens of bank vaults, jewellery stores and private safes. Lundy immediately saw the potential. He approached his Scotland Yard chiefs who agreed to supply more officers, including a detachment from the Special Patrol Group. In two days his team identified all the main suspects and the main crimes they had apparently committed. He then put together an 'army' which arrested some thirty people 'in one hit'. Many of them admitted their crimes. Several turned supergrass themselves.

For two weeks we were charging people by the dozen, in and out of court, working day and night. We recovered firearms and even police uniforms. The pressure on me and my officers was immense. In some ways I don't blame others when they say, 'Oh, no, slow it down, take your time', because it's a hell of a way to do it. For days on end I was scarcely going to bed. You have to work out which police stations each of the arrested men are to be taken to – they're spread out all over North London – then you have to decide who's interviewing which suspects, and then brief everyone on what they have to ask. Then you have to bring all the troops back together, to find out who's achieving what, and which suspects are saying what. We had a lot of help, of course, from Detective Superintendent Reg

Dixon, and other chief inspectors joined in with their teams. Even so, it was hell.

The entire job became known as 'Operation Jenny', and resulted in seventeen men being convicted of robbery, and eighty-three robberies and conspiracies to rob being 'cleared up'. A further 105 burglaries and attempted burglaries were also solved. The total value of cash and goods stolen in these crimes was over £3 million. One of the biggest jobs which Wren admitted was a £500,000 jewel raid on the Savoy Hotel arcade on 19 June 1978. When it occurred, the police learned that the team included Douggie Weafer, Michael Chick and Ronnie Johnson. They were arrested but had to be released for lack of evidence. 'We knew they'd done it,' says Lundy, 'but we had to let them go.'

Almost two years later Wren named the entire Savoy team, including Weafer, Chick and Johnson. Weafer confessed and told Lundy's officers where he had hidden police uniforms, guns and other robbery gear. Ronnie 'Brains' Johnson admitted 119 burglaries and robberies. 'He was a compulsive professional thief,' recalls Lundy, 'but he decided to clear the books of anything he'd ever done so that when he came out of jail again he'd be completely clean. Just taking his statements took a month.' Johnson's honesty was not as well-rewarded as he had hoped. He was jailed for fifteen years. His confessions, however, added to those of other Wren confederates, helped 'Jenny' charge another fifty-three people, clear up 190 more offences and boost the amount involved in all the crimes which it had solved to £10 million.

One big breakthrough came when we hit some lock-up garages Wren had told us about. They were an Aladdin's Cave full of the best gear any burglar could want: thermic lances, petro-chemical lances, radios tuned to police wavelengths, stuff that villains dream of. Wren claimed Tony Fiori had stockpiled the lot over many years (the garages were very near Fiori's home) so he too rolled over and became a supergrass. Now we could really crack the organized burglary side of London crime. A separate squad was set up at Whetstone under Reg Dixon and Bill Peters to deal with Fiori and Micky Gervaise, who had also offered to turn supergrass.

I didn't agree with Gervaise being used as a supergrass. He wanted help and started to talk but I said, 'No way! He's an out-and-out liar.' He was admitting loads of burglaries but he was denying three or four robberies we knew he had committed. Cunning bastard that he was, he'd taken part in a £400,000 jewel raid in Hatton Garden in May 1978 [Patel] and another worth £800,000 in April 1980 [Gemco] but he kept them both back until my deputy, Pat Fleming, and I dragged them out of him! We were getting him down from Whetstone back to Finchley and strapping him about crimes he would not admit – until we got to the N'th degree. Then he'd have to admit them and also admit he'd lied.

I said, 'You can't use a man like that. What kind of a supergrass is he? He'll be the destruction of the entire system!', but I was over-ruled. I was told to keep my place and told Gervaise would be used. As I predicted, he backfired on us when all charges were dropped against Tony Colson, whom he had eventually named on both the Patel and Gemco raids, because Gervaise had told so many lies. Colson was later arrested for other offences but we were sick at the time because we knew he was a major robber.

Lundy did not know the half of what Gervaise was holding back. Even now he was concealing his role on a massive robbery, worth far more than all his confessions put together. Luckily Lundy did not rely solely on Gervaise for news of his activities. Another source would soon come forward.

8

A Rewarding Profession

Snout, Nark, Slag, Fink, Squealer, Stool-pigeon, Budgie, Canary, Grass. In every age police informers have been branded with abusive names, for they are the enemy within. Most are criminals themselves. The exceptions are usually relatives with motives little better than criminals': a two-timed wife, a jealous brother, a father-in-law trying to rid his daughter of a parasitical spouse. Good citizenship rarely comes into it.

Informing is not an honourable profession – its patron saint is Judas Iscariot – but at least Jesus knew the identity of his betrayer. The professional criminal does not know which familiar might give him away. Anyone, no matter how close or 'staunch', could be a secret snout. That is why gangsters claim to detest informers, and yet the biggest crooks are usually the biggest informers. That is how they got big. Even in the Mafia, for all its code of *Omertà*, the greatest Godfathers have always been ready to 'drop a dime' to eliminate a rival, to avenge an offence, to return a favour to a helpful cop, or simply for the hell of it. Lucky Luciano, La Cosa Nostra's 'Boss of Bosses', and his boyhood buddy Meyer Lansky, the Mob's financial brains for fifty years, used to betray their brethren whenever it suited their purpose.[1] There are two things any top informer must always remember: grass before you are grassed, and don't let your victims know you're doing it.

Modern supergrasses do at least gesture towards decency by testifying in open court. Traditional snouts are more insidious. They never go public. They take the greatest care to remain accepted in the circles they are informing against, not only for safety's sake but because continuing treachery can earn them big rewards. Only by remaining the trusted confidant of active gangsters can an informer earn serious money. He must never 'show out'.

One of Tony Lundy's outstanding strengths, and the source of many of his successes, was his dedicated cultivation of informers. At its finest this skill is not only rare, it is extremely dangerous for its practitioner. That is because the best informers are often the most devious criminals, capable of playing individual coppers off against each other and of manipulating entire police hierarchies. One man who was Lundy's boss in later years sums up the relationship between detective and snout in brutal terms: 'You must keep your boot on his neck or assuredly he will have his boot on yours.'

Lundy refuses to talk about any sources by name but in the 1980s his relationship with one much-publicized informer, Roy Garner, was subject to so much hostile speculation that it would cripple the detective's brilliant career. The controversy revolved round these questions.

1. Was Lundy using Garner legitimately – that is, solely to assist the police apprehend criminals, solve or prevent crime, and recover stolen goods? Or

2. Was Garner using an unwitting Lundy, not just to gain authorized rewards but to so ingratiate himself with the Scotland Yard hierarchy as to acquire immunity from investigation into his own criminal activities? Or

3. Were Lundy and Garner using each other? Was Garner benefiting from rewards, a criminal licence and police intelligence – all courtesy of a conniving Lundy? And was Lundy receiving not just information enabling him to make spectacular arrests, but also a cut of very substantial rewards which he had nominated Garner

to collect? Was the detective in a continuing conspiracy with a man whose crimes were allegedly far worse than those of the criminals he informed against?

If the answer to the first question is Yes, then Lundy is 'in the clear' and has been cruelly wronged by some sections of the media. If the answer to 2 is Yes, he joins an illustrious line of thief-takers whose love of results blinded them to the risks in an informer's embrace, but who committed no crimes themselves. If the answer to 3 is Yes, then Lundy deserves a far worse fall than he has suffered and should have gone to jail. To have any hope of discovering the truth, we must review what has already been made public about how the Lundy–Garner relationship began.

The pair met around 1968 when Lundy became involved with Finchley Boxing Club. One would-be fighter there was Garner's son Mark, whom Lundy helped train alongside dozens of other youths. Soon the detective was tipped off that Roy had a record. He checked with Criminal Intelligence and found Garner had convictions for the relatively minor offence of receiving stolen property, the latest in 1965. There was nothing in the file to indicate he was a villain of any importance but Lundy updated it and continued to eye him, like any other criminal, as a target for arrest and a potential source.

If Garner was much of an 'active' criminal in 1968 he had already built a legitimate cover that had for years fooled far older and more experienced detectives than young Lundy. Born in the late 1930s, Roy had followed his humble, respectable father into the near-hereditary job of meat porter at Smithfield Market. He then joined his uncle in a shopfitting business while handling stolen meat, for which he gained convictions. He set up a van-hire firm with his partner, Kenny Ross, until they switched to quasi-legitimate money-lending. At the same time they were buying a lot of real estate. If any investigative agency had scrutinized the pair in the early 1970s it might have had difficulty tracing a legitimate source for their capital, but at that time there was nothing to set Garner and Ross apart from hundreds of other mini-entrepreneurs enriching themselves on the margins of crime. Many years later a supergrass claimed Garner had organized a plot to set fire to his own properties, to oust sitting tenants and thus increase the properties' values. Another supergrass claimed that in the early 1970s he had been an active armed robber with a sadistic twist. There was even talk of murders. Neither grass's claims led to criminal charges – more than ten years after the alleged events, no supporting evidence could be found – but the arson case, revived as late as 1985, appeared strong and Garner may well have been guilty.

For the upwardly mobile criminal, public houses have always been an ideal business. A pub is a perfect place for a crooked landlord to receive stolen goods, meet detectives as well as criminals, and pass information to and from the underworld. Ross and Garner acquired The Horns in Shoreditch in the 1960s, then bought The Eagle in Tottenham in the early 1970s. The Eagle was next to Tottenham Police Station, so naturally it was patronized by local detectives. After a few years Garner tarted it up and renamed it 'Elton's Disco'. He was obviously making a lot of money, and certainly Elton's was showing a sizeable profit. He bought a big house in one of North London's lusher suburbs, built a swimming pool and owned a Rolls-Royce. He also turned himself into a country squire, buying a farm in rural Hertfordshire and developing a passion for 'trotting' or harness racing. In America this sport attracts large crowds and a lot of gamblers. In Maryland USA Garner established a large stable of trotting horses and raced them in New York State and Florida. Back in England he established a second family with his mistress, Phyllis Warren, and set them up in a fine house in Highgate. He also ran girlfriends on the side who crossed the Atlantic with him, staying at his apartment on Florida's Gold Coast.

Most of this information on Garner's colourful lifestyle was gathered in the 1980s when he was targeted by a special inquiry set up by Scotland Yard and by a separate Customs and Excise fraud probe. In 1982 some investigative reporters were set on his trail and started raising questions in the press and on television. Some of their material came from criminals worsted by Garner and a lot more from disgruntled cops who claimed their inquiry into the man had been blocked. Yet back in 1970 none of it could have been known by Tony Lundy, as detective or boxing trainer: not Garner's alleged penchant for robbery or arson, not his VAT frauds, not his large investments on either side of the Atlantic. All this lay in the future.

By the time Garner was found guilty of any major crime (in 1984) Lundy's dealings with him had long been strictly limited. Confidential sources (not Lundy) have disclosed to me that he had long been meticulously documenting every aspect of their relationship, which simultaneously was being closely monitored by senior officers. This system was in place right from the start of 1981, when he had been instructed to report all his meetings with Garner *before such meetings happened*. This was mainly for Lundy's own protection and he rigorously complied with the order for the rest of his service. He was therefore in no position to shield, connive at, participate in, or even know about Garner's nefarious activities. From 1980 his sole dealings with the man were in his authorized role of informant 'handler'. He had no authority to question Garner over any other matters. His job was mainly to listen, but this also meant drawing Garner out about any information he was offering.

Attempts to taint Lundy with any of Garner's crimes, whether committed before or after 1980, are misplaced. What Garner was doing – beyond informing – was no more Lundy's responsibility than, say, the private offences of Wellington's army ('the scum of the earth') may be blamed on the Iron Duke. Fighting crime *is* a war, and folk like Garner are part of the weaponry. That he was a criminal is no shame to his 'handler'. Indeed, it was a qualification, although Lundy had no idea what rackets the man was into. As John Grieve, another senior detective, told an inquiry into Lundy in 1987, Garner 'was an outstanding informer who cost the public purse little. He was dangerous and undoubtedly deeply criminal. So are nearly all the top informers.'[2]

Mayby Garner had corrupt relations with other London officers. He certainly had two former police on his payroll, working at his pubs and clubs, but these had been uniformed constables – not detectives.[3] Whether he ever paid detectives while they were in 'the job' has never been proved. In 1973 one senior Criminal Intelligence officer targeted Garner but he says today that despite his best efforts he was unable to discover any evidence to justify criminal charges. In the later 1970s several anti-Garner intelligence operations were started, then stopped on guidance from above. At one time there were hints that he was helping with other matters and was better left alone for the moment. On another occasion it was said there were more pressing tasks. For sure, he was never the 'the overlord of London crime' or 'London's top gangster', as alleged by one retired detective in 1986 and endorsed by Lundy's main media adversaries in 1990.[4] Such claims display breathtaking ignorance of London crime as a whole. Garner certainly became 'big' but there were bigger criminals even more worthy of investigation who had never received the scrutiny he later attracted. Detective work, like all sides of modern policing, is governed by 'priorities'. Not targeting Garner, or calling a squad off him, was probably due to 'prioritizing' – right or wrong – or ignorance or apathy, not to a conspiracy of protection. In any case, such decisions would have been taken way above Tony Lundy's head.

If Garner was getting protection, he would probably have got it from someone more senior than a chief inspector, which was all Lundy was until November 1980. Indeed, the last person Garner would sensibly have involved would have been the detective who was nominating him for rewards. For that task he would have wanted an upright man, someone above suspicion with credibility at the top of the CID. For any dirty work, to get information out of the Yard for example, he would have wanted a man he could buy. Whether he paid for them or not, Garner did benefit from leaks from many CID officers, including some within the very squads investigating him.

It is illogical to heap up all the evidence gathered against Garner by those massive inquiries in the decade up to 1990, and then claim Lundy should have done something about him ten to twenty years earlier. Never was Lundy himself told to investigate the man. If he had been, he might well have done the job better than the detectives who were told to do so, but who never brought Garner to trial and then bleated in retirement. Refusing to be specific, but speaking of all his informers, Lundy claims, 'There's no question that I would have charged them if ever I'd found out they were at it – and I said so to each and every one of them.'

What Lundy did know in the early 1970s was that Finchley Boxing Club was desperately short of funds. There was an unrelenting struggle to pay for new gloves and other equipment. Many boys could not afford the sub-scriptions, although none was turned away. Fund-raising was the obvious answer so Lundy helped organize charity nights with the local CID. Up to 200 people would turn up to dine and then watch the fights. All profits were split between the boxing club and divisional police social funds. When the Regional Crime Squad joined in, the functions became more ambitious. Seats were sold in tables of ten. Many were paid for by the boxers' fathers, including ex-convicts. On other tables a few feet away sat high-ranking detectives.

Such socializing might raise eyebrows today but twenty years ago it was the norm. Boxing has always been a sport where gangsters and detectives rub shoulders. This has something to do with its macho image and the passionate affection of both cops and robbers for the 'Noble Art'. A more sinister overlap goes back to the 1940s and 1950s when much of British professional boxing was effectively run by gambling racketeers who had squads of cops in their pockets. One hopes such bad old days are over, but even now any copper – no matter how Simon Pure – who is involved in amateur boxing will touch gloves with villains, if only in the ring. It is a sport which inevitably attracts the underworld.

At Finchley such connections were kept at fists' length. For sure, men like Garner would pay for a dinner table and stack it with confederates, but Lundy maintained some distance. As he told a later inquiry:

I didn't go with these people. I have never been physically anywhere with Garner. In those days we're all part of the boxing club scene . . . I'm there in an innocent capacity . . . It's easy to interpret it in reverse by other people with ulterior motives later, but I don't believe for one minute that I did wrong.

Roy Garner himself set up two spectacular fund-raisers

in a banqueting suite at Enfield Football Club. He used big-name entertainers to attract a large audience including many faces from the North and East London underworld. Lundy stuck to the boxing side of such events. The benefits for Finchley ABC were immense. In the early 1970s it paid £27,000 for an old Boys Brigade hall, to be refurbished as club premises. The building is now worth £250,000.

Scotland Yard was also benefiting from Lundy's boxing activities, in a different way. Social mixing between police and villains is always open to hostile interpretation, but in this case it gave Lundy excellent cover. 'The more functions you attended, the more you had a chance to drink and chat with these people, so that when someone *did* start volunteering information, it was easy to meet without any members of that fraternity becoming suspicious. You could chat on the side without it looking rum.'

Boxing functions led to other charity gatherings, such as the 1974 dinner of the Lady Ratlings (a female offshoot of the Grand Order of Water Rats). A photograph of this occasion, held at the Dorchester Hotel, would return to haunt Lundy eight years later, for near the detective stood a number of North London malefactors including Roy Garner. A similar photo of a later occasion also emerged. For Lundy such open association would prove unfortunate in an unforeseeable way, but at the time it worked only to the good of Scotland Yard. Lundy made sure everyone in the chain of command knew of his connections and what results they were yielding in terms of arrests and convictions. Chief officers who had risen through the detective ranks understood his approach. Besides, even today, what is the alternative?

If you had a policy saying you must not socialize with anybody with a criminal record, you could not really have a CID. Where do you get criminal information from? You don't get it from meeting people in church. Imagine there's a particular force that says, 'We don't believe in any officer, uniform or CID, having any informants. We don't *want* informants, we don't talk to them, they're a very dangerous breed. We shall now operate on the basis that our intelligence, our phone-taps and our surveillance techniques are so good that henceforth we shall not use informants anywhere any time. If anybody's ever caught speaking to anyone with a criminal background, in a pub or anywhere, he will be guilty of an offence.'

Terrific! Everybody would know where they stand! The trouble is, your crime detection rates might not be the best in the world now, but in future they would go rock bottom!

Lundy never mixed with criminals to the point where the socializing got in the way of the job. Indeed, by the CID standards of the day his social life was puritanical. This was an era when Soho club-owner and vice syndicate boss Bernie Silver sat at the top table at Flying Squad dinners next to Commander Dave Dilley, head of Criminal Intelligence;[5] and when Jock Wilson, no less than Assistant Commissioner (Crime) until 1977, held his daughter's wedding reception in a hotel owned by his friend Charlie Taylor, a notorious criminal. Wilson was even photographed sitting next to Taylor at a police dinner at the Dorchester. Taylor's other friends included Deputy Assistant Commissioner Reg Davies and senior Fraud Squad men.[6] Strange as it seems, such associations were the norm until the mid-1970s when it struck some journalists and a few police that this kind of thing was no longer 'on'. At least Lundy could show results from keeping doubtful company.

Dwarfing all individual friendships was the biggest social club of all, the secret society of Freemasonry, behind whose temple doors and at whose unphotographed dinners many leading detectives bound themselves in solemn oaths of mutual defence to leading London criminals. For

instance, Obscene Publications Squad chief Bill Moody
introduced his convicted pornographer friend, Ron 'The
Dustman' Davey, into his Surrey lodge.[7] All the underworld figures in the Lady Ratlings photo with Lundy were
Freemasons. They were all members of lodges containing senior police. Garner belonged to the Bishop Ridley
Lodge, number 6196, along with a detective sergeant
named Peter Dougherty. The detective shot on Garner's
farmland and even kept a caravan on it, but he had broken
no police rules.[8]

Almost the only non-mason in this story is Tony Lundy.
Many of the criminals he sent to prison were 'on the
square'. So were some of the police chiefs who later tried
to ruin his career. With the benefit of hindsight, it seems
he would have done far more for his future by becoming
a Freemason than by working most nights for the boxing
club or cultivating sources. But that was typical of the man.
He was a workaholic.

From the detective's point of view, if you're keen you're
always going to be seeking information because you want to
get results and better jobs. But if you're a lazy detective, with
no ambition, you only do the job in hand. You get a prisoner in
for, say, grievous bodily harm, you deal with him for that – and
finish! You don't bother asking him about anything else. But I
was keen, and if you're keen you're always going to be trying.

The over-riding importance of informers was dinned
into him early in his career during a junior CID course
at training school.

I'll always remember one old instructor saying 'the be-all and
end-all of CID work are informants'. Everybody you arrest is a
potential informant. The greatest way of encouraging informants
is arrest, not as blackmail but as a form of pressure. There's
nothing underhand in saying to a man, 'Look! If you can help me
with other things – local burglaries or that piece of shoplifting,

this robbery or that knifing – then I'll put a word in for you at court, I'll speak up a bit.' That's the natural starting way.

Anybody who's going to inform wants help or favours of some sort: either money or a deal. It's always a *quid pro quo*. No one's going to do something unless they get something in return.

For Roy Garner the *quid* was clearly thousands of quid. His main motive had to be money because, it seems, Lundy never had anything on Garner to justify an arrest and thus bring pressure upon him. Yet for many years, as leaked documentation shows, Garner gave Lundy information when no reward – from police or insurers – was on offer. What, in the psychological make-up of such a man, drives him to volunteer information? Another retired senior detective talks from his own experience:

Some informers get a buzz out of squealing. It's an adrenalin thing. They seem propelled by the risk of discovery. Years ago they may have been involved in physical crime, armed robberies. But even if they've stayed out of jail long enough to build a safer way of making a living, they still miss the thrill of hold-ups on the pavement. It's like smoking: they can't give it up. It's in their blood. Of course, some ex-robbers get so rich they would be mad to go back on the streets. Instead they get their kicks from shopping active villains. In earlier days they may have started informing to protect themselves, as an insurance policy. Later on, maybe, they're worried about the past catching up. That's when they like to think, 'If it does, at least I've got a bit of credit in the bank.'

Whatever their motives, all informers are meant to be handled with great care by Metropolitan detectives, according to a code which has become increasingly strict over the years.[9] The officer must make sure his informant does not 'counsel, incite or procure the commission of a crime' or act as *agent provocateur* by persuading others to commit crimes so that he may inform on them. Nor, when the informant is expected to take part in a crime by those he is informing against (for example, when they have recruited him for a robbery) may he play a major part in its planning or execution. The police must always do their best to conceal their man's role as an informant, even to the point of aborting a trial if that role is likely to be revealed. This does not give him immunity from prosecution if it turns out that he did fully participate in the crime concerned, or if he commits any other crime. However, if he is later arrested for any crime and convicted, it is wholly in order for police to give the judge or magistrate a letter explaining his past assistance, so his sentence may be adjusted downwards if appropriate.

Rules governing payments to informers have also been tightened. Even snouts have expenses, for which they may be later recompensed, but the really controversial issue is rewards. There are two main kinds of reward: small sums – rarely reaching £1,000 – which in London come out of the Metropolitan Police Informants' Fund and are paid at the discretion of the force; and large sums – usually ten per cent of the value of goods stolen and recovered – which are paid by loss adjusters or assessors acting for banks, security firms or insurers who would otherwise bear the loss. Obviously, loss adjusters want to reward only the true informer, so they usually confirm his identity with senior police. However, the decision to pay, and the size of any payment are entirely in the discretion of the institution paying the reward. The police have no say.

With percentage rewards, of course, the bigger the 'take', the bigger the reward. By the 1980s that meant very big bucks indeed. There used to be far less on offer, as Lundy recalls from his days as an 'aid to CID' in the 1960s:

In every CID office you used to have what they called the ACC's Consolidated Instructions manual. It laid down guidelines, for example, how you were to claim for rewards or what sort of reports you had to put in. If you had little jobs off, here and there, you'd put in a report to your governor saying this or that had happened as a result of information given by such and such a name. And they'd pay out the odd few pounds or whatever was needed. The whole idea was that you didn't pay money out yourself.

In the 1960s and early 1970s no detective had to identify his informant: 'When you submitted your reports you just gave the informer a pseudonym and he was paid out on that basis. You didn't have to reveal his true name to anybody. Nobody knew who he was except the detective who handled him. Confidentiality was strict. Nobody leaked anything.' Yet, as Lundy acknowledges, this system was open to appalling abuse by crooked cops. On the Metropolitan Police Drugs Squad by the late 1960s it became the custom to 'license' some drug dealers in return for information on lesser dealers, who would then be arrested and jailed. The bigger the dealer, the wider his licence.[10] In a parallel and equally appalling epoch on the Obscene Publications Squad, it was a case of 'the higher the detective the bigger the bribe'. Massive sums were paid by leading pornographers, stripclub and dirty-bookshop owners. In return the 'Porn' Squad would arrest their competitors and put them out of business. The only way those competitors could survive was by paying even bigger bribes to join the club.[11]

The 'Porn' Squad officer with the longest reign (and the deepest pockets) was Detective Chief Superintendent Bill Moody. With another officer he took at least £100,000 a year in bribes. He rationalized the system in an intriguing way. In areas of so-called 'victimless' crime, such as pornography and drugs where there will always be substantial public demand, Moody felt it made no sense to jail the leading operators. That would only create a vacuum which would be promptly filled by other criminals. Far better to 'license' the big fish and leave them to eat the minnows. In this way the 'Porn' Squad surrendered its detective role to the pornographers themselves who would simply inform the squad's commanding officers (Moody among them) when to knock out which opposition. The detectives seemed to believe the current Kings of Soho were less violent than anyone who might replace them. Unfortunately the main men they licensed had very violent reputations: Jimmy Humphreys, who was later jailed for eight years for a vicious four-man knife attack on his wife's lover; and Bernie Silver, a ponce who was jailed for six years for living off immoral earnings. In 1975 Silver was sentenced to life imprisonment for conspiracy to murder but was later cleared on appeal.

These vice kings did not inform for conventional rewards. After all, they were paying the police fortunes. Their prize was being allowed to continue their booming business with no fear of police interference or commercial opposition. Eventually public outrage, press exposés and the integrity of some Yard detectives brought the rotten system tumbling down. When Flying Squad Commander Ken Drury was exposed by the *Sunday People* in 1972 for holidaying in Cyprus at Jimmy Humphreys's expense, all he could bluster in defence was that he, Jimmy and their wives were all on the island pursuing a tip-off about fugitive 'Great Train Robber' Ronnie Biggs.[12] This was a lie but it betrayed the top detective's instinct that collaboration with an informer could be used as a cover for almost anything, however corrupt. It was a feeble lie which helped earn him eight years in jail in 1977. At his trial he justified meeting the pornographer so often – fifty-eight times at restaurants and clubs, with Humphreys always paying the bill – on the grounds that he was cultivating an informer. Indeed, Humphreys was an informer, but not a legitimate one. If he had been, he would not have paid Drury (London's top operational detective) a total of £5,000 or ten times that amount to the far greedier Bill Moody who was sent down for twelve years.

There was one other twist in the tangled web of police–informant relations in the 1970s. This involved the Wembley Robbery Squad which had handled the first supergrass, Bertie Smalls (see Chapter 2). Its considerable success was tarnished by the manner in which an informant, 'William Wise', was put up to claim a series of rewards totalling £2,175 over the 1972 robbery which had led to the 'Smalls' inquiry. It later emerged that a true informant, 'Mary Frazer', had been deprived of her due rewards, and that contemporary records justifying her claim had disappeared or been deleted. Her handler, WDC Joan Angell, protested to Commissioner Sir Robert Mark, and eventually 'Mary Frazer' was given £1,000 by Barclays Bank. Joan Angell quit the force in disgust. The case left some nasty questions unanswered. Was 'William Wise' really an informant? Did he exist, even without his pseudonym? Did the police who nominated him already know the information – notably about the two robbers' safe deposit box stashed with robbery proceeds – before Wise allegedly gave it to them? Did one of those detectives steal £25,000 from that box and why did he run away to Miami just when John Shirley of *The London Programme* was seeking to interview him about the affair in 1976?[13]

As these scandals broke one by one through the 1970s, receiving graphic exposure in newspapers and on television, they simultaneously forced and freed Metropolitan Police chiefs to restructure London's CID on an anticorruption basis. The job of cleansing the stable shared by bent cops and fake informants fell to David Powis who, as Deputy Assistant Commissioner (Operations), was in charge of all London detectives from 1977 until he retired in 1984. He reformed the reward system to curb opportunities for detectives who – unknown to him – might already be corrupt, but also to protect clean ones from poisoned whispers. Far from cursing this reform, the rising star Lundy wholeheartedly supported it. He assumed, of course, that the new system would always be totally secure from the informants' point of view (a false assumption, as it turned out).

David Powis said, 'From now on the true identity of inform-ants has to be revealed. When you submit any report relating to an informer, his/her identity may still be disguised with a pseudonym, but you must put the true identity in a sealed envelope. Your informant report will be passed up the detective hierarchy for comments on the value or truth of the information supplied, but the sealed envelope containing the informer's name may be opened only by me. Only in my office will any record or index of informers be kept.' In practical terms this meant that the only people who knew informers' true identities were David Powis and his staff officer. For years there was not a single leak from that office.

Lundy's respect for Powis seems to have been recipro-cated. When Powis took over as DAC 'Ops', Lundy had just come on stream as Scotland Yard's biggest thief-taker. While crooks and backwoodsmen were being forced out by the hundred from the 3,000-strong CID, he not only soared in rank, he was surging in reputation. Commissioner Sir David McNee and Assistant Commissioner Kelland both visited Finchley to thank Lundy's team personally for their fine work. And when ITV's *London Programme* wanted to film an 'Action Man' sequence about Scotland Yard crime-busters, the Yard nominated Lundy and his Finchley Robbery Squad. The programme also included a muscular interview with David Powis. Determined to bring London's violent crime rate down, he saw Lundy as one of his main weapons. It might be claimed that this gave Lundy a special degree of influence over Powis. 'That was not my experience,' said Powis's staff officer, Detective Superintendent John Grieve, in 1987. 'I find the suggestion that DAC Powis had a corrupt relationship with any officer or informer totally incredible. [His] behaviour was always scrupulously honest.'[14]

What Powis may have admired in Lundy was the street-wise detective he had once been. When he was made 'chief' of detectives, Powis had been out of the CID for twenty-one years, a fact which his detractors distorted by falsely claiming that he lacked crime-fighting campaign medals. He also needed capable allies against the rump of the 'Old Guard' who kept trying to undermine him and his boss, Assistant Commissioner Gilbert Kelland, precisely because they had come to power on an anti-corruption ticket and were determined to shake the CID out of its age-old complacency and 'bent' habits. Lundy was certainly not part of the Old Guard despite serving in one of its last bastions, the Flying Squad. Indeed, he must have seemed the finest of a new breed. Yet officers with scarcely an arrest to their name, and even some dispassionate observers, were spreading rumours that he was just too good to be true.

Powis himself was curious about Lundy's *modus operandi*. For reasons which had nothing to do with Lundy (see Chapter 10), he had introduced another anti-corruption reform. He had decided that he should pay informers himself, not leave the task to junior detectives. Lundy recalls Powis's first such encounter in Lundy's presence. The beneficiary was not Roy Garner.

The first time Mr Powis ever came to pay a man out, I was sitting in a pub with the informer, waiting for him to arrive. So the man – let's call him 'John' – says, 'Why does he have to come? You've paid me out all this time.' I said, 'It's new rules, and unless you accept it, you're not going to get the money. He's

got to pay it and that's it!' So in walks Powis, he looks round
and he comes and sits on the other side of the man from me.
I say, 'Hello, sir, this is John.' And he stretches out his right
hand and says, 'Pleased to meet you, John!' Now John was not
used to shaking hands or genteel civilities. So I'm thinking, 'Oh
God' and I say, 'Can I get you a drink, sir?' 'I'll have an orange
juice, I don't drink.' So the geezer, a little bloke, knocks his pint
back and says, 'Well, I'll have a pint.'

I go up and get the drinks and I come back and sit down, and
Powis says, 'I want you to know that there's no reflection on this
officer in my being here to do this payment . . .' – and the geezer
looks at him because he doesn't understand half the words Powis
is using – 'It is merely a new policy to safeguard the interests of
this officer and people like him. And we thought it right that,
above a certain amount, I . . .' And he goes on and on, but all
the bloke wants is his money!

Then Powis starts, 'I'm very interested in this type of psychol-
ogy, in the motivation of informants. Why do you do this sort
of thing?' And by this time I'm sitting there burying my head
in my hands, thinking, 'What *is* he going to say to him?' Of
course, I *know* why the informer had started doing it: because
I sort of blackmailed him, when he was on offer for grievous
bodily harm or whatever! It was a case of 'does he get bail or
doesn't he?' That was how I started him off. And he says to Mr
Powis, 'Well, he had the blag on me, didn't he?' And Powis says,
'Pardon?' 'Well, when he had me nicked once, you know . . . he
said it would be in my interests if I started to give him a bit of
help, like. And I needed a bit of help, so he blagged me. And
since then we've stayed pals. And I've put up a few bits and
bobs here and there. And things work out, don't they?'

Powis then asked the bloke, 'Have you read my book?' And
he said, 'No, what book?' It was *The Signs of Crime – A Field
Manual for Police*.[15] Well, this man had never read a book in
his life and probably didn't have one in his house, but Powis
just carried on, saying something about writing a book on
informants. Now when the bloke talked about 'blagging', Powis
must have realized he meant a kind of blackmail, so I butted in
and said something like, 'How are you ever going to get started
with anybody?'

Now I'm sitting there cringing, but eventually Powis gets
round to paying him. Then he starts dictating: 'You have to write
out these words – I have received X amount from such-and-such

a body at this time – and sign here.' It was a proper form. And as the man signs, Powis looks at his watch and says, 'at 7.29 and 46 seconds p.m.' or whatever.

You might think that paying money to an informant ought to be done in secret but Powis *insists* he counts it all there and then. The bloke says, 'That's all right! I trust you, don't I?' 'No,' said Powis, 'I insist you count the money.' (Another time he made an informant count out more than £30,000 in cash!) So this time he pays John, says his farewells and leaves. I stay on with the bloke, chatting about other odds and ends, then I get up to buy another pint. But while I'm waiting at the bar, Powis suddenly walks back in again. He'd done it deliberately, to see if the informer was giving me any of the money. I'm convinced of that. But when he sees the bloke sitting down there while I'm up at the bar, he just says, 'Oh, sorry' and turned and walked back out again. When he finally left, the geezer turned to me and said, 'Jesus, what was all that about?'

The story is to Powis's credit, for if he had indeed returned to see if Lundy was taking any of the reward money, he was only doing his job as he saw fit. Powis has told me: 'I had strict attitudes towards the registration, supervision and payment of informers. I successfully recommended stringent changes of procedure, one being that I would personally convey rewards of any size to informers, and then only to those whose true identity and addresses I knew, and who were properly registered. I performed this duty many scores of times.' Powis's behaviour when paying out Lundy's informants was not a sign of any particular suspicion. Indeed, another detective has told me that, during a similar pay-out to one of his informers, Powis went far further and told the man he must not split his reward with the detective, and that any such deal would be illegal. After Powis departed, the pair collapsed in laughter because, had they made such a deal, they certainly would not have told him.

Lundy had originally met the informer 'John' while serving in Finchley as a sergeant. When Lundy first arrested him, 'John' knew he was certain to be jailed for a year or two, so he offered information in the hope of bail. Lundy leaped on the information but gave nothing away.

Quite often you know you might have difficulty keeping the man in custody anyway so you let him have bail. There's nothing underhand or devious in this. It's the way you have to work. So 'John' thought I had done him a favour over bail and later he got a 'result' at court. Then he rang me up and gave me one job, then another – local things, burglars, odds and ends – until in 1978 he put up a big job: he named Dave Smith – and that, of course, led on to so much more.

In later years it would be suggested that the man who informed against Dave Smith was Roy Garner, but Lundy says it was this man 'John'.

The bloke who put up Smith got a lot of money: all paid out, official. Yet in all the years when people have attacked me, no one's ever mentioned him. Nothing has ever leaked. If they were just attacking me, they would have leaked police intelligence about this informant who put up big jobs and was paid big rewards, but no one has ever attacked my relationship with anyone except one man. To damn him it was necessary to damn me too.

It is indeed likely that Roy Garner, not Lundy, was the leakers' original target because he had trodden on powerful vested interests. It may be significant that the first anti-Garner police leaks occurred only after mid-1980, when he disturbed the masonic bonds which for generations had united many London criminals not just with crooked cops but with straight ones too. These bonds are explored in Chapter 25.

Perhaps Lundy was not Garner's first police 'handler'. It seems he may previously have been handled by a high-ranking officer who served on the Wembley Robbery Squad before retiring at the end of the 1970s.[16] For the record, however, it should be stated that Roy Garner was not the 'William Wise' put up to claim a controversial reward by other Wembley officers. Nor did any previous Garner handler nominate Lundy to succeed him. Garner was never a subject of discussion between Lundy and the man alleged to be his predecessor. The two officers never worked together in the force. Certainly the older detective lived close to Finchley and supported the boxing club indirectly, through police social organizations, but he had no other connections with Tony Lundy.

Records show that Garner's first reward (as a result of information he gave Lundy) came through Hertfordshire, not Scotland Yard. Early in 1978, following an armed robbery in which shots were fired, Herts Police set up a special unit including two officers from Lundy's Finchley squad. It was this operation which led to the arrest of Leroy Davies who turned supergrass. Davies named a man as having taken part in twenty robberies, including some for which rewards had been offered. The man was in hiding hundreds of miles away and Garner knew where he was. Lundy passed on the news, the man was arrested and later convicted. Garner received a reward but Lundy played no role in the payment and no publicity resulted. Even years later, when Scotland Yard was leaking like a sieve with anti-Garner and anti-Lundy stories, nothing ever came out about this job, perhaps because it was impossible to use it to denigrate that pair alone. Other officers were involved, so if it was portrayed as bent, they must be bent too – or so a libel lawyer might think.

Garner and Lundy's first collaboration for Scotland Yard was over a series of attacks on the vans of one security company in 1978 and 1979. The raids were very similar and had obviously been committed by the same robbers. Information from Garner led to their surveillance, their arrest within hours of yet another robbery, and the recovery of a large sum of money and an arsenal of guns. The gang all went to jail for many years, and Roy Garner had earned another pay packet.

Early in 1980 (again, according to records) Garner helped police over a kind of crime – jewel thefts – that he knew well. He had long been a suspected receiver of stolen jewels, and several specialist gem dealers in London's diamond quarter, Hatton Garden, were his regular customers. It turned out that a pair of them had been involved in a fake robbery. The 'victims', Wilfred Hogg and John Heath, had recruited a pair of violent robbers to steal £778,000 worth of gems which the jewellers were about to export to Saudi Arabia. The scheme was that the robbers were to return the gear, and receive a share of the proceeds of a fraudulent insurance claim. Hogg was duly attacked, kidnapped and dumped in a van in Islington, claiming he had been robbed. Within days Roy Garner found out it was a set-up and he named the likely robbers as two men whom he said he saw and recognized when he himself had visited Hogg and Heath's premises a few days before the crime. He now presumed they must have been checking the place out.

By 5 March Lundy set up photographic observations on the suspects but these yielded no hint of where the stolen property might be. Lundy's squad continued to watch Hogg, Heath and the alleged robbers, but on 24 April – seven weeks after Garner's tip-off – a Sussex officer came forward with information from a source who was also claiming the robbery was bogus. The source said that Heath had hidden some of the jewellery at the address of his girlfriend who was taking it abroad very soon. This news forced Lundy to arrest Heath and his girlfriend next day, but his officers found nothing at her address. In that respect the Sussex informer proved dangerously wrong, but during a long interrogation Lundy forced Heath and

Hogg to admit their guilt and reveal that the jewellery was hidden in a barn on farmland owned by Heath and in four safe deposit boxes. It was recovered in full.

Hogg also named the two 'robbers' as the same men named by Roy Garner. They were, police sources say, 'first division villains'. They were charged but then Hogg lost his nerve, apparently fearing reprisals if he testified. This forced the Director of Public Prosecutions to drop charges against them because of insufficient evidence. However, Hogg and Heath both pleaded guilty and were sent to prison for five years.

There now arose the question of who should have the £75,000 reward. DAC Powis and Sussex's Deputy Chief Constable decided it should be split down the middle: £37,500 for Lundy's man and £37,500 for the Sussex source. Lundy thought no more of the affair but, three years later, another detective would claim the only valuable information had come from Sussex and accuse Lundy of falsely nominating his own informer. The story behind this allegation is told in Chapter 14. In the meantime, the reader may be sure Garner was a genuine informant on the Hatton Garden job, and that in 1980 he would prove his value again over a far more spectacular crime.

Silver Bullion, Golden Egg

In the three weeks since Chrissie Wren and co. had been arrested, Finchley Robbery Squad had worked non-stop: on raids, interrogations, remands and a mountain of paperwork. But at last Lundy snatched a day off. It was the morning of Saturday 31 May 1980 and he was at home. Then he got the phone call. According to Scotland Yard's official records, the caller's name was Dave Granger but in a year or two it would leak out that his true identity was Roy Garner. Despite Lundy's home-loving objections, 'Granger' insisted that they meet at once.

There was a pub in East Finchley where the pair used to meet. Lundy did not want to go but 'Dave Granger' never wasted Lundy's time. When he arrived, 'Granger' came straight to the point – the Silver Bullion job.

Every keen detective in London wanted to solve the Silver Bullion job, the biggest armed robbery there had ever been in Britain at the time: three and a half million pounds-worth of East German-owned silver stolen from a lorry hi-jacked on its way to Tilbury Docks on 24 March 1980. The lorry had been waved to a layby on the A13 road by a bogus uniformed policeman, accompanied by two equally bogus Ministry of Transport officials in white smock coats and dark glasses. They pulled out a pistol and a sawn-off shotgun, kidnapped the lorry's three occupants and later dumped them, tied up in a locked garage. By the time they broke free, their silver had disappeared. Now, ten weeks later, 'Granger' – or Garner, as it is less confusing to call him – was telling Lundy that the police already held one man who had been on the Silver Bullion job: Micky Gervaise. Roy Garner now knew the identities of Gervaise and the other main robbery conspirators because one of them, Micky Sewell, had approached him the previous night, wanting to do a 'complete runner': to disappear from all his known haunts by leaving London.

At first Lundy was disbelieving. He thought Garner was joking, but the mention of Micky Sewell rang true. Lundy already knew a lot about Sewell. At that moment he was wanted for questioning because his old buddy, supergrass Micky Gervaise, had revealed they worked together on several big burglaries. They had been like brothers, never apart, but when police officers went to arrest the people named by Gervaise, one suspect they had not been able to find was Micky Sewell.

Sewell was also wanted for the conspiracy to rob Lambeth Town Hall in August 1978. Ray Fowles had grassed him over that job, Sewell found out and disappeared for months. Lundy learned where he was and tracked him down. Although Lundy had 'turned' Fowles, pressure of work had obliged him to hand the entire Fowles inquiry to other detectives (see Chapter 5). Lambeth Town Hall fell to Chief Inspector Bill Peters, under Superintendent Corbett. Lundy dutifully told Peters where Sewell was. Peters arrested him but Lundy was later surprised to hear that Sewell had been given bail. Sewell promptly went 'on the lam' again and was nowhere to be found.

Lundy was incensed. How could Sewell have been given bail when he had just spent months on the run and had only been recaptured through Lundy's efforts? Bill Peters later explained that he had not opposed bail because Sewell, as the alarm man, had not played a major role in the conspiracy. He also had a family, a fixed address and people prepared to stand surety for him, so he seemed unlikely to abscond. It has also been suggested that Sewell was an informer himself. Whatever the rights and wrongs

of his bail, once he had got it he was free to take part in
other crimes, including (it seems) Britain's biggest-ever
robbery: the Silver Bullion job.

When he found out that Gervaise had been arrested
on 18 May and had turned supergrass, and then that the
police were looking for him, Sewell had been driven into
even deeper hiding than usual. He was worried sick over
what Gervaise might have revealed, but he need not have
worried so much because Gervaise had named him only
on burglaries. Even if he were convicted, these crimes
would bring him only seven years' jail. With remission
and parole, that meant less than three years inside. For
the Silver Bullion job, however, Sewell knew he could get
twenty years, but Gervaise had held this back. Sewell had
almost worked this out himself (when he realized that no
one else on the Silver job had been arrested either) but,
even so, he decided to flee and went to Garner to borrow
money. As usual, avuncular advice was dispensed. Garner
told him to lie low because the police would have only
Gervaise's evidence to rely on and that would not be
enough to get Sewell convicted on the burglary offences.

Apparently, that helpful hint had drawn Sewell on to
make his fateful admission about the role of both himself
and Gervaise on the Silver Bullion robbery. Garner could
scarcely believe his ears. There had never been a whisper
about the job – not even in the close North London crime
circles in which he and Sewell both moved. Now from
nowhere the fly Sewell had flown into the spider's web
and 'spilled his guts'.

A few miles away at Enfield Police Station Micky
Gervaise had shut up about the Silver job, not because it
would have brought him a long sentence – as a supergrass
he could have confessed it without adding to his probable
five years – but because he was still hoping to get his
half-million-pound share of the loot when he came out.

That would not be possible if he admitted he was on it and had then, under his supergrass obligation, been forced to name his co-conspirators who still had the silver.

Lundy was already furious about Gervaise's failure, in the two weeks since he turned supergrass, to volunteer the truth about other robberies in which £1,200,000-worth of jewellery had been stolen (see Chapter 7), but he knew he could not just go in to Gervaise and blast him head-on for concealing his role on an even bigger crime, because he would surely realize he had been informed against. Lundy had to proceed with cunning or his informer would be in extreme danger. Garner, naturally concerned for his own safety, wanted Gervaise to be deluded into believing he was confessing the Bullion job of his own free will. With that hint Garner went on his way, and the detective kissed goodbye to a quiet weekend at home. By now Lundy's preoccupation with police work was having a catastrophic effect on relations with his wife, Vi.

Our marriage was almost on the rocks that year. I don't know how we survived. It's funny looking back on it, but at the time there was a lot of bad feeling between us. The kids were having to live through it all, and I'm sure they all thought I was neglecting them. As far as they were concerned, nothing I was doing could be right, but I was working all hours for the Metropolitan Police. I'd let the job take over my entire life.

Fleeing from Vi's justifiable fury, Lundy went off to Whetstone and told the story to Superintendent Reg Dixon, the detective in overall charge of the Gervaise inquiries. As ever, Lundy did not identify his source even to this senior officer. Dixon was just as angry as Lundy over Gervaise's continuing failure to admit *all* his crimes, so now they both went straight to Enfield to make him talk, without Lundy revealing what he knew or how. 'When we went in to Gervaise, we tried to steer the conversation so that it was him telling us what happened, not us telling him.' According to Lundy's statement, he and Dixon told Gervaise they felt he was holding something back. For the previous three weeks Lundy had been grinding out the same tune, 'You've still not told us the whole truth, there's still things to come out.' Gervaise had brushed these remarks aside (he assumed Lundy was fishing) but on this day he could tell that Lundy knew something very bad indeed. Lundy recalls the encounter.

When he looked at me, his bottle dropped out and he knew. I never told him, I didn't have to. Here were we, coming in on a Saturday afternoon, out of the blue, when he knew we were all supposed to be having a weekend off, and he was locked up in peace at Enfield. He knew it had to be something special when all of a sudden we're there: the superintendent and the chief inspector!

According to the two policemen's statements, Gervaise prevaricated. Then, assuring Dixon he meant no disrespect, he asked to speak to Lundy on his own. Dixon, a blunt down-to-earth Cockney, took the request very well in the circumstances. According to Lundy, Dixon pretended to be annoyed: 'I'm the bloomin' superintendent, aren't I? And you want a word with Lundy on his own? I'll go and get the teas, won't I? That's good, innit? Here's me, *Superintendent* – yeh! You get the teas, *Superintendent*!'

This act turned the encounter to the detectives' advantage, for so long as Gervaise told one of them about the Bullion job it did not matter which one. As soon as Dixon left, Gervaise said, 'You know, don't you?' 'I don't know anything,' said Lundy, 'but I know you've not been truthful.'

According to Lundy's statement, Gervaise then approached the point which, he thought, might bring difficulties: 'You don't understand, Mr Lundy. It's a personal problem that could also affect you. What are you going to do? Look at the embarrassment you're going to have!'

Lundy dismissed the suggestion: 'I don't have any embarrassment from anybody, me. I don't have any allegiances. Whatever you've got to tell us, tell us! I've no worries or fears.'

After restating his family worries, Gervaise edged nearer the abyss.

'It involves Lennie.'
'You mean Lennie Gibson.'
'Yes, but you don't realize how serious it is.'
'Get one thing straight: Lennie is a likeable type but I have no allegiances to him or anybody else. If they are involved in villainy, they will be nicked and dealt with like anyone else.'
'But I thought he was a very good friend of yours.'
'No way. I have known him socially from drinking in the same pub – but we are no more friends than that.'
'I understood you were in the same lodge together.'

This remark set Lundy going.

'Look. I don't know what stories people have been spreading but I assure you, that is completely wrong. I have never had anything to do with Freemasonry. And obviously somebody has frightened you by suggesting associations and friendships which don't exist. Now tell me what it's all about.'

Put a little at ease, Gervaise finally spat it out:

'Well, perhaps you will understand why I have been worried – I was on the Silver Bullion job with Lennie Gibson.'
'Now I understand. Tell Mr Dixon all about it.'

At this point Reg Dixon came back into the room with the teas, and Lundy told him why Gervaise had been so hesitant to name Gibson. Then Gervaise offered up the names of the men he claimed were his main co-conspirators – Bob Deanus, Micky Sewell, 'Dolph' (Rudolpho Aguda) – and explained their various roles. 'I was the policeman,' said Gervaise, 'but the uniform and guns were provided by the others.' 'The others' had also laid down the bullion. 'But I honestly don't know where.' Lundy recalls:

That was it. We sat there for a couple of hours as he told us all the ins and outs of the robbery, but he insisted he had no idea where the silver was hidden. We then called in a sergeant who'd taken earlier statements from Gervaise and we said, 'You take a written statement from him now, no matter how long it takes. You stay here all night if needs be, and you take down every word about this job.'

The senior officers left Gervaise with the sergeant and went straight to the pub where Lundy had arranged to meet the informant again. Dixon stayed outside while Lundy asked for more details but Garner refused to say any more until he was sure Gervaise really was 'spilling his guts'. To prove it, Lundy mentioned some of the men Gervaise had named: 'Micky Sewell, Lennie Gibson and Dolph Aguda, also some bloke called Ron who has a transport firm. You said I'd be shocked, and you were absolutely right.'

What Lundy needed to know above all was where the bullion was. Garner said he did not know but he knew that Gibson and Aguda controlled it. He then offered an insight into the two men's psychologies: they would be more likely to admit everything if they were allowed to talk things over between themselves. Once they knew Gervaise was going to testify against them, they would realize that the only way they could lighten their sentence would be to give the silver back; but if they were seen separately, neither would admit anything because the one would not let the other down.

Lundy left Garner and rejoined Reg Dixon. The pair then reported to their boss, Chief Superintendent Mike Taylor, at his home. They also called in Superintendent Dave Little, head of Walthamstow Robbery Squad, who was in overall charge of Silver Bullion inquiries because the robbery had occurred in Barking in his East London territory. He had visited Finchley in previous weeks in the hope that one of Lundy's supergrasses might know something about the job but, until his latest coup, none of Lundy's budgies had sung.

By now it was late on Saturday so the detectives decided to send surveillance teams out next day to locate the men named by Gervaise, preferably at home. In addition to Gibson, Sewell, Dolph Aguda and Bob Deanus, the detectives wanted the man Gervaise called 'Ron', who was now identified as Dolph's nephew Renalto. Gervaise had also mentioned an 'inside man', working for the firm which owned the hi-jacked lorry. This seemed to be its transport manager, known on the North London boxing-cum-masonic circuit as 'Bolster' Parker.

All Sunday and Monday went by but still the surveillance teams had not 'housed' Gibson or even seen him, while Sewell had repeated his disappearing act. The others had all been located but there was no point in arresting them if Gibson was still free, because he would soon find out and then shift the silver. The decision to hold back was taken by Lundy, who was running the operation even though it was not his job; his senior colleagues trusted him to make the arrests because he had successfully carried out dozens of similar operations in the past four years. 'In all my dealings with Tony', says Dave Little today, 'I found him 100 per cent positive. I've never once doubted his integrity.'

On the Tuesday Lundy was committed to attend the funeral of a South Wales detective who had become a close friend when both men had collaborated on a major supergrass investigation. Lundy travelled down to Cardiff in a police car, but as he returned that evening he heard his radio operator say, 'Gibson located, and he's on the move.' Even better, Gibson was in a car with Dolph Aguda in London's East End. Lundy listened to their movements until he returned to Finchley. He then talked tactics through with Dave Little and decided on a swift end. Everyone agreed.

Gibson and Aguda were seized, and instantly all other arrest plans were put into operation. The entire gang (bar the elusive Micky Sewell) was picked up and locked inside various North London police stations while squads of police searched their houses. Later Lundy would wonder if he had made the right decision – it turned out Gibson and Aguda had been on their way to meet Sewell – 'But if we'd let it run, I was desperately worried in case we lost them. They could have "sussed" our lads on their tail and disappeared. Then we might never have found them or the silver.'

Now came the moment for Lundy to confront his old acquaintance from Finchley Boxing Club and the Torrington Arms: 'I could have interviewed any of the gang in any order but, obviously, my first one has to be Len Gibson. I go in to him, and he just shrugs his shoulders and shook his head in a sad sort of way.' Lundy cautioned him, then, according to his interview statement, he laid out what Gervaise had said about the silver job.

'There you are, Len. You don't have to say hardly anything! You know why you're nicked and you're due to go inside for a long time.'
'Jesus, I'm sick. It's no good me trying to lie to you. What can I do?'
'Len, if you have got control of the silver, I think the best thing is to give it all back – throw yourself at the mercy of the

Court and hope you can mitigate yourself that way and get a reasonable sentence . . .'

'You can have it all back and I'll do everything you say, but I don't want things to look worse for Dolph. Can I have a word with him for a few minutes and tell him I trust you and that I think what you say makes sense – and maybe we can get reasonable sentences . . .'

'Superintendent Little is in overall charge, so I will have to see if he agrees . . .'

Dave Little was up at Finchley, questioning Dolph Aguda who was denying everything. Lundy took Gibson to that station, but at first Little would not let Gibson see Aguda. Then he agreed provided he was present with Lundy. The encounter took place in Lundy's office. It went just as expected: 'Lennie's trying to talk Dolph into admitting and giving back but Dolph's not playing ball.' Eventually, according to Little's statement, Gibson begged Little,

'No disrespect to you but please leave us alone with Mr Lundy. I'm not trying to pull any strokes, but it will be easier to talk to Dolph with just Mr Lundy present. I know you think there is something funny going on – but there isn't. It's just that I know him personally and trust him.'

Little relented and went to have a cup of tea. Lundy stayed in the room. Now Dolph Aguda started to shift, 'Ah, fuckin' hell, Len! What are we doing?' After some hour and a half's discussion, he agreed to give the silver back. According to Lundy's statement, at 11.15 that night Aguda announced: 'All right, Mr Lundy. We will admit we've done it and make statements and give the property back. I think it's all there. Will it reflect on us if there's some missing?' Lundy said, if they were honestly trying to give it all back, the court would take it into account. 'If someone else had taken some, there's not much you can do about it.' They would still get at least seven years, he said, but 'I'm not the judge. I can't guarantee anything.'

At around 11.30 Lundy called Little and Chief Superintendent Taylor into his office and said the two robbers had agreed to give the bullion back. Gibson would take the police to the hiding place while Aguda made a statement.

When all the senior officers and a support team were assembled, off they drove in a convoy led by Len the robber, in handcuffs. He told Lundy's driver to head for Oakwood, near Southgate, then directed them to Belgrave Close and pointed to a lock-up garage, saying 'that one'. Neither Gibson nor the detectives had a key on them, so it fell to the highest-ranking officer, Mike Taylor, to jemmy open the garage door.

Sure enough, behind a stack of wooden pallets, in the back corner, were the silver ingots. It was almost midnight. Lundy gave instructions for Gibson to be taken back to Finchley to start making statements. The detectives now had to wait two or three hours while forensic officers and photographers recorded the scene. That done, the police formed a human chain, passing the silver bars out of the garage, one by one, and loading them on two lorries. The senior officers Little and Taylor counted every bar, marking each one off until the entire 10 tonne load was transported to the Prisoners' Property Store at Chalk Farm, with an armed escort.

They had counted 309 ingots. That was twelve fewer than had been stolen ten weeks earlier. In later years it would be alleged that at some time this night either the silver was left unattended, or Lundy was left alone with it. There were also suggestions that earlier in the evening, either after Lundy's first session with Gibson ended at 7.10, or during his session alone with Gibson and Aguda between about 9.45 and 11.30, Lundy and/or other officers had slipped out and paid a secret visit to the garage. Then, using a key from among the property taken from Aguda when he had been arrested, he/they had stolen the missing ingots.

None of these allegations was true. Lundy paid no secret prior visit to the lock-up nor was he ever left alone at the scene. 'On the night', he says, 'there was an army of people there. There's no question that anybody could nick anything without being seen by other officers. Mike Taylor never left the scene, nobody left the scene.'

The explanation for the missing bars came out later, as Lundy explains:

The robbers had apparently moved the silver around in a seven hundredweight mini-van. First they had shifted it to a garage in Walthamstow but, when they heard Gervaise had been arrested, they moved it to the lock-up. They did this a dozen bars at a time, like a shuttle service. There were 321 bars in all. When the time came to shift the last little load, it went somewhere else. Either Micky Sewell had it as his share, or they never completed the last run, and it was still elsewhere when we arrested them. So they thought, 'Bollocks! We're not going to tell the police about *them*.'

The most surprising thing, perhaps, was that only twelve bars had disappeared in the ten weeks since the robbery.

Lundy points out that Aguda had already hinted some bars had gone when he had asked (around 11.15), 'Will it reflect on us if there is some missing?' Lundy's enemies, in the underworld and the press, have suggested he simply invented that remark and attributed it to Aguda, to cover up his own role in stealing the missing bars earlier that night. Lundy rejects this allegation by pointing out that from the moment he first spoke to Gibson at 6.45 he was either at Golders Green Police Station, or in transit direct to Finchley or at Finchley Police Station.

But what about Aguda's key? Surely, there was no need

for the garage door to be jemmied open because the police had his key all the time! The anti-Lundy camp claim this again shows jiggery-pokery: Lundy and any confederates had clearly used Aguda's key earlier in the evening to steal the missing silver.

The truth allows for no such conspiracy. The day after the recovery of the 309 ingots, Inspector Pat Fleming was turning over the entire case in his brain. He suspected Aguda might yet scheme up some way to plead not guilty. The fact that everyone, except Deanus, was now admitting the crime might not stop them retracting their admissions at the Old Bailey. Gibson probably had no chance after leading the police to the silver, but Dolph Aguda might still wriggle out, so Fleming kept thinking how to make a conclusive case against him. 'How come there are no keys?' he pondered as he examined the lock which had been removed from the garage door. He checked the prisoners' property lists and saw that some keys had been taken from Aguda after he was arrested and detained at Enfield Police Station. Fleming now went to Enfield and asked the property officer (a uniformed sergeant) for Aguda's property bag. He saw that its seal was unbroken, indicating its contents had not been disturbed since they were taken from Aguda. He booked the keys out and tried each one in the lock, until one fitted – just like Cinderella's slipper.

'Initially', says Lundy, 'we couldn't do anything with Aguda's keys because we didn't know about the lock-up.' But why had the police not taken the keys with them when they set off with Gibson? Because, says Lundy, although Aguda was appearing to co-operate, both he and Gibson claimed they had no keys to the garage. Anyway, at that point the main thing was to get to the garage and find the silver. 'Why worry about the keys', says Lundy, 'when Gibson's taking us straight there?'

In the rush no one had checked Aguda's property bag at Enfield, which was five miles from Finchley Police Station where the pair had confessed. Only in relative calm, next day, was that done. Aguda's failure to volunteer the fact that he had a key may have been because he knew that, if it had never been discovered among his property, he could still claim he had nothing to do with the robbery – a lame defence but one which might convince an Old Bailey jury. 'Aguda would have played silly buggers,' says Lundy, 'he would have fought it. He would have turned round and said, "I was conned into admitting. I wasn't really on it . . . It was Gibson who . . ." but he had no chance once we had found the right key in his possession. That was good detective work.'[1]

The allegation of skulduggery over the key has obscured the more fundamental question. If Lundy really was corrupt, why would he have stopped at stealing a measly twelve bars? Why did he not take twenty-four or forty-eight or more? Ah, his adversaries might say, he only had time to nick twelve bars before popping back to Finchley to sit in on the encounter between Gibson and Aguda! But again, if he was the villain he has been painted, why did he bother to tell his fellow-detectives what Garner had told him? Why did not he and Garner keep this to themselves, allowing Lundy to go in to Sewell or Gibson and demand a huge slice of the loot? Why go through the bother of interrogating Gervaise, and the risk of involving so many other detectives? Why not just extort Gibson direct? After all, if he and Lundy were such close buddies, they could easily have sorted it out between them. No need for arrests, guilty pleas or any years in jail.

Instead, Gibson, Dolph and Ron Aguda pleaded guilty at the Old Bailey in January 1981 and were each jailed for ten years. The inside man Bill 'Bolster' Parker also pleaded guilty and went down for seven years. Bob Deanus denied taking part. That he was able to do so may have had something to do with the fact that he was the only principal defendant who had not been interviewed by the highly persuasive Lundy. When he came to trial in January 1982 he was acquitted, a verdict which excited the attention of some sceptical reporters (see Chapter 12). The elusive Sewell, whose indiscretions to Garner had started the ball rolling, eluded the police for many months but was eventually arrested. By then Gervaise was a discredited and reluctant witness, so there was no point in trying Sewell over the Silver job, but there was still a case against him over Lambeth Town Hall, for which he was jailed for three years.

Solving the Silver Bullion robbery was one of Lundy's greatest triumphs, especially as it was not even his case! It was the climax to four extraordinary years, into which he had packed more thief-taking than most detectives achieve in their entire careers. Yet it was speculation over the Bullion job which, more than anything else, would cause the thief-taker's downfall.

East Enders Bearing Gifts

On 11 June 1980, eight days after almost all the silver bullion had been recovered, Chief Inspector Lundy sent his commander a report on the subject, <u>Reward to Informant 'Dave Granger'</u>. The name was in inverted commas because it was of course a pseudonym. To Lundy's profound anger and regret, it has been revealed elsewhere that Dave Granger's real identity was Roy Garner.[1] Indeed years later the entire report would leak out to reporters, in murky circumstances.

Under whatever name, the man was due for a reward. He should have been paid almost immediately, for here was an open-and-shut case (or so it seemed) of a reliable source passing information leading to the recovery of over three million pounds-worth of silver, the charging of six robbers and five confessions – all in less than four days. Lundy stated that without 'Granger's' information, the police would not have been able to push Gervaise into admitting he was the 'prime mover in planning and perpetrating the robbery'. Before that, he never had any intention of revealing his part. 'He had been in custody for two weeks at that stage and, although he had admitted numerous offences and named accomplices, he had made no mention of this robbery.'

'Granger' had not just named names, said Lundy, 'his assistance was invaluable in locating Gibson and others throughout the following days. Even more important, his assessment of the individuals' characters proved to be extremely accurate and enabled interrogating officers to achieve an immediate breakthrough which resulted in the almost total recovery of the property.' Lundy stated

that missing robber Michael Sewell 'is known to have
possession of the twelve missing ingots' but 'Granger' 'is
confident that he will locate him in the near future and
thus we hope to recover the outstanding property'. The
detective ended by saying:

'GRANGER' has proved once again that he is an outstanding
informant and in this particular case he has exposed himself
to great personal danger, particularly in locating dangerous
professional criminals, and is deserving of exceptional reward,
as the case is probably unique in criminal history.
'GRANGER' has never been rewarded from public funds and
no such reward is recommended on this occasion. However,
a reward of £300,000 was offered shortly after the Bullion
Robbery and it is respectfully requested that a letter be sent
to Douglas JACKSON and Company (Adjusters) Limited . . . in
order that consideration may be given to reward monies being
paid to 'GRANGER'.

With that effusive backing 'Granger' should have
had a big pay day coming soon, especially since loss
adjusters (who advise insurance companies on whether
they should pay rewards) generally have no qualms
about handing out ten per cent rewards, whatever their
size. In this case, loss adjusters Douglas Jackson had
publicized a £300,000 reward because the silver was
worth £3,397,047 on 24 March 1980 when it was stolen.[2]
As 'Granger' had supplied the crucial information, he
naturally assumed he would have no problems getting
most of that £300,000.

Yet there were problems – severe ones – not at first
over 'Granger' but because Scotland Yard had recently
got itself into a mess over rewards. Between 1973 and
1977 the number of robberies committed in London each
year had doubled. To stop this alarming rise, the force
felt it could not rely solely on the efforts of detectives
like Tony Lundy, however brilliant. It wanted the robbed

institutions – mainly banks and security firms – to spend more on rewards. Unlike percentage rewards set by loss adjusters to recover whatever has *already* been stolen, these kind of rewards are standard pay-outs aimed at inciting information from the underworld in order to stop armed attacks *before* they happen.

At first the strategy seemed to work. In 1978 the high street banks raised the level of their rewards to £5,000, and attacks on their premises had fallen. On 25 July 1978 Scotland Yard's chief of detectives, DAC David Powis, told a meeting of Britain's biggest transport security firms that they should follow the banks' example because it appeared to have been a success.

The firms agreed that later in the year they would raise their rewards to £5,000. In the meantime Sergeant Derek Hall, a City of London detective attached to Barkingside Regional Crime Squad, had put Securicor (Britain's largest security firm) in touch with someone he described as a 'good informant whose information had been reliable in the past'. Hall soon proved that a hard-working snout is worth his weight in gold to both the police service and the public, especially if his name is Gold as it was in this case. 'Tommy Gold' and his half-brother, 'Johnny Silver', were apparently able to give Hall advance details of robberies 'going off' all over the East End – and all on Securicor vehicles!

Hall's relationship with the men had started in July 1978 when a guard working for Mint Security had asked them to perform a fake robbery on him when he would be carrying £150,000 in cash. The guard, Martin Darkins, had planned that 'Gold' and 'Silver' would then split the proceeds with him, but they decided they did not want to do the job. Instead the devious 'Gold' told Darkins he was interested while simultaneously shopping him to Sergeant Hall. He then introduced Hall to Darkins, claiming Hall was in his gang and would be doing the robbery. The detective was wearing a tape-recorder and Darkins said enough during their conversation to justify his arrest and, later, a six-year jail sentence.

For informing on Darkins, 'Gold' and 'Silver' received a Mint Security reward of £1,000, but not directly from Mint. Instead it came from none other than DAC David Powis who gave it to them in person in his car by Old Scotland Yard, with Sergeant Hall present. This was because of Powis's decision that when a reward exceeded a certain amount he should pay informants personally. Powis was trying to reduce the opportunity for corruption (by officers who might be tempted to pocket rewards in whole or in part) and to ensure rewards were paid to genuine informants, not bogus ones as sometimes happened in the past (see Chapter 8).

In this case Powis's intervention may not have prevented malpractice. 'Gold' later claimed that, on the very day he received his reward from Powis, he placed £200 under the front passenger seat of a junior policeman's car. Later, for the same information, 'Gold' and 'Silver' received another £200 from Scotland Yard's own Informants' Fund.

On this occasion the pair had at least supplied information about a genuine crime, but worse was to come. In September 1978 'Gold' told Hall that he knew of a robbery soon to be executed on a Securicor vehicle in the East End of London. Hall set up a meeting between 'Gold' and two Securicor representatives on Monday 25 September in Battersea Park. He then went for a walk, leaving 'Gold' and the Securicor men, Joe Goyder and Dick Hellaby, to negotiate an appropriate reward. That done, 'Gold' duly told Hall the names of three men who were going to rob the vehicle outside National Westminster Bank in Bow Road. Sure enough, three days later the suspects were caught by police on the 'plot'.

Four days after that, Securicor's Joe Goyder paid 'Gold' and 'Silver' £1,000 which the informants felt was not enough. About this time a Securicor guard was shot dead during a raid. In response the firm increased its rewards immediately, complying with DAC Powis's earlier suggestion. In early November Securicor advertised rewards of £5,000 'to any member of the public who gives information to the police leading to the conviction of persons attacking their crews, stealing or attempting or conspiring to steal any of their property'.

The prospect of such rich pickings provoked 'Gold' and 'Silver' into supplying a stream of tip-offs about imminent attacks on Securicor vehicles. The first tip-off seemed to come true on 11 November when two men were captured outside the Express Dairy in Southwark. The circumstances should have struck the Securicor men and their go-between, Sergeant Hall, as disturbingly similar to the Bow Road job, yet a few days later the firm paid 'Gold' and 'Silver' £1,500. This was meant to be the first instalment of a total of £5,000. The rest was to come when the robbers were convicted and jailed. Early in 1979 the ravenous 'Gold' and 'Silver', still working through Hall, sacrificed three more criminal teams. Each was captured as they were about to rob Securicor vehicles: outside a branch of Keymarkets in Romford; the Co-op dairy in East Ham; and the Inland Revenue offices in Gants Hill.

For all these efforts 'Gold' and 'Silver' picked up a total of £14,000 in Securicor rewards, including two full £5,000 pay-outs according to the Powis tariff. In six months the pair had delivered Derek Hall thirteen 'bodies'. All had been caught red-handed and ten were jailed. The other three would also have gone to prison – and 'Gold' and 'Silver' would have picked up another £10,500 on the Powis tariff – had not Operation Countryman intervened. From September 1979 Countryman detectives had been gathering statements from petty, mostly young, villains in jail, all making similar allegations against two East Enders in their thirties or forties. They claimed these men, identifiable as Montague FitzMaurice and Frederick Skipp, had persuaded them to commit robberies which had all gone strangely wrong. They had all been arrested on the 'plots' just prior to committing the crimes, yet FitzMaurice and Skipp had never been questioned.

In April 1980 Inspector Bernard Coleman of Countryman arrested FitzMaurice and Skipp. They turned out to be none other than Derek Hall's informants, 'Gold' and 'Silver'. They had adopted their mocking pseudonyms to conceal their true identities when drawing rewards, but some of their victims knew who they were, so Countryman had little difficulty in tracking them down. Both soon admitted their activities and in a rare moment of contrition Skipp blurted out, 'I know we was bad bastards setting them jobs up, and there ain't no excuse for it.' Bad bastards they were. In the moral calendar there can be few worse offences than inciting people to commit crime and then delivering them straight into the arms of the law, just to pick up rewards.

It was an obscenity worthy of Jonathan Wild (the notorious eighteenth-century thief-taker who set up robberies, then betrayed the robbers to the authorities and sent them to the gallows). On 26 January 1981 the dreadful duo were jailed for four years. They were the first people to be convicted by Operation Countryman. This struck interested outsiders as strange because Countryman had been set up to catch crooked cops, not common criminals! Its main interest, therefore, was in an officer to whom, the *provocateurs* were claiming, they had paid over £3,000. On several occasions, FitzMaurice/Gold said, he had slipped this officer payments of £500, but the only evidence to support his word was the word of Skipp/Silver. In legal terms this was not corroboration, so the man was never charged.

The alleged offender was not a Metropolitan Police officer so none of his actions could be blamed on Scotland Yard, yet Scotland Yard was acutely embarrassed because it was a largely Metropolitan-staffed Regional Crime Squad which had carried out all arrests arising from the bogus 'Silver' and 'Gold' tip-offs. Worse still, Scotland Yard had paid the pair a total of £1,000 for their information about four of the bogus crimes. For the Express Dairy robbery they were handed not just £5,000 by Securicor but £250 by Flying Squad Commander Don Neesham. Then DAC Powis handed 'Gold' an extra £300 because one of the 'robbers' was also wanted for a genuine murder in Kent. 'Gold' later collected £200 for Romford, £200 for East Ham and £350 for Gants Hill – all courtesy of the Yard's Informants' Fund.

Egg would also stick to Securicor representatives Joe Goyder and Dick Hellaby. They would not have paid 'Gold' and 'Silver' £14,000 had they known the robberies were set-ups, but in retrospect they seem to have been remarkably gullible. Surely any experienced investigator might realize no informants could know about so many similar crimes on the same security firm without having engineered at least some of them.

When setting up the robberies 'Gold' and 'Silver' had left a trail of evidence linking them to the petty villains they had incited, but at the time they felt they had immunity from Barkingside Regional Crime Squad, and never imagined that within a year a load of country coppers would be re-examining the cases with fine toothcombs. Even when they heard Countryman was poking around, they said to each other that nothing would be done as it would make everyone look silly from DAC Powis down. Talking of Powis, 'Gold' later told Countryman:

> It is a bit funny really. I mean I've sat in his office in that big chair, had tea with him, talked to him like old friends . . . and then he says to me words to the effect 'Get back out on the streets again and get a few more bodies in. Results, statistics, that's all people think about, get back out there and help us.' So we figured that if this is the kind of bloke we'd been working with, he's going to stop Countryman doing anything, as it would make them all look stupid.

'Gold' and 'Silver' misread Powis who, far from stopping anyone investigating genuine cases of corruption, was himself dedicated to rooting it out. The pair made their crucial admission statements in April 1980; only two months before Roy Garner made his legitimate claim for a share of the Silver Bullion reward. Inevitably, the 'Gold–Silver' fiasco had a catastrophic impact on his claim. The reward he was after – at £300,000 – was twenty times larger than their entire take! The fact that his information was as genuine as the Bullion robbery itself may not have been obvious to a Yard hierarchy worried stiff that another bogus informant scandal might be just round the corner.

The 'Gold' and 'Silver' scandal rumbled on for seven more months until they were sentenced in January 1981. In the meantime it must have dawned on Yard chiefs that the act of raising rewards to £5,000 had played little part in reducing robberies. Indeed, it had helped increase them because some crooks had discovered that setting up robbery was now more lucrative – and less risky – than robbery itself.

Once again Scotland Yard redrew the lines. On 22 August 1980 Gilbert Kelland, who as Assistant Commissioner (Crime) was one rank above David Powis, wrote to the banks, loss adjusters and security firms suggesting guidelines on the <u>Payment of Rewards to Informants</u>. He confirmed the 'fundamental principle that informants, properly controlled, are of significant value in the effective prosecution of professional thieves, and in the recovery of high value stolen property'. Nevertheless, a reward should never be so large as to generate the crime in question, or future similar crimes.

To put it in a nutshell, informers must never think it worthwhile to arrange a crime, with the intention of betraying the active criminals involved, so as to lay their hands on the reward money. That such behaviour is counter-productive, and against both the public and commercial interest, is plainly self-evident. However, such conspiracies have occurred – indeed have been attempted recently – and this is my main reason for writing this letter.

Kelland explained that Scotland Yard had laid down procedures for its officers to follow whenever a reward was likely to be paid, and whether the money was to come from police funds or private sources.

Individual officers MUST NOT
(a) make approaches to interested parties with the intention of securing a reward for an informant
(b) vouch for an informant to such parties
(c) give authority to such parties for a reward to be paid to an informant.

He referred to a recent case of 'grave dishonesties against the public and private interest' which had led to criminal proceedings. It had involved direct contact between a security consultant and a junior detective 'without the knowledge of any senior CID officer'. There had been 'no dishonesty on the part of police', said Kelland. He was, presumably, referring to 'Gold' and 'Silver'.

He said only DAC Powis, or someone of equal rank, was permitted to discuss or negotiate the rewards payments concerning crime in London. If anyone wanted to pay a reward through the police, they could forward a cheque to Powis, payable to the Commissioner, but lower down 'the handing of cash or cheque to any Metropolitan police officer for later conveyance to an informant, quite apart from being undesirable generally, is forbidden by our regulations'.

Kelland added there were grounds for believing 'strict adherence' to Yard policies over informant payments had contributed to 'a healthy twelve per cent' fall in robberies on banks and security firms in the first six months of 1980. This was correct partly because 'Gold' and 'Silver' were no longer setting up robberies at £5,000 a go! To prevent similar rackets the Yard now turned its policies upside down. Whereas in 1978 David Powis had encouraged security firms to *raise* rewards to £5,000 in order to elicit true information, in 1980 the Yard wanted them to pay *no more than* £5,000 to discourage *false* information. Precisely how the number 5,000 alone had the magical power to encourage honesty and to discourage lies was never explained. While that stayed a kabalistic secret, what did need sorting out was the conflict which a £5,000 limit caused with the ten per cent reward usually offered by loss adjusters for the recovery of stolen cash or goods. Kelland tried his best:

Occasions may arise when certain matters are known to us which, of themselves, render the payment of a full or fixed percentage reward most inappropriate, but where a much smaller sum may be suitable. In these cases, which arise only rarely, Mr Powis is available to discuss and inform you confidentially of our views.

This hint placed loss adjusters in difficulty. Generally

they were happy to pay rewards of ten per cent. As one
of them put it:

It seems to me that [where] you have a loss involving half a
million pounds, to offer a reward of £5,000 is not realistic, and
I do not think you will get the information that you require to
recover this property for your insurer clients, by approaching the
matter along those lines. So the reward has got to be realistic, and
it has got to form a temptation to somebody to come forward
and give you the information. And I think that ten per cent is
probably about right.[3]

Tony Lundy, who seems to have had more success in
winkling information out of sources than any other recent
detective, agrees:

Every agency, every private concern should be free to pay
what they think anything's worth to clear something up. Ten per
cent is the norm for professional organizations in the commercial
world, but some of those would pay fifty per cent. When Powis
argued for a maximum of £5,000 that reflected Scotland Yard's
embarrassment over 'Silver' and 'Gold'! It was pointless to say,
'We now have a policy of never recommending over £5,000 to
anybody' – just when the newspapers were saying a £300,000
reward was being offered for information about the missing
Silver Bullion – because it was bound to be ignored.

The loss adjusters' prime concern is to recover stolen
property for their clients, whatever that may cost. A police
force may see this as conflicting with two of its concerns:
to prevent the incitement of crime and eradicate, where
possible, opportunities for corruption. High rewards may
tempt criminals to set up crimes just to claim the rewards,
and they may increase corruption because it is usually only
on a policeman's recommendation that a reward will be
paid. The higher the reward the greater the kickback to
the crooked cop.

The 'Gold' and 'Silver' fiasco demonstrated both dan-
gers but it had no bearing on the relationship between

Lundy and his informers. There is no evidence that they provided information about anything other than genuine crimes, and they all seem to have been genuine claimants for any rewards they received. It also seems extremely unlikely that Garner could have been involved in the planning of the Silver job. If he had been, he would not have been so stupid as to betray the other robbers, especially one who was already a supergrass. By naming Gervaise he was forcing him to name the other conspirators including Garner, had he been one of them! In any case, if Garner had been one of them, he would have made more money by keeping quiet and waiting for his share than by going after a reward.

In the bad old days of the 1960s, when detectives could keep their snouts' identities to themselves, it might have been easy for an informer to have been involved in a robbery and still pocket a reward for betraying his confederates. This was why DAC Powis introduced his sealed envelope routine: so that at least he knew who the informers really were. With this safeguard it should no longer have been possible for a detective, straight or bent, to harbour a bounty-hunting *agent provocateur*. Yet despite this, the 'Gold' and 'Silver' scandal had happened.

Powis's reforms helped purge the system of past evils; they should also have ensured that proper relationships between detectives and informants would now be above reasonable suspicion. Unfortunately, early in 1981 Powis's top-secret 'Who's Who of Informants' sprang a leak, and great damage was caused to the whole structure of police–informant relationships. For Garner and Lundy themselves the leak would prove disastrous, adding flesh to rumours already circulating in the underworld, in the media and in that huge rumour-factory known as Scotland Yard.

11

Roy Gets His Money,
Billy Takes Revenge

When Garner/Granger applied for the Silver Bullion reward in June 1980 he was already well-known to Deputy Assistant Commissioner David Powis. They had met several times since 1978 when Powis, applying his policy of paying informers in person, handed over the first of several rewards from insurance companies for tip-offs leading to the recovery of stolen goods and the jailing of criminals.

First there was the £4,000 Garner received for informing on robbers who kept attacking the same security firm's vehicles because they knew that firm carried larger cash sums than the others. Next there was the £1,500 he received over a stolen jewellery job. Then, of course, there was the £37,500 reward he had earned for exposing the bogus Hatton Garden robbery which Messrs Heath and Hogg had perpetrated on themselves with the intention of pocketing a £750,000 insurance pay-out. From opposite poles, therefore, Garner and Powis had established a working relationship.

Over the Silver Bullion reward, however, Powis suddenly told Garner he was only going to get £5,000, in accord with his new limit. Garner was furious. He threatened to sue the loss adjusters, Douglas Jackson & Co., and briefed a solicitor. For their part the loss adjusters were willing to pay him. So were their clients, the East German government. After all, it was largely through his efforts that they had recovered almost all the silver. Their legal advice was that if his information was genuine, he should be paid. The only obstacle was Scotland Yard.

To settle the issue DAC Steventon told the loss adjusters they could interview all the senior detectives on the case and make their own decision. An executive from the firm borrowed Steventon's office for a day to question Mike Taylor, Reg Dixon, Tony Lundy and Dave Little one by one, taking written statements from each. This satisfied him that the man he knew of as Granger was indeed entitled to a very large chunk of the reward, yet still no money reached the informer. On 10 March 1981 Garner asked Lundy to arrange a meeting with Powis. Records show that two days later he drove to Tothill Street, near New Scotland Yard, where he met not only Lundy and Powis but also Ron Steventon. The two DACs climbed into the back of Garner's car, while Lundy slipped into the passenger seat. They all listened as Garner complained about the continuing hold-up over the reward and expressed fears of violent underworld revenge.

Two more months passed with no sign of the money, so another Tothill Street summit was arranged for 28 May, three days less than a full year since Garner had supplied the information. This time Powis had to cancel at the last minute, leaving Lundy to apologize to a furious Garner who drove off, ranting about broken promises and breach of trust. Lundy went straight to Powis's Scotland Yard office and wrote a bitter report in long-hand for the DAC to read on his return. It was the testament of a very angry man and contained sentiments which a more politically astute, but less honest, detective would not have put in writing.

The report made the scarcely exaggerated claim that 'Granger' had 'achieved successes in the war against major criminals far in excess of any other informant, possibly, in the history of the Metropolitan Police'. For many years he had never claimed rewards, but over the Bullion job it was Lundy – encouraged by Superintendent Dave Little – who had referred 'Granger' to the reward advertisements to spur him to 'greater successes'. Lundy said that he had heard of no restriction on those advertised rewards 'until after the bullion had been recovered'.

He stressed that if 'Granger' went ahead with his action, and the case reached court, he would not only risk his life but 'considerable embarrassment will be caused'. Lundy meant embarrassment to the force because many internal Yard papers and interviews would be brought into the public domain. 'Granger' was not even claiming the entire £300,000 reward; he was merely asking police not to restrict his share to £5,000 and to let the assessors decide. The issue had gone unresolved for a year. Now it 'needs finalizing one way or the other'.

Lundy left this 1,400-word report for Powis's staff officer to type and give to Powis. Had Lundy seen it in its typewritten form – which later leaked out to the media (again in mysterious circumstances) – he would have revised it, if only to correct many spelling errors not in his original. Nevertheless, its seething tone and whiff of trouble ahead appear to have jolted Powis into meeting Garner four days later. Again he brought Steventon along, and again they all climbed in Garner's car. They talked for forty-five minutes, and, although he was angry about the Yard's behaviour, Garner volunteered information about another active criminal conspiracy. A further month passed before Powis and Steventon met him again in Tothill Street, on 1 July. This time their purpose was to identify him to the loss adjusters as the true informer. The same day the firm sent his solicitor a cheque for around £180,000. At last the crude justice which applies to such rewards had been fairly applied.

A smaller but substantial chunk of the reward was

paid to Lundy's supergrass, Christopher Wren, whose solicitor argued that he had started the whole thing by first naming Gervaise (for other crimes), who eventually named his Silver Bullion confederates. It was Lundy who had made Wren 'sing' but the detective was vexed that any supergrass should profit from rewards. He opposed a pay-out on the grounds that Wren was already being rewarded with a much-reduced prison sentence. On this point his Yard bosses agreed with him: Wren should get nothing at all. Nevertheless, the loss adjusters paid him. To end the affair, they settled with both claimants. Later Lundy would think it strange that Wren's outrageous pay-out aroused no hostile press comment, whereas Garner's legitimate reward would be exposed, attacked and scorned in the media for years on end.

If one reason for the opposition to Garner's due reward was the Yard's crippling embarrassment over 'Gold' and 'Silver', there was now another area for alarm. Lundy himself was attracting flak. He saw this as inevitable. The more successful a detective the more enemies he makes, not only among criminals. He was already London's most productive detective in living memory, and his thief-taking triumphs were showing up the inadequacy and laziness of many colleagues. Some detectives had a personal reason for being upset: he had jailed their informants. Anti-Lundy sentiment became rife when certain officers found out their 'snouts' were on remand in Brixton prison and would shortly go down for fifteen years. Eventually revenge rumours concerning Lundy's relations with Roy Garner reached the Scotland Yard bosses who had so often climbed in Garner's car: David Powis and Ron Steventon. As DAC (Operations), Powis's main concern was catching criminals, so Lundy was one of his main assets. As DAC (Administration), Steventon's concerns were the organization, structure and discipline of the entire Metropolitan CID. He saw Lundy as a dangerous liability.

In July 1980 Lundy had been expecting promotion to superintendent, when he received a completely unexpected telephone call informing him that he was being transferred sideways to Chingford, to be deputy head of 'J' Division CID. In just under three years he had led Finchley Robbery Squad to unmatched achievements. Only one month ago he had pulled off his astonishing Silver Bullion triumph. Now he was being sent to an obscure station to perform routine duties. Such a move was rare, especially for a senior officer awaiting promotion. Devastated, he was told that his transfer was the decision of DAC Steventon, so he asked to see him. An audience was granted and Lundy asked why he was suffering this downward move. According to Lundy, Steventon retorted, 'I don't have to give you reasons. You do what you're told. I've listened to you, the decision's still the same. Go to Chingford, do as you're told, and you'll get your promotion eventually.'

Lundy queried the decision with David Powis who said he was sorry but there was nothing he could do, though Lundy would get his promotion shortly. So Lundy had to stomach the move, despite its clear implication that he had been a naughty boy. Inevitably, tongues wagged and some hostile colleagues guessed any naughtiness must have involved the recent Bullion job. Others felt he was the victim of his own success.

As it happened, Lundy spent very little time at Chingford. He reported there on 28 July, but found the natives unfriendly once they realized that, for the foreseeable future, their new detective chief would be fully occupied at the Old Bailey supervising trials and giving evidence. What little hope Chingford had of his services was smashed at the end of August when he ruptured an Achilles' tendon and had his foot in plaster for two months. As soon as he was fit, he was promoted to superintendent and transferred to Wembley where he would supervise all 'Q' District's criminal investigation and conduct a series of complex murder inquiries. He was also trusted to investigate complaints against the police. Whatever the rumours, he seemed to have re-established his credit and credibility. The high point came on 5 January 1981 when Gibson and the Agudas pleaded guilty and were each sentenced to ten years in jail. Without Lundy, and without Garner's information, they would still have been free and the best part of £3 million richer.

Fate has a nasty habit of toppling people just when they achieve their greatest triumphs. So it was with Superintendent Lundy. Just as his career was lifting off he received curious news. A North London thief named Billy Young had turned supergrass and was making allegations against the Finchley Boxing Club crowd, including Garner, Gibson and Lundy himself.

Young had first come to Lundy's attention through the Torrington Arms crowd around 1978. The detective soon learned he was a full-time thief. He checked the man's Yard record which showed him living in Islington, North London, but a friend said Young now lived in Hertfordshire and volunteered his telephone number. Lundy used this to discover Young's address, which he passed to Herts CID. Until then they had no idea he existed, let alone that he lived on their patch.

In October 1980 Young was arrested by Number 5 Regional Crime Squad which investigates major crimes running across several counties west, north and east of London, including Hertfordshire. Lundy soon found out because a Herts detective named Brendan O'Connor telephoned him at home where he was still stuck with his foot in plaster. The pair had worked together on many inquiries and O'Connor knew Lundy had long maintained an interest in Young and supplied information on him. O'Connor now asked for more information against Young which would help his interrogators break him. At the moment they were struggling.

Lundy then recited all he could remember about Young: rumours and bits and pieces going back years. Later O'Connor told Lundy that this information broke Young. Later still, however, Lundy learned some other detective had told Young it was Lundy who had provided the dirt on him. This provoked Young into fulfilling an old vow against Lundy and Lundy's boxing club friend, Dave Spicer.

Spicer was not only Lundy's friend. He had been close to Young, a fact which now had dangerous consequences as Young concocted a cunning mix of fact and lies which would condemn Spicer to jail, and Lundy to ten years' investigation by police, newspapers and television shows. They were all desperate for the same thing: proof that Lundy was 'bent'.

Of all Lundy's connections, his friendship with Spicer proved the most difficult for his pursuers to grasp. With Roy Garner, Len Gibson and other criminals whose sons attended the boxing club, Lundy always kept his distance. They were acquaintances, not friends, and if he attended social gatherings where they were present, it was to raise money for charity, often for the club itself. In any case, he never shared a dinner table with them. Dave Spicer was different. The biggest difference was that he was 'clean': apart from a £2 fine for a prank when he was seventeen, he had no record. He was also on the club committee, with Tony Lundy, from which the obviously criminal fathers were excluded. Spicer was good company, hail-fellow-well-met, and Lundy enjoyed being with him on some of the few evenings he was not on duty. Both

Lundy and Spicer insist that there was nothing improper about their friendship.

Dave Spicer was an independent bookmaker, not always an honourable profession, but Spicer operated legally and above board. Inevitably, many of the customers at his Finchley premises were not so respectable. They included Billy Young. Lundy recalls:

Hell! He was a baddie. The other characters around the Torrington were personable people, but he was a horrible bastard. A growler, sullen, surly. I used to say to Dave Spicer, 'How is he on the scene?' – because he was known as 'Burglar Bill'. It turned out they all knew him through Freemasonry. I couldn't believe it! Here was an allegedly moral fraternity with a member whom all these other masons used to call Burglar Bill! And who genuinely believed he was still at it as a burglar! 'How come he's part of all your masonic crowd?' I used to say. Nobody liked him.

Today Lundy might be accused of blackening Billy Young's already 'black' character just to discredit allegations which Young has made against him. However, many other folk who frequented the Torrington Arms in the late 1970s say he was odious. One Monday night a crowd of them ended up at the Hertfordshire home of a man named Stevie Salter who ran a car repair business, among other activities. Among the crowd was Dave Spicer who had come to pay for a battery. He was counting out the money onto the kitchen table when Young came up and asked him a question. Spicer asked Young why he wanted to know the answer, at which point (says Spicer) Young took umbrage and walked off growling 'Bastard!' or a similar expletive.

A little later everyone was in the Salters' large lounge, standing around eating sandwiches, when Young suddenly strode across to Spicer shouting, 'You fat bastard!' and slinging punches at him. Spicer parried the blows, then, back against the wall, he smacked Young hard with his fist. Other people rushed over and pulled Young away but, as they dragged him off, he shouted, 'I'll fix you and that bastard Lundy!' The host, Steve Salter, then quietly asked Spicer to go home so that he (Salter) would have a better chance of calming Young down. The following day Spicer rang Mrs Salter to apologize for the incident. According to Spicer, she told him not to worry because everyone knew what Billy Young was like. At least some people present that night believed he was a dangerous 'nutcase' and that 'fix Spicer and Lundy' he certainly would (although why he should have had any animosity to Lundy at that time is unclear).

On 5 March 1981 Lundy dropped Spicer off at his home after a night at the boxing club and the Torrington. Spicer was an epileptic and could not drive so Lundy often gave him a lift. As they stood on the pavement Lundy paid Spicer hundreds of pounds collected from friends for tickets to a charity 'do'. At five o'clock next morning, officers from No. 5 Regional Crime Squad rang the doorbell and told him they had a warrant 'to search these premises for stolen property, i.e. money'. Spicer was then taken to the police station at Dunstable outside London, locked in a cell and questioned.

According to police statements, many of the questions ranged far wider than the matters for which Spicer had formally been arrested. One of his interrogators (provincial detectives from Number 5 RCS headquarters at Reading) was particularly interested in the Finchley Boxing Club and its committee, but also in why Spicer kept the company of Len Gibson, the Silver Bullion robber. Spicer said he had not known Gibson was an armed robber but he did say he used to attend meetings of Gibson's masonic lodge as Gibson's guest.[1] The detectives were also keen to get

Spicer to discuss his association with a senior London police officer, but he ran off a long list of officers with whom he used to drink – not just Tony Lundy but far more senior men such as commanders and even 'Jimmy Crane' who, as Sir James Crane Kt CBE, was at that very moment Britain's highest-ranking police official: Her Majesty's Chief Inspector of Constabulary for England and Wales!

The reason why Spicer (whose epilepsy put him in chronic need of medication) had been roused before dawn and stuck in a police cell was that Billy Young had finally taken his revenge. A few weeks earlier, as part of a wide-ranging investigation known as Operation Carter, 5 RCS had arrested the robber Fred Sinfield. He turned supergrass and named Young as a burglar. Young was arrested and he too turned supergrass. He made long statements incriminating more than 60 people. In 1982 he received a jail term of just six years despite admitting 123 crimes, mainly robberies and burglaries. It was a standard supergrass deal.

Young had accused Dave Spicer of passing him information about suitable places to burgle. Young also claimed that Spicer was Tony Lundy's middleman in corrupt dealings with criminals, including Len Gibson and Young himself. That seems to be why Spicer's inquisitors were so keen to ask him about his friends in the force. They then confronted him with Young, in the hope that Spicer would crumble and confess. This was a technique often used by Tony Lundy with great success, but on this occasion Spicer denied everything Young threw at him and said: 'You used to play with my kids, Bill. They used to call you "Silly Billy". What are you doing to them now by having me locked up?' Young responded by claiming Spicer had once levied a bribe of £1,000 from him to ensure that the police did not raid Young's home. He also said that the

RCS had corroboration for this claim (which it had not). He then said: '. . . Lundy, Garner and fucking Ross. They couldn't give a shit about you, Dave.'

The Young–Spicer confrontation did not in itself produce results for the police, but it may have weakened Spicer's spirit. Certainly, in circumstances explained below, he did sign a statement saying that some of what Young had said in his statements was true but the rest was not. He was then charged with conspiracy to burgle and in June 1982 went on trial at Snaresbrook in Essex, alongside five other alleged Young confederates none of whom he had ever met, let alone conspired with.

Many of Young's allegations against Spicer could not be believed by anyone who knew Spicer or the victims he had allegedly set up. One such victim was Mrs Bartlett, the mother of the Torrington Arms landlord, Alan Bartlett, who was Spicer's friend. Young claimed that in 1979 Spicer had tipped him off that Mrs Bartlett had a collection of antiques. Young claimed he did not know where she lived until Spicer showed him the house. In fact Mrs Bartlett, a widow, lived very near the pub, as any Torrington regular like Young could not help but know because she was always behind the bar, talking openly to all and sundry. Young also claimed it was Spicer who rang him one afternoon to say she was going to a dinner-dance that night so her house would be empty. This again was knowledge which Young, who drank in the pub almost daily, could have learned from Mrs Bartlett herself. Indeed she regularly went out for social evenings as everyone in the Torrington circle knew. Young did not need to be told that by Spicer. The only likely truth in Young's tale was that he did indeed burgle the old lady's home.

Mrs Bartlett herself bore no animosity to Spicer, even during the trial. One day when she was due to give evidence, she asked the Spicers for a lift to the court in their car: scarcely the request of someone who believed that Dave Spicer could ever have arranged to have her burgled. Dave himself suggested a lift would be unwise because someone would surely cite it as proof that he was interfering with a prosecution witness. Today Spicer still drinks in the Torrington, buying alternate rounds with Alan Bartlett who clearly does not believe Spicer could ever have plotted to burgle his mother.

Another example of Spicer's treachery, as alleged by Young, involved Spicer's bookmaker role as a local football pools collector. Every Friday Spicer or his wife would deliver an envelope containing completed coupons and payments to the collector for the entire area. Young claimed that, one week, Spicer took him along to the area collector's premises so he could plan a burglary at a time when they would be bursting with pools-punters' cash. In the event Young abandoned the scheme but, as Spicer says, there *never* would have been any point in burgling the place because the pools company insisted on collectors paying in all monies by cheque. There would never have been any cash to steal, so not even if he was a crook could Spicer have dreamed up such a crime.

Young also claimed that Spicer had suggested a burglary on the home of his half-brother, Leslie Dare. He said Spicer had a grudge against Dare, relations had become 'a bit strained', and the two men were not on speaking terms. Spicer denied the entire story and Leslie Dare himself testified in court that there was no ill-feeling between them. Young also claimed that Spicer suggested that a man named Halliburton was worth 'a few bob' but that Spicer did not know his address. One night at the Torrington, therefore, he told Young to give Halliburton a lift home to find out where he lived. That was Young's story, but Spicer stated that no such subterfuge would have been necessary because Mr Halliburton was on the

Finchley Boxing Club committee with him, so they both had a list showing each other's address. Mr Halliburton himself testified that Spicer knew his address, for they sent each other Christmas cards. He also insisted that his colour television had not been stolen. This destroyed another part of Young's evidence: that it had been necessary to bring a van close to Halliburton's home to take this large item away. Young's entire case was that Spicer had provided verbal tip-offs and taken him on occasional trips to spy out targets. No one else witnessed these dealings and not even Young suggested that Spicer went on any burglaries himself.

At the end of the trial Spicer was cleared on two charges but convicted on one charge of conspiracy to burgle. The judge branded him 'a viper who has sunk about as low as a man can' and sent him to prison for three years. He spent one year inside before being released on parole, but in July 1983 he was cleared by the Court of Appeal, on the grounds that his defence had not been fully or fairly left to the jury by the trial judge in his summing-up. Spicer's conviction and sentence were quashed. So were orders that he pay a £10,000 fine and a further £10,000 costs, and be made a criminal bankrupt.

Throughout the time that Spicer had been held in police custody, was out on bail and then in prison, Tony Lundy could have nothing to do with him. There is a regulation that policemen must not associate off-duty with anyone charged with criminal offences, unless they have higher authority. Only later could Spicer tell Lundy what, he says, had happened during the eight days immediately following his arrest back in March 1981. After he had been charged, he had been taken aside by a very senior RCS officer who said he knew that Spicer should 'not be here' but explained that if he now made a statement supporting Billy Young's claims – including his allegations of criminal conduct by Tony Lundy – he would be given an easy time. He would get bail and then be put in the care of an inquiry, based at Albany Street Police Station in London, which was investigating Young's other claims (why it was not already handling those against Spicer was never explained).

By this time Spicer was not well. As his wife Laura would later testify in court, when she visited him in police custody on 9 March he looked very ill and she feared that his medical condition (always a concern to her because of his epilepsy) was far worse than when he had been taken away four days earlier. She insisted on an examination by an independent doctor who confirmed that Spicer was extremely unwell. He diagnosed problems with Spicer's kidney and heart and noted he had not eaten for days. Mrs Spicer was also distressed by the fact that, although soon after her husband's arrest she had delivered several sets of clean clothes to the police station, he was still wearing the (now very dirty) clothes he had hurriedly put on during the raid on his home. He had also slept badly because officers, ostensibly checking on his epilepsy, kept on waking him at night. Dishevelled, unshaven and run-down, he was in the same clothes when he appeared before a magistrate's court. Despite his sick state, he was *compos mentis* enough to notice that he was the only defendant who was not handcuffed. Some of his co-accused also noticed this and interpreted it as a sign of police favour. They instantly accused him of being a grass. Spicer certainly was not a grass but, even if he were, he had never seen any of the other men before and so knew nothing to grass them about. However, he does say that, because of all the pressure upon him, medical and psychological, and the inducement of bail, he did sign a statement even though what Young had said was lies.

Sure enough, after spending eight days in custody

(barely eating), Spicer was freed on bail but he promptly made a statement of complaint to his solicitor alleging that two detectives had threatened to put the word round the underworld that he had grassed the other defendants. He claimed they had told him that his house might be burned down in revenge and his children would be in great danger. On the other hand, if he turned informer, they said his family could be relocated to a safe address.

Spicer says that they also kept throwing in remarks such as, 'We know Lundy's bent.' He then realized that if he did not help send Lundy to jail, he would go to jail himself. This was a grim prospect, but he had no choice. He knew nothing to Lundy's discredit, he believed he was an honest detective and he would not tell lies against him, whatever the penalty. Thus, it seems, it was for his *honesty* that Spicer served a 'three-year' term in jail, not for criminal dishonesty. At the time of writing, he is still pursuing a claim for damages and wrongful arrest with the Home Office through his local MP, former Prime Minister Margaret Thatcher. It seems to me that, if what happened to Spicer had happened to a prisoner in Tony Lundy's care, his story and complaints would have been published long ago, instead of being told here for the first time ten years after.

Billy Young made very serious hearsay allegations against Lundy. These are examined in Chapters 23 and 24. Lundy's name came up again in February 1981 when an anonymous letter arrived at Scotland Yard addressed to 'The Commissioner'. This alleged that Lundy, his deputy, Inspector Pat Fleming, and his boss, Chief Superintendent Mike Taylor, had conspired together to obtain the Silver Bullion reward for an informant who was not entitled to it. It was two years before any of these detectives were told of the letter's existence, at which point each strenuously denied the allegation. The identity of the sender was never established, but the signs were that it came from a very senior Metropolitan detective who did not have the courage to declare himself.

The coincidence of that letter's arrival early in 1981 and of Billy Young's allegations was too much for Scotland Yard. Detective Chief Superintendent Alan Stagg was chosen to conduct an inquiry, under the supervision of DAC Steventon, into all complaints levelled against Lundy and the other Silver Bullion officers. For two and a half years this team laboured mightily investigating the minutest allegation.

Running parallel with 'Stagg' was a criminal investigation. This was also inspired in part by Billy Young who had made allegations against Roy Garner, Len Gibson, the Agudas and many other London villains. It was not considered appropriate that these should be investigated by 5 RCS to whom Young had first made them, so they were handed to a veteran detective, Superintendent Harry Clement. He was already conducting 'Operation Albany', so-called because it was based at Albany Street police station, on the basis of allegations made against Garner by another supergrass, John Moriarty. He had been arrested on 20 November 1980 and was later moved into the cells at Albany Street as a 'resident informant'. Had Spicer accepted the deal which he had been offered, it was to this Albany set-up that he would have been sent.

Harry Clement, leading forty-five detectives, worked for over a year on the Young–Moriarty allegations without nailing any of his main targets. His explanation is given in Chapter 13. In the meantime the war against Garner, Lundy and the Silver Bullion reward was being fought elsewhere – in the media.

12

The Fourth Estate

Six people had been charged with the Silver Bullion robbery. Five pleaded guilty and were jailed, largely as a result of Tony Lundy's detective work. The only main defendant he did not interrogate was Bob Deanus, a self-employed jeweller. He admitted nothing and fought the case at the Old Bailey in January 1982.

One reporter covering the Deanus trial was Graeme McLagan of BBC Radio who had chronicled the dirty dealings of cunning crooks and bent detectives for many years. He had followed the Silver Bullion affair from the start and had been in court when supergrass Micky Gervaise pleaded guilty and received the standard five years in April 1981. McLagan was now on hand to hear Gervaise credited as the source of the information leading to the robbers' arrest and the silver's recovery, but it also came out that the reward had gone elsewhere. This struck McLagan as curious and he said so on radio.[1]

Another puzzled observer was Duncan Campbell, a long-standing, perceptive and witty commentator on the London underworld. As he wrote in *City Limits*: 'If Gervaise provided the information for the retrieval of the bullion, how is it that someone else got the money?' Later Campbell added, the reward must 'be within the knowledge of Det. Supt Tony Lundy'.[2] Neither reporter so much as whispered 'corruption' but other folk might have read it into their stories.

The reward had come up in Deanus's trial when the defence questioned Gervaise's motives. As Judge Peter Slot put it: 'Is he giving this evidence because he has hope

of financial advantage?' In Gervaise's absence, Slot read
the jury a statement of 'agreed facts' prepared by Scotland
Yard. This stated the reward had been paid on 1 July 1981
but not to Gervaise, no further reward would be paid, and
'the police believe that Gervaise does not know the identity
of the person who has received the reward and that he does
not know any reward has been paid'.

Had Gervaise even aspired to the reward? Yes, according to Detective Superintendent Dave Little. In court
Little said that back in June 1980 Gervaise had asked,
'what his position would be if he requested it. I told him
it wasn't on, there wasn't the remotest chance, and I said
that came from the Assistant Commissioner.'

In the witness box 'Skinny' Gervaise, cadaverous and
balding, cut a poor figure. In his summing up Judge Slot
remarked: 'You would not honestly hang a dog on his
evidence, would you? You would not dream of finding
a man guilty on the basis of his evidence alone, would
you? Well, I would not.' After this outburst, it was no
surprise that the jury appeared to agree with the judge.
They acquitted Bob Deanus.

In normal circumstances the Silver Bullion affair would
have ended with the Deanus trial. The only alleged co-
conspirator still wanted was the fugitive Micky Sewell,
but even when he was recaptured he would not be tried
for this crime because the only witness against him would
have been the catastrophic Gervaise. Most of the silver
had been recovered, and the insurers were satisfied their
rewards had gone to the right people. But these were not
normal circumstances, and many folk had an interest in
keeping the pot on the boil.

One was John Goodwin, a 'dealer', of Bishops Stortford,
Hertfordshire and also of London's East End. In the
early 1980s Goodwin became one of the Old Bailey's
most talked-about defendants. His celebrity came not

from being convicted but from winning two retrials and an eventual acquittal on charges of burgling a bank in Whitechapel in 1978. In the first trial the jury could not agree. The second had to be abandoned when Goodwin successfully feigned a heart attack. In the third trial in February 1982 he was acquitted after he produced a tape-recording of a detective taking money from him. He had gathered this crushing evidence while out on bail between the second and third trials by hiding a recorder in a Christmas tree at the home of a friend shortly before two officers called for a festive drink.

The Old Bailey had not seen the last of John Goodwin. In April 1982 he reappeared with a co-defendant Brian Reader to face charges over three burglaries totalling £1,250,000. The main witness was the mendacious Micky Gervaise, but by now Micky had turned into a 'double-agent' supergrass. He said he had made it 'abundantly clear to everyone that I didn't want to be here. I even wrote to the prosecution saying I didn't want to get involved.' He withdrew his evidence, claiming Robbery Squad officers had told him to falsely implicate the defendants in burglaries in which he had participated:

I went along with what was required. Goodwin's name was suggested – he should be involved as an extra. I was expected to involve him. I was doing a deal and I just went along with it . . . The police officer said Goodwin and Reader were to be implicated – they had to go, to use police terminology – to be put away. It was left to me to involve them in whatever role.

He also claimed that a former Robbery Squad inspector had committed a string of burglaries with him in the 1970s, and that when he turned supergrass other detectives told him to say nothing about corrupt dealings with police.

After Gervaise's extraordinary turnabout the defendants could have expected to be found not guilty, but the judge abandoned the trial because of 'jury-nobbling' claims. A retrial took place in October 1982 without Gervaise. This time the defendants were cleared, but by now Goodwin had been charged with trying to nobble the first jury. In March 1983 he was convicted and jailed for seven years but in May 1984 he was cleared by the Court of Appeal and freed. The same month three detectives faced trial for taking a total of £8,500 from Goodwin over the 1978 bank burglary charges. Two were cleared, including Peter Bignold who was heard on the 'Christmas Tree Tape' taking £1,000 from Goodwin. His smart defence was to admit he had taken the money but had told only the truth about Goodwin, so there had been no corruption and no perversion of justice. The third officer was convicted but he too was cleared on appeal.

There were times, however, when Goodwin benefited from straight policing without buying it. In April 1983 his wife Shirley was kidnapped. From jail he told police of a long-standing feud with a South London villain, Charlie Pitts, who was demanding a ransom. Working with police the family pretended to agree to pay £10,000, but the kidnappers were arrested and Shirley was released three hours later. Pitts and four confederates were jailed for up to eighteen years.

Amid these extraordinary twists and turns, the lean and wiry Goodwin became something of a cult figure among investigative journalists, some of whom he invited to his daughter's wedding. They were particularly intrigued by Micky Gervaise's antics, which seemed to confirm their suspicions that 'supergrass policing' was nothing less than a liar's charter to fit up minnows, and put big villains back on the streets fast to rob all over again. The irony was that the most successful exponent of supergrass policing, Tony Lundy, had always argued against giving Gervaise supergrass status because he was an unregenerate liar who would be a disaster in the witness box and would bring the entire policy into disrepute (see Chapters 7 and 9). He was over-ruled, so the 'Gervaise' trials went ahead with other officers in charge.

Lundy had nothing to fear from Gervaise. Indeed, in the long stream of criminal allegations he made against named detectives during Goodwin's trial, Gervaise never implicated Lundy. It was only when the Silver Bullion reward came up again that Gervaise mentioned the detective who had made him confess. 'I was put in a dream world that I would receive a reward for the Silver and Gemco, but that's all been pushed aside. I was told by Lundy and Dixon. I didn't know whether to believe them or not. I was originally under the impression I would.' The judge queried Gervaise, asking if he 'really seriously' expected the police to help him get a reward for a crime in which he himself had been involved. Gervaise replied, 'Other people who have been on robberies have received a reward', but did not offer any examples.

It is inconceivable that a sophisticated criminal like Gervaise could ever have believed he would get rewards for informing about crimes in which he admitted taking part. He must always have known he would never get a reward for informing on either Gemco or the Silver Bullion job. Nor would Little, Lundy or Dixon have been so naive as to have tried to delude him into thinking otherwise.

Lies though they clearly were, Gervaise's remarks helped muddy the already murky Silver Bullion waters. Now John Goodwin joined in. Free on bail in early 1982, he introduced a reporter to a certain Mr Bob Deanus, freshly acquitted and anxious to avenge himself. His motives were obvious and understandable, but why was Goodwin so keen to keep the Silver Bullion pot on the furnace?

The answer may have something to do with what happened soon after Goodwin was arrested in May 1980 over Gervaise's allegations. At this point *Goodwin himself offered to turn informer*. He approached Chief Superintendent Reg Dixon, in overall charge of the Gervaise inquiry, offering this deal: *he* would assist in recovering bullion, or solving the crime, provided he was given a written guarantee that he would be let off the Whitechapel bank burglary charges. These pre-dated his problems arising from Gervaise's supergrassing and so (I presume) could not have been wiped out even if Goodwin had turned supergrass himself.

Dixon took Goodwin seriously enough to ask the Director of Public Prosecutions if such a deal could be sanctioned. The answer was that it could not. Around this time, of course, Tony Lundy gathered his own information leading to the bullion's recovery. This smashed Goodwin's chance not just of a deal but of the massive reward which would have come with it. Were his later behind-the-scenes efforts to discredit Lundy the actions of a thwarted bounty-hunter? He certainly had something against Lundy, for on his own 'Christmas Tree Tape' recorded in December 1981, Goodwin grossly exaggerated the evidence against the detective: he said Billy Young had named Dave Spicer, which was true, and that 'Spicer made half a dozen statements at least against Lundy', which was untrue. He had made not even one such statement. Goodwin seems to have wanted to spread the idea around that Lundy was in deep trouble and was happy to tell this false gossip to Detective Sergeant Bignold to whom he paid £1,000 cash a few minutes later.

One of the journalists whom Bob Deanus approached was Duncan Campbell. In April 1982 Campbell published a piece in *City Limits* entitled 'The Silver Bullion Mystery'. This tied Tony Lundy more closely into the reward controversy than any previous report. Campbell had an interest in Lundy, having previously written a long piece on Danny Gowan and Charlie Smith, both cleared of robbery charges based initially on evidence from Lundy supergrasses (Smith at trial, Gowan controversially on appeal).[3]

Campbell now published a photograph of Lundy at a social function at the Dorchester Hotel in the 1970s (the Lady Ratlings 'do' of 1974). It was only half the photo (the other half had been cut off before the photo reached Campbell) but it showed Lundy standing close to Roy Garner and Garner's business associate Kenny Ross. Campbell wrote that any detective's job means 'mixing with the underworld' but this photo was 'compromising' because Ross had a criminal record and 'it is doubly troubling because of allegations that Ross and Garner have knowledge of what happened to the reward money'.[4]

Campbell said there was now a Scotland Yard inquiry into the reward and the twelve missing silver bars. He presumed this inquiry was looking into possible corruption for, he surmised, it was working under Commander Mike Taylor, head of the anti-corruption squad, CIB 2. Back in 1980 Taylor had been in overall charge of the Silver Bullion job, jemmying open the garage where the silver was found. Campbell said this 'must make his appearance of neutrality shaky'. (In fact, though Campbell did not know it, Taylor had no authority over the inquiry, which was being conducted under the direct authority of DAC Steventon.) After referring to the recent suspension of the detectives whom Goodwin had taped as they discussed fit-ups and bribes, Campbell ended by saying: 'Scotland Yard knows that it is facing one of its biggest internal crises for years.'

An equally persistent seeker after truth in the Silver Bullion mystery was the BBC's Graeme McLagan. The more he looked at the 'Agreed Facts' produced in the

Deanus trial, the more they perplexed him, particularly paragraphs 4 and 5.

> 4. In consequence of Gervaise's statements about the bullion robbery a number of persons were arrested and pleaded guilty to it in January 1981. These pleas of guilty amounted to convictions within the meaning of the offer of the reward. In consequence of the arrest of the others named by Gervaise a substantial part of the silver bullion was recovered.
>
> 5. The reward was paid on 1st July 1981 but not to Gervaise. It has been paid to someone else . . .

McLagan understood the principle that no supergrass, or any informant, should ever be paid a reward for informing on a crime in which he had participated. Manifestly Gervaise was not entitled to the reward, but on the basis of the 'Agreed Facts' neither was anyone else. Who, then, *had* got the reward, and why?

On 8 November 1982 McLagan presented an edition of BBC TV's current affairs flagship, *Panorama*, in which he investigated the reward. Bob Deanus also appeared on the programme but anonymously. He said he understood that the supergrass Christopher Wren had grassed Michael Gervaise who grassed Lennie Gibson who gave the silver back. 'So we feel that the reward should never have been paid.'

McLagan then referred to Lundy's statement of his June 1980 interview when Gervaise admitted he was on the robbery. McLagan reconstructed the exchange in which Gervaise raised the relationship between Lundy and Len Gibson.

GERVAISE: I thought he was a very good friend of yours?
LUNDY: No way. I've known him socially from drinking in the same pub, but we're no more friends than that.

GERVAISE: Well, perhaps you understand why I've been worried? I was on the Silver Bullion robbery with Lennie Gibson.

To cement that point, McLagan showed the full colour photograph of the Lady Ratlings 'do'. This revealed Len Gibson in the line-up as well as Lundy, Garner and Ross. McLagan observed, 'What's clear is that the interview reveals Gervaise confessed voluntarily. Gervaise didn't get the reward, so why should anyone else qualify?' Certainly the reward had not gone to Gibson or Dolph Aguda who had stashed the silver in the garage. Dolph's brother, Ferdinand, appeared on the film to say both imprisoned men felt that whoever had got the reward was not entitled to it.

McLagan then looked into the £300,000 reward and the obvious conflict with DAC Powis's suggested limit of £5,000. He then put a figure of £180,000 on the Silver reward paid in July 1981 and named its probable recipient as Roy Garner, 'a successful businessman who owns property in London and Hertfordshire'. Yet through his solicitor Garner was denying he had ever been a police informer. Thus, said McLagan, 'the mystery of who got the bullion reward and why, remains'.

In the rest of the film McLagan scrutinized the supergrass system and revealed Gervaise as someone ready to tell lies to fit people up unless they paid him a lot of money. McLagan was correct, and no one would have agreed with him more on this point than Tony Lundy. McLagan also showed that two of Lundy's supergrasses, Norman Jones and Dave Smith, had been involved in very violent crimes and had got off lightly. Again Lundy would have agreed that these were men of extreme violence, but would have pointed out that sentencing is up to judges, not mere detectives.

McLagan then produced a disturbing piece of new

information. He had talked to Mrs Christina Price, the widow of a supermarket manager named Walter Price. On 19 October 1967 Price had been driving home from his Swiss Cottage branch of Sainsbury's when he was attacked by Dave Smith and George Williams who knocked him unconscious with a cosh and stole his keys. (Their take from the supermarket was £4,000.) Mrs Price told McLagan that her husband 'fell in the back door in a dreadful state with this big lump on his head, big as an egg'. Eight weeks later he died of heart failure. Mrs Price felt it was murder. Ten years later she received a phone call from police asking to speak to Mr Price. She replied that he had died ten years before. She was then told that one of his assailants had confessed and was in custody, but she heard no more. It was only from Graeme McLagan, five years later still, that she learned Williams had turned supergrass, been charged with no more than robbery and been jailed for just five years. 'That seems a very light sentence for murder,' she remarked. It was the most poignant moment in a programme which raised far more questions than it was able to answer.[5]

In 1982 almost every national newspaper carried some piece about the Silver Bullion controversy, but often in a coded way to avoid legal action. Thus on 4 April 1982 John Shirley wrote in the *Sunday Times*:

One officer is alleged to have stolen bars of silver bullion, the proceeds recovered from a major robbery. It is also claimed that he passed crucial information about the silver bullion raid to two wealthy criminals and then shared a large sum of reward money with the criminals when they 'traded' the information back to the police.

On 26 April the *Daily Mail* said: 'well-known underworld figures have claimed "Sweeney" detectives . . . were involved in the disappearance of 12 silver ingots seized in a £3 million bullion raid and have taken a share of reward money paid out to mystery informants.' The newspaper also stated Commander Mike Taylor was in charge of the inquiry and 'is understood to have twice visited the US to try and establish whether a corrupt officer purchased property and land with money from the sale of the silver bars, each worth £10,000'.

The most persistent onslaught came from reporters David Leigh and Paul Lashmar in the *Observer*. Over the next seven years this award-winning pair published dozens of pieces on Lundy and Garner, undermining Scotland Yard's faith in its most successful detective and its most effective informant. On 25 July 1982 they published a sensational full-page article entitled 'Secrets of the Bullion Job'. This explored 'friendships' which Micky Gervaise, Lennie Gibson and Micky Sewell each had with police officers and asserted, 'had it not been for these friendships (some of them corrupt, others merely "cosy") the £3 million of silver bullion might never have been parted from its rightful owners'.

The writers alleged that Gervaise used to bribe detectives 'to escape their unwelcome attentions', but the only such officer named was Chief Inspector Alec Eist who was dead and could not sue. They went on: 'Gervaise was no minnow in the silver bullion case: he was in fact the instigator. Had he been behind bars at the time, as he should have been, the robbery would probably never have happened.' As for Micky Sewell, at the time of the Silver Bullion job he was at liberty despite facing charges over Lambeth Town Hall. According to the article, the detective in charge of that case, Chief Inspector Bill Peters, later said in court that he had agreed to Sewell's bail application so he could act as an informant (Peters would later successfully sue the *Observer* for libel). Regarding Len Gibson, Tony Lundy was a 'long-standing drinking companion' of his. However, Leigh and Lashmar took care to state, 'we have no evidence to suggest any corrupt behaviour on his part'.

Much of the information on which these reporters based their article came from public sources such as police statements and trial evidence. What gave the piece an acute edge was that it seemed to have been written with access to the contents of highly confidential statements made by two supergrasses. The authors stated that both Billy Young and Fred Sinfield were claiming that Lundy's friend, Dave Spicer, was a go-between for criminals and corrupt detectives. Again the authors took care to say Lundy was 'apparently unaware' of Spicer's role in passing bribes to senior Robbery Squad officers but, as Lundy was the only past or present squad officer named as knowing Spicer, this scarcely lessened the hint that Lundy himself was 'bent'.

Leigh and Lashmar were emboldened to name Spicer because he had been convicted on 2 June 1982 of receiving stolen property and sentenced to three years' imprisonment. On that basis the *Observer*'s lawyers must have taken the view that anything the supergrasses had alleged about Spicer could be printed without him suing for libel, but one year after the article's appearance he was cleared on appeal (see Chapter 11).

The article also contained barely concealed references to Roy Garner and Kenny Ross as two powerful Mr Fix-its who were themselves 'major receivers of stolen goods and organizers of armed robberies'. Again Billy Young was cited as claiming Spicer was their go-between when bribes had to be paid to police. Leigh and Lashmar then turned to the night Gibson led Lundy and other detectives to the Silver Bullion garage. They referred to Rudolpho Aguda's key and the twelve missing bars, then said, 'no-one knows what happened to them or when they were spirited out of the garage'.

As for the reward, the reporters said the entire £300,000 had been paid to recipients 'who must have been recommended by Chief Inspector Lundy'. Scotland Yard would not say but 'sources have said that the money went to Kenneth Ross and Roy Garner after a public-spirited tip-off'. Because of all the allegations surrounding this affair, the Yard had appointed Chief Superintendent Alan Stagg to investigate. His 'secret unit appears to by-pass both the Yard's official anti-corruption department CIB 2, and the orthodox CID command structure.' Stagg, said Lashmar and Leigh, was 'working with' DAC Ron Steventon.

When Lundy saw the article he was outraged, not least because its innuendoes were heightened by a blow-up of the photo previously published in *City Limits*, showing him close to Garner and Ross. He read the piece again and again, trying to fathom the injustice it had done him. There was the long passage about the robbers' 'friendships' with police, without which 'the £3 million of silver bullion might never have been parted from its rightful owners'. If, as the authors asserted, Gervaise should have been in prison at the time of the robbery, which detective *did* cause him to be arrested and jailed? Tony Lundy. If Micky Sewell should have been in custody over the Lambeth Town Hall job – not free on bail – who was the detective whose information had got him arrested in the first place and was outraged when he was given bail? Tony Lundy. And if Len Gibson was Lundy's 'friend' – albeit through the detective's voluntary work at Finchley Boxing Club – who was it who broke him, persuaded him to give back the silver and then had him put in jail for ten years? Tony Lundy.

As for Billy Young's corruption allegations, this was the first Lundy had heard of them. Not that he believed he had anything to fear from Young. Had not everybody at the

Torrington called him Billy Liar? They all knew he was a professional thief. That was why they also called him Burglar Bill and why Lundy never had anything to do with him. He says he knew that Young could allege nothing directly against him because he had never done anything wrong. However, Young's allegations against Dave Spicer had already sent that innocent man to jail, so who else might he manage to 'fit up'?

In July 1982 when the *Observer* article appeared, Lundy knew nothing of the attempt by a very senior Regional Crime Squad officer to persuade Spicer to make statements claiming he was corrupt. But now he read of Fred Sinfield's allegation that Spicer had 'channelled a £10,000 bribe to a senior officer so Sinfield could avoid arrest', he could not help wondering if Number 5 Regional Crime Squad was involved in a vicious whispering campaign against him, for he knew it was 5 RCS which had arrested Sinfield and Young. Lundy of course recalled that, far from helping Sinfield avoid arrest, *he* was the detective who had wanted to ambush Sinfield and the other Lambeth Town Hall robbers back in 1978, but had been over-ruled and had a blazing row because of it. If Lundy had got his way, Sinfield would have been captured on the spot (see Chapter 5). So if any Metropolitan detective had been bribed on Sinfield's behalf – which Lundy doubted – it certainly was not him. He had never met Sinfield or had any dealings with him.

Lundy's main concern about the article was that he felt it must have been based in part on a leak either from the Stagg inquiry or 5 RCS. He also felt it could not have been written without breaches of confidence and the Official Secrets Act by police officers. Certainly, he felt, anything that either criminal had said about corruption should have been a matter of the strictest secrecy until any charges were brought.

In a passage about the bullion reward, Leigh and Lashmar wrote that some 'sources' had said the money went to the club-owners Kenneth Ross and Roy Garner. In fact Ross was not paid any reward. Nor had Lundy recommended all the 'recipients': he had totally opposed the payment to supergrass Chrissie Wren. The reporters also claimed that Lundy shared the services of a solicitor with Garner and Ross. This was untrue, although on one occasion the solicitor had acted for Lundy's wife over a traffic accident. They recycled Gervaise's claim that he had believed he himself would receive the Silver Bullion reward. They also said there was 'no record of what understanding, if any' was reached during a two-hour private meeting between Lundy, Gibson and (later) Aguda. In fact there had been two different meetings and Lundy did make a record. Two days later he wrote up a statement, based on contemporaneous notes, in which he detailed the only understanding arrived at: that the pair were admitting their role and were giving the silver back. He did not record the opaque conversation which they had between themselves before coming to this understanding.

Then there was the matter of Dolph Aguda's garage key. The article implied that police could have used it to remove the missing twelve bars of silver before the official police convoy arrived near midnight. No such skulduggery seems possible because none of the police had any idea where the silver was stashed. Lennie Gibson had no key nor did he state the lock-up's address before navigating the police convoy to the site. Aguda did not go along. Whether he had a key or not, he was not there to ask. That was why the door had to be broken. It also seems likely that the twelve bars were elsewhere long before Gibson and Aguda's arrest – maybe in the clutches of the fugitive Sewell before the load was even moved to the lock-up. And if they had never been in that garage, they could not have been 'spirited out' (see Chapter 9).

Neither Scotland Yard nor Tony Lundy had been happy with earlier articles linking him and Roy Garner, but this *Observer* piece was far more damaging. Its content made it no easier for either man to face the pressures it would bring. Henceforth Garner lived in fear of physical attack, even assassination. The pressure on Lundy was different. Naturally his colleagues expected him to sue. They called him 'Top Man' after all, so what had he to fear?

If he sued, surely he would 'clean up' in the High Court and win huge damages? If he did not sue, would he be admitting guilt?

13

The Lone Granger

Tony Lundy wanted to sue the *Observer* but there were two severe constraints on him. One was financial. When he solved the Silver Bullion robbery he belonged to the Police Federation, the 'trade union' for all officers ranked chief inspector and below. With 125,000 members it is rich enough to maintain a large legal fund and supports libel actions brought by many officers. Lundy could have been one of them but when the *Observer* article appeared he had risen to superintendent. This obliged him to join the Police Superintendents' Association which has only 2,000 members and barely any resources. Far from funding libel actions, it had a ceiling of just £1,000 for legal advice. Nor could Lundy get legal aid – there is none for libel – and funds were not going to be forthcoming from Scotland Yard, even though he had been defamed 'in the line of duty', because DAC Steventon had refused him representation by Metropolitan Police solicitors. If he were to sue the *Observer* or any other publication to clear his name, he would have to risk his own money – at least £50,000, and maybe £200,000 if he lost.

There was a far more serious constraint, one which touched on the essence of all honourable detective work. In court Lundy would have to refute this severe slur in the *Observer*: 'Lundy may well have been unwise to spend as much time as he did with Gibson and Spicer. The two club-owners, Ross and Garner, similarly fell into the category of men it was perhaps unwise of a senior officer to become too well acquainted with.'[1]

Most of Lundy's senior officers believed his relationships

with all four men were legitimate. They also knew that his Finchley Boxing Club connections had greatly helped their force in the war against crime. Yet if Lundy were to demonstrate all this in open court, certain people would be placed in grave danger. Each relationship would be exposed in fine detail, then prominently reported in the press. Once that happened, the underworld would take revenge on at least one of the four.

The main, if unstated, questions posed by the *Observer* were, 'Who received the reward?' and, 'Was he/were they the true source of the information?'; in other words, 'Who were Lundy's snouts – genuine or bogus?' Leigh and Lashmar suggested they were Ross and Garner, and there the pair were standing alongside Lundy in the photo at the top of the page! The photo was genuine – in legal terms it was 'fair comment' to publish it – but the overwhelming drift of the full-page spread was that the relationship between the three men was corrupt.

In court Lundy would refuse to say anything about that relationship, not to protect himself but because he believed that, when police start naming informers, they breach a moral code. On a practical level they would also destroy the basic tool of their trade. Lundy recalled what he had been taught twenty years before at training school: 'Informants are the be-all and end-all of detective work.' Name your sources, and your sources will dry up. If the criminal world were to read in newspapers or see on television that London's most successful detective was sacrificing 'snouts' just to clear his name and pocket a fortune in damages, the number of high-level informers would tumble overnight.

No 'profession' ought to understand this principle better than journalists. 'I cannot reveal my sources' is one of the most well-used phrases in a reporter's knapsack. No doubt David Leigh and Paul Lashmar would go to prison rather than reveal the names of any police officers or public servants or, indeed, private citizens who have helped them confidentially on any story. Certainly such 'whistle blowers' would expect that degree of protection from investigative journalists. Similarly, although Lundy wanted to defend himself against character assassination, his informers would still expect him to 'button his lip'. In the moral scales he had to balance their lives against his reputation, and the scales came down on their side.

His legal advice, through the Superintendents' Association, confirmed he had a better-than-even chance of success, but only at immense risk to his informers. A libel action was therefore 'not on'. Instead he would have to stomach the lies being spread among his colleagues, and just hope his informers could fend off people's suspicions and survive. His counsel also pointed out that if he sued, the *Observer* would certainly seek 'discovery' of all documents relating to matters in the article. During any action both Lundy and Scotland Yard might be ordered to disclose highly confidential and sensitive papers: another compelling reason for not suing.

But Lundy was not the only policeman reading the *Observer* with a view to going to court. So was Detective Chief Inspector Bill Peters who believed the Leigh–Lashmar article suggested he was a corrupt policeman, which he was not. He felt there was an imputation that he had received a large bribe to obtain bail for Micky Sewell who later absconded and earned the right to be considered a prime Silver Bullion suspect. Peters sued for libel and won £10,000 from the *Observer*, which also printed an apology.

Another irate reader was the ultimate boss of both Peters and Lundy, David Powis. He was mentioned only once in the *Observer* spread but in dangerously inaccurate terms. Leigh and Lashmar had written, 'The insurance

company paid out a staggering £300,000 reward money',
which 'was handed over by Deputy Assistant Commissioner David Powis, but to this day the Police will not
say who received the cash'. These lines contained several
errors. The insurance company paid not £300,000 but
around £200,000. The sum was handed over not by Powis
but by the insurance assessors. Far from collaborating in a
'staggering £300,000' pay-out, he had gone out of his way
to assert that no more than £5,000 should be paid. Furthermore, 'Secrets of the Bullion Job' was not the only crooked
cop story in the *Observer* that Sunday. Leigh and Lashmar
had also written a front-page piece entitled 'Met Bribes
Revealed' in which they stated: 'There have been question
marks put against two deputy assistant commissioners in
the present secret inquiry.' The only DAC named in either
article was David Powis so the two pieces, read together,
might convey that Powis himself was under suspicion. This
was all too much for Powis. He sued.

In May 1985 the *Observer* paid him substantial damages
for any implication that he was suspected of improper
practices. It did not accept that the two articles were open
to this interpretation but apologized 'for any distress and
embarrassment' caused to him and his family.

Lundy, of course, had suffered far more distress and
embarrassment but if Powis could take money off the
Observer without endangering informers, good luck to
him thought Lundy. This is not how it turned out. In
the course of the Powis action the *Observer* did exactly
as Lundy's counsel had predicted: it successfully applied
for discovery of all Scotland Yard documents relating to
the Silver Bullion reward. The newspaper hit the jackpot! Powis's lawyers – in this case, the Metropolitan
Police's own solicitors – handed over a batch of papers
containing details of rewards paid over many years *and
of the informers who received them*. As for the *Observer*'s

fulsome apology, *Private Eye* commented: 'This will be no consolation to the informers who will be fearing for their lives nor to Scotland Yard officers who will be wondering who to turn to for their underworld information.'[2]

The *Eye* was right. In the three years since the *Observer* 'exposé', Roy Garner had 'toughed it out', denying he was an informer. Despite being named repeatedly in newspapers, he 'fronted' all comers. His sheer nerve convinced many underworld faces he might not be a snout after all: otherwise, how could the guy still be walking around? But now, because David Powis had sued to save his good name, Garner's bad one would soon be returned to him stamped 'official'. To protect informers Lundy had let far worse libels go unchallenged, but for all the good this had done them, he might as well have sued and let them hang – literally, if some of the folk they had 'grassed' ever laid hands on them.

Responding to *Private Eye*, Powis said the documents handed to the *Observer* gave only informers' pseudonyms, not their true names, but this was no comfort to the informer whose pseudonym 'Dave Granger' gave him no protection whatever. The mass of other information in the documents made it only too easy to identify him as Roy Garner, especially since the name of his handler, Tony Lundy, was not obscured. Much of the information had nothing to do with the Silver Bullion reward but related to other payments on other jobs. These incidental disclosures were a further catastrophe for 'Granger'.

Powis stated correctly that the documents were given to the *Observer* solely for the legal proceedings and that their use for any other purpose 'may amount to a contempt of court'.[3] Yet, according to *Private Eye*, the newspaper had quickly struck a deal with the makers of a programme in the BBC's *Brass Tacks* series, in which seven informers would soon be named. As it turned out, the programme was never shown (see Chapter 15), but photocopies of highly sensitive police documents which had been disclosed in the Powis–*Observer* action – concerning the Silver Bullion reward and naming 'Granger' – did reach journalists working in other places and were distributed far and wide. The *Observer* never quoted them in its pages – that would have been a clear contempt of court – but in years to come extracts from them appeared elsewhere time and again.

The truth – if we can believe official records – was that Garner had been a phenomenally fruitful informant whose full value was known to only one police officer other than Tony Lundy: that was David Powis, who had often met Garner on official business. Three times between March and July 1981 they sat and talked in Garner's car, along with DAC Steventon. At this time Garner was supplying information almost every week, through Lundy, on jewel robberies, bank raids, two separate counterfeit currency operations, numerous drug-smuggling rackets, American organized crime connections with Britain, and the movements of fugitive bullion robber Micky Sewell.

Many arrests resulted, including those of the three Barry brothers in May 1981, captured with two million pounds-worth of forged five pound notes, and an entire forger's den, including printing presses, a guillotine and photographic plates with fifteen different serial numbers. Two of the brothers and four confederates pleaded guilty and were jailed in March 1982, Patrick and John Barry each getting nine years. Naturally Lundy nominated Garner for a Bank of England reward, and so did Superintendent Dave Little who was in charge of the case. Powis knew how much Garner had done on this job because he had dealt with him directly while Lundy was on holiday. As a result Garner expected a big payday but Powis restricted the Bank's reward to £5,000, in line with his new policy.

Garner was appalled. The next time he saw Powis he called him 'Bastard!' Powis announced he would pay him an additional £1,000 out of the Metropolitan Police Informants' Fund. He thought the sum appropriate to cover Garner's expenses while informing. Garner did not say thanks. He called Powis a few more names.

The Yard's schizophrenia over Garner through these years was paraded to tragi-comical effect in 1981 over a West End robbery, in which some very valuable jewellery was stolen. Lundy was taking a rare day off from his duties as head of CID on 'Q' Division, when he received a call from an inspector on Finchley Robbery Squad where Lundy himself had been 'Top Man' only a year before. Could he identify three raiders snapped by a video-camera at the jewellers? The Squad had drawn a blank with the other robbery squads, criminal intelligence and local station CIDs. No one knew the raiders. Lundy was their last hope. He agreed to look at the photos which were brought to his home that day. He recognized no one, but he asked the inspector if he wanted him to show the photos to his informants. Yes, said the inspector. As the matter was urgent, the off-duty Lundy made instant arrangements and, according to police records, he went that September evening to see Garner at home where he was preparing to go out to work at his club. Within two minutes Garner identified one man by his first name but could not remember his surname. Lundy promptly left and reported to the inspector. Next day Lundy was told the raider's full name and where he could be found.

There had been a further development. Garner had been contacted by a close acquaintance who was a receiver of stolen jewels. He was asking to borrow £9,000 to buy the jewellery stolen on the self-same raid. Garner was loath to lend the money, only to inform on the man soon afterwards and then see the purchase

seized by the police. He might just as well give £9,000
to charity. Yet if he did lend the money, the receiver
would have the stolen jewels, and the police could raid
his house where, for a short while, the jewels would be
kept. In the end Garner agreed to lend the cash.

Finchley was kept fully informed of these developments,
and told that the receiver would shortly pick up £9,000
and collect the jewels. Soon after, Garner reported that
the receiver had collected and buried them in his garden
under a rose bush. It was then decided that Robbery Squad
officers should raid the house and search the garden next
morning but later that morning the Finchley inspector
called Lundy to say nothing had been found in the garden.
A few hours on Garner himself called to complain about
the police: 'What a load of wallies! They've cocked it up
again!' He said the receiver's wife had called him to say her
husband had been arrested over a few watches, and could
he come round. Garner went to the house and found out
the police had searched the garden with metal detectors
but had failed to look under the rose bush. After the police
left, she recovered the parcel of jewels from under the bush
and asked Garner to take it away for safe-keeping until
her husband was released. Garner did not want to do this
but his partner had already agreed and quickly took the
parcel away.

Garner was in a pickle, which he rightly blamed on the
clodhopping cops who should have found the parcel in the
first place. Lundy explained the situation to the Robbery
Squad superintendent, and then went to do the work he
was being paid for. All his efforts on Finchley's behalf
were voluntary, coming on top of his divisional duties
at Wembley and his almost daily involvement at the Old
Bailey supervising trials resulting from his earlier Robbery
Squad work. At the Old Bailey next day he was astonished
to receive a call from a high-ranking Yard officer saying he

had been ordered by DAC Steventon to arrest Garner as a participant in the jewel crime, and to search his premises! Lundy was livid. As soon as the court rose, he rushed to prevent the impending catastrophe. He insisted on seeing Steventon to explain the idiocy of this course of action.

First, Garner would not be at home or at any of his premises. Secondly the jewels would not be found because Garner's partner had hidden them elsewhere, and even Garner did not know where. Thirdly, it was only as a favour to the Robbery Squad that Lundy had asked Garner to identify the raiders from the photos. Fourthly, Garner had identified one of them and was the sole person to recognize anybody; as a result, that man was watched, he met the other two raiders, their identities were established, and all three were detained along with a small portion of the stolen gear (they later pleaded guilty). Fifthly, it was only through Garner that the police knew who now had most of the stolen jewels. Sixthly, it was not his fault that the search party had failed to collect the 'tom' and stick it in a police safe by now. And seventhly, was this how to treat a man who 'had been responsible for the arrest of more major criminals than any other informant'?

Despite Lundy's plea, DAC Steventon insisted that Garner should still be treated as a 'participating informant'. He would be raided, detained, and then released while papers were submitted to the DPP. Lundy was even instructed to tell him to make sure to have the stolen jewellery at his home, so it could be recovered later in the day. Garner was not dumb enough to fall for that one. Sure, he wanted police to recover the jewels, but not by finding them in his own place. That way, he would be fitting himself up! It would be impossible for him to get out of any 'verbals'. Imagine his defence: 'I was a snout for the fuzz. They told me to keep the "tom" safe at home till they came to get it. Honest!' No jury would believe him. Guilty! Fifteen years. Besides, he could never admit he was a snout.

And what would his partner think if he asked him to bring the jewels back, only to be caught with them hours later? He would know instantly Garner was a snout. Naturally Garner refused to play, but that night his home and premises were raided. So were his partner's. Nothing was found, of course, but his partner must now have suspected he was a grass anyway. What clinched the suspicion was that the police had told the partner they knew the pair had taken stolen property from the receiver's home. The aftermath of this fiasco was that the missing jewels were never recovered, so there was no reward for Garner to collect; a resentful Garner disappeared abroad, vowing never to assist again; and relations with his partner were not in good shape. Again records show that, at the time, there was concern that if his partner knew Garner's secret, he 'would be in extreme danger, as many of his partner's friends are serving long terms of imprisonment because of Garner's information'.

Garner broke his vow never to assist Scotland Yard again. He resumed the collaboration as soon as he returned to Britain in November 1981. Yet even as he was giving the Yard so much help, the Yard was trying to put him in jail. Since September 1980 he had been under continuous investigation by Operation Albany, the special task force under the direct authority of DAC Steventon. Soon Albany was forty-five 'hand-picked' officers strong, led by Chief Superintendent Harry Clement.[4] Garner found out about Albany early on. He even told Powis and Steventon he knew he was being investigated. It was meant to be top secret, but it was as leaky as a sieve.

One person Clement might have arrested was a member of his own team. In July 1981 Garner named an Albany detective who was leaking information from Clement's inquiry. Garner's action would seem to have been self-defeating, for surely he could have made use of continuing inside intelligence about how hot Clement was on his tail. Instead, it seems, Garner sacrificed his 'bent' source because he thought he was doing Scotland Yard a favour. The information was passed upwards but no action was taken against the leaky detective who remained on Albany. Either the Yard was turning a blind eye to a corrupt cop, or the leaker was leaking with official backing.

Not that Garner needed leaks to know what Albany was doing. Sometimes he caught them at it. On 7 October 1981 he and his business partner Kenny Ross were travelling round North London in Ross's van, buying goods for their pub operation from cash-and-carry premises, and so carrying a lot of cash. After some time they realized they were being followed, and thought they were about to be robbed. To shake off their pursuers they took many detours round back streets but without success. Being rather hot-headed, Ross decided to retaliate. He suddenly reversed, ramming into the van behind him. He then jumped out and grabbed the driver, only to see motor cycles and taxis hastily departing the scene. Realizing his pursuers were not robbers but surveillance cops, Ross got even angrier and shouted abuse at one of the mock taxi-drivers. He and Garner then complained to the local police.[5]

Records show that later that day, Garner kept an appointment with Lundy and expressed concern that, if the surveillance team had not been so incompetent, it might have spotted them having this very meeting. Lundy told him that different sections of the police had different tasks and if Garner was suspected of offences they would do their duty, which would include following him. Lundy had already done his duty by giving his commander advance notice that he would be meeting 'Granger' – a wise precaution.

Albany's longest probe concerned a series of arson attacks in the 1970s on properties owned by Garner in Islington and Hertfordshire. They seemed to have been organized by Garner himself, to winkle out sitting tenants or as insurance frauds. According to another Albany leak, the inquiry suspected that a man named David Austin was the chief fire-raiser and that he had been murdered. To dispel that misconception Garner revealed that Austin had disappeared for his own reasons. He later revealed Austin's whereabouts. Lundy passed any information upwards. In due course Albany had Austin arrested.

Albany was not wholly dedicated to Garner. Its task was to investigate all allegations against criminals made by supergrasses Young and Moriarty. For example, Young had placed Len Gibson and Dolph Aguda on forty-two and thirty-five robberies respectively. He said Gibson and Renalto Aguda had been on a £30,000 robbery in Tottenham just one month before the Silver Bullion job. Yet the only charge Clement could stump up against any of these men was against Gibson for receiving a stolen television set! Later even this charge was dropped. Despite its huge staff Albany had few successes. They included Patrick 'Parky' Barry, grassed by Young for the same Tottenham robbery on which he had placed Gibson. As Patrick Barry was also grassed by Garner over the 'forged fivers' job (for which he would receive nine years) this Albany triumph did not add a day to his time in jail. One curiosity is that if Parky Barry could be done for Tottenham, why not Gibson or Renalto Aguda?[6]

One man never arrested or even questioned by Albany, while it was under Clement's leadership, was Roy Garner. He was adamant that Young and Moriarty's allegations were malicious and vengeful because they thought he had grassed them in the past. He never discussed Albany's progress with Lundy nor did he ask his 'handler' to intervene, yet it may have struck both men that Albany's length might have had as much to do with 'getting Lundy' as getting him. Certainly Albany overlapped with the Stagg inquiry into allegations of corruption, mainly against Lundy. 'Stagg' did interview Garner, but to no effect for he had nothing to say against Lundy. Looking back, it seems strange that the man whom Clement's deputy, Superintendent Gerry Wiltshire, later branded 'the overlord of serious crime in London' was interrogated about the acts of a copper but not (until after Clement's departure) about his own alleged crimes.

Lundy says he never interfered with Operation Albany. He says he knew very little about its investigations and nothing about any acts of arson by Roy Garner. It is clear from Lundy's leaked report of 28 May 1981 that he did tell Powis of Garner's view that the supergrass allegations against him were malicious – a view which Garner himself forcefully expressed to Powis face-to-face.

However, Lundy also stated that he owed 'no allegiance' to Garner. Unlike many detectives, Lundy did not shield his informers from other officers' inquiries. He says he always told them they could expect no help from him if they were caught committing crime. Indeed, he would arrest them himself if he had evidence they were 'at it'. A person with no axe to grind – for or against him – is John Grieve, who was staff officer (right-hand man and office manager) to both DAC Powis and his successor. To a later inquiry Superintendent Grieve stated:

My view is that Mr Lundy did all he could professionally for his informer, and this was no more than many others did, and less than some . . . It has been put to me . . . that Mr Lundy was exceptional in the pressure he applied for his informer. I repeat that was not my experience.[7]

Despite his criminality, Roy Garner was an informer Scotland Yard badly needed if it was to keep the lid on violent organized crime in London. But was Garner part of that same problem? He certainly was, according to the man who ought to know best. In May 1983 none other than London's chief of detectives, David Powis, launched an astonishing attack on Garner from a witness box at Wood Green Crown Court. The occasion was a shotgun licence hearing on behalf of Garner's brother, David, who was appealing against a previous decision to revoke his licence. Roy too had lost his licence but had withdrawn his appeal. Even so Powis turned up and said: 'It could never be in the public interest for either Roy or David Garner to possess any firearm. It would be a danger to public safety and the peace.' How so? Powis offered this evidence against brother Roy:

I consider him to be the close associate of organized habitual criminals that are preying on the public in the Metropolis. I have come to the conclusion that Roy Garner has connections in the US with certain criminal factions. My colleague Ronald Steventon is conducting an intense inquiry into allegations against Roy Garner of crimes of violence, mainly robberies, arsons and conspiracy to pervert the course of justice in a murder inquiry and similar matters . . . I suspect that he funds criminals. Major crimes have to be funded with substantial funds and I believe that it is in this area that Garner is involved.

Powis was supported by Superintendent Wiltshire who said he believed Garner had been involved in five armed robberies between 1970 and 1978, and conspiracies to pervert justice and commit arsons. Wiltshire added that Garner's Tottenham club (Elton's) was a hangout of armed robbers and his associates were the 'top criminals in London today'. A final report on Garner's activities would be sent to the Director of Public Prosecutions in three months, said Powis. His onslaught had the desired effect: David Garner was refused a shotgun licence. A devastated Roy blasted back in purple prose matching Powis's: 'This is not Sicily and I don't belong to the Mafia. I'm no gangster. If I am a murderer, robber and arsonist, what am I doing walking free?'[8]

There was no answer to that, except that most of what Powis and Wiltshire had thrown at him came from the mouths of supergrasses Young and Moriarty. There was nothing to corroborate their hearsay allegations. As even the *Observer* pointed out: 'Police have no shred of proof of what they say that would stand up in court.'[9] Indeed, since the 'evidence' was almost all hearsay, it would not even be admissible in a criminal trial. Only in a non-criminal licence hearing, where hearsay evidence may be given in order to assess a person's character, could Powis have got away with his script. Overall, the unrestrained police act at Wood Green had the air of a show put on at a provincial theatre by a cast who knew it would never reach the West End.

Why Powis took such trouble to attack Garner at his brother's shotgun hearing is a mystery. It occurred almost a year after the *Observer* article, and two years before the *Observer* paid Powis and apologized. Soon after the hearing Tony Lundy had reason to see Powis. The Deputy Assistant Commissioner seemed anxious to justify his performance and said, 'Nobody will ever think he's an informant now, will they?' Powis seemed to think that by attacking Garner he had done him a favour.

Powis's remarks in court were widely and sensationally reported. Only the *Sunday Times* highlighted the paradox that in 1980 and 1981 Powis himself had been involved in the payment of huge rewards to the man he now painted in such evil colours.[10]

Powis himself seemed unaware that he might have done

Garner any harm. In a bizarre twist on 4 May 1984, a year after his ferocious tirade against Scotland Yard's prize informer, he rang Garner direct to ask him for information about a murder. Fortunately, Garner was not there to take the call.

In November 1984 the Yard's inability to jail its 'Mr Most Wanted' turned into public embarrassment. That was because Her Majesty's Customs and Excise had just done what the Yard had failed to do: it had won a conviction against Garner, his first in almost twenty years. He had been unable to resist the easy pickings of a new form of crime: VAT fraud.

The racket was astonishingly easy. All gold transactions were subject to Value Added Tax. If a firm sold gold to anyone it was obliged to charge an additional fifteen per cent VAT. On one million pounds-worth of gold, therefore, the VAT would be £150,000. This fifteen per cent was meant to be handed on to Customs and Excise within three months. The trick was to import Kruger-rands – South African gold coins on which no VAT was payable when brought into the country – and sell them on, charging VAT. By the time Customs realized what was going on and came to collect, the firm would have disappeared with all that VAT. It was not just fifteen per cent, however, as the racketeer could recycle his million many times over in a short space of time. As soon as a legitimate bullion dealer paid him back his million plus fifteen per cent, that sum could be used to buy more Kruger-rands abroad, instantly import them and sell them to the same dealer. Even if the racketeer sold the Kruger-rands at a loss, he would still make a rapid profit by pocketing the VAT.

From August 1982 until March 1983 a firm called Jencorose, controlled by Roy Garner, imported over £14 million-worth of Kruger-rands. Bullion dealers paid Jencorose almost £2 million VAT on these coins, and a further £130,000 to another Garner-controlled company. Garner had imported the coins from Jersey in quantities worth no more than £50,000 (thus benefiting from a postponed accounting system). They were brought in by tame couriers or in freight through three different airports. After some while Customs found out and kept observation, but by the time its officers pounced on Garner, his son and five confederates, the VAT had disappeared. Garner had spirited it abroad.[11]

Roy's runners (including his long-time partner Kenny Ross) pleaded guilty but he did not. He went on trial at the Old Bailey, was convicted and on 26 November 1984 was sentenced to four years' jail for conspiracy. He was also fined £150,000 and made criminally bankrupt. At his request, Scotland Yard drafted a letter charting his career as an informer for presentation to the judge. This was shown to a senior Customs officer on 21 November 1984 – prior to Garner's conviction. Next day Superintendent Grieve took it to Judge Richard Lowry who read it, not in open court but in the presence of only defence and prosecuting counsel. He said he was not surprised to learn Garner 'had a foot in both camps'. Grieve pointed out that it was 'an extraordinarily dangerous document' so its contents were recorded privately in the judge's chambers.[12]

In May 1985 Garner's case came before the Court of Appeal, and the Yard again supplied a letter chronicling his services as an informer. His sentence was reduced to three years and the fine quashed. This Yard effort was not because of any pressure from Lundy. It stemmed from David Powis who, on retiring in September 1984, honourably told his successor Brian Worth, 'had the decision been his, he would have provided "help"'. John Grieve saw nothing odd in this.

It has been suggested to me that this illustrates in some way

a special relationship or a degree of influence of Mr Lundy
with Mr Powis. This was not my experience and up to that
time I only saw him in the vicinity of the DAC's office on
two or three occasions. Other officers, some of much junior
rank, were [there] in connection with informers or other covert
matters much more often . . . [Steps were taken to protect
Garner in prison.] I have no direct recollection of Mr Lundy
requesting anything in connection with these events. I was in
any event doing far more for another informer at this same time
whose position was even more perilous in terms of exposure
then and there . . . I would be surprised if Mr Lundy had not
pressed his informer's case at this time, but it cannot have been
noteworthy, as many officers did so, some of whom stick out in
my mind.[13]

Nor did the fact that Garner had committed a monstrous
fraud reflect badly on Lundy. He had known Garner for
sixteen years but 'The Man' had never come up in any
investigation to which he had been assigned or which
he had generated through cracking supergrasses. He had
turned twenty supergrasses and jailed 200 major criminals
on their evidence, but none had so much as mentioned
Garner. Nor could his VAT fraud have been investigated by Lundy or any other policeman. Only Customs
had that power. In the early 1980s many people perpetrated the same Kruger-rand racket. Most were outwardly
respectable businessmen with no criminal record, who
opportunistically seized what seemed a once-in-a-lifetime
chance to steal a fortune with no risk of getting caught.
It was a kind of crime for which there was no typical
perpetrator, and there was no reason for Lundy to suspect
it was in Garner's repertoire.

He therefore had every excuse for not nailing Garner.
In contrast Operation Albany targeted Garner as its main
suspect but did not arrest or charge him, let alone put him
in prison. Of course it was difficult to find corroboration
of offences committed up to a dozen years earlier, but

it might be that Garner had not committed some of the crimes alleged by supergrasses Young and Moriarty. Even if he had, that would not invalidate him as an informer. Indeed criminality is the hallmark of a snout.

David Powis made this point in a BBC interview on winning his libel damages in 1985:

> The assertion made by some people that there is something intrinsically improper in a senior detective accepting information from a suspected criminal – who himself is likely to be involved in other organized crime, and who might be a 'target criminal' himself – that assertion is naive . . . You will not get information about armed robberies, those involving shootings and even murders by desperate men, by going to the Women's Voluntary Service or to a church bazaar. You get such information from other active criminals.[14]

Powis never referred to Garner by name, but the interview's introduction made it clear whom he was talking about. Garner himself was appalled when he heard the entire report in prison for the VAT fraud, and tried to steer clear of avenging inmates. Even so, he refused to go into Rule 43 accommodation (for prisoners in danger from other inmates) and has never accepted it since.

Albany's strongest case was made in 1985 when Superintendent Wiltshire submitted a report to the Director of Public Prosecutions concerning the arson attacks a decade earlier. John Grieve read the report and concluded, 'Garner was guilty but it was unproven.' The DPP came to the same conclusion and brought no charges. So what was Scotland Yard to do about this man who excited such wildly different reactions among senior detectives? The Yard's hierarchy was caught in a dilemma with extremely spiky horns. As a considerable criminal Garner ought to be pursued and, if a case could be made, he should be put on trial. As a top informer, however, he should not be cast aside. Using him was a two-edged sword, 'a high risk initiative', as they say in top-cop talk. Around this time, says John Grieve:

The grave legal and moral risks involved were discussed but in the light of other actions we were taking at the time, and problems being faced in policing the capital, my advice was that we should continue to maintain a 'responsive' contact with 'Granger' and that we were obliged to fulfil our responsibilities to him in terms of protection and help.[15]

Albany finally got its man in October 1985 when he was charged with forgery over a false passport. This earned him a nine-month jail term to run concurrently with his VAT sentence. He continued to inform even when he was in prison, and kept going when he came out again at the end of 1986. It is difficult to see what good this did him – in some ways it destroyed him – but Garner was a compulsive grass. For him, informing was almost an addiction.

As for his handler, Detective Superintendent Tony Lundy, he was having his own troubles. Most could have been avoided if he had sacrificed informers as readily as some sections of the force for which he worked. Instead he fought back in his own tenacious way.

14

'A Corrupt Officer'

Throughout 1981 Tony Lundy served as detective superintendent at 'Q' District headquarters at Wembley, which
serves a population of 450,000 people. Under a chief
superintendent he was now responsible for the investigation of all major crime including murders. He led one
inquiry into the gruesome death of Mrs Margaret Cross, an
elderly woman who was found naked and mutilated on her
living-room floor, with dozens of knife wounds. Suspicion
fell on a relative but Lundy's intuition led him to suspect
a nineteen-year-old youth who lived next door. His family
had provided him with an alibi, but Lundy interrogated
him and eventually he confessed. Through solving this
and other killings, Lundy built up an 'excellent' record
as a murder investigator.[1]

While at Wembley Lundy was trained as a hostage
negotiator and took part in a large operation on Cyprus
with military and security service personnel. Perhaps
the strangest duty he performed during these years was
investigating complaints against other policemen – strange
only because he was himself being simultaneously investigated by the Stagg inquiry. The early 1980s, therefore,
were even more tempestuous years for him than his time
on Finchley Robbery Squad. Indeed, supergrass trials
continued to occupy much of his time:

I was being investigated from pillar to post, but for three years
I seemed to be living at the Old Bailey. I had six courts running
at one stage. I was getting out of one witness box, jumping into
another one, out of that into another, days at a time. And the
same defence barristers kept strapping me. I was investigating

murders half the time, and I was the victim of attempted murder – character assassination – for the other half.

Like the boxer he was, Lundy appeared to absorb all this punishment unflinchingly, taking it as part of the job. His stamina and resilience seemed to be overcoming all career difficulties, and by January 1982 he was chosen for an intermediate command course at Bramshill, the national police college. Completing the three-month course, he wrote a thesis on supergrasses, 'Accomplices in Crime'. It was highly commended, which was not surprising; he knew more about 'supergrass policing' than any other copper and was its most successful practitioner.

When the course ended, Lundy transferred to the head-quarters of 'X' District, in Ealing, next door to Wembley. Here again he led investigations into many murders and was applauded as 'a dedicated professional with a constant urge to get on with the job', but his career had again come to a halt. In 1982 he was eligible for promotion to chief superintendent but was not even seen for an interview. He realized that until he was cleared by 'Stagg' he would have to mark time as a superintendent. So ambitious a man was bound to feel frustrated. More upsetting still, the steady drip of hostile press stories was affecting his family. The first time anyone gets bad headlines is always a shock to relatives but from 1980 Tony Lundy suffered ten years of media attack. His family were particularly upset by the *Observer*. In April 1982 its tenacious reporter David Leigh called Lundy at work about the Silver Bullion affair. The detective refused to discuss it, a decision confirmed by Scotland Yard's Press Bureau. Leigh and his colleague Paul Lashmar then turned up at his home at ten at night demanding to speak to him. They were turned away. After another brush-off from Lundy, on 5 May 1982 Leigh called a solicitor named Roland Pelly and spoke as if Pelly acted for Lundy. Pelly had once represented Mrs Lundy over a traffic accident but he had never acted for Lundy and told Leigh so. Later the *Observer* wrongly claimed Lundy 'shared' Pelly's services with Roy Garner and Kenny Ross.[2] The point of that comment, it seems, was to bond Lundy even closer with men who, the newspaper mistakenly claimed, had *both* received the bullion reward on his recommendation.

The *Observer* reporters had only been doing their job, of course, by visiting Lundy at home. Equally, coping with a hostile press ought to be part of a detective's job description these days – and written on his wife's marriage contract – but the Lundys were also victims of a bizarre crime which some newspapers later reported in such a way that the real felon seemed to be Lundy himself. In April 1981 Vi Lundy arrived home with her three young daughters after spending the weekend in the North of England. It was around lunchtime and she knew Tony would be at work, so she was surprised to see the swing door of the integral garage up, and an unfamiliar car parked inside. She parked her own car on the road and sat for a moment wondering if some workers were doing a job for Tony in the house. Then she saw a head at the back of the garage and a flurry of activity. Suddenly two men jumped in the car and drove out of the garage across the front lawn in order to avoid Vi's car parked across the drive. This manoeuvre involved smashing into an oak tree before the pair steamed north up the road to the village of Shenley in Hertfordshire.

Vi ran in the house, saw there had been a burglary and rang the police. She jumped in the car, turned round and sped off in hot pursuit of the burglars. The road to Shenley is countryfied, and there are woods on either side. When Vi reached a sharp bend she saw the burglars' car. It had rolled over and lay upside down in a ditch. The burglars were nowhere to be seen, but scattered all around was the property they had stolen: television sets, Olympic coin sets which Tony had brought back for his daughters from his official trip to Montreal, a stamp album, a clock, a few old pens, and lots of almost worthless domestic junk.

Very soon the police arrived. The burglars could not have gone far, so the Lundy girls jumped in patrol cars to try and spot them in the neighbourhood. The girls recognized one in a telephone box and soon both were captured. By this time Tony Lundy had been called home. He saw the trail of damage and went to Boreham Wood Police Station to find out who had been arrested. He wanted to know if the burglars already knew him – had he arrested them in the past, for instance – or had they hit his house by chance. The local detective constable, John Compton, told him their names were Bryson and McCarthy and they came from Hayes in Middlesex. This struck Lundy as odd. Most household break-ins are committed by people who live nearby, but Hayes is some fifteen miles from the Lundys' home. Also the house was on a main road, easily visible to passers-by, so it was hardly a good place to burgle.

Lundy played no part in the case. He never interviewed the men or saw them. Nor did he make a statement as the victim; his wife did. All the stolen property was taken to the police station and listed. The Lundys did not get it back for weeks. Later Tony heard that Keith Bryson had been released on bail. In January 1982 he was jailed for twelve months. That should have been the end of the matter but in February 1983 Lundy received a phone call about a 'conspiracy to rob' trial going on at Willesden Crown Court. The defendant, Keith Brown, was claiming he had been fitted up by police because, they allegedly said, 'Mr Lundy was very annoyed with him.' Brown, it transpired, was the person who had organized bail for Bryson when he was caught burgling Lundy's home. To keep him out of jail Brown had put up a £5,000 surety and agreed to give him a job.

Bryson had come to court on Brown's behalf to say that in Lundy's house he had found a black attaché case containing over £40,000-worth of American and Spanish currency but he was charged with stealing goods worth only £3,670. The case and its contents had vanished. Bryson claimed this made him very pleased – 'I thought, "Cor, that's a result"' – because, instead of getting as much as five years in jail for a big theft, he would now get only one year.[3]

The prosecution asked Lundy to rebut this claim, which he was more than willing to do. He never had such sums of foreign currency – at home or anywhere else – and never had such a case. He recalls telling the court: 'You'll never find anyone to say they've seen me with a black executive briefcase 'cos I've never had one. The only briefcase I have is a pigskin thing I've had for twenty years. It's out-and-out lies. There's no such thing.'

Lundy reflected on the nonsense of it all. If the burglars *had* hit upon a fortune in cash, why did they bother to steal near-worthless TV sets, pens and coin sets as well? And *when* did the briefcase disappear? Bryson claimed it was by the car when they rolled it over in the ditch. How remarkably dumb of him not to take it with him when he ran off! Bryson said that DC Compton knew about the missing money. The case must therefore have been picked up by police. If so, twenty officers may have been in the conspiracy to make it vanish: uniformed men, traffic patrol cops, tow-truck drivers, as well as detectives.

Compton testified at Brown's trial denying Bryson's tale. Denials also came from two Barnes Robbery Squad men accused of framing Brown on Lundy's behalf. Lundy said he had never met those men and never discussed his case with anyone on their squad. Indeed, he did not

even know that Brown was on trial until after the trial
started.

Brown was acquitted, mainly because the direct evidence against him was weak. Bryson's evidence must have
helped, of course, just as it harmed Lundy who saw it as
another orchestrated assault. On arriving at this obscure
and rarely reported court, he found the press box packed.
The case was prominently reported in *City Limits* and the
Observer. It was also featured on *Private Spy*, a tacky
videotape mixing peep-show pornography with exposé
journalism, distributed in the autumn of 1983. It was
fronted by John McVicar, the robber who served eighteen
years in jail before becoming a journalist, and featured
Bryson, Brown and two men cleared of charges brought
by Lundy: Danny Gowan and Charlie Smith. There were
some amusing lines – amusing for anyone other than
Lundy. Smith said he was 'very full of himself. I don't say
he's a normal person. There's something wrong with him.
He really thinks he's been sent on a mission by somebody
above.' When hauled in for questioning by Lundy's men,
Smith said he was told, 'Don't upset Top Man. He's just
lost a game of squash. We'll all suffer.' The squad built
Lundy up in a frightening manner: 'It's like you're going
to face God!' When 'Top Man' saw the video, however, he
was more upset by the accusation that he had a Yorkshire
accent.

Merely by reciting Bryson's claims, such a programme
could make it seem that Lundy really did have this vast
fortune in currency. And, as he could not have saved
it from his modest cop's pay, he must have come by
it corruptly. Indeed, 'Lundy-watchers' might have concluded it was either his kickback share of the Silver
Bullion reward or his profit from selling the twelve missing ingots. *Private Spy* certainly gave that impression by
re-hashing all the old allegations over the Silver Bullion

job, yet at the time of the burglary the reward had not been paid.

Detective Chief Superintendent Stagg interviewed Keith Bryson for a day but found no evidence to support his story. There again the matter might have ended, except that on the night of 1 May 1984 Bryson's partner on the Lundy job, Mark McCarthy, was arrested for another burglary and taken to Hayes Police Station in West London. The following morning he was interviewed by Detective Constable Bob Caldecourt who had dealt with him in the past. In small talk after the interview, Caldecourt asked McCarthy how his wife and family were getting on. The detective then mentioned the *Private Spy* video which he had heard of but not seen. According to a statement made by Caldecourt later that day:

McCarthy stated he hadn't seen it and that it was a 'load of bollocks anyway'. I asked him what he meant. He said, 'Look, we did it and I did me bird [prison sentence]. I want none of that.' I said, 'Are you saying it's all nonsense?' He said, 'They think we were put up to do it. We were over that way doing screwing [burglaries]; me and Bryson saw a crate and fruit juice outside a house. We knocked, there was no one in so we got in by the side window. I got a brief-case. It was the only one there. It was empty. I used it to cart the stuff out we nicked.'

I said, 'So there wasn't any money?' He said, 'No, of course not.' I said, 'Are you prepared to speak to someone else about this?' He said, 'Yes, but I'm not grassing anyone.'

At this point Caldecourt left the interview room to tell his chief superintendent what McCarthy was saying. Caldecourt then returned and asked if McCarthy had ever been asked to back up the allegation against Lundy.

He said someone had asked him to, but he wanted no part in it. I asked him what else he knew about it. He replied that Bryson had the needle because he'd been turned over twice since, and on one occasion he had rung McVicar who sent a photographer along. The 'Old Bill' [police] had searched Bryson's house and found nothing but had left it okay. Bryson emptied all the drawers and things before the photographer arrived. McCarthy had been present throughout and was there when the photographer had asked Bryson to appear in the photograph and to try and look distraught.

Caldecourt informed McCarthy that other persons might wish to speak to him about his story, and then took him back to his cell. Returning to the CID office, Caldecourt was told that officers from CIB 2 (meaning, the Stagg inquiry) would be arriving at midday. They arrived on the stroke of noon and interviewed McCarthy. Caldecourt meantime was told not to leave the station. From the investigators' manner, he felt they were not pleased. He was also struck by the contrast between the speed with which they arrived at Hayes that day and the fact that they had not spoken to McCarthy at any time during the fifteen months since Bryson had made his damaging attack on Lundy in open court. Surely, 'Stagg' should have spoken to McCarthy straight after that outburst, for he was the only possible witness to the truth or otherwise of Bryson's claim. Caldecourt scarcely knew Lundy and was not a friend of his, but he did feel that it was time someone in the Metropolitan Police hierarchy stood up in public and defended Lundy against attacks such as Bryson's which were manifestly untrue.

Tony Lundy himself had first been interviewed by Alan Stagg on 5 November 1982, three months before Bryson made his allegation. By that time Stagg had been at work for nearly two years, a period so long that it may indicate he had difficulty finding much wrong in Lundy's conduct. At this opening encounter Stagg raised allegations made by Billy Young and other criminals. Lundy denied them all. Many were instantly dismissible, all were hearsay, few were ever raised again. Those few are investigated elsewhere in this book, in the order they were leaked to the media and published. However, one is best examined here: the row over the 'bogus Hatton Garden job'.

As explained in Chapter 8, early in 1980 a pair of Hatton Garden jewellers, John Heath and Wilfred Hogg, pretended to be robbed of £778,000 worth of jewellery. They hired two top-grade crooks to attack, kidnap and dump them, then give back the jewels and get a share of the fraudulent insurance claim. Unfortunately for the conspirators, Roy Garner knew both the jewellers and found out that it was all a set-up. He had been visiting the premises a few days before the crime and recognized two professional criminals who were there at the time.

As is clear from Scotland Yard documents leaked later in an attempt to discredit Lundy, Garner gave him this information by the beginning of March 1980. This caused Lundy to set up an intensive surveillance operation on all the suspects. Some seven weeks later he received a phone call from Nigel Dungate, then a detective superintendent with Number 6 Regional Crime Squad, based at Brighton. He told Lundy about a Sussex constable who had useful information. The pair visited Lundy and the constable told him he had an informant who was saying that the Hogg and Heath robbery was a fake. According to Lundy:

I say, 'As it happens, we believe that too and we're working on it.' I had already got the surveillance squad working on the jewellers and robbers, photographing them. We're ticking along on it, watching all four, before Dungate had even got in touch.

Then the Sussex man says that his informant had said Heath's long-time girlfriend was involved. She was supposed to be leaving the country next day, taking all this nicked jewellery with her. So I say, 'Oh, that's interesting!'

This forced us to act quicker than we wanted to. We weren't ready, because we still did not have enough evidence to justify arrests. What the Sussex connection did was trigger off events too soon. Next morning we nick the girlfriend and pull her in. Sure enough, she was going abroad, so we keep her in custody and interrogate her. She was a lovely woman, and I was ashamed to have to lock her in a cell for a night. She missed her flight, of course, all on the strength of what this Sussex informer had told Dungate's man.

It turned out that she was nothing to do with it whatsoever. She'd never even spoken to Heath for a year. She was totally innocent and she was later paid compensation for wrongful arrest and detention. This compensation was paid willingly. What had happened to her was diabolical.

Meantime I crack Hogg and then Heath. They tell us to look in a barn on land owned by Heath in Buckinghamshire, and in safe-deposit boxes, and we recover the entire three-quarter million pounds' worth of jewels. Heath only admitted his role, but Hogg named the robbers who did the job. They had picked the top league of villains to fake it! We then drag the robbers in, they won't admit it, but with what we knew – and with Hogg as a potential witness – we charge them. Then Hogg lost his nerve. No way will he give evidence, he'll just be pleading guilty to his own part. So the DPP decides there's insufficient evidence against the robbers and he drops their charges, but the jewellers plead guilty and get five years.

Again, leaked documents make it clear that Lundy put in a reward application through David Powis as soon as arrests had been made and the jewels were recovered. He stated that it was his information about the robbers which had broken Hogg. Lundy now says:

At first Hogg wouldn't admit even knowing them, but by then we had surveillance photos of him with them. That was what forced him to collapse. Never mind the fact that he later chickened out of giving evidence against them, the prior information had proved vital. Without it we'd never have broken Hogg or Heath. The information from Sussex came afterwards – and it was absolute cobblers, as it turned out!

Now the jewellery had been recovered, the insurers no longer had to pay out £778,000 on a bogus claim. Instead their assessors were obliged to hand over a ten per cent reward, rounded down to £75,000. They accepted the recommendation of DAC Powis and the Deputy Chief Constable of Sussex that it should be split down the middle: £37,500 to 'Dave Granger' on Lundy's recommendation, the other £37,500 to the Sussex informer, whose pseudonym was 'Sean Murphy'. Powis paid 'Granger' his share on 8 September 1980 (in the presence of DAC Steventon) and 'Murphy' his on 22 September (in the presence of Sussex's Deputy Chief Constable). 'No problems. All sweet and above board. End of story,' says Lundy, until some two years later when David Powis sent for him.

I go up to his office, he's sitting there, and on his desk is the big batch of papers on the Hogg and Heath job, which was dead and buried by that stage. He says, 'Tell me again about that Hogg and Heath job.' So I told him the background. 'Oh yes. Right. Now I remember that clearly.'

So I say, 'What's the matter with Hogg and Heath? What do you want to know about that?' 'Nothing, I just needed to know some of the background.' I said, 'There must be something?' 'No, no. Don't worry about it,' and then he chatted about other things.

Then he said to me, 'Nigel Dungate: would he want to do you any harm?' I was mystified. I looked at him and said, 'Dungate? No. Shouldn't think so. I've given him some good jobs, over a period, but I've not seen him for a long time. Why do you ask that?' 'Nothing. I just wondered how you got on with him.' 'I've not spoken to him hardly at all.'

Powis says no more, and I hear nothing else until I'm being interviewed by Stagg when they suddenly start asking me all about the Hogg and Heath job. I'm being accused of having put in a false reward application. Then I find out that – after all the publicity about Roy Garner and me – Dungate had gone to the Yard complaining he had always thought I had made an 'iffy' reward application, and that the information had come from the Sussex informant.

The truth is, the Sussex informant got his £37,500 reward for wrong information. Not only that, he had *cost* the Metropolitan

Police a compensation pay-out to Heath's ex-girlfriend for wrongful arrest and detention!

Lundy was even more surprised when he learned that Nigel Dungate had been transferred onto the Stagg inquiry and was investigating other complaints against Lundy. He was shortly promoted to chief superintendent and stayed on 'Stagg' until it finished. As Lundy sees it, 'I had all that hassle over Hogg and Heath for nothing!'

By a curious coincidence, while Dungate was busy investigating Lundy's dealings with informers, he chanced to bump into one of his own. A motley bit-player in Britain's pageant of crime is a character named Francis Attard. Or is he David Attard? Or is he Frank or Francis Giles or Jarvis? Or David Levy? Or Bill Oliver? Or Laurie Upshon? Or John Monfort? Or Mark Bayliss? Forever changing his name, Attard had been an informant of Nigel Dungate's since 1976.

On 22 September 1982 Dungate visited the secure 'supergrass unit' at Reading jail to interview Micky Gervaise. This was months after Gervaise had turned against the prosecution when testifying in the Old Bailey trials of Bob Deanus and John Goodwin. Goodwin's re-trial was imminent but Gervaise was not to testify and would soon lose his supergrass status. In the meantime he had made allegations against police, including Tony Lundy, 'to the effect that you had shared in the reward money paid out after the Silver Bullion robbery on 24.3.80, and that you had been a party to the theft or retention of a number of bars of silver after its recovery'.[4]

Reading's supergrass unit contained only some half dozen prisoners and, while visiting Gervaise, Dungate happened to see his old informer, Francis Attard. The pair had a chat, which Gervaise observed. Attard later claimed that, after Dungate left, Gervaise asked him if Dungate trusted him. When Attard said 'he's always found me reliable', Gervaise offered him 'five grand in readies' (£5,000) to tell Dungate some 'Jack and Danny' (misinformation) 'about Old Bill corruption that we were involved in.'

When you see Dungate, we want you to tell him that you heard from us that Lundy and his pals had the missing twelve bars of silver and part of the reward money. Lundy and some of his mob are due to be put in the frame, and Dungate will believe whatever we tell him . . . I have done the business on Tony Lundy good and proper. Now he will know what it is like to be fucked.

But the supergrass Gervaise was about to be grassed! On 5 November 1982 Attard told this story in a statement he made to Dungate alleging that Gervaise was telling lies against Lundy to fit him up. He said that in truth Gervaise and Fiori had told him they had only ever had corrupt dealings with one detective and he was not Lundy.

In an earlier statement to Dungate on 27 October, Attard claimed that Gervaise had said that he, Gervaise, had the twelve bars missing from the Silver Bullion haul, and had them hidden away abroad. Then Fiori had said that when he got parole, he would be selling the silver on Gervaise's behalf. Gervaise and Fiori had both told Attard they had contracted their corruption tales to the *Observer* for thousands of pounds, for publication after their release. This was untrue. Fiori said his story detailed 'corruption up to the rank of assistant commissioner', while Gervaise said he had put in a 'fat chapter on Lundy'.[5]

Attard was claiming that a 'fit-up' of monstrous proportions was being constructed against Lundy. On 21 June 1983 he sent a letter to Lundy at Ealing Police Station. Signing himself 'Francis Giles', he said he wrote 'in a voluntary capacity' about 'a long standing matter which "others" have – wrongly – challanged [sic] your integrity. After much consideration I feel I have a duty to come forward.' He said he would not speak to police, only to Lundy's solicitors. Lundy discussed the approach with his commander, then sent his solicitor to find out what 'Giles' had to say. That was how Lundy discovered that 'Giles' was in Reading with supergrasses Fiori and Gervaise, both of whom Lundy had forced to 'turn'. 'Giles' told the solicitor this pair were telling lies about Lundy to 'fit him up', and had offered him a lot of money to help them. He said he had already made statements to Superintendent Dungate, but that Dungate was annoyed with him for alleging there was a fit-up. (There is no evidence to support the claim that Dungate expressed any annoyance.)

Lundy reported all this to his commander but, as 'Giles' had already spoken to Dungate, there was no need to do any more. Then in October 1983 'Giles' made an extraordinary request through Lundy's solicitor: would Lundy pay money to the convict's girlfriend to meet a rates bill? Lundy was not amused: 'I absolutely refused to have anything to do with Giles. He seemed to think I owed him something for having made a statement to Dungate which proved I was being fitted up.'

The solicitor wrote back saying Lundy would not assist. 'Giles' replied that he was 'disappointed and really gutted that a person I saw it proper to assist had shut the door in my face'. He asked Lundy to make a statement to help when his conviction came before the Court of Appeal. Lundy refused. In January 1984 'Giles' again wrote saying he was disappointed, but when the Court of Appeal heard his case in March 1984 Chief Superintendent Dungate described him as a valuable source of information, and his sentence was cut by eighteen months to three years.

Lundy had refused to help for the compelling reason that he knew nothing about 'Giles', so how could he speak for him? Had Lundy known *anything* he would have run a mile, for 'Giles' was that most dangerous kind of informer: a chronic and compulsive liar.

In his long career as a petty criminal and con-man, the man born Francis Peter Attard in Poole, Dorset, in 1948 has caused endless grief. By 1983 he had been sentenced twenty-one times over a total of 185 crimes, mostly burglary, theft and deception. He had spent more than half his life in approved schools, borstals and prisons. Within months of coming out of jail he would always get caught again, plead guilty and go back inside. His victims were not only householders and shopkeepers: they included fellow-criminals (whom he would betray for any deal he could get with police), the police (to whom he would tell any lie to get a deal), and reporters (to whom he would tell anything they wanted to hear, preferably for money). In 1975 he was arrested for handling stolen property and obtaining goods by deception. That was when he first came across Nigel Dungate to whom he offered information about a drugs deal and a conspiracy to murder a prosecution witness. In 1976 he gave evidence for the prosecution in that case.

For years Attard has claimed that, on remand in Wandsworth prison in 1976, he was visited by Special Branch officers accompanied by Dungate, who had recommended him as a helpful source. The Special Branch men suggested he gain the confidence of another remand prisoner in his cell. This was Khalil Waffai, a Jordanian charged with the theft of the 'Harold Wilson Papers': documents stolen two years earlier in a burglary at premises where the Labour Prime Minister's belongings had been stored while he was in opposition. Some of the papers had already been recovered but the idea was to get Waffai to disgorge the rest. Attard has claimed that Special Branch suggested he offer to buy the remaining papers from Waffai. He claims the Jordanian agreed and that, after £15,000 was paid into his bank account, he had the papers delivered to Attard's solicitors. Attard claims that, after these efforts for the nation, he was told he would get a suspended sentence for his crimes, but when he appeared at Kingston Crown Court in June 1976 he was jailed for two years. Nigel Dungate, then an inspector, did what he could. In mitigation he said Attard had helped him over the drugs case, yet Attard still felt double-crossed by Special Branch.

It should be said that the burglary in which Waffai was involved was not political. The intention had always been to sell the papers for money. Waffai was duly convicted and jailed, but he never made any deal with Attard. Whatever papers had been in his hands had already been recovered when he was arrested selling them to a pornographer who 'shopped' him to the police. As Waffai said later, he recognized Attard as an informer as soon as he came in the cell, so he told him nothing and never made any deal. He never gave him any papers because he had none left to deliver. Thus Attard has never had any Wilson papers.

By 1977 Attard was out of jail. He committed at least fourteen more offences and was caught again. While at liberty he approached national newspapers offering them the missing Wilson papers. He was already back in jail when his offer came to the attention of Gerry Gable and myself, two reporters on *The London Programme*, a TV current affairs show made by LWT. He was then calling himself David Levy. We met his girlfriend who was acting for him. When asked where the papers were, she seemed embarrassed but said they had been buried on a golf course outside London. We made frequent visits to see 'Levy' in Pentonville. Seeking confirmation that he was reliable, I even met Inspector Dungate. At that time the media were obsessed with finding the Wilson papers which were believed to hold the key to Wilson's mysterious, sudden resignation in 1976. I was as gullible as other reporters and thought, by supplying 'Levy' with large bars of chocolate and one-ounce pouches of roll-your-own tobacco, I could persuade him to part with the papers so they could be splashed on television. I must have legally supplied him with enough Old Holborn to make him a Pentonville tobacco baron, yet I never got my hands on those papers. After several months I gave up the hunt. I decided 'Levy' had no papers and was just trying to con me into some deal, presumably financial. I even met someone purporting to be his 'literary agent', but I am relieved to say I never paid 'Levy' or his agent any money.

In October 1978 he was sentenced to four-and-a-half years in jail for his usual: theft, burglary and deception. In 1981 he escaped from prison, and then obtained over £130,000 worth of goods by deception. He was caught, escaped again, recaptured and sent down for a few more years. He was still informing when he was placed in Reading's 'supergrass unit' in August 1983. By November 1984 he was out again on parole. He got straight 'at it' – using yet more names – and was back in jail by December. Astonishingly, in January 1985 he was freed on police bail and went on the rampage again.

During his short spell at liberty before Christmas 1984 Attard performed at his vintage worst, especially with the media. He met a TVS reporter named Mark Bayliss and spun him the old tale about having copies of the Wilson papers and tapes of the 'Tiger' talks (between Wilson and Ian Smith, the UDI Prime Minister of Rhodesia). He wanted money; TVS were not prepared to pay, and neither tapes nor papers materialized. Attard also talked of prison beatings and an IRA escape perpetrated with the connivance of prison warders, but his most tempting tale concerned a certain detective. He told Mark Bayliss that:

> while in prison, he had been approached by a solicitor acting for a police officer called Lundy. He said he had been asked to give false evidence to assist Lundy. A supergrass called Gervaise was making allegations against Lundy. Attard said he signed a statement that Gervaise had confessed to him that the allegations against Lundy were untrue. Attard said he had subsequently given evidence in court to this effect and 'got Lundy off the hook'. He told us it was quite untrue that Gervaise had made any such confession to him. He said in return Lundy had arranged for £2,000 to be paid to him into a bank in Bournemouth. We asked him to provide the bank statement, which he never did. We asked him to tell us the name of the bank manager. Eventually he gave us a name, but there was no bank manager of that name in Bournemouth. We asked him to give us the right name but he never did.[6]

TVS staff eventually rumbled Attard, whom they were calling 'Bill Oliver', but not before he had conned them out of thousands of pounds: ten days' hotel and living expenses, drinks on the tab, taxis back and forth from Southampton to Bournemouth, and a £1,000 car-hire bill in London. Purporting to work for TVS he had also conned an electronics store into handing him equipment worth £30,000. TVS found out only when the invoice arrived. Having taken TVS's money, 'Oliver' stole the names of three of its staff: Laurie Upshon, John Monfort and reporter Mark Bayliss. Worse still, he adopted Mark Bayliss's identity while perpetrating further acts of deception. When arrested, he called himself Bayliss and even gave evidence at the Old Bailey in that name. The occasion was the December 1985 trial of a man accused of murder by stabbing. 'Bayliss' claimed that in a chance meeting in the 'cage' at Marylebone Magistrates' Court, the defendant – a complete stranger – had confided he had killed the man.

He then asked 'Bayliss' to go to an address and hire a hit-man to kill the only witness. This evidence was as false as the name in which it was given. The defendant, Sean O'Neill, was cleared.

Defence counsel told 'Bayliss': 'You make up information and you try to sell it.' That was certainly true of his claims against Lundy. First he sought to ingratiate himself with Lundy. Then he tried to get money from him. When Lundy refused, he invented false evidence against him and peddled it round the media. TVS were very near to broadcasting a documentary built on his allegations, when staff realized he was a liar and con-man. However, the *Observer* went one stage further. A few days before Christmas 1984 Attard inveigled Lundy's solicitor into meeting him. The solicitor suggested the main bar at the Cumberland Hotel where Attard made a number of remarks suggesting that, after all he had done for Lundy, the detective owed him a substantial payment. The solicitor knew of nothing done by Attard which deserved any payment so he made a series of non-committal answers. He was vaguely aware of people staring at him in the bar, but it was so crowded that he thought nothing of this. He was later told that Attard had been wired with a tape-recorder, and that *Observer* reporters had made a transcript of the tape. As the solicitor had said nothing on it to justify Attard's claim that Lundy owed him money, nothing appeared in the newspaper.

But Attard was not easily defeated. In July 1986 Lundy was served with a Form 163 saying:

A Mr David ATTARD alias Francis GILES has alleged that you, and a solicitor . . . conspired to pay him certain sums of money as an inducement for him to give false testimony at any subsequent Criminal or Disciplinary proceedings which might be held to adjudicate on the allegations made against you by a Mr Michael GERVAISE.

Even though this was palpable nonsense, it still had to be investigated by the Complaints Investigation Bureau and a report sent to the Director of Public Prosecutions. In September 1986 the DPP responded by saying 'criminal proceedings are not being contemplated' against Lundy over this matter. The man who should have been 'done', of course, was Attard for perjury and wasting so much public money. The chronology shows conclusively that he made his allegations against Gervaise seven months before he even made himself known to Lundy. *If* what he said about Gervaise *really was* false testimony, he had made it up for his own benefit, not for any bribe from the long-suffering detective. As Lundy says: 'It makes a change for someone to accuse *me* of paying *them* money. Usually it's the other way round.'

Back in August 1983 all the best efforts of Alan Stagg, Nigel Dungate and co. were submitted to the DPP in the Stagg inquiry's final report. Its contents were summed up in an *Observer* story headlined 'Corruption Net Widens':

A senior detective has been named as a corruption suspect in eight major criminal cases, in an unprecedented 4,000-page report sent to the Director of Public Prosecutions. The policeman, based in London, is linked in the report to allegations that he watered down evidence in court for favoured criminals, fabricated evidence to obtain convictions and arranged for criminal associates to receive rewards . . . The DPP's office, which has been in possession of the report for six months, is treating the case with the utmost secrecy. For legal reasons it is not possible to name the detective.[7]

The detective was Tony Lundy but, after digesting the 4,000 pages, the DPP found no evidence on which to prosecute him or any other officer. The Director saw that 'Stagg' contained no hard evidence, only hearsay allegations, impossible to substantiate, from criminals or even anonymous sources. There was not even enough dirt to put Lundy through internal discipline hearings. Indeed, in November 1984 Lundy was awarded the Police Long Service and Good Conduct Medal, and early in 1985 he was given final clearance on all the 'Stagg' allegations.

It took all that time – four years – and eventually a number of us were sent for and given words of advice. Mike Taylor, Pat Fleming, virtually everybody who had been inquired into in some shape or form, had words of advice about odd little faults in pocket books – a blank line left here . . . petty things. At the very end there were just these words of advice. And that was it! So after all that damned time I'm cleared of everything!

By then, however, the Stagg inquiry had done Lundy immense damage. Not only had it leaked to the press, its very duration had paralysed his career. In the early 1980s, as always, he received glowing annual reports from commanders yet in June 1983 he failed a board for promotion to chief superintendent. He felt particularly aggrieved because Steventon had sat on the board, even though he was in charge of 'Stagg': he was his 'prosecutor' and his 'judge'. Lundy had assumed that out of fairness Steventon would withdraw during Lundy's interview, but he did not. Instead he questioned Lundy over his informants, the bad publicity and why he was not suing the newspapers. Lundy explained his difficulty about naming informants, and over money, having been refused representation by Metropolitan Police solicitors. What vexed him was that Steventon was already aware of that refusal: he himself had made the decision. In contrast, David Powis had been granted legal support and used it to win substantial damages from the *Observer*.

Lundy was so upset that on 27 June 1983 he sent a confidential report to London's top cop, Commissioner Sir

Kenneth Newman, requesting a private interview. Everyone in the force has the right to make such a request, and to send it under sealed cover, marked for the eyes of the commissioner only or his personal staff. Lundy pointed out that, despite his outstanding record, officers with less service had been promoted ahead of him. He then said:

I find it impossible to put out of my mind that there is prejudice because of attacks by criminals and in the media, and the prolonged investigation by officers under the command of DAC STEVENTON. I accept that a thorough investigation into allegations which have been made is essential, but I am concerned about the length of time which has passed since such investigations commenced . . .

I have personally been responsible for the arrest and conviction of numerous major criminals, probably more than any other CID officer ever, and it is my success in that field which has led to all the allegations being made . . . There is no doubt that criminals serving [life imprisonment or up to twenty-five years] see their only hope for early release is to attack me and then appeal or petition accordingly. Officers who have not been in the forefront of the operational field are not subject to unfounded allegations and it is not right if, as I suspect, I am being punished because of my successful career as an operational detective . . .

I have not complained before, but it is disturbing when one considers that I was responsible for the arrest and conviction of over 200 major criminals in less time than a squad of officers have taken to investigate the complaints.

I believe that I have been deprived of justifiable promotion because of unjustified allegations, particularly as such matters were raised at my selection board by DAC STEVENTON. I believe that it was unfair that the officer in overall charge of investigations against me should participate on my selection board . . . I have spoken to many senior officers, and none can remember a similar situation where an officer in charge of 'current' investigations into allegations has participated in the selection procedure of a junior officer . . .

I feel it is inevitable that allegations will be made against me for a long time to come, and I wish to discuss my unfair treatment and future career prospects.

Soon after sending this report, Lundy was called in by Assistant Commissioner Gilbert Kelland, head of the entire Criminal Department, one rank above Steventon and only two ranks below Commissioner Newman. As Lundy waited to enter his office, Steventon walked out. Lundy was ushered in and to his horror saw his own report – for the eyes of the commissioner only – open in front of Kelland on his desk. Kelland immediately fell into the sympathetic, avuncular style which was his hallmark. He said he had been asked by the commissioner to see Lundy on his behalf to discuss the confidential report. Lundy told him he had no right to see it but Kelland proceeded to tell him he was unwise and wrong in his opinion of Steventon. Far from being his enemy, Steventon was on Lundy's side and would not do him any harm. Things would be different at the next selection board. Meantime he should think seriously about dropping his request to see the commissioner, as it would not do him any good. Lundy recalls, 'It was obvious I had no choice in the matter and I left totally demoralized.'

Lundy had little alternative but to drop his request, yet even so Steventon did him immense harm. Less than six weeks later, when Steventon sent the 'Stagg' report to the DPP, he also sent a copy to Deputy Commissioner Albert Laugharne (in overall charge of force discipline), appending a minute destroying Lundy's character. Lundy found out about this minute only three years later, when parts of it were quoted on a programme in ITV's *World in Action* series. The programme is dealt with later in this book, but the essence of Steventon's minute is clear from this sentence which, while not quoted in the programme, was read out in parliament instead: 'It is my belief that

Mr LUNDY is a corrupt officer who has long exploited his association with GARNER . . . '

In the programme the minute appeared to be objective: the measured view of a most senior officer who had overseen a nigh-three-year inquiry and so must have known all Lundy's ins and outs. The programme's makers clearly did not know the minute was inaccurate nor could they have fully understood its final paragraph: 'I have recommended on other papers which deal with a request for an interview with the Commissioner by Det. Supt LUNDY that consideration should be given to removing him from specialist duty.' Here Steventon was saying that Lundy should be taken off detective work and put into uniform. This was very damaging, but when Lundy first read the whole minute four years later, it confirmed what he had suspected in 1983: Steventon *had* seen his request to see the commissioner *including his remarks about Steventon acting unjustly and unfairly towards him*. This meant Steventon not only knew that Lundy had tried to criticize him to Scotland Yard's 'boss of bosses'. He also knew that Lundy had never seen the commissioner anyway.

Lundy himself has no doubt what the impact of Steventon's minute on his career must have been: 'That, effectively, was me finished: I can't pass any more selection boards then. I fail another four or five.'

Lundy even failed a board when he swallowed his pride and applied for the job of *uniform* chief superintendent. Yet he still had admirers at the top. One was Deputy Assistant Commissioner David Powis, who sent me the following comments, for publication if I saw fit.

I have the highest and most genuine respect for my old colleague, Mr Ronald Steventon. Nevertheless, I did not agree

Above: Some of the guests at the 1974 dinner dance of the Lady Ratlings at the Grosvenor House Hotel, including (1) Len Gibson, (2) Detective Sergeant Tony Lundy, (3) Kenny Ross and (4) Ross's business partner Roy Garner

Right: Informer Roy Garner at his North London club with the American singing group, the Inkspots. Their greatest hit came in 1940 with 'Whispering Grass', from which 'grass' (meaning informer) is derived

Above: Robert Speed (in rubber mask) and Edward Kelly (with sunglasses and moustache) attempting to rob a North London bank in June 1979: the first raiders in Britain to be jailed through identification by bank surveillance cameras

Right: Part of the Finchley Robbery Squad in 1980, led by Chief Inspector Tony Lundy (centre, front) and Inspector Pat Fleming (right, front). This was probably the most successful squad in Metropolitan Police history, jailing 200 major criminals in less than three years

Below: Former Commander Phil Corbett, Tony Lundy's chief on the Flying Squad from 1978, and later at Criminal Intelligence

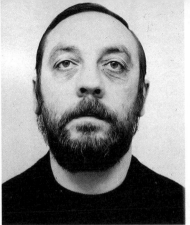

Above left: Alf Berkeley, named by supergrass David Smith and jailed for 25 years for armed robbery (reduced to 20 years on appeal)

Above right: Danny Gowan, also named by Smith and jailed for 25 years but cleared on appeal

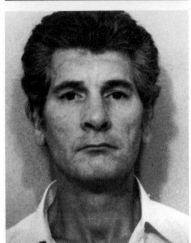

Left: Contract killer Harry 'Big H' MacKenney, jailed for life in 1980 for six murders. Tony Lundy first uncovered the crimes when he cracked an informer in 1979

Below: Micky Morris (left) demonstrating on the roof of Wormwood Scrubs Prison in 1980 against alleged brutality and bad conditions. He had been sentenced to 14 years for armed robbery after being named by Billy Amies, another supergrass 'turned' by Tony Lundy

Right: The mugshot of armed robber Len Gibson reproduced in Scotland Yard's *Handbook of Violent Thieves* shortly before he took part in the Silver Bullion Robbery at Barking on 24 March 1980

Below: The 309 bars of silver worth £3 million, discovered in a lock-up garage in Oakwood, North London on 3 June 1980 after Gibson had confessed to Lundy and led Robbery Squad officers to the hiding place

Bottom: Detectives loading the silver bars on board lorries which carried them to the Prisoners' Property Store under armed escort

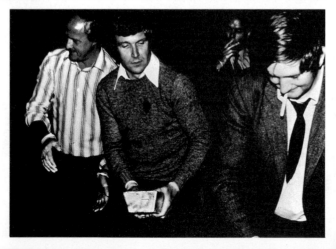

Above: Ronald Steventon, Scotland Yard's Deputy Assistant Commissioner (Administration), who in August 1983 expressed the belief that Detective Superintendent Tony Lundy was a 'corrupt officer'

Right: A 1978 photo of David Powis, Deputy Assistant Commissioner (Operations), handling a sawn-off shotgun of the kind used by London robbers. He has 'no doubts' about Lundy's integrity and 'never knew him to speak or write a falsehood'

Below: Customs officer Barry Terry (left) and ex-Customs officer Graham Branton, both jailed in 1988 for involvement in a VAT swindle. Terry was later cleared on appeal

Above: Howard Marks, one of the world's biggest cannabis smugglers, arrested in 1988 in Majorca following close co-operation between Scotland Yard and America's Drug Enforcement Administration. He was jailed for 25 years

Above right: Brinks-Mat Gold Robbery suspect John Fleming. While fighting deportation from Florida in 1986, he successfully appealed to Scotland Yard to take Lundy off his case. Later the case collapsed

Below: The fugitive Lord Moynihan in Manila, the Philippines, in 1987. Moynihan collaborated with the DEA by going undercover against Howard Marks

Above: Convicted drug-racketeer and suspected triple murderer Scott Errico, enjoying an adventure holiday in 1985 while a fugitive from American justice

Above right: Journalist Andrew Jennings of Granada TV's *World in Action*

Right: Solicitor Michael Relton, jailed in 1988 for 12 years for laundering £7.5 million in proceeds from the 1983 Brinks-Mat Gold Robbery

Below right: Tony Lundy, after completing the 1988 London Marathon

Below: Con-man and fraudster Francis Attard, one of many criminals who made false allegations against Tony Lundy

Above left: Nikolaus Chrastny, the prime mover in a £100 million cocaine conspiracy, who escaped from a West Yorkshire police cell in October 1987 and has not been recaptured

Above right: Roy Whitehorne, the cocaine conspirator who testified against Roy Garner

Left: Tony Lundy attends the Old Bailey to give evidence in the cocaine trial

with all he said or wrote. No evidence was forthcoming of any corrupt behaviour by Mr Lundy during the whole time he was in my charge and, as far as I am concerned, there was no existing compelling suspicion.

I never knew him speak or write a falsehood. Although he was sensibly discreet, I have no reason to believe that he was otherwise than frank to me concerning his dealings with informers, violent criminals and their families.

I may have had the reputation of being a disciplinarian and a suspicious man, particularly in relation to corrupt persons within or without the Service. As far as I am concerned, Mr Lundy's general fidelity was never in question. His industry in operational work and in administration was on the highest plane. I have no doubts about his fundamental integrity. He expressed feelings of moral responsibility towards his duty of protecting the public against the style of criminal he specialized in, the arrogant armed robber. I believe these feelings were genuine. He did deal with many evil and, I believe, vengeful men who may well have borne him grave animosity upon release from prison. Many of these had control of wealth.

Regarding Lundy's style, Mr Powis told me, 'Some persons may have come to the conclusion that he was of an impatient and over-abrasive nature. Maybe so, but he was disciplined and proper in his contact with me. Our association was a close one, bearing in mind our different ranks, and lasted several years.' After making other positive observations about Lundy, Mr Powis closed his letter by saying, 'There it is. That is what I think. It is not the most popular view. I did not have to write these truths to you.'

Powis's strong support was one reason why – in stark contrast to Steventon's wish – Lundy was never put into uniform. He stayed a detective for the rest of his career, during which time he did his most outstanding work. Having waited more than three years to find out about Steventon's minute, Lundy had to wait even longer to discover that early in 1985 Assistant Commissioner John

Dellow had reviewed his personnel papers. Dellow felt that if Lundy's name was clearable, it should be cleared. After reading the papers, he consulted senior detectives who vouched for Lundy in the strongest terms, and concluded there was no evidence to substantiate any allegations that Lundy was corrupt. He then asked Scotland Yard's three other assistant commissioners to review Lundy's papers. They each assigned a view agreeing that there was no such evidence against Lundy.

This unanimity overruled and wiped out the force of Steventon's minute. It freed Lundy to return to front-line detective work of international importance. In September 1985 he was selected for promotion to detective chief superintendent and was about to be given that rank when he fell victim to a media campaign even more hostile than before.

15

'The Untouchable'

Cleared at last of all the 'Stagg' allegations, Tony Lundy had good reason to believe, as 1985 began, that his career would blossom anew under the Metropolitan CID's new leadership. Not only had John Dellow become Assistant Commissioner; Brian Worth had recently taken over as DAC (Operations) from David Powis who had retired. Lundy's most powerful detractor, Ron Steventon, had retired as DAC (Administration) in August 1983 after firing his devastating minute. Lundy still had no idea it existed but, as the top brass had now effectively struck it out of the record, he should have had nothing to fear from it anyway.

On 11 March 1985 Commander Phil Corbett, the new head of C11 Department (Criminal Intelligence) recruited Lundy to be deputy head of an investigation into what had happened to the proceeds of a robbery in which 26 million pounds-worth of gold was stolen from a warehouse at Heathrow Airport on 26 November 1983. This 'Brinks–Mat Gold' job had overtaken the 1980 Silver Bullion heist as Britain's biggest-ever robbery, and Lundy was the obvious person to lead a money-laundering probe which was bound to be complex and protracted. His brilliant work in the specially-created post of 'senior intelligence co-ordinator' is chronicled in Chapters 19 to 22. It overlaps in time and interweaves with events in coming chapters but, if the reader is to understand two highly serpentine tales, they must be told separately.

Five years after the Silver Bullion job an outsider might have thought that public interest in the Lundy–Garner show had run its course. There had been many media exposés but nothing had stuck to Lundy and, if some journalists regard catching bent cops as a vocation, they had plenty of other targets to aim at. Indeed, the affair might have died if it had not been for the tenacity of just one journalist, Andrew Jennings.

Jennings, wavy-haired, of medium height, in his forties, is a foot-in-the-door veteran of BBC Radio's crusading *Checkpoint* series. His infectious, waspish humour and street-wise wit have enlivened many a court press box and won him friends among reporters who might otherwise be his rivals. He also has a quality rare among 'investigative journalists': he does not hoard information. Most muck-rakers are anal-retentive, rarely parting with a fact or document lest anyone steal their story. Jennings operates on a different basis, sharing many fruits of his researches with other reporters. This style would prove valuable in the later 1980s when, with a few other journalists, he convinced even some of London's usually pro-police correspondents that Lundy might be partly, if not diabolically, 'bent'.

By early 1985 Jennings and a TV producer, Vyv Simson, were well into researching a programme for *Brass Tacks*, a current affairs series made by BBC Manchester. The show's working title was 'The Untouchable' and its premise was that Roy Garner was simultaneously a highly-paid police informer and one of London's biggest criminals. The implication was that he had been granted a licence to commit crime, hence he was 'Untouchable', and that one detective who knew a lot about him was Tony Lundy. In the film Garner was to be branded a bank robber, a landlord who had set fire to his own property to oust tenants, and a perverter of justice who threatened to kill a witness if he testified against a friend of Garner's who was facing trial for murder. The allegations were unproved, coming largely from supergrasses Billy Young and John Moriarty, but they helped build an image of a monstrous gangster unfit for enrichment by the insurance companies.

The imprisoned Garner first heard about the *Brass Tacks* project in the spring of 1985 when several cronies let him know that they had been visited by BBC journalists claiming proof he was a 'grass' and mentioning crimes other than the Silver Bullion job on which he had informed. Garner's sources said the reporters claimed they even had copies of reward receipts with his pseudonymous signature, 'Granger', upon them. Meantime his family told him that *Brass Tacks* had filmed his home and business premises. He feared that any fresh publicity would damage his appeal against the VAT conviction which would be heard just when *Brass Tacks* was due to be shown. He was also concerned because he feared the programme would provoke reprisals against him in jail. He had always refused to go in Rule 43 accommodation (for prisoners in danger from other inmates) because that would be an admission of guilt. It would also finish him as an informant. What also worried him was that, if the BBC men were telling the truth, they must have a 'leak' within the very squad investigating him, Operation Albany.

How right he was. What gave 'The Untouchable' its startling new edge was that, for the first time in public, the mud was being slung by a detective, Harry Clement, who had led 'Albany' against Garner and other criminals until he retired in 1983. On film the former chief superintendent expressed outrage that so big a crook had survived so long without charge, even as London's best publicized thief-taker was handling him as an informer. This implied that Garner's links with Lundy had given him immunity. The programme also queried Lundy's ignorance of Garner's criminal activities, despite his social familiarity with him and other villains. It did not say he was corrupt, but clearly it would severely damage his reputation just when the Yard had restored it intact.

Lundy soon had evidence that the BBC team had high-level police contacts. Shortly after starting work on the gold bullion inquiry (at Tintagel House, on the south bank of the Thames), he took a call from Don Neesham, his former Flying Squad Commander. Neesham had retired in 1979 after a long dispute with Scotland Yard superiors. This was brought to a head when he was told he was being transferred from the Squad to a job on district. Contrary to stories reported in the media, he was not moved because he had obstructed Operation Countryman or to appease Countryman's chief officers, although this seemed possible at the time. Nor was he demoted or facing demotion when he quit. When he called Lundy in 1985, he was working as a consultant to the Tobacco Advisory Council. 'Neesham tells me that he's been approached by these people Jennings and Simson from *Brass Tacks*, and they're asking about issues such as dealing with informants.' It was also clear to Neesham that they had talked to a senior serving officer and were inquiring into Lundy himself. 'So there they were, trying to get information out of Don for a programme attacking me and my informers!'

Lundy promptly wrote a report to Commander Corbett about Neesham's call. Corbett consulted with DAC Worth and on 18 April he went to see Neesham who told Corbett he was not going to co-operate with the BBC. Corbett explained his fear that *Brass Tacks* might name informants including 'Granger', whom Neesham himself knew about from his days as Flying Squad boss. Corbett added that he was even more concerned about David Powis's impending libel action against the *Observer*, in which there might be similar dangerous disclosures. Neesham took the point that police would be placed in an impossible situation if informants were identified, and their lives and families imperilled. He agreed to help Corbett.

Corbett was now instructed to inquire into possible breaches of the Official Secrets Act and the law of confidence by Yard detectives, retired and serving. The OSA also applied to journalists. Probing their activities might be seen as a gross invasion of press freedom, but Corbett's job was to assert a paramount principle of policing: the *identity* of informants must be protected. This is not to say that *informants* must be protected. Both Corbett and Lundy asserted they would arrest any 'snouts' they knew to be committing crimes. However, with allegations surfacing that the BBC men were telling the underworld they had proof which crimes Garner had 'grassed' and copies of reward receipts he had signed, Corbett felt he was justified in digging deep. After all, Lundy had been investigated for four years on the basis of mere allegations. Corbett's task was to establish if these new allegations against other people were true or false.

He discovered that some detectives were indeed helping *Brass Tacks*, not just the retired Harry Clement, but at least the problem of Powis's libel action suddenly seemed to go away. On 2 May the *Observer* paid him substantial damages and then printed a full apology. There would now be no contest in court, so no sensitive informant material was likely to be disclosed for public consumption. This was a great relief to Corbett, Lundy and the Yard hierarchy, but twelve days later *Private Eye* claimed a deal had been struck between the *Observer* and *Brass Tacks*.[1] The *Eye* said the programme had secret details of informants disclosed by Powis, and seven would be named in the show on 29 May.

Brass Tacks had no intention of naming seven informers, but the story made Roy Garner even more nervous. He was now reeling from the cavalier way in which his

confidential role was being publicized, and had become
almost hysterical. On 7 May he asked Scotland Yard to
make every effort to stop the show. One week later the
Yard did put pressure on the BBC. On 14 May Assistant
Commissioner Dellow wrote to its director general to say
that naming an informer would be a grave disservice to the
public interest and would put him at risk of 'serious injury
at the hands of those against whom he had purportedly
informed'.

It is possible that some of the documents upon which your
programme is based . . . were released in the course of a
procedure known as discovery of documents in a civil action.
These documents, which were of a highly confidential and
sensitive nature, were disclosed solely for the purpose of that
action and their use for any other purpose could amount to a
contempt of court.

After this heavy hint Dellow said: 'As with journalists
and television reporters it is impossible for police to work
without protecting their informants . . . Journalists, as you
are aware, have gone to prison sooner than betray confidential sources.' He added that steps had recently been
taken to 'enhance the methods of informant handling',
but stressed the special need to protect sources in the field
of major crime. He acknowledged that police corruption
was a legitimate matter of public interest but added that
such allegations should be reported to the Metropolitan
Commissioner.

This letter put the BBC hierarchy in the usual dilemma
of having to defend muscular programme-makers while
not recklessly offending an institution of state. The suggestion that informers might be injured – even murdered
– after being named by *Brass Tacks* was not relished
by senior BBC figures. They took the safest decision:
postponement. Further legal opinions were canvassed and

the script was repeatedly revised to eliminate all reasonable risk of being sued for libel by Garner, Lundy or
Powis. Two massive problems remained. One was that
the programme's main allegation – that Garner had been
allowed to play the dual role of highly-paid informer and
major crook – could not be made without naming him as
an informer. While this would increase the danger for him
and his family, he had already been exposed elsewhere,
and the 'public interest' might now lie more in exposing
than protecting him. At least that position could be argued
if the matter ever came to court.

The second problem was still worrying the BBC nine
months after the film was first meant to be broadcast. This
was the thorny issue of the programme-makers' access
to internal Yard papers. One lot had indeed come from
Powis's *Observer* action. On 5 March 1986 the BBC's
in-house solicitor, Tony Bostock, wrote a memorandum
saying:

We have used those documents to the extent of background
research material and the facts disclosed have been checked and
used by reference to other sources, and not to the privileged
documents. Nevertheless, it is known that we have had access
to such documents and this would give Scotland Yard grounds
for an application to the Court to prevent transmission, if they
were so minded. There is also the fact to be faced that we
may, technically, be in contempt of court, having made use of
documents to which we should not have had access.

Bostock said the BBC would argue that the matters
revealed in the show were of 'over-riding public interest',
but there was another difficulty.

We have had access to, and made use of, documents in
the possession of Harry Clement who, before his retirement,
conducted Operation Albany, and we could be said to be
acting in breach of confidence. This would give grounds for an

injunction. However, the Yard, knowing he has such documents, do not appear to have made any effort to recover them from him, and this could be a strong point in our favour.

Bostock's view was that the issues raised by *Brass Tacks* justified all remaining libel and contempt risks. Yet the BBC eventually dropped the show 'because of insoluble legal difficulties', announced Assistant Director General Alan Protheroe, 'not following representations from Scotland Yard'. This was scarcely accurate. The BBC had 'copped out'.

Commander Corbett, meantime, had continued to pursue breaches of the Official Secrets Act. He took a trip to see Harry Clement in retirement in deepest Devon and found him very helpful. In a quite separate move Andrew Jennings was placed under covert surveillance, followed and photographed. Jennings found out in 1987. He demanded an investigation and protested to the Home Secretary:

This affair surely raises huge worries about the freedom of journalists in our democracy to make legitimate inquiries into policing. How can it be proper for senior Yard officers, who so frequently lament their lack of resources, to divert detectives to spying on a journalist who has never been convicted of – or is guilty of – any crime?[2]

The aim of the surveillance was to discover if any crime had been, or was being, committed. Similarly Corbett needed to know precisely what police documents had been disclosed in the Powis–*Observer* action and on whose authority. He reached a stage where he felt he could go no further without interviewing Powis and Powis's former chief, Gilbert Kelland. They had both retired so Corbett needed Scotland Yard clearance to approach them. He made a formal request to the serving Yard hierarchy, listing pages of matters he wished to raise, but he never received a reply. His probe was ended in November 1985, even though secret internal material on Garner and Lundy continued to be leaked to the media. The Yard had decided not only that there would be no prosecution; there would not even be a full inquiry. There seemed no need. After all, the BBC had suppressed *Brass Tacks* so why bother about possible breaches of the Official Secrets Act? The battle had been won.

Or so it seemed, but Andrew Jennings had other ideas. He was not a career BBC man and he quit. He then offered the idea round other TV companies and in August 1986 placed it with Granada's *World in Action*. He would now make an enhanced version of the abandoned *Brass Tacks* with new witnesses, additional research and *World in Action*'s sharper edge. This time Scotland Yard would have no chance of stopping the show.

16

The Unstoppable

Still in jail, Roy Garner became distraught as the *World in Action* film came ever nearer to being broadcast. Again he tried everything to persuade Scotland Yard to block it. He even informed – vaguely – on a massive cocaine conspiracy, to prove his continuing value, but this time the Yard was reluctant to assist. DAC Dellow did write to Granada along the same lines as he had written to the BBC, but to no effect. On Monday 3 November 1986 the show went out. It was called 'The Untouchable', just like the banned *Brass Tacks*, but this version was even more damaging to Garner than the first. Testament to his villainy was provided by two retired detectives: not just Harry Clement – head of Operation Albany from 1980 through its 1981 shutdown and its 1982 revival – but also his deputy, Superintendent Gerald Wiltshire who led it from 1983 until 1986.

In the film's first minutes Garner came over as a monster. Working from allegations by supergrasses Moriarty and Young, 'Albany' had gathered evidence of nine arson attacks on properties connected with Garner. In 1973 he bought a building in Upper Street, Islington, with a butcher as a sitting tenant. In 1975 he apparently arranged for the butcher's shop to be torched, forcing the man to quit. He then bought a four-storey building next door which was also encumbered by a sitting tenant, an optician named Sydney Arnold. He refused to quit even when Garner announced plans to demolish the upper three storeys. Up went the scaffolding and in succeeding months two fires broke out, one next door and one in Arnold's own premises. 'It was pretty obvious that Mr Garner wanted to get rid of me and possibly wanted to take over the entire block,' lamented Arnold who refused to budge. When 'Albany' checked these stories with the fire brigade and the local council, it found that all these fires had been classed as arsons. Meantime on his country estate in Hertfordshire Garner had told a woman to quit a cottage she rented from him. She refused to go. Soon her barn burned down. According to the woman, Garner 'drove slowly round the barn with a big grin on his face. Two weeks later I gave up. I quit.'

Clement submitted a report to the Director of Public Prosecutions, adding a minute suggesting Garner should be charged, but 'the report bounced at the DPP's office: we had circumstantial evidence but not sufficient to take him before a court.' Clement said all the officers who had seen the report were 'absolutely devastated' by the decision.

'Albany' investigated an even worse crime: the 1976 death of Raymond Hoy. A former Garner employee had been charged with his murder but was acquitted when vital witnesses suddenly changed their stories. In 1981 'Albany' officers found a petty criminal who had seen the killing. He was now ready to testify that Garner had told him to keep quiet, and that later Garner and some associates told him to go to the accused's solicitors and make a false statement. If he did not, they said he could be charged with the murder himself. 'Albany' found a young woman who said she too had been pressurized into making a false statement, in return for drugs and money. When she told Garner's men back in 1976 that the police had cracked her story and she would have to tell the truth, they threatened her. Soon after, she was attacked in the street, burned with a cigarette and told to stick to her original story.

'Albany' had also investigated claims by supergrass Billy

Young that Garner had organized armed robberies: on
a KLM security van in 1970 (proceeds £117,000), on
the merchant bankers, Brown Shipley 1972 (£62,000), at
Stratford station 1973 (£3,000) and on Marks and Spencers in Putney 1977 (£18,000). *World in Action* flashed
these jobs on screen and then stated: 'But as Operation
Albany began investigating Young's allegations, they were
unaware that Roy Garner was playing a double game with
Scotland Yard. For years he'd been one of the Met's best
informants.'

The programme said Garner had received rewards totalling £250,000 even as 'Albany' was proceeding, but his
secret relationship with the Yard was never disclosed to
Clement 'who was busy trying to lock him up'. Clement
asserted:

> Most certainly I should have been told . . . At that stage I
> think they should have called a halt to using him as an informant,
> irrespective of his worth . . . We should have been privy to the
> fact that he was an informant – at least I and my deputy should
> have been – there should have been a conference and we should
> have been allowed to take it on from there.

World in Action commented that, far from dropping
Garner as an informant, 'the Yard helped him collect the
biggest reward in criminal history', over the Silver Bullion job. DAC Powis opposed rewards exceeding £5,000
but Garner threatened to sue the insurers for the full
advertised reward of £300,000 if they did not pay. At
that point, the programme claimed, Tony Lundy secretly
wrote to Powis: 'He outlined Garner's case for the reward
and passed on Garner's fervent denial of the "Albany"
allegations.'

Clement was then asked if it was proper for Lundy to
put Garner's case to the head of CID:

> No! No! No! No! This should have all been dealt with at a

conference. We should have all got together round a table, and
he'd have said, 'He's our informant', and I'd say, 'Well, he's
my number one suspect' – no secret, no secret – where are we
going to go? That's how it should have been done. None of this
here hole-in-the-corner business.

The commentary said Powis 'was even prepared to hold
a private meeting with Roy Garner to discuss the reward
dispute'. On 1 July 1981, with his superiors' consent, 'he
even identified Garner to the insurers so he could collect
the money' – £178,000, said the programme. 'Almost
beyond belief,' said Clement. 'When I learned of this
I was shaken . . . it was absolutely amazing that this
should have happened without my knowledge . . . I was
the officer leading a whole team in the investigation of
this man!'

World in Action asserted that the Yard's help to Garner
over the reward while 'Albany' was proceeding 'illustrates
their confused approach'. Should they have treated him as
a criminal or an informant? 'They shouldn't have had any
difficulty in making up their mind that he was a criminal,'
said Clement, 'my reports showed most certainly which
way they should go.' Far from pressing ahead, said the nar-
rator, 'Albany' was abruptly closed at the end of 1981.

Gerry Wiltshire said he was never told why 'Albany'
was stopped. 'We were just told to go back to our various
duties. The whole inquiry team was broken up . . . I did
think in my mind, perhaps we were getting too close to Roy
Garner.' Clement added, 'Perhaps if we'd proceeded with
this, certain people would have egg on their face. They'd
have been embarrassed. We would have shown up that
the top informant, as he is alleged to have been, was in
fact a very active criminal.' 'Were you blocked?' Andrew
Jennings asked. 'I don't know. It's hard to say. You can
have suspicions without the proof.'

This was the programme's half-way point. Tony Lundy

had only just returned from inquiries overseas, but when he later saw a videotape, he was angry and dismayed at these retired detectives' complaints. If they *had* been blocked, which he doubted, he had played no part in the blocking. He was also astonished at how Clement conducted his inquiry. If Clement had evidence of Garner's role in nine arsons Lundy felt that he should have charged him, not submitted a report to the DPP and waited for a knock-back. That was how Lundy had run Finchley. His three years there had resulted in 200 major criminals going to jail, few acquittals and only two convicts cleared on appeal. In contrast Clement, described in the film as 'one of the Yard's most experienced detectives', spent well over a year without securing a charge against his 'number one suspect', despite finding two witnesses who claimed he had covered up a murder. Lundy had just twenty officers on his squad. Clement had a 'hand-picked' forty-five. Lundy was never instructed to nail Garner, nor had any of his supergrasses or other sources ever named him. 'I never had to investigate him in my whole service. Yet these men had a licence to investigate him! Wiltshire had him as a target for five years!'

Nor could Lundy understand why Clement did not lock Garner up for a few days and interrogate him over Young's claim that he had organized four robberies. Other 'Albany' targets were Len Gibson and Dolph Aguda of Silver Bullion fame. 'Why didn't Clement do Gibson and Aguda for all the robberies this man Young put *them* on?' Lundy later railed. '*They* weren't informers, so they couldn't have got any of my alleged protection! They were locked up for years and could easily have been talked into pleading guilty in return for a concurrent sentence – *if* they ever did those jobs, that is. Since the allegations came from "Billy Liar", I very much doubt it.'

As for Clement's claim that he should have been told

Garner was an informant, Lundy found it ridiculous. Whether Garner was a 'snout' or not should have made no difference to Clement. Lundy was sure he himself had jailed dozens of crooks who were other detectives' snouts, and he would have interpreted any officers telling him, 'so-and-so is my man' as a heavy hint to 'lay off'. If Garner was Clement's target, his role as an informer was irrelevant. Also from the Yard's point of view, it made a lot of sense to have one squad trying to put Garner in jail while blind to the fact that another cop was extracting valuable information from him.

In any case, the whole point of concealing informers' identities is to protect them from retribution. That was partly why David Powis had brought in the sealed envelope system for officers recommending informants for rewards: to *prevent* other detectives finding out their names and leaking the news back to the underworld (see Chapter 8). Lower down, 'Albany' was as leaky as a sieve, as Garner well knew: one man on the squad was informing to the underworld! So it would have been unwise of Powis or anyone else to tell 'Albany' of Garner's role.

Besides, Lundy was very surprised to learn that Clement had not known about that role. He assumed that Clement had been liaising with Alan Stagg's corruption probe – both inquiries stemmed largely from supergrass Billy Young – and Stagg certainly knew Garner was an informer. Also, as Garner was his 'number one suspect', Clement must have used his vast squad to put the man under near constant watch. The proof lies in what Gerald Wiltshire and David Powis told Wood Green Crown Court in 1983: Garner was a target criminal. He was closely shadowed and photographed, his phones tapped and his home and premises probably bugged. Powis said Garner had been the subject of target surveillance 'as close as we could make it' for three to four years. That includes the time Clement was running 'Albany'. If so, he must have noticed that Lundy met Garner almost once a week. Questions upward, to Powis or Steventon, would surely have resulted in word that these meets (of which Lundy always forewarned Powis) had been cleared by Scotland Yard and were legitimate. Of course, 'Albany' surveillance might well have revealed that the two DACs were meeting the target quite often too.

Lundy also scorned Clement's claim that Scotland Yard should have stopped using a particular informant, 'irrespective of his worth'. Following his *Observer* victory, David Powis had expressed a wiser view.[1]

The assertion made by some people that there is something intrinsically improper in a senior detective accepting information from a suspected criminal, who himself is likely to be involved in other organized crime, and who might be a 'target criminal' himself – that assertion is naive.

Whilst it is incumbent upon senior detectives to regard such information with suspicion, it cannot be disregarded and must properly be investigated. If corroborated, it must be acted upon. The acid test is this: is the information TRUE? If it is and it leads to lawful arrests of violent thieves, and murderers, and to the recovery of victims' property, then a reward commensurate to the success of the operation should and would be paid to encourage further information.

In the case of a current 'target criminal' giving information, any refusal to accept the information from him would be bound to arouse suspicion in his mind that he was himself the subject of secret investigation, with bad results as far as the investigation and the public was concerned.

These remarks more than counter Clement's attack. As for Lundy's letter outlining Garner's right to the Silver Bullion reward, he had every justification for writing it. He had properly recommended the reward in the first place, and a year had gone by with no money paid. As for passing on Garner's 'fervent denial of the "Albany" allegations',

Lundy did not mention 'Albany' but simply said Garner believed that 'malicious allegations from supergrasses who suspect him of being a grass' were being investigated. In passing on Garner's view – without endorsing or supporting it – Lundy was doing nothing improper. Indeed, he was duty-bound to do so.

The letter should be seen in the context of the frequent meetings Lundy and Powis were then having with Garner. Despite their disparity in rank, the two officers had to communicate directly because Powis had taken it on himself to authenticate all reward claims but could only meet Garner through his 'handler', Lundy. In contrast, Lundy had never met Harry Clement and had no need to consult him. Indeed, it would have been odd if he had consulted him, and would probably have been interpreted as an attempt to interfere. In any case Lundy had never been told officially of 'Albany's' existence and only knew what Garner had told him: it leaked! Lundy had reported this intelligence upwards, with the express goal of getting the leaking detective removed. This was hardly the action of a detective protecting the criminal interests of his informer. It fully justifies Lundy's statement elsewhere in the letter: 'I owe no allegiance to "Granger" and he knows I would arrest him if he participates or had participated in crime.'

As for why 'Albany' had been shut down, Lundy believed *World in Action* unwittingly contained the answer. It was not that there was any risk of it 'getting too close to Roy Garner', as Gerry Wiltshire claimed, nor would certain people have had 'egg on their face' as Harry Clement alleged. Lundy felt it was terminated probably because it had occupied forty-five officers for far too long without bringing charges against any major target.

Tony Lundy could already see many holes in 'The Untouchable' but the programme-makers had not finished yet. Half-way through they turned the spotlight on to the 'Steventon Inquiry' – the title they gave to the corruption probe led by Chief Superintendent Alan Stagg – and focused on evidence indicating that 'Mr Lundy has been unwise in some aspects of his conduct as a police officer'.

Showing the old photograph of Lundy, Garner, Gibson and twenty-six others at the Dorchester in 1974, the programme stated: 'Such friendships were frowned on by Scotland Yard and the picture led the Steventon inquiry to look closely at the Silver Bullion case.' However, it was not the photo which led 'Steventon' to look at the Bullion case but the anonymous letter which followed hard on Billy Young's allegations (see Chapter 11). Nor in 1974 was socializing between cops and criminals necessarily frowned on. Indeed, the kind of community work which had brought Lundy into social contact with Garner and Gibson at Finchley Boxing Club was encouraged. Lundy says that the 'Lady Ratlings' charity do, at which the photograph was taken, was an outcrop of that work. How the Yard regarded such links would depend on whether they helped or frustrated its war on crime and on whether any 'friendship' was corrupt. With Lundy no corruption has ever been found because, he says, none has ever occurred. On the contrary, his social links only helped his force to fight crime. By getting to know underworld figures in boxing and charity circles, he developed many informers and, over the Silver Bullion job, used 'friendship' as a tool to coax Gibson not only to confess but to return the loot.

All the more outrageous, thought Lundy, that *World in Action* should air the view that he had soft-pedalled on Gibson at his 1981 trial by saying, 'I had no idea he was involved in criminal matters'. In contrast, Clement said of the gang: 'You only had to look at their past records and intelligence files . . . They were professionals . . . There was sufficient knowledge at the Yard that these were very active people.'

The programme did not interpret Lundy's remarks about Gibson but implied he had done a big favour to a close buddy and allowed him to get off lightly. The truth was entirely different. For a start, it was Lundy who had ended a period of fifteen years during which Gibson kept a clean sheet. It was to Lundy alone that Gibson owed his ten-year term in 1981. Nor was ten years that light. As prosecution counsel Tim Cassel later reflected: 'Bearing in mind that the robbers were pleading guilty and had returned most of the silver, I thought ten years was what they deserved.'

The programme did not point out that Harry Clement himself had both Gibson and Dolph Aguda as targets. They may have been 'very active people', as he claimed, but this only makes it all the odder that the only charge he could raise against Gibson was for receiving a television set. It was no surprise when even this charge was dropped. Gibson was already serving ten years in jail – thanks to Lundy – and so petty a charge would not have earned him an extra five minutes inside. Clement did not charge Dolph Aguda at all.

Even so, could or should Lundy have 'put the boot in' any harder? The answer is no. He was not the prosecuting officer – all he did was solve the crime – and he spoke in court only because that same day the defence had requested he appear in mitigation. Scotland Yard agreed but, like any other witness, he could only answer questions which were put to him. He was asked just two about Gibson's criminality.

Q: The fact of the matter is that as far as his past record is concerned, for the last fifteen years or so, certainly for the last twelve years since you have known him, he has rehabilitated himself.
A: As far as I knew, he was a successful businessman who had

put his past behind him. I had no idea he was involved in criminal matters.

Q: Can you help us, from your practical and professional knowledge, there is no evidence at all of any involvement in any sort of crime in recent years by Mr Gibson.
A: There is no evidence to support any question of him being involved, no.

World in Action claimed: 'This came as a surprise to those detectives who, like Mr Lundy, had access to the Yard's criminal intelligence files.' But what *was* in those files? In early 1980 the Criminal Intelligence section issued a list of London's top hundred robbers. Lundy was given a copy. Entitled the *Handbook of Violent Thieves*, it contained an entry on Gibson which revealed ancient convictions for nothing more than 'going equipped to steal, handling stolen goods and shop-breaking'. This hardly indicated he was Public Enemy Number 1, or Number 42 which the alphabet accorded him in this list, as Lundy confirms.

It was a total shock to me when I was told Gibson was on the Silver Bullion. To all intents and purposes he made a respectable living buying old houses, converting them and letting them off as flats. Whether he was named as a suspect along with ninety-nine people in a black book was neither here nor there. Some people in that book had never committed another crime in their life.

With hindsight it is clear that Gibson was rightly in the top hundred but his entry did not solve the Bullion robbery, perpetrated a few weeks after the *Handbook* was printed. Such intelligence is not *evidence* and does not solve crimes: Lundy cracked the Bullion job without checking *any* intelligence files. Nor should the contents of such files be trotted out in court – least of all by a detective summoned to give evidence in mitigation.

Any defence counsel who's mitigating only puts questions that you can answer without damning his client. He's not going to put anything in a way that you can do him harm. I wasn't interviewed in advance, nor did I volunteer. I was just told *that day*, 'Go into the witness box. You're a fully-bound witness. They want to put some mitigation.' All the Yard top brass were in court. If I had said anything untrue or out of order, they would have jumped up or got hold of prosecuting counsel to halt proceedings. I'd have had to be an idiot to help Gibson, and why would I bother? He never got favours out of me! I got the information, I arrested him, I questioned him, I got all the admissions and I recovered the bullion. It wouldn't have made a blind bit of difference to me what happened to Gibson from then on. I'd done my job. Before all this I hadn't the faintest idea what he was doing, but I'd told him repeatedly over the years, 'If you are at it, then one day I'm certain to find out and I'll have you.' And I did.

No one else 'had' Gibson – certainly not Harry Clement, even though he had the benefit of all the fresh 'intelligence' which Billy Young coughed up. Lundy knew the difficulties. Back in 1977 Gibson had been a Flying Squad target so Lundy told Commander Don Neesham that he knew him and offered to help. When the inquiry came to nothing, Lundy assumed he had been doing nothing provably wrong. Not long after, however, an informer told him that Gibson and the Agudas might have been involved in a daring robbery on a security vehicle in the Blackwall Tunnel. This caused them to be arrested, but they were released when it was clear they had nothing to do with the crime. So when Lundy gave evidence at Gibson's trial he knew of two occasions when Gibson had been pursued on the basis of wrong or inadequate intelligence.

Ironically, officers from 'Stagg' accused Lundy both of playing down Gibson's criminality at his trial, and of *falsely* accusing an innocent Gibson of the Blackwall Tunnel job four years earlier. The allegations were incompatible. Indeed, it was the Blackwall Tunnel job which taught

Lundy not to believe mere 'intelligence' about Gibson, and explains why he did not blacken his past when he captured him for a crime he really did commit.

It was material of that quality which filled most of the 4,000 pages which 'Stagg–Steventon' sent to the Director of Public Prosecutions in August 1983, and on which the Director ruled no action. However, quoting that decision, *World in Action* threw in the bombshell which almost blew Lundy out of his chair: the 'Steventon Minute' about which, until then, he knew absolutely nothing. He gaped open-mouthed as four hostile sentences were flashed on the screen. The minute's inaccuracies are shown up in detail in Chapter 19, but its crushing verdict – that Lundy should be disciplined and taken off all detective work – appeared to have merit simply because it was written by Steventon. *World in Action* was perplexed that it

. . . had no adverse effect on Mr Lundy's promotion . . . Mr Lundy was not returned to uniform and there was no discipline hearing. Within a year the Yard had awarded Mr Lundy a long service and good conduct medal, and he now runs investigations on the Special Operations Task Force, the Yard's elite crime-fighting squad. Today Mr Lundy is Scotland Yard's top detective.

This part of the script was also incorrect. Steventon's minute *did* have an adverse effect on Lundy's career: it blocked his promotion for a further two years. And he was not Scotland Yard's top detective. He was outranked by dozens of other officers. He was, however, the Yard's most successful detective. In that sense he was 'top'.

The rest of the show catalogued Roy Garner's decline and fall: Powis's ferocious onslaught at Wood Green; his VAT conviction at the hands of HM Customs; and the decision to re-start 'Albany' in 1983, with the goal of discovering where he had stashed his fraudulent £2 million. Gerry Wiltshire, who led the new team of just three officers, claimed that when he found out the money had been moved to America he was inexplicably refused permission to go and get it. The programme stated that Garner took advantage of this decision to shift his money beyond British reach. It said Garner was now getting Christmas and weekend breaks from Ford open prison as rewards for continuing to inform. Wiltshire said he had charged Garner with travelling on a false passport, but the Yard had intervened to ensure he got a light sentence – nine months concurrent – and did not serve a day longer in jail.

Lundy was curious to learn all this from his TV because he had played no part in any such moves. He was even more bemused when Wiltshire said his two sergeants had been approached by senior Yard officers threatening to 'do their legs' if they pursued the Garner inquiries. One man had even talked of a plan to push Wiltshire under a train. He himself claimed that as his retirement approached, one of these same senior officers had told him: 'Why don't you quietly return to Wales and take ten per cent.' Wiltshire added: 'He was offering me a bribe.'

The programme's final twist was that Garner might yet get his biggest reward ever. Lundy had recently been on American TV announcing a dramatic breakthrough in his search for the proceeds of the 1983 £26 million gold bullion job.

Among detectives who know Roy Garner well, there's little doubt that he's been grassing again. Having got his own millions to safety in America, they believe he's revealed the secret money-laundering route to Scotland Yard. For money. We asked the Yard whether they expected to pay a reward for this latest information. They declined to comment.

This 'belief' was rubbish. Sure, Lundy had tracked down

millions of pounds and dollars of drugs-related monies following on from his Brinks–Mat investigations (see Chapters 19 and 20), but this owed nothing to Garner. Lundy and his task force had traced many money-laundering routes, cracking new supergrasses and informers on both sides of the Atlantic. In comparison any sums Garner had shipped abroad were peanuts. The idea that he was 'the overlord of serious crime in London', as Wiltshire claimed on *World in Action*, was risible. Bigger criminals were shifting far bigger sums. And there was no question of him getting any Brinks–Mat reward. Neither Lundy nor anyone else had any intention of nominating him. That was bunkum but Lundy could see it was too good a tailpiece for the programme-makers to resist.

Fair or unfair, the film's impact on Lundy and Garner was very serious. Next morning almost every national newspaper carried sensational reports of the alleged plan to push Wiltshire under a train. 'BENT COP "IN THREAT TO KILL A YARD BOSS"', screamed the *Sun*, but for Lundy the worst blow came from the House of Commons. Briefed by *World in Action*, Labour MP Clive Soley stood up and read a section of the Steventon minute which even Granada's lawyers had balked at. Sheltering behind parliamentary privilege, he quoted Steventon saying: 'It is my belief that Mr Lundy is a corrupt officer who has long exploited his association with Garner.' He then cited another paragraph about the Bullion robbery and another raid in Hatton Garden for which Garner was paid rewards. Some evidence had been deduced 'in respect of both these cases which suggests that Garner was not the informant he was claimed to be and he was merely exploiting information which he had received from Mr Lundy.'

Not even *World in Action* had dared claim Garner was a bogus informant, for that would imply Lundy had falsely nominated him for the reward and taken a corrupt share. There was no evidence – only underworld canard – but in the House of Commons Soley could say anything without fear of being sued for libel. He recited some of the programme's claims and called for an adjournment debate.[2] This was refused, but the machinery of state was already turning against Lundy.

On the night of the programme Scotland Yard issued a statement saying all but one of the allegations had already been 'the subject of probing and totally unrestricted inquiries', but 'no evidence has ever been revealed to indicate any Metropolitan police officers acted improperly'. The one fresh allegation was Wiltshire's claim that he was threatened with murder, but the Yard said he had never made this allegation 'while he was a serving officer or since'. Now he would be 'invited to substantiate his claim' in an immediate investigation. The statement added: 'The suggestion that Mr Garner contributed to the success of the investigation of the gold bullion robbery or the laundering of the proceeds is utterly false as are many of the alleged "facts" contained in the programme.'

Lundy was furious, and with Yard approval he issued a lengthy statement branding the programme 'a repetition of malicious and unfounded allegations which have been going on for a number of years. They have already been investigated and I have been fully exonerated.'

I have been in the front line of operational detective duties for more than twenty years. During the last ten years in particular I have been responsible for the arrest and conviction of numerous major criminals, including murderers and armed robbers . . .

Because of confidentiality and the Official Secrets Act, I have remained silent during the past few years and have continued to do my job with outstanding results. However, the latest series of allegations on my character have taken different and sinister lines of attack . . . The fact that Members of Parliament can irresponsibly make unsubstantiated general allegations that I am

corrupt whilst hiding behind parliamentary privilege is absolutely
disgusting . . .

I have no doubt that numerous criminals backed up by
certain sections of the media are determined to discredit me
and thus open the floodgates from prison. I will not give in
to such pressures and will continue to do my job to the best
of my ability.

This tirade was justified, but Commissioner Sir Kenneth
Newman had already bent to pressure from Home Secretary Douglas Hurd. The day after the programme Newman
announced that Peter Wright, Chief Constable of South
Yorkshire, would be investigating its allegations. These
obviously included claims that Lundy and Garner had an
improper relationship. Although in theory Newman had
appointed Wright, the inquiry would be supervised by the
newly formed Police Complaints Authority, and its deputy
chairman, former Labour MP Roland Moyle.

Lundy was appalled. He had been investigated from
pillar to post for over five years, yet nothing worthy even
of a discipline hearing had ever been proved. Now the
whole process was to be gone through again over the
same old ground. *World in Action* contained nothing new
against him – he was not among the officers alleged to have
threatened Wiltshire or his sergeants – yet a new inquiry
was now being set up with him as the main target. How
long it would last, how much it would cost, and how trivial
its search for dirt would become, neither he nor anyone
else could have predicted.

'One of Your Officers is Plotting
to Kill Me'

Two days after 'The Untouchable' was screened South
Yorkshire began work. A team of fifteen to twenty officers, led by Detective Chief Superintendent Robin Herold,
headed for London and set up office on the sixth floor of
Wellington House, a Metropolitan Police office building
not far from Scotland Yard. From the start the inquiry was
in the bizarre position of having its agenda laid down by
a journalist: Andrew Jennings. Its brief was to 'investigate
allegations raised against Metropolitan Police officers in
the *World in Action* broadcast on 3 November 1986', which
Jennings had researched and master-minded.[1] At the time
no one was more steeped in the Lundy–Garner affair than
Jennings.

On 25 November Herold had a short first interview
with Tony Lundy and served him with a Form 163 – a
formal notice of allegation – stating that 'your relationship
with one Roy Garner' was being investigated. Lundy
said he had been told that his imminent promotion to
chief superintendent (which had been approved fifteen
months previously) would now be delayed until South
Yorks completed its work. He pointed out he had been
exonerated by a past inquiry and asked if there were any
new allegations against him, by which he meant that there
was nothing new in 'The Untouchable'. Herold called in
his chief constable, Peter Wright, who said that at this
stage he could not tell what was new and what was old
in his inquiry, while Lundy's promotion was a matter for
the Metropolitan Police.

It took South Yorkshire well over a year to investigate a lot that was old and much that was 'new'. That was because Jennings, in servicing the inquiry, went far beyond the programme. On 28 November he handed over a dossier laying out sixty-four separate allegations. Many had already been investigated by 'Stagg' which had found no evidence that Lundy had committed criminal or disciplinary offences, but Jennings threw in fresh claims gleaned from the underworld, police sources and other hard-won contacts. Not that the South Yorks officers were restricted to his offerings. They canvassed for complaints against Lundy, approaching some people unsolicited on what seemed like fishing expeditions.

I was among those who received a surprise call from a senior officer on the team. He had earlier approached a newspaper journalist who knew little of the affair but said I might know more. In fact I knew little more than I had read or seen on television. I had not written articles or made programmes on Lundy or Garner. For an entire year I had been researching another book – on Freemasonry. I explained this to the officer, but he still wanted to bring another detective to see me at home. Over coffee I told them I had seen various exposés, and I had met Lundy, but I still did not see any case for him to answer. He had been investigated for years, no evidence had been found against him, and the odds were that none existed. I understood him to be London's most successful thief-taker. If that was true, complaints from criminals and jealous rivals in London's CID were bound to follow.

We chatted affably, but the South Yorks men could not have found me much help because they did not contact me again. In any case, they had plenty of other material to keep them busy. At that time it was 'open season' on Lundy; anyone and everyone was making allegations. One unsubstantiated piece of dirt was flung just three weeks before 'The Untouchable', when the Complaints Investigation Bureau (CIB) served a Form 163 on Lundy, raising this complaint: 'From an anonymous source it has been stated that you are having a house built in the Boreham Wood area, the cost of which is in excess of your earnings. It is alleged that the money for its purchase has been obtained from your corrupt practices.'

Lundy soon found out that, far from being anonymous, the allegation had come from a high-ranking policeman living nearby, who had made little of his property and was jealous of Lundy's career success. This accuser was allowed to shelter behind bogus anonymity – offering no evidence in support of his claim – while Lundy had to give the CIB details of his domestic finances going back seventeen years. The Lundys had moved home three times in that period, so he had to prove they had bought each house from within his earnings, their mortgage loans and identifiable private borrowings. He soon satisfied CIB over every house, including the one he was currently building. In 1984 Tony and Vi had sold their home for £95,000 and bought a dilapidated bungalow, next to an electricity pylon and power-lines, for £75,000. What the Lundys had spotted, but which could not be seen from the road, was three-quarters of an acre of land behind the bungalow. After a year they won planning permission to knock down the bungalow and build a far bigger home way back from the road. They achieved this with an £80,000 loan, and with Tony doing much of the labouring and trench digging himself whenever he had a few spare hours. He and Vi then did the decorating inside and out. All this took three years, during which the Lundy family lived on the site in the bungalow until July 1987 when the new house was ready and Lundy demolished the old one. When questioned by CIB, Lundy produced genuine receipts showing substantial amounts had been paid to the main builder, plasterers, plumbers, glaziers, bath and kitchen suppliers. These all demonstrably came out of the Lundys' income and loans. Now it was finished the new house was worth £250,000 (according to a hostile article),[2] but was encumbered by a £90,000 mortgage. They were to sell it in 1989 for £590,000. For sure, Tony and Vi had greatly increased their wealth but they had done so legitimately through their own hard work and initiative. No need for silver bars or kick-backs from crooks.

While Lundy was proving all this, South Yorks came on the scene and scooped up allegations that his lifestyle was above his earnings. Even his daughters' private education was put under the microscope. When this titbit was published, newspaper readers may have imagined a hugely expensive boarding school but the girls went to day schools with modest fees. To defend himself overall Lundy produced details of all his earnings since 1976, authenticated by the Inland Revenue. These proved that for years one of the Yard's hardest-working detectives had been putting in many hundreds of hours' overtime, so that his annual earnings often exceeded those of even the Assistant Commissioner, Crime. 'So how could that jealous commander claim to know my house cost in excess of my earnings?' South Yorks were obliged to accept the Inland Revenue figures, but they still scrabbled round for evidence of illicit income. On occasions Lundy saw their plain-clothes surveillance teams in unmarked cars watching his house. He wondered what they were hoping to see: twelve bars of silver loaded on a van, perhaps? He assumes they must have clocked up a good deal of overtime themselves.

A far nastier allegation surfaced three weeks after 'The Untouchable'. In September 1986 a convict called John Bryant had been charged with violently assaulting a woman but was surprisingly given bail. It seems that another criminal then introduced him to a Yard detective who gave him a copy of a criminal intelligence report on Bryant himself, and told him the information on it came from a man named Chris Robinson. This was not true but John Bryant assumed that it was and went wild. Chris Robinson was living with Bryant's former girlfriend at the time, so Bryant went to their flat, threatened the girlfriend and attacked Robinson. The police re-arrested him but again he got bail. He lured the girlfriend, with her children, out to meet him and abducted them. According to Robinson, Bryant then rang him to say, 'I've got her and the kids, and you're dead,' vowing he would get an IRA man to kill him. Fortunately Bryant was caught before the deed could be done. This time he was remanded in Brixton prison. (In 1987 he would be cleared on the original assault charge, and given a conditional discharge for attacking Robinson.)

In the meantime a nervy Robinson was trying to get his hands on the leaked intelligence report. He was a videotape producer who in 1985 had been cleared of video-piracy in a civil action. Both Robinson and Bryant knew Ian Cutler who had co-produced the 1983 *Private Spy* video on Garner and Lundy, and had hired the convict-turned-journalist John McVicar to present it. Robinson had helped edit the programme's master-tape at Cutler's North London home. In 1986, while Bryant was still at liberty he had shown Cutler the intelligence report on Robinson, and named the detective who had allegedly supplied it. When Robinson found out, he complained to CIB about the named detective. He was told that this officer had retired two years earlier, so he could not have been the man who met Bryant.

The idea was then fed in to Robinson that he might be Tony Lundy instead. This was a dangerous fiction. Lundy had never met Bryant, he knew nothing about him or

Robinson, nor had he ever drawn any file relating to Chris Robinson, if there was one. However, once Robinson had been fed Lundy's name, he went at Lundy with a vengeance. On 26 November 1986 he sent a letter to John Bryant in Brixton prison saying,

If you give me that piece of paper from the police computer saying all those lies about me, <u>I will help you</u>. Your friend Chief Superintendent Tony Lundy who gave it to you is going to be in big trouble. Ian came to see me last week. He told me everything you were up to with Lundy . . . Lundy told you to blame another policeman named – –. Well he retired 2¹/₂ years ago. That was just to put me off the scent. It did not . . . If you want me to still be a friend of yours, you must stop all the threats and give me that print-out.

When Lundy was told about this letter (which had been properly opened at the jail for security reasons) he asked for it to be brought to the attention of the Prison Liaison Department and a copy handed to Scotland Yard. Three days later, on the morning of 1 December, he answered a telephone at work. The caller asked for his boss on the Brinks–Mat inquiry, Brian Boyce. According to a contemporaneous note, Lundy – who had no reason to announce himself – replied that Boyce was not there and asked if he could help instead. The caller identified himself as Chris Robinson and insisted on speaking to Boyce. Lundy suggested Boyce could ring him back. Robinson agreed and left his telephone numbers. Lundy then asked what the call was about. Robinson replied: 'One of his officers is plotting to kill me.'

It is not often that a detective finds out he is plotting to kill a man from the mouth of his alleged victim. This time Lundy was well and truly 'gob-smacked'. So would Robinson have been, had he known he was talking to the very man he believed was having him murdered. There

was no truth in this fantasy but Lundy had been the victim
of so many crazy conspiracy theories in the past that he
could not ignore Robinson's extraordinary call or what
was in his prison letter. He promptly wrote a report to
his commander adding: 'There is obviously an extremely
sinister conspiracy going on at the moment to "fit up"
myself and other officers. I request urgent consultation
and appointment of investigating officers to look into this
matter.' An inquiry was started but it soon faded away, in
sharp contrast to the way the pettiest allegations against
Lundy were scrutinized for years on end at huge public
expense.

Ian Cutler has convictions for theft, criminal damage
and arson. In 1970 he was sent to prison for five years for
fire-bombing a restaurant. His connection with Robinson
and Bryant, and his involvement with John McVicar,
continued to haunt the 'Lundy Affair'. On 22 January
1985 Cutler's home was raided by police. They smashed
down the front door with a sledge-hammer, caused £7,000
worth of damage, and seized videotapes and recording
equipment. Cutler, who had already suffered a stroke,
claimed the raid had caused a relapse. At the time rumours
flew that it was an act of vengeance for the *Private Spy*
onslaught on Lundy back in 1983 – but Lundy had nothing
to do with the raid and knew nothing about it until
days later.

In March 1990 another version was told in the High
Court when an action brought by Cutler was at last heard.
He was claiming damages against the Metropolitan Police
for the 1985 raid. On the sixth day he accepted £15,000
and the police agreed to pay his costs. For once Lundy
did not get blamed. Cutler's case was that the raid was
connected with another piece of John McVicar journalism.
On 5 December 1984 the *Daily Express* had published a
story in which McVicar claimed to have been to Spain to

interview two criminals, Christopher Hague and Marek Raczynski. They had escaped three months earlier from a Harrow police cell after being caught red-handed robbing a building society. According to McVicar, Hague was claiming he had paid a £2,000 bribe to a police officer before they escaped. However, on 14 January 1985 they were re-captured in Berkshire. It turned out they had never been to Spain, or even left England. In the words of Cutler's counsel, McVicar's story was 'pure fiction'. However, it seems he did interview the pair in hiding in London but they had insisted he say they were in Spain to throw the police off their trail. Hague was later jailed for fifteen years, Raczynski for ten, but McVicar was not charged with wasting police time, or sued over the bribe allegation.

During Cutler's court case in 1990 the police denied that McVicar's tale – fact or fiction – had provoked their 1985 raid on his home. Their justification was a drugs warrant. In fact they were looking for John Bryant. As Chris Robinson told that violent cell-dweller in his November 1986 letter: 'The police are blaming you for when Ian got his raid. They say they were after you.'

This sordid story says nothing uplifting about the Metropolitan Police, but at least Tony Lundy emerges with credit. South Yorkshire did not pursue the 'murder plot' claim, which was handled within Scotland Yard, but much of what they did have to investigate was as baseless. A few days after Robinson made his complaint, a hatful of allegations hit the headlines during Lundy's first public test since *World in Action*.

In December 1986 two long-standing criminals, Micky West and Jimmy O'Loughlin, went on trial at Southwark Crown Court for possessing two kilograms of cocaine in 1985 with intent to supply. They were acquitted, partly because Lundy, who had taken over the case after it began, was confronted in court with the damning allegations so recently raised in 'The Untouchable'. These included Steventon's view that he was 'corrupt' and the claim that he had played down Gibson's criminality in the Silver Bullion trial. The allegations were hollow but to the jury they may have rung true. In the witness box Lundy asserted they were false, coming from 'bitter and twisted' former policemen who were part of a 'malicious trial by media'. As a mere witness, he had no opportunity to prove his innocence but, even if the jury wanted to believe him, the controversy surrounding him must have helped the defence. In inner London, juries only have to get a whiff of police corruption to be tempted to acquit.

Neither West nor O'Loughlin gave evidence but, through the defence's cross-examination of police witnesses, it emerged that they were claiming they had become involved only at the instigation of an informer whom they named as Geoffrey Stack. Back in 1985 both had been in jail: O'Loughlin at the end of a seventeen-year sentence for the 1975 Bank of America job, and West on remand for burglary. West claimed that, while inside, he was visited by Stack who suggested he could earn credit with police by helping them catch a Colombian cocaine dealer known as 'Diego'. After their release, both defendants seemed to be claiming, they had met the Colombian who sold them the cocaine. Stack then introduced them to a buyer, but he turned out to be an undercover cop and they were promptly arrested. The Colombian escaped, they were alleging, even though they had given the police his address soon after their arrest.

There was no such target Colombian, say the detectives on the case, and they did not employ West and O'Loughlin to catch any drug dealer. Nevertheless, the prosecution case was not helped when the tape of a conversation with the defendants disappeared and apologetically was declared 'irretrievably lost', then reappeared three days later. A defence expert claimed that it had been edited, and although defence counsel offered no evidence that Lundy had been responsible for these mishaps, they had dragged in so much dirt that no one was surprised when West and O'Loughlin were acquitted.

Lundy was furious. He realized that, if this onslaught was going to hit him every time he gave evidence, his days as an operational detective were over. Juries would not know that the allegations were untrue, so silver-tongued QCs would trot the same rubbish out every time. He was particularly incensed at the grinning presence of *World in Action*'s Andrew Jennings in the press box. Lundy was sure it was no coincidence that his cross-examination read like 'The Untouchable' script.

He was even more infuriated because he knew the defence case was false, including the claim that Stack was his informant. Lundy had never met such a person. Stack existed somewhere in the underworld but now he had been branded a 'grass' in court and in the press he would have to watch his back.

In fact Geoff Stack did exist, as journalist Andy Bell found out some two years after the trial. Bell was news editor of *Time Out*, a magazine which does the police no favours but keeps its objectivity. Preparing an article on Tony Lundy, Bell interviewed Stack who 'made a persuasive case that he was never a police informant'.[3] Bell's doubts about West and O'Loughlin were increased when he learned that, a few months after their trial, they had hawked a wholly different tale to the newspapers. They were no longer claiming that Lundy's informer in the case was Stack. It was Roy Garner! The crooked duo had changed their story in the hope of getting a big pay-out, but even Fleet Street refused to run their brand-new lie and sent them off empty-handed.

The true story was even nastier. There *had* been an informant but he did not 'belong' to Lundy. He was known to an officer drafted on to the Brinks–Mat squad where Lundy was senior intelligence co-ordinator. This source claimed that West and O'Loughlin, then out of jail, were involved in drugs in a big way. The job required a policeman to go undercover, as a participating informant. The Yard hierarchy approved this dangerous operation and authorized Lundy's boss, Brian Boyce, to supervise it personally. At the time, however, Boyce was busy running a series of complex trials of gold bullion robbers and receivers at the Old Bailey. That is how the job landed on Lundy's plate when it was already under way.

It went like a dream. The undercover cop was introduced to West and O'Loughlin as a villain looking to buy cocaine. He agreed to buy two kilos, so Lundy had to get permission to make £64,000 available for the 'buy'. The next meeting was secretly videotaped and tape-recorded. The undercover cop showed up with the cash and an armed minder (another plain-clothes man). The minder stayed with West while the buyer drove off with O'Loughlin. They returned with two kilos of cocaine. As the money was about to be handed over, dozens of police suddenly swooped and captured West and O'Loughlin. That was the police version.

The pair were now quivering. They knew they could get twenty years for so much cocaine, so they tried for a deal. They begged for bail, but Lundy ruled it out. They then turned informer themselves and claimed that a violent North London villain had recently been handling a load of heroin. This led to raids on a hotel where he and several other men were found with much money but no drugs, and on the villain's home where some drugs were found. His wife was later charged and convicted.

At the time West and O'Loughlin were in custody

in Wormwood Scrubs, screaming for bail. One day a prison security officer rang Lundy's office and told how O'Loughlin had been caught in possession of a tiny radio microphone transmitter. He had violently resisted a search straight after a visit from his woman friend, so it was obvious she had given him the bug. It seemed likely that he planned to use it next day at Marylebone Magistrates' Court where he was to appear for his weekly remand. Past police experience indicated he probably intended to trap the two sergeants on his case into saying something compromising, which could then be used to discredit the prosecution in the cocaine trial.

Lundy told the sergeants to take an extra squad of officers next morning, to scour the streets all round the court. Sure enough, not far away they found O'Loughlin and West's spouses along with a criminal in a car equipped with a radio tape-recorder. They were arrested and questioned, and their homes searched. At one place some notes were found, apparently written by one of the prisoners. They were addressed to John McVicar, they named Lundy and said the women would explain what this was all about. The notes were presumably intended to accompany the tapes, but there was no indication that McVicar knew of the scheme. When questioned by police, neither the women nor the accomplice would say anything. They were charged with possessing stolen cheque books and a cheque card, but were never prosecuted over the bugging attempt.

A few days after this scheme was discovered, a prisoner in Wormwood Scrubs alongside West and O'Loughlin spoke to the officer in charge of his case, which had nothing to do with Lundy. The prisoner volunteered words to the effect: 'I may be a villain but I don't agree with what they're doing. There's a big plot to stitch up Lundy. They're going to plant two kilos of heroin at his house, and they're bringing somebody over from Belgium to do it.' Scotland Yard appointed a senior officer to investigate. He took a written statement from the prisoner and found his story checked out. A friend of the accused pair had served a prison sentence in Belgium, had criminal contacts there and had been on a recent visit. Lundy was used to being the victim of dirty tricks but this news scared him stiff.

The heroin was on its way, they knew where I lived, and when it had been planted they were going to make a phone call to the police saying 'Lundy's got drugs in his house.' The police would go and search it, find the heroin and that would be my lot! Who's going believe me after that? You can imagine: suddenly the drugs squad or CIB get a call, 'Lundy's got two kilos in his house' – up they come and steam in! I would have been hung, drawn and quartered. It would have been the easiest thing in the world to plant drugs at that house because it was so wooded and isolated.

Then my boss Phil Corbett says, 'We're going to put full surveillance on your premises, Tony, we'll install alarms and cameras, we've got to do it!' I don't want all that. At this time, remember, I'm tearing across the world after the gold bullion proceeds and I'm worried what impact all this harassment – from TV, newspapers and villains – is having on my wife and kids back home. We've already moved house once to get away from the press, after that nonsense over the burglary and the briefcase stuffed full of notes, so I daren't tell them about this latest effort to fit me up. How *can* I say what might happen? So I tell Phil, 'You want to have people there watching all night long? The family will never sleep or relax again! It's not on. I'll just have to live with the threat. But at least it's on paper, everyone in the job's been forewarned, including CIB and the Commissioner.' The only person not informed was my wife Vi. I didn't dare tell her till three years later!

Eventually the plot fizzled out – they may have got word that we knew – but it was definitely going to happen. Of course, when they got to court they didn't need a heroin fit-up on me to get off. They had all the ammunition from what appeared on *World in Action*. It happened that the jury came back on a day when I was being interviewed by South Yorkshire. During the interview I got a phone call saying West and O'Loughlin had got off. The South Yorks officers could see I was gutted, because I knew from that day forward there was no way I could ever go to court again in this country – no point – because there was always going to be the same attack.

What grieved me wasn't just what happened to me. It was that two bad drug dealers had got off. They weren't into just two kilos of cocaine, they had access to eighty! My plan was to go after the whole lot. I wanted to let the £64,000 go, we'd take the two kilos and then make a meet for the full eighty. But the Yard hierarchy didn't dare do it, they hadn't got the bottle. I said, 'You're playing games at it. In America they'd do it. At the very worst you'll lose £64,000, but you'll still have the two kilos and still be able to arrest them. But if you let them run, they'll be so greedy at the thought of getting *two and a half million pounds* for eighty kilos, they're bound to come back. We'll film it again, get a record load and probably bag their supplier too.' Of course, I couldn't convince my masters, which was a pity because when we analysed the two kilos, it turned out to be over ninety per cent pure, packaged direct from Colombia. Cut up, it would have been worth tens of millions.

Two astonishing twists were still to come. Following their acquittal, West and O'Loughlin had to be given back all their seized property. This included several rolls of £50 notes. As they were about to leave the room, O'Loughlin dropped one of the rolls in the waste-paper bin. One officer noticed this. He retrieved the money and forced O'Loughlin to take it all back, before making sure that both men left police premises without dropping any more money.

Then, weeks later, word reached the Brinks–Mat squad that the pair were offering to set up drug dealers for arrest, in the same way that, they claimed, they themselves had been set up. The squad rejected the offer, first, because the use of *agents provocateurs* is unlawful, second, because it smelt like yet another set-up for the amusement of the media.

A Big Result

For Roy Garner 'The Untouchable' spelt the beginning of the end. He had feared as much ever since October 1986 when it dawned on him that any day *World in Action* would broadcast a revamped version of the banned *Brass Tacks*. Highly vulnerable in jail, he tried hard to stop the show but, far from reducing his problems, these efforts merely sealed his downfall.

At the time the copper to whom he would normally have aired his fears, Tony Lundy, was searching America and the Caribbean for laundered Brinks–Mat monies, so Garner went straight to DAC Brian Worth. Worth was surprised to get a call from a serving convict but Garner had told the authorities at Wayland Prison he had information 'of national importance'. On the phone he would not tell Worth what it was, instead insisting on delivering it in person at the Yard.

Aware of Garner's tortuous relationship with his predecessor David Powis, Worth discussed this approach with Assistant Commissioner Dellow. They both felt Scotland Yard should have no more to do with him. The force's stance, as Worth wrote at the time, was 'to keep Garner at arm's length and not initiate any contact'. Yet he had always been a superb informant and the Yard was reluctant to spurn his intelligence even now. That was why Dellow authorized Worth and his staff officer, Superintendent Roy Ramm, to see him. On 29 October prison authorities allowed him a day trip to London. When Garner met the officers he had no idea Ramm was tape-recording the conversation.

The transcript shows Garner indeed claiming to offer information 'of national importance', but in return he wanted the Yard to block *World in Action*. He believed the programme had access to 'all the evidence that Mr Powis took to court' to obtain his substantial damages from the *Observer*, including receipts for reward payments signed by Garner.

If the programme were to be shown, he said, he was a dead man. The prisons were full of drug addicts who would murder him for a pittance. 'I'll be the first to go if that television comes out . . . if you want a scandal it'll come if me or my family are hurt.'

Without waiting for a promise from the Yard, Garner said 710 kilograms of cocaine had been smuggled into Britain in July 1986: 'Now if that ain't a national problem to you, God knows what is!' He claimed to know the organizer only as a slim, 6 feet 2 inch, fifty-five-year-old Dane called Jan, but he described the distribution system in some detail: 'Now up until Tuesday there was 26 kilo left, that 26 kilo is being transported to Glasgow tomorrow. That is positive. How it's going I don't know, I'm guessing by train because I understand the previous lot went by train. With the arrival of this 710 kilo came fourteen mules – carriers, peasants, dead bodies – sell their heart and soul for a pound of sausages.' The cocaine was Colombian, 'packed, wrapped three times with Colombian newspapers in between each pack.'

Garner claimed that on various visits to America he had established credibility with the syndicate to which 'Jan' belonged, by helping a South London criminal, Freddie Foreman, who had also been in America in recent years and was known to members of the New York Mafia.[1] This made Garner look a good contact for organizing drug imports into Britain. When 'Jan' arrived he found Garner was in jail so, 'someone else jumped in and tried to do the job'. However, there was a big problem with so immense a load: 'There's no way that London can absorb 710 kilo . . . I would think that if London can handle five kilo, seriously, five kilo a week uncut, that's it.'

He predicted another huge consignment was on its way: 'There's the biggest load of cocaine that's ever left Colombia on its way here. I'm telling you, it's arrived and sold and gone. Now it comes over by sea, now you've got a choice of coming in June, July, or October, November, when you're going to come.'

Garner indicated his information was coming from 'Henry Radley' (a pseudonym, for legal reasons) who had been convicted with him on the Kruger-rand VAT fraud. Radley had been released from jail eight months earlier but had since been charged with a passport offence and vanished. If he turned up, Garner did not want him arrested because he had been handling 'Jan' while Garner was still in jail: 'Radley had to do part of what I was expected to do.' He should be allowed to remain free, said Garner, so he could keep supplying him with intelligence.

'Now what I want, sir, please,' Garner begged Worth, 'I want the press off me back and I want Granada off me back, and in return 710 kilo will be arriving here. I know how it's coming, I know approximately when it will come, and I would like to deal for it.' He suggested invoking the Official Secrets Act to stop *World in Action*. Worth ruled that out.

They'll take a lot of stopping, certainly the Official Secrets Act won't do it . . . I don't have the sort of power to stop the programme. They are a very high-grade investigative set-up who pride themselves, as I understand it, that they are totally unapproachable and they do their own thing for the good of whatever . . . And even trying may make it worse because they'll say, 'you've got something to hide' because they will no doubt expect us to try . . .

Garner left empty-handed. As he took the train back to his Norfolk jail he must have kicked himself for informing on the cocaine job *before* extracting a guarantee to stop the show. Yet DAC Worth could never have given a guarantee. He rightly gauged the futility of trying, although his boss, Assistant Commissioner Dellow, did send a letter to Granada next day. Three days more and the show was broadcast. It provoked no attacks on Garner or his family. His underworld victims were either biding their time, or they cynically accepted that each of them would grass too if the price were right, or they had decided that not even 'mega-grasses' like Garner are worth killing.

Garner himself had sensed another kind of danger. During the taped conversation he had complained about Gerry Wiltshire, Operation Albany's newly retired head, who 'feels he's had a bad deal from all round. He went for me like a terrier dog. Now there was nothing. I haven't been on armed robberies. I haven't done any of that. I know that, he knows that.' Turning to the Wood Green hearing when Wiltshire testified against him, he said: 'If you want to read the script over the gun licence it would make a good play.' Four days after Garner made these remarks, Wiltshire appeared on 'The Untouchable' and blasted off again.

Garner had also complained about Wiltshire's sergeant, Gordon Bain, who was still in the force pursuing Garner's assets to recoup £2 million VAT for the Official Receiver. Garner told Worth he was sure that 'Bain was working with the press.'

This belief had driven Garner into a paranoid fit earlier that day when, waiting to see Worth and Ramm, he sat in the Yard foyer only to see Bain and a colleague walk out. Worth assured him this was a coincidence 'because they didn't know you were coming'. Garner also feared that, as he left the building, he would be confronted by a wall of cameramen. 'To clinch everything, a photo of me coming out of here will just about hit. That's the last nail in the coffin.' To avoid that embarrassment Roy Ramm arranged for an unmarked car to be driven out through the garage, with Garner lying on the back seat.

Two weeks later, on 14 November, Garner was freed. He immediately rang Tony Lundy, now back from his trans-Atlantic inquiries, saying he wished to see a senior officer because he was dissatisfied with the assistance given him by the Yard. Lundy passed the request to Brian Worth who arranged for Garner to see Roy Ramm again on 17 November and also Chief Superintendent Robin Herold of the South Yorks inquiry. Herold would want to see Garner sometime, and here was an appropriate occasion. Again the conversation was to be recorded without Garner's knowledge. He was told to go to Wellington House, not far from Scotland Yard, where the South Yorks team had set up base. Horror of horrors! Who should he see again as he came into the building but Gordon Bain.

As he was introduced to Herold soon after, a jaundiced Garner told Ramm: 'Before we start, sir, there's little point in calling me "Granger" because our friend Mr Bain was in the foyer calling me Mr Garner . . . To help you I've come here and the very man that *shouldn't* see me is in the foyer.' Ramm said Bain did not even work in the building: 'I chose here because it's away from the Yard. I've no idea what he's doing here. What can we say?' 'I've got to believe you,' said Garner, 'because it's just too coincidental to be a coincidence.'

Herold then revealed that in the past few days Bain had been giving South Yorks a statement, but he had no idea he was coming in this afternoon. 'If apologies are necessary, then I apologize, but believe me, it was sod's law.' Herold said, the less publicity his inquiry received the better. He would see Bain, 'if I can get my hands on him', and tell him to say 'absolutely nothing whatsoever to anybody . . . about your visit here as a direct order'.

The revelation that Bain was collaborating with South Yorks upset Garner, and ruined Herold's attempt to get his co-operation. Herold tried to explain his mission, but Garner was not interested. He wanted help over his son Mark's court appearance next day, alongside the elusive Henry Radley, on passport offences. Roy was upset because none other than Sergeant Bain was running the case.

Now all I am really looking for is some help . . . is he going to – as he's done at every other meeting – go completely off his rocker at court, and try and stop my lad's bail, therefore keeping him away over Christmas?

Roy said he needed his lad home because his own father was dying at the time. Ramm offered him the straw that Bain would be replaced by a more senior officer at court. This calmed Garner whose second request was that Radley should not have his bail withdrawn despite the fact that he had not shown up at court last time. He would be surrendering tomorrow, said Garner, but, 'If you bang Radley up, you sever me completely from any chance I got of seeing what's gonna take place in a month or two's time.' That would cut Scotland Yard's best informer off from his best source on the largest cocaine importation this country had ever known, or so Garner wanted the police to believe.

Herold meantime was trying to appease Garner so he would help South Yorks get to the bottom of the Lundy allegations. If anybody knew the truth Garner did. Only now did Garner ask if the conversation was being recorded. He was told 'No'. This fib may have been told because his inquisitors hoped he would now 'dish the dirt' on Lundy, if there was dirt to dish. Instead he gave this response: 'If there's anything bad going on with Lundy and me, you'd have heard it way before now. I mean, there is no secrets in your job, only venom. And it's become personal. Someone has got venom, terrible venom, against Lundy and [is] using me to draw it out.'

At his meeting with Worth, Garner had been more forthcoming, but no help to anyone looking to send Lundy to jail.

They are trying to say that Lundy and I had something going – now you know that is complete and utter rubbish – [that] I escaped prosecution for giving bodies. Now let me remind you that while Lundy was in his job he had over two hundred arrests, all aided with supergrasses. Now if I was 'active' there's no way you people wouldn't know. It's impossible. You know everyone that's active from the supergrasses that you've had come through your books. Now my liaison with Lundy was purely that I've known him many years. He was at my boy's boxing club and saw fit to favour my boy . . . He seemed decent, straight, upright and we formed a liaison.

If you go back and look at Lundy's records there never was no money [rewards] for years and years and years. I don't like bad thieves, I don't like plastic gangsters, I was nicely situated to give him all the help I did – pubs and clubs, silly talk, loose talk – I haven't lied for my fifteen years that I've been associated with Lundy, there's no lies anywhere. I haven't been misleading. I told the truth or I said nothing . . .

Lundy is not crooked. Now I look you both [Worth and Ramm] in the eye and say that – as many times as you need me to say it – you, Granada and no one else could make that right. For some reason, he's the straightest thing on two legs . . . Now we grown together . . . and then he went to that college of yours and learned how to interrogate me without knowing, and he drew me out, and once you're in, you put your big toe in, and you're in, aren't you? And that's how Lundy got me in.

The idea that Garner was somehow tricked or trapped into informing may have been hard for Herold to swallow.

He tried a different tack. He appealed to Garner for any
dirt on *any* crooked London cops: 'If you can make waves
for anybody in the Met, through malpractice or anything
at all, then I want to know. I make no promises. I simply
put my cards on the table and say, "Look, Roy Garner, if
you can – please do."'

There could be no clearer incitement to inform on bent
'old bill'. Yet, far from telling tales on Lundy, Garner made
this reply:

> Well, the only suggestion I've got – and there's no way you
> can call it a malpractice – . . . you'd think you'd been sold
> down the river if a man in Mr Powis's position took confidential
> paperwork and information to court . . . and expose half of
> what the Metropolitan Police would consider was confidential
> and secret information.

Ramm then explained to Herold how, during Powis's
Observer libel suit, documents emerged that caused Garner's informer role to become 'common currency'. Herold
listened with apparent sympathy and must have been
interested to hear so soon from his potential number one
source that Lundy was as clean as a whistle.

In the next few weeks Garner had more fraught exchanges
with the Yard, mostly over his insistence on talking to the
only cop he trusted. On 20 November he called Tony
Lundy at work and asked to see him. Lundy repeated
what he had already told Garner many times: he had been
instructed not to meet him and he must report his request.
Garner said he would talk to no one else because every
time he went to the Yard he bumped into Gordon Bain.
Lundy reported the conversation and next day he called
Garner from Brian Worth's office, with Herold listening
in. This time Garner was told he was being tape-recorded,
and Lundy again said he could not meet him alone because
of the inquiry. Garner exploded: 'I'm not interested in

your inquiry. What the fuck has your inquiry got to do with me? . . . If you want some help, I'm available but it isn't my problem. You've given me fuck all. I don't know what you think you're going to give me in the future.'

Garner was so fed up over the Yard's failure to stop *World in Action* and over Gordon Bain, that he threatened to refuse all future help over the cocaine:

Now you all go stew in your own juice, you all go fuck one another up, which you're plainly doing, and at the end of the day when I feel like it, and you and your lot up there have this country such a fucking problem you can't deal with, one of you come cap in hand and make me some proper promises and guarantees and I'll help you. But for the minute, no thank you. You're not going to talk me into it. I've got my family to consider.

Later that day Lundy made another recorded call to Garner who had calmed down. He talked of the latest twists and turns in the cocaine saga. He indicated that his man Radley had been minding a large sum for him in California – £1 million, it later emerged – and had entrusted it to an English car dealer named Peter. This Peter placed the money with some dubious character who had subsequently stolen it, to Radley and Garner's understandable fury. According to Garner's information, an unidentified Yard detective had then told a Los Angeles cop that Radley was just waiting for his US visa before coming to 'do the business on Peter' (to kill him) over the money. This provoked Garner to ask Lundy: 'Now what is someone in your place doing liaising with American officers and filling them full of that fucking shit?'

Lundy was bemused: 'Well, I don't know, and I don't know that it's happened because I'm not part of it . . . I'll only pass it on and we'll see.'

All these calls, made with the knowledge and consent

of Scotland Yard and South Yorks, were ruffling the
feathers of people who wanted to stop all contact between
the two men. From the beginning of 1981 Lundy had
complied with orders to report all meetings with Garner
before they occurred, but since South Yorks began work,
those orders had been tightened. A few hours after his
florid conversations with Garner, Lundy was ordered by
Assistant Commissioner Dellow to 'strictly adhere' to this
text when talking with 'David Granger'.

I have been instructed to say to you if you have any information about crime you must give it. If you do not then I am further
instructed to tell you that I must have no further contact with
you during the currency of the inquiry by the Chief Constable
of South Yorkshire, Mr Wright.

If Garner asked how he should pass information, Lundy
was to say: 'We will make arrangements but you will have
to accept who we nominate to accept the information
and see you.' Dellow insisted: 'No further contact will
be allowed.'

Lundy had already made Garner fully aware of the state
of play but this new script was such a mouthful that Garner
would have spat it back in his ear, had the detective been so
pompous as to quote it. Anyway, there was nothing Lundy
could say to stop Garner contacting him. On Sunday 7
December he even turned up in Lundy's local pub and
asked to speak to him as he drank with his family. Garner
said he knew he should not contact Lundy but he did
not know who else to trust. Lundy said he must report
their conversation immediately. Garner did not mind and
talked of his latest efforts to recover the cocaine, and of
his partner Henry Radley.

Lundy had never met Radley, or even heard of a man
named Roy Whitehorne whom Garner suddenly started
talking about. He said that Whitehorne was a jeweller in

Fort Lauderdale who hailed from Sheffield, England. He was also Radley's contact in the cocaine deal. The previous day this Whitehorne had phoned Radley, who promptly phoned Garner. Garner said: 'Whitehorne was leading a conversation in such a way that Radley believed it was being taped and thought Whitehorne might be involved with police in Florida.' Garner then made this offer to the Yard: he was willing to go to the USA 'to tape conversations with Whitehorne and was still sure he could lead to the seizure of the 710 kilos'. After telling Lundy all this, Garner left the pub.

Lundy himself went straight home and called Commander Corbett about what had just happened. Next day he wrote a full report of Garner's conversation, which Corbett sent to DAC Worth. Corbett noted that London cocaine prices had fallen by twenty-five per cent in the past year, which indicated large amounts had recently been smuggled in. Now it seemed that more was on its way: 'Since this informant is seldom incorrect, the possibility of the suggested massive import of cocaine is a real prospect.' However, he cautioned, there might be other motives behind Garner's offer to help in the USA, notably his need to act over his huge losses in California.

This offer set the cat among the Yard pigeons. DAC Brian Worth wrote that it placed the Yard

. . . somewhat on the horns of a dilemma here. Operationally it might be thought inconceivable not to pursue the potential of a seizure of 710 kilograms of cocaine whether off our coast or in the USA. And to this end one would have to 'sup with a long spoon' with Garner again . . . Obviously, as is the way with these things, Garner's potential information may come to nothing, either because of some game he is playing, for some advantage, or for reasons beyond our control in the USA. It seems unlikely he will lie down of his own volition, so some contact will have to be made with him. To allow him to go to the USA as an agent (as he appears to be suggesting) would

in my opinion be unacceptable, even supposing the Americans
would grant him a visa. I advise only debriefing.

Assistant Commissioner Dellow agreed and wrote that,
'The magnitude of the consignment or its potential cannot
be ignored.' However, he said, there could be no deals
with this man. Worth meantime had read transcripts of
the recent taped conversations and became convinced
that Garner was trying to use Scotland Yard: 'He has
come up with nothing concrete. That is not to say he
won't but reading between the lines it looks as if he wants
our valediction [sic] for a trip to the USA. This cannot
be.' Dellow also feared that if the Yard assisted him this
way, 'we could be in unproductive contact with the man
for evermore'. He ordered no further contact 'unless and
until Garner by his own initiative provides information
that can be acted upon'.

Far from helping Garner, Dellow and Worth went the
other way and canvassed the US Embassy to stop him
getting into America. Dellow told Ramm to call Garner
to check on his plan to leave Britain on 10 December.
Unwisely Garner revealed he had a valid passport with
a life-time US visa, but feared there was a block on
him entering the States. Ramm offered to find out and
to let him know next day. Ramm told Dellow, Dellow
spoke to the Embassy's resident FBI agent, who would
'attend to the visa'. Sure enough, when Garner flew to
Los Angeles on 5 January 1987 he was refused entry. He
protested to an immigration officer that a lot of money
belonging to him and his partner had been stolen from
a safe deposit box, and he had come to get it back. The
officer, acting on instructions from the London Embassy,
said he must refuse him entry because of his recent jail
sentence. Garner had no choice. He was put on the next
flight back to London.

By the time Garner had made his offer through Lundy, some South Yorks men had already visited America. Neither Dellow nor Worth knew the reason for the trip, only that it must have related to Garner's US activities and allegations of police corruption. Dellow therefore sent South Yorkshire's Chief Constable, Peter Wright, copies of all the Yard's documents on Garner's offer. He added: 'If your recent inquiries in Florida revealed anything that throws light on Garner's alleged information about a cocaine assignment, and you felt able to comment, I would appreciate a personal word from you . . . there is little enough to test Garner with at this stage, and every little would help.'

Shut out of America, Garner was soon off to western Europe where he could come and go without a visa. Records show he kept calling Lundy to complain about his US ban and the theft of his fortune, but said he would prefer England's Official Receiver to have that million rather than the bent lawyer who had stolen it. He also complained that South Yorks had raided his premises and taken correspondence he needed to settle the bankruptcy order imposed after his VAT conviction.

He now had another worry. Following inquiries by the tireless Sergeant Bain, Kenneth Colquhoun, an officer at Ford Prison in Sussex, had been charged with corruption: taking £3,000 from Garner for smuggling in hampers of goodies such as smoked salmon, champagne, vodka and cigars for Garner when he was serving his sentence for the VAT fraud. South Yorks had now taken over the case and wanted to question Garner. A warrant was issued for his arrest but he could not be found. Whenever he called Lundy in the early months of 1987 he would not give his exact whereabouts. Lundy kept telling him to surrender, but Garner refused because his request that his solicitor be present throughout any subsequent interrogation had been turned down.

On 23 April 1987, still abroad, he called Lundy again. He said that Henry Radley, who along with Mark Garner had received three months for passport offences, was soon due out of jail. Now Garner was claiming he feared that Radley might disappear to the USA on some valid passport. However, if his US visa was withdrawn Radley would have no choice but to do his cocaine business on this side of the Atlantic where Garner could know what was happening and inform to Scotland Yard. Then he promised, 'We would have a big result.'

A big result was on its way, but not the one Garner was hoping for. On 21 June 1987 Customs and Excise raided a flat in Harley Street, central London, and found 52.4 kilograms of cocaine hidden in three suitcases in a cupboard under the stairs. It was all that was left of an original consignment of 392 kilos which had been shipped from Panama to within forty miles of Cornwall, transferred to a catamaran, then smuggled onshore on 20 August 1986.

Two days before the London seizure, Customs had arrested a Mr and Mrs Nikolaus Chrastny in another Harley Street flat. Chrastny was the prime mover in this conspiracy and Customs had been after him for seven months. He was a German national, born in 1943, a convict and still wanted in Munich for the 1973 robbery of £250,000-worth of precious stones. Portly, bald, of medium height, with a penchant for disguise and using the alias Charles Flynn, Chrastny was now a bogus US citizen, an international jewel dealer and a drug smuggler who had risen from the rank of armed guard on other people's runs to become a leading smuggler in his own right, trafficking marijuana and cocaine across the Caribbean. He was also suspected of murder. For eighteen months, from the beginning of 1985, Chrastny had travelled frequently between

Colombia and England purchasing the 392 kilos of cocaine, overseeing the shipping arrangements and checking on the British distribution set-up. When arrested, he soon shopped two of his 'gophers', Brian Van Den Breen and Robert Cermak, who were captured with the 52.4 kilos. Two days later, on 23 June, Customs arrested another man at his home in Southgate. It was none other than Roy Garner.

Garner was soon charged with conspiring in the very drugs deal on which he had been informing for eight months. His trouble was that he had been informing to Scotland Yard but was captured by Customs. The biter had been bit. Just as Henry Radley, Garner's sidekick, had feared back in December 1986, the jewellery store owner Roy Whitehorne was in league with police. He had been coerced into co-operating. In December 1984 his former girlfriend had gone to Florida's detective force, the Department of Law Enforcement (FDLE), and shopped him over his drug connections. These included Nikolaus Chrastny, alias Charles Flynn, who had come to know him through their common interest in precious stones.

Working on the girlfriend's information, FDLE had made use of an imprisoned jewel thief named Jimmy Tullevere who was looking for a way to get his sentence reduced. He was allowed out to infiltrate Whitehorne's circle. He visited his jewel store in Fort Lauderdale and, after a few meetings, gained his confidence. Wearing a body-microphone, he then recorded 125 hours of tapes with Whitehorne who often yapped on about Charles Flynn as he himself planned various drug deals. By October 1986 FDLE arrested Whitehorne. In November he pleaded guilty to conspiracy to distribute drugs (within the USA) but was not jailed because he had turned informer. He received a mere ten years' probation and duly talked of the separate UK cocaine conspiracy, and his crucial role in introducing Chrastny to Radley and Garner. He co-operated with law enforcement, making phone calls and other helpful moves. By then FDLE was working with British Customs, which arrested Chrastny seven months later. This was a full six weeks after German police had given Customs his Harley Street address. While he was under Customs surveillance, in those six weeks Chrastny and his team shifted some 60 kilos of cocaine, worth £15 million.

When Customs put its case together to fit England's judicial system, it gave Whitehorne total immunity even though he had played a fundamental role in a conspiracy which had successfully smuggled £100 million worth of cocaine into Britain. No British police force could have engineered such a deal. Ever since the 'Bertie Smalls' judgement in the Court of Appeal (see Chapter 2) no supergrass in a major police case has been able to get off scot-free. Customs investigators have far greater powers. They may grant immunity to whomever they like. In this case it suited their books to bring Whitehorne across the Atlantic to testify against Garner, having promised to let him return a free man.

News of Garner's arrest perturbed many of Scotland Yard's top brass. To that date they had told Customs nothing of his passing information on Whitehorne, Radley and the cocaine. Now Customs had to be told, as Garner was certain to try and use this fact somehow in his defence. If Scotland Yard did not tell Customs before that happened, it could be severely embarrassed, especially when the story was leaked out to the media, as it assuredly would be. DAC Brian Worth now pressed his boss John Dellow to meet Customs chiefs, with South Yorks, to exchange intelligence. In order to brief Dellow, Worth talked through the Garner interview transcripts with Tony Lundy and the Drugs Squad head, Chief Superintendent Roy Penrose.

On 26 June a 'summit' took place in Dellow's office. Customs was represented by Dick Lawrence, chief investigation officer, and his deputy Arthur Rigby. Also there was Robin Herold of South Yorks who later claimed the credit in a statement he made to his own inquiry:

> Because of my unique position in being privy to at least part of the information supplied by Garner to Lundy in the last two or three years, and also being privy to certain aspects of the operation being conducted by HM Customs, I felt there was a need for the two agencies to meet and exchange intelligence in the public interest.

Garner's role as some kind of an informer on the conspiracy was duly revealed to his captors, but when he came to trial in 1989 he was portrayed as one of the prime movers. Rolling Customs evidence up with Scotland Yard's, the prosecution offered this scenario. Whitehorne had brought Chrastny together with Radley and Garner as early as 1984. The North London pair offered £1 million to buy the cocaine, and the deal was set to go ahead when, in November 1984, both were jailed over their VAT racket. This caused them to drop out and to be replaced by others, but in February 1986 Radley was released and joined in again, visiting Garner in jail to keep him informed. Whatever he told Garner, he may now have played a very active role. In August 1986, allegedly, he travelled to Cornwall and, using his pilot's licence, rented a plane to fly over the smuggling boats on the very day the cocaine was landed, to make sure Customs were not about to pounce. The cocaine was then moved to London, stored in rented flats, and Radley used to take several kilos at a time to distribute, or so Customs would later claim.

As for Garner's missing million, Radley had indeed entrusted it to a Peter in Los Angeles, an Englishman named Peter Davy who was a fraudster but appeared to earn a living selling second-hand cars. He had met Radley in January 1986, when they were both in Wandsworth prison for separate VAT frauds. Davy was soon released; he re-entered the USA and returned to Los Angeles. On 20 February he received a surprise call from Radley, asking him to help shift instantly £1 million (in fact, $1,262,000) from a bank account in New York. The money's whereabouts had just been discovered by none other than Sergeant Bain in London who had found some account documents when searching a briefcase belonging to Mark Garner. Davy promptly obliged, using a Hollywood lawyer to transfer the money to a Los Angeles bank account opened for Davy in a false name. Davy and the lawyer then creamed off $120,000 each for their services. The lawyer traded the remaining million dollars for Kruger-rands and other gold coins, and secreted them in a safe deposit vault. This rapid response took the money beyond the reach of Sergeant Bain and Superintendent Wiltshire on Operation Albany. Having reported Bain's earlier discovery, they had not been permitted by Scotland Yard to pursue the money themselves. Now it was under the total control of villains just as big as Radley and Garner. When Radley was able to go and collect it in September 1986 it had gone, disappeared. The deposit box was empty. The fraudsmen had been defrauded of what seems to have been the million they had earmarked to buy the cocaine.

When the cocaine trial began at the Old Bailey in January 1989 Radley had still not been found. Meantime mastermind Chrastny had escaped in farcical circumstances from a police cell in Dewsbury, West Yorkshire, where he had been hidden for safe and secure keeping. Of the alleged major players, only Garner now faced prosecution. The jury did not believe his secret defence (disclosed *in camera*) that he was a passive participant, gathering information for Scotland Yard. They found him guilty of conspiring to smuggle drugs, and the judge sentenced him to twenty-two years in jail. The main evidence against him – other than the Scotland Yard tapes – was the word of Roy Whitehorne. For various reasons Whitehorne included a number of lies in his evidence. Even so, the jury believed him more than Garner.

Had Garner not tried to stop *World in Action*'s version of 'The Untouchable' or told the Yard anything about the 710 kilos, he might have been able to claim he knew nothing of Whitehorne or the cocaine deal, but he was the author of his own misfortune. He had made a fatal mistake: he had informed against himself.

Out of a sackful of questions surrounding this case, at least two demand answers here. The first is: Should Scotland Yard have told Customs back in October 1986 that Garner was offering to inform on the cocaine job, rather than wait until his arrest eight months later? The Yard's CID chiefs have been criticized in the press for this apparent failure, but it is not clear if they even knew that Garner had come up in Customs drug inquiries before his arrest. In contrast the South Yorkshire inquiry *must* have known that as far back as November 1986 when some of its officers travelled to Florida. In addition, on 9 December 1986, John Dellow had asked their chief constable Peter Wright 'if your recent inquiries in Florida revealed anything that throws light on Garner's alleged information about a cocaine assignment . . . I would appreciate a personal word from you . . . there is little enough to test Garner with at this stage, and every little would help.'

It is now clear that South Yorks were already liaising with officers in Florida's Department of Law Enforcement, over what their witness Whitehorne might know of any corrupt Yard connection. As the FDLE was already working closely with British Customs, South Yorks must have learned of Customs' interest in Garner by that November. Yet it was not until his arrest seven months later that the inquiry chief, Robin Herold, saw the need to bring Yard and Customs together, due to his 'unique position in being privy to . . . information supplied by Garner to Lundy . . . and also being privy to certain aspects of the operation being conducted by HM Customs'. He clearly did not think it necessary to bring them together earlier, so possibly the Scotland Yard hierarchy did not know of Customs' special interest before Garner's arrest.

The Yard, of course, had decided to leave Garner and his information alone because it no longer wished to sup with this man even 'with a long spoon'. On 11 December 1986 Dellow had told Worth not to pursue this matter 'unless and until Garner <u>by his own initiative</u> provides information that can be acted upon'. The trouble was that Garner, keeping his options open, had given the Yard very little to work on: only the names of his partner, Henry Radley, and Roy Whitehorne. The Yard decided to ignore this morsel. One Yard man with the tenacity to pursue it, Tony Lundy, had been expressly forbidden to initiate contact with Garner or follow up anything he said. Garner might well have performed as a prime informant yet again but, with no Lundy to goad him, he failed to inform enough on the plot to avoid his ultimate conviction as a co-conspirator. However, the affair was confounded by two long-running sub-plots of distrust and animosity: between Customs and the Yard and between the Yard hierarchy and the last survivors of Operation Albany. This leads on to the second major question demanding an answer here: Just what was Albany's Sergeant Bain up to, with South Yorkshire and over in America?

Garner was right to believe that Bain was the source of many of his recent troubles. Pursuing Garner's and his VAT fraud millions, Bain had 'flagged' Garner's VAT accomplice, Henry Radley, as a target.[2] By mid-1986 Radley had come up on FDLE tapes of Roy Whitehorne's conversations. Bain was notified and realized, on talking to Florida officers, that Garner was also involved. By now Bain was well-steeped in the view that Tony Lundy was corruptly bound up with Garner, that they were a criminal double-act. His superior officer, Detective Chief Superintendent John Bates, felt there was nothing to justify such a view and that, after all these years, 'Albany' should 'put up' about Lundy – present enough evidence to justify criminal charges against him – or 'shut up'.

Bain appears to have regarded much of the Yard hierarchy as involved in a cover-up to protect Lundy and Garner, so he took the extraordinary step of handing the Florida intelligence not upwards within the Yard but outwards to Customs, without informing Bates or seeking his authority. According to a book which applauds Bain,[3] he made contact with the Customs cocaine squad which then set up Operation Redskin to work with the FDLE. To cover himself, and to get authority to go to Florida, Bain wrote his own report for the Yard about the cocaine job in July 1986 but, fearing sabotage, he did not mention Roy Garner. On the basis of his report, the Yard set up Operation Distant Drum and Bain was given permission for the Florida trip.

If 'Distant Drum' was ever brought to the notice of the Yard's detective chiefs, Dellow and Worth, the fact that Garner was not one of its declared targets would have made it almost impossible for them to see any connection between it and the information offered by Garner later that year. It seems, therefore, that they did not tell Customs of Garner's information, before he was arrested, because they had no idea he was being investigated by Customs, or even by their own man Bain, over any drug-related activity.

In the coming months Bain and some people in British Customs became convinced, wrongly, that Tony Lundy was 'Scotland Yard's Cocaine Connection': the inside man protecting the Chrastny–Garner conspiracy. The South Yorkshire inquiry never made anything of this notion but other folk did. They would make a television programme, a series of *Sun* newspaper articles and even a book out of it.

The Brinks–Mat Job

While journalists picked over Lundy's entire detective career, and police inquiries scrutinized dozens of complaints against him (old and new), Lundy himself did not sit paralysed, like a guilty man awaiting a dawn raid, handcuffs and a long spell in jail. He got on with police work with all the zeal and directness that his bosses valued and most of his immediate colleagues admired and respected – even if it was accompanied by an abrasive intolerance of detectives less able or less dedicated than he was.

This chapter and the three chapters which follow tell the story of one of the finest periods in Lundy's career: the two and a half years he spent as deputy head of the Organized Crime Task Force and as its senior intelligence co-ordinator. The entire operation stemmed from an investigation into one massive crime committed against one of the world's biggest security companies: Brinks–Mat.

It had all seemed too easy. At 6.40 on the morning of Saturday 26 November 1983 the Brinks–Mat warehouse on the Heathrow International Trading Estate was penetrated by a team of robbers and looted of 3 tons of gold worth £26 million. They had opened the door with a key, they knew the security guards' names, and they knew all about the complex series of locks and alarms protecting the vault and three huge safes within it. Even so, they had to extract the current combination numbers from the senior guards by soaking them in petrol and threatening to burn them alive. They had already knocked one guard senseless so the threat seemed real, especially when matches were struck.

Then one robber produced a knife and threatened to cut the genitals off a guard who had genuinely forgotten the numbers for the final locks defending the safes. 'It looks like we've got a hero,' the guard overheard the bully saying.

As that guard struggled to recall the numbers (they were written in a diary he had left at home), another was asked what was in the grey shoe-box-sized containers stacked in the open vault outside the safes. Gold, he declared. Suddenly the robbers forgot the safes, drove two vans into the loading bay and shifted 6,400 gold bars of various sizes on board. With a last punch to the brain-scrambled guard's belly, the gang tied up and bound all six guards and departed wishing everyone 'Merry Christmas'.[1]

It looked an unexpectedly Merry Christmas for the robbers, who had no idea so much gold would be there. One million pounds-worth was all they reasonably expected. Had they arrived any later, they would have found none at all, for in just a few minutes it was to be taken straight to Gatwick Airport and flown to the Far East.

It was not a Merry Christmas for Tony Black, the last guard to arrive that morning, ten minutes late, and only seconds before the robbers. Their easy entry and detailed knowledge meant they must have had inside help. Eight days later Inspector Tony Brightwell took Black from his New Cross home to Hounslow Police Station where he was questioned for hours, then arrested. The story he had told in his original statement did not add up: neither his account of what happened during the raid nor his version of his movements the previous night. He knew he was done for as soon as Brightwell asked him what his brother-in-law thought about the robbery. That meant Brightwell knew he was related to Brian Robinson, for years a targeted south-east London criminal and an associate of some of the capital's most notorious robbers. 'The Colonel' (as the intelligent, disciplined Robinson was known) was on the 1978 Williams and Glyn's robbery; he was one of the gang who escaped trial initially through City Police corruption, and again in 1981 because of unlawful conduct by Number 5 Regional Crime Squad officers (see Chapter 25). Had 5 RCS not mishandled that inquiry, this Brinks–Mat job – still Britain's biggest proved robbery – could never have taken place.

Black soon confessed he was the 'inside man' and explained how Robinson (the common-law husband of his sister Jennifer) had organized the raid with his complete co-operation. Robinson had also introduced him to 'Mick' and 'Tony'. These were two more notorious south-east Londoners: Tony White – another Williams and Glyn's survivor – and Michael McAvoy, a hot-tempered gunman who was the thuggish bully on the raid. Black did not know their surnames but, as he had taken them on several recces, he identified them instantly from police photos of Robinson's known associates. On 6 December all three were arrested. They were charged the following day. Robinson had an elaborate alibi proving he was in deepest Kent during the raid, but one guard positively identified him as 'the Boss'. Three guards identified McAvoy as 'the Bully' but none picked out White. The case against him consisted largely of admissions he allegedly made during interviews, but which he never signed and always denied. In December 1984 an Old Bailey jury pronounced him not guilty, but they convicted Robinson and McAvoy who were both sentenced to twenty-five years in prison. Black had already been handed a modest six years for pleading guilty and testifying against his co-conspirators, including his sister's husband.

This was the state of play on Brinks–Mat in January 1985 when Tony Lundy was finally cleared by 'Stagg' and all Scotland Yard's four assistant commissioners agreed that there was no evidence to substantiate the allegations against him. Now Phil Corbett, commander of C11 (Criminal Intelligence), was free to recruit him to the gold bullion team – soon to be called the Organized Crime Task Force – in the specially created post of senior intelligence co-ordinator. The inquiry clearly needed someone of Lundy's calibre, for it was now over a year since the crime and, although two robbers had been jailed, no gold had been recovered. Lundy's job was to lead the hunt for the proceeds but, well before he joined, one line of inquiry had been pursued with some success. A long and painstaking surveillance operation had pieced together a chain of handlers and receivers moving huge amounts of gold from London's south-eastern outskirts to a bullion firm in Bristol called Scadlynn. When stolen, the gold was in the form of 6,400 distinctively marked ingots, all of extremely high purity. The police and the insurers had circulated these details throughout the gold market so, if the stolen gold was to be sold to legitimate dealers, the ingots had to be smelted and disguised by the introduction of other metals such as silver and copper. The police had worked out that the gold was being smelted twice: first by persons unknown, second by Scadlynn. Between September 1984 and January 1985 this ramshackle, small-time firm received, smelted and sold on almost half the original Brinks–Mat gold. Ironically, most of it ended up with Johnson Matthey, the dealers from whom Brinks–Mat had collected the gold in the first place.

According to evidence later believed by a jury, the pivotal figure in these movements was a millionaire businessman with criminal connections named Kenneth Noye. The prosecution claimed he had access to regular supplies of Brinks–Mat gold which, having been through a preliminary smelting, Noye's runners then handed to Scadlynn for re-smelting and onward sale to legitimate dealers. The dealers paid a total of £10.5 million into Scadlynn's account at the Bedminster branch of Barclays Bank, from which Scadlynn personnel then withdrew huge sums in cash: £270,000 in notes was once taken off in a paper sack. Security guards twice delivered even bigger cash amounts – £320,000 and £500,000 – from Barclays to Scadlynn's offices, where they were casually told to leave the bags on the floor so the notes could be counted. The bank did not have to report such large transactions to any authority, because it was bound by a duty of confidence to deposit-holders.[2] When police embarked on a search for Noye's assets they found £1.8 million in bank accounts on the Isle of Man and in the Bank of Ireland. Noye claimed this money was not his but belonged to two Florida businessmen who needed to disguise 'illicit profits from property and gold'. Whatever the truth, the police could find no trace of most of the Scadlynn millions – at least not in Kenny Noye's tangled financial affairs.

Back in 1984 the police knew little about Noye's bank deposits or Scadlynn's cash flow, but in December that year the Brinks–Mat probe was taken over by Chief Superintendent Brian Boyce. Meticulously he planned a complex surveillance operation on Kenny Noye and the man who seemed to be doing most of his running around, Brian Reader. The idea was to discover from whom they were getting any gold and to whom they were passing it. Within weeks a catastrophe hit Boyce's operation. On Saturday 26 January 1985 a surveillance officer named John Fordham was stabbed to death within the 10-acre grounds of Kenny Noye's million-pound home at West Kingsdown, Kent. At 6.15 that evening when it was already dark, Fordham and a colleague had been ordered into the grounds to scout out covertly what was going on between Noye and Brian Reader, who had just driven through the estate's security-gates. The police already had a search warrant and their intention seems to have been to order a raid if any 'gold' activity was spotted. None occurred. Instead, Noye's three Rottweiler dogs cornered Fordham and barked, attracting the owner's nervous attention. He went to the spot and saw what he later claimed was a terrifying figure clad in a Balaclava. 'I just froze with horror. All I saw when I flashed my torch on this masked man was just the two eyeholes and the mask. I thought that was my lot. I thought I was going to be a dead man.' He jumped to the conclusion that he was confronted by a robber, rapist or assassin. In a frenzy of alleged self-defence Noye stabbed him eleven times, ran off and returned with his wife Brenda who was carrying a shotgun. He then cried out to the figure on the ground, 'Who are you?' Back came a faint reply, 'SAS, on manoeuvres.' Noye did not believe him. By now Fordham's colleague, Neil Murphy, had called for assistance. It arrived too late. By the time he reached hospital, Fordham was dead.

Noye was charged with murder, but when he went on trial in November 1986 he argued that he had no idea Fordham was a policeman and had acted entirely in self-defence. However, the autopsy showed that most of Fordham's wounds had been inflicted while he was immobile (and so difficult to justify as self-defence). Even so, the jury declared Noye and Brian Reader not guilty, but both men stayed in custody to await another trial for handling Brinks–Mat gold. In July 1986 they were convicted, along with Garth Chappell (a Scadlynn director) and a notorious but dying old Hatton Garden racketeer named Matty Constantinou who had been paid a modest £30,000 for allowing Scadlynn to list two of his companies in its books as the legitimate supplier of £9 million-worth of the stolen gold. Three other men were acquitted. Reader was jailed for nine years, Noye for fourteen. It might have been less had he not tactlessly cursed the jury: 'I hope you all die of cancer.' His defence was that he was a gold *smuggler* and VAT fraudster, not a thief or receiver. This time the jury did not believe him. Yet although the state eventually seized several million pounds-worth of cash and property from Noye, only a small proportion of that wealth may have come from the sale of Brinks–Mat gold. He was into other rackets which might have generated large bank deposits, and the only gold recovered in the entire inquiry – eleven bars, worth £100,000, found on his property – had a metallic content which meant, almost certainly, it could never have formed part of the original Brinks–Mat haul.

One man whom police wanted to try alongside Noye was John Palmer, a West Country jeweller and recent Scadlynn director who was located on Tenerife in the Canary Islands the week after Detective Constable Fordham was killed. There he stayed until June 1986 when, following pressure from Scotland Yard, the Spanish authorities ordered him out as an undesirable. He boarded a flight from Madrid to Rio de Janeiro where he was refused entry because his passport had run out. Giving up the fugitive game, he chose to be deported to London and was arrested on arrival. In March 1987 he was tried on charges of conspiring dishonestly (with Noye and his co-defendants) to handle the bullion. His defence was that he had resigned as a Scadlynn director in March 1984 – before any alleged Brinks–Mat gold had passed through the company's books – and that any gold he had smelted thereafter (in £200,000 lumps in a furnace on his own land) was, he had assumed, part of a 20-ton consignment which Garth Chappell had told him was legitimate. If it was Brinks–Mat gold he must have been deceived by Chappell and was therefore guiltless. The jury was sufficiently impressed to acquit Palmer, and another former fugitive, so the jeweller was free to drive off triumphant from the Old Bailey with his beautiful wife, and to enjoy the huge profits he was receiving from a villa timeshare business back in Tenerife in which he had reportedly invested £5 million in 1985 and 1986.

The mixed outcome of all these trials was a long way off when Tony Lundy joined the Brinks–Mat team at Tintagel House on 11 March 1985. Fordham's recent killing had necessitated the premature arrest of some twenty people who, ideally, would have been left alone until further evidence had been gathered. This 'cart-before-the-horse' start imposed an immense workload on Chief Superintendent Brian Boyce, so it was decided that he should concentrate on the Fordham murder and the serpentine gold-handling inquiries while his new deputy, Lundy, pursued all fresh operations. Lundy says:

First I read up on everything that had happened on the Gold Bullion job. Then I got hold of the officers who had been on the team right from the robbery itself: Tony Brightwell, Sergeant Owen Griffin and several others. I found they were annoyed, frustrated, and critical of the way the inquiry had been handled before Brian Boyce took charge. After the initial arrest of McAvoy, Robinson and White, it seemed the only interest lay in getting those men convicted whereas these boys, keen as mustard, were bursting to nick the other robbers and recover the gold. They knew who these robbers were, but had received no backing to get them. They had put forward proposals on what to do but were getting nowhere. They'd had a very frustrating year.

Lundy discussed with Boyce and Corbett what to do next. He proposed intensifying the pressure on the other suspects who were now living lives of luxury with no fear of arrest, but simultaneously he set about trying to recover whatever gold the robbers, or their confederates, had not yet sold on to the market. All reports indicated that this was about half the load, some £13 million-worth. Lundy's

mind was already working along its usual lines: go to the
criminals who are already doomed, who need help, and get
them to tell you more. The accomplice guard, Tony Black,
had no more to tell – he had identified everyone he knew
– but two other people obviously knew a whole lot more
and might welcome a chance to earn a reduction on their
twenty-five-year jail terms: the convicted Brinks–Mat robbers, Michael McAvoy and Brian Robinson.

I asked, 'What efforts have been made to get them talking
and telling all?' None, I was told. I knew they were going to
the Appeal Court so I said, 'They've got to be desperate for
a reduction, otherwise they'll be old men before they come
out. Can't we get in to them and try to twist their arms?' So
I arranged for an officer who had dealt with McAvoy in the past,
and who had remained on reasonable terms, to visit Leicester
prison where they were in a secure wing, more or less created
for them after they were caught plotting to escape by helicopter.
Now they even took their exercise under cover. I asked this
detective superintendent, 'Go in and have a general chat, and
see if they're interested in talking about their appeal and any
ways we might be able to help each other.' Lo and behold! They
agreed to talk. So Brian Boyce and I went up to see them.

By now we knew that, while inside, McAvoy had come into
a lot of money because his girlfriend Kathy Meacock (for
whom McAvoy was getting divorced so he could marry her)
had suddenly moved from a council flat into a £250,000 house,
where – pisstaker that she was – she kept two Rottweiler dogs
named Brinks and Mat. Micky was fairly even-handed: he'd
also bought his current wife a £150,000 house, even though
she was divorcing him! We were already questioning Kathy
so he knew that we were still after his money and there was
no guarantee that, when he came out after doing time, he'd
have any Brinks–Mat profits left to enjoy the good life.

As we chatted, I asked what he thought he would get on
appeal. I had two angles: either he could name everybody else
and get a big reduction, or he could help us recover what was
left of the gold and still get a big slice off his twenty-five years.
I never really thought that McAvoy – or Robinson – would
grass the others because they were in the same jail. This

was unfortunate because you can't really talk to two robbers together, as neither wants the other to see he's harming their mates. If they'd been split up in different jails, I think they would both have grassed. As it was, we talked to both together and said that if they named everybody, the Appeal Court would have to take a lot of notice. As I predicted, they wouldn't listen to any such suggestion, but they were very interested in what result they might get if they gave back all the gold which had not yet been smelted and – according to our information – was still buried somewhere. I regarded recovering that gold as even more important than jailing the other robbers, because if it was converted to cash, like the other £13 million-worth, it would go to fund other criminal activities, especially drugs. Indeed, because the price of gold had gone up, this unsold half was now worth £18 million.

I said, '*We* can't tell the Appeal Court what to do, but if your defence can say you've been responsible for giving back half the gold, it's got to help.' So we saw them a couple of times, and it really looked likely we were going to get it. At one point McAvoy said point-blank, '*I've* got control of half the bullion. Nobody else can touch it unless I give the instruction.' Once he had gone that far, he was over a barrel. First he's saying he wants to do it, then he doesn't; then he rants and raves about how could he be sure, if he gives it back, that we're not going to arrest everybody in sight for handling. We say that won't happen but I'm also saying, 'Look, you've told us point-blank that you control half this gold, so what's going to happen now when you go to appeal? We'll have to tell prosecuting counsel and the DPP what you've said, so no judge is going to cut your sentence when you're saying, "I've got the gold but I'm not giving it back!"'

McAvoy has a flaming temper and this drove him absolutely potty, but now he realizes he's *got* to give it back, and Robinson's agreeing with him. So McAvoy tries to dictate terms: he wants a guarantee he'll not get more than ten years, but we can't give guarantees. Then he says, 'There's no way I'm going to tell you where you can just go and get it, because you'll have to nick the people looking after it – it's where somebody will have to be nicked – but if you get a call one day to go urgently to a certain street where there's a lorry parked and nobody with it, that way you can't nick anybody because you won't know who's put it there. So that's what we're going to do. It's just going to be left somewhere, you'll be told immediately, and you go and get it.'

Lundy and Boyce put this scenario on paper and passed it via Commander Corbett to Deputy Assistant Commissioner Brian Worth. Lundy was optimistic: 'It was magic because, even if you didn't nick anybody, to recover the gold rather than let it stay in the hands of villains to fund future crimes, it was worth cutting McAvoy and Robinson's sentences to say eighteen years.' Almost immediately, however, Lundy was off abroad pursuing other crucial aspects of the Task Force inquiry. As Boyce was pre-occupied with the Fordham–Noye–Scadlynn investigation, this left the field open for DAC Worth to take personal charge. When Lundy returned from one foreign trip, he found that lawyers had become involved. He feared this would kill the deal stone dead.

Instead of keeping it simple as we had arranged – with the gold suddenly popping up in an abandoned lorry one day – everything had turned cripplingly formal. The next thing is, defence solicitors were demanding written guarantees. There were even meetings with the DPP. I'm sure that, if we'd done it our way, we could have got the gold back. You see, we refused to be dictated to by McAvoy and Robinson. They knew they would get no written guarantees from us – because no guarantees could ever bind the Court of Appeal – but they would still have co-operated because they had no choice, except to do 25 years.

They were desperate, but as soon as I go abroad they try it on. While I'm away they involve solicitors, and then, with so many people involved, news leaked out to the underworld, and other villains with an interest in the gold started jumping around saying: 'Bollocks to them! They've got their bird and they'll just have to do it. If we'd been nicked, we'd have had to put up with it, so that's it: we ain't giving it back!'

One man McAvoy thought he could trust was Tony White who had stood trial with him at the Old Bailey but was cleared. We knew that White and another villain called 'Harry Handy' [a pseudonym for legal reasons] were running round during these negotiations because we had them under surveillance, but they couldn't pull off the deal because the other people involved

– among them a fierce South London clan who've still never been nicked over Brinks–Mat – were saying, 'No way you give it back!' So although McAvoy believed he was the boss – and may indeed have controlled half the gold – once word got around that he wanted to give it back, the danger was that these other first-division robbers would just step in and take it, and he would lose it altogether. Later he tried to recover it involving only Kathy Meacock but that also failed.

In the end both he and Robinson dropped their appeals. They daren't go ahead once McAvoy had boasted about controlling half the gold. They couldn't do a damned thing. It had become a huge bureaucratic balls-up, so as far as we know, a lot of the gold may still be underground.

It is a tantalizing thought that £18 million-worth of gold is still buried somewhere in greater London – and still controlled by some of the capital's toughest organized crime figures. At one point the Task Force heard that it lay buried in the home of an East London villain: 'We dug up his swimming pool and grounds but we never found it.' On another occasion Kathy Meacock said it was in the basement of a house in Dalston belonging to some old folk who did not even know it was bullion when McAvoy had first asked to store it. They knew he was a crook, but it was only after he was captured and charged that they realized they were sleeping on top of a golden fortune. They had never dared touch it but, as Kathy explained, McAvoy could not tell the police where it was because the old couple would have had to be arrested. 'So half the load is probably stuck in a Dalston basement to this day. We tied it down almost to a street, but we couldn't find the people Kathy was talking about. So Micky may still be sitting on a fortune for when he comes out in ten years' time.' Or his mates may have stolen it.

When Lundy returned from his official duties abroad and found out about the failed negotiations, he told senior officers that if they were not going to get the bullion, it was time they charged McAvoy's go-betweens, notably 'Harry Handy' the middleman in the 'lorry' negotiations, and Kathy Meacock (who had married Micky in Leicester prison in 1985). Only then, as the detectives looked into Handy, did they discover a new subterranean layer to the bullion conspiracy: the laundering of Brinks–Mat monies through the London Docklands property boom.

The squad had picked up a rumour that a firm named Selective Estates was moving a lot of money on McAvoy's behalf. This involved Handy, it seems, and a prominent solicitor named Relton, neither of whom had been implicated in the Kenny Noye side of the story. Although McAvoy may still have controlled the unsold gold, it was clear from his uxorious house purchases that he had received a cut of the £10.5 million which had already piled up as Scadlynn sold the first half. Indeed, Kathy Meacock's house had been bought in the name of a Cayman Islands company with money kept in Florida by Michael Relton. Lundy says:

As we understood it, to that date all the main men had accumulated nearly £2 million apiece – less pay-offs to smelters and runners. This led us into Selective Estates which was dealing in Docklands property. Some people in Docklands had the right to buy council homes in which they lived as tenants at a cheap price. Many had no wish to buy or they hadn't got the money, so along came Selective who lent them the money to buy the dwellings in their own names as fronts for Selective. This way the firm made a killing, especially at that time when property was booming. This activity was not legal but it wasn't strictly criminal either. The huge profits Selective made when selling these properties were a windfall. The company's main function was to act as a cover for investing Brinks–Mat money for whatever return, before moving it into Swiss banks.

By doing rather more than stockpiling little people's homes, Selective used a total of £7.5 million (all Brinks–Mat

money, claim the police) to build a property portfolio worth
£18 million. Its assets included three Dockland wharf sites
– one of which had increased in value from £4 million to
£6 million in little over a year – and £800,000 worth of
residential property in Cheltenham. The brains behind
Selective was Michael Relton, who in 1984 had been
approached, allegedly, by a former client, 'Alfred Roach'
(another pseudonym for legal reasons), who asked him to
launder Brinks–Mat money on the robbers' behalf. The
forty-six-year-old Relton had been a defence solicitor
for many years and had built up a lucrative practice.
Among some policemen he was highly regarded, though
not necessarily for the right reasons: he often represented
detectives prosecuted for corruption. It is said that out of
twenty-eight officers he had defended in court, all but
one were acquitted. He had even represented the Police
Federation. In reality, however, he was a sophisticated
crook, as Lundy recalls:

Suddenly Relton closes his legal practice and goes full-time
into Selective, so you can imagine the sort of money he knew
he would be dealing with, to make it worthwhile packing in his
practice, the greedy man. That's what it was all about – greed.
Once he was in the frame, we were all the keener to pursue every
aspect of Selective's finances, but suddenly we found he had a lot
of friends in the force. Some of them were even on our squad!

Fortunately, most of the Task Force detectives were
not Relton's friends and they were doing outstanding
work, accumulating masses of evidence on Selective's
international banking rackets. At the same time 'Bill
Front' (also a pseudonym), who had recently moved off
the squad, turned out to be very friendly with Michael
Relton.

Somehow Front was always bang up-to-date on our planned
inquiries. Soon after he'd left the squad, we found out he'd had

a meet with Harry Handy (who we were after) without our sanction. This upset us greatly for he knew we had targeted Handy. He also knew our strategy against Selective. When we discovered he had met Handy, we were livid. Front had not even reported the meeting to our Task Force chief, Brian Boyce, who was outraged.

By early September 1986 the squad had lost track of Relton. He had disappeared. Then an industrious inspector, David Sandlin, informed Lundy and Boyce that Bill Front had told him Relton was in Florida, scared out of his wits, and was threatening to kill himself unless he could do a deal. By coincidence Lundy was due to fly to Miami on 8 September so he asked Sandlin to ask Front to arrange for him to see Relton in America, in the hope he could talk the crooked lawyer into coming back and 'rolling over'. While Lundy was in Florida he kept ringing London to find out when the meeting was going to take place, but it never happened. When Lundy returned to London, Sandlin told him that Front had said the meeting had not come to fruition.

Soon after his return, on 8 October Lundy held a briefing with all his inspectors. Their teams had done a massive amount of work, piling up bank details and chasing large sums through Switzerland. There was now almost enough evidence to charge Relton, if only he could be found, so a timetable was drawn up with the aim of arresting him in another two weeks. After the meeting, the detectives went for an evening drink in the Black Dog pub just across from Tintagel House. Lundy was not intending to stay long but one of his juniors hinted he wanted a private chat. As Lundy stated in a formal report, this 'dedicated professional detective was obviously emotionally upset'. Almost in tears, the man blurted out to Lundy that he had been offered £100,000 if he stopped pushing the inquiries into Relton.

At the end of a very long conversation the two officers left the Black Dog and went home. Lundy was horrified by what he had heard, so next day he told his chief, Phil Corbett, what had happened. On 13 October there was another meeting, to which the tearful detective was summoned to join Corbett and Lundy. Commander Corbett put it to him that he had been offered money to protect Relton, but he denied that had happened. He looked at Lundy in a very embarrassed manner and appeared to be upset that Lundy had reported their conversation. Today Lundy wonders if there was anything else behind the incident.

I've got a feeling it was an attempt to compromise me. Perhaps some people hoped I would say, 'Oh yeh, a hundred grand, what a good idea!' But when this officer is suddenly called to see Corbett and asked, 'What's all this?', he just gulped and tried to minimize it, saying he had not really been offered that money after all.

Either way, Corbett went straight to Assistant Commissioner Dellow and got it in writing that he and I were to pursue Relton as a matter of urgency. For the moment we concentrated on Relton himself. We put a surveillance team together to house [locate] him, because another DI had given us information that he was going to do a runner. We house him and within a day or so we realize he's flying round all over the place. He's seen running between his homes in London and the country with a couple of suitcases, so our boys chase him round until I say, 'Right! Nick him!', and on 15 October he's in a car when they jump on him, and he's brought into Rochester Row Police Station, where I see him.

I introduced myself and explained that he had been detained in order to be interviewed. He had been drinking heavily so we delayed interviewing him until next day. That's when he was told he'd been arrested over Brinks–Mat and his part in moving cash into concerns such as Selective Estates. 'Do you want to talk to us?' I asked, and suddenly he decided to roll over and tell all.

The Task Force officers pursuing Relton already knew

that the Zurich branch of the Hong Kong and Shanghai Bank was a focal point in Selective's money movements. Prior to Relton's arrest they had been to Zurich to inspect the HK&S account, but Relton instructed Swiss lawyers to block the request on the grounds that it contained tax money and was therefore protected by Swiss law. However, on 16 October 1986 at his home in Haslemere, Surrey, in the presence of Inspector Sandlin, he called his Zurich lawyers to say that the money in the HK&S account was not tax money after all. Over a cup of tea he then revealed the account had earlier contained £2.3 million, which he knew at the time was Brinks–Mat money. This confession was a spectacular breakthrough, but then Lundy learned of a dangerous familiarity between Relton and some detectives on his squad.

For years and years he had known dozens of Yard detectives. I wasn't one of them but now I was given conclusive evidence that some officers were being over-friendly, soft-pedalling, saying, "Don't worry, Mr Relton, everything will be all right,' and undermining the pressure which I and other detectives had applied. One officer, who was above suspicion, told me: 'I can't carry on doing interviews with "X" [another detective] present, because every time I try to be hard, he turns round and says: "Don't worry, Mr Relton, everybody will look after you.'"

Somebody then suggested to me that the pair had masonic bonds, so one night I gave this man a right dressing-down about him bending over backwards to help his friend. I told him, if this had anything to do with Freemasonry, to keep out of it because Relton was going to be dealt with, whatever any secret society might think. I said he was in deep trouble and would be charged, so all this extra-niceness had to stop.

Lundy removed the over-friendly officer from the interviews. Relton then made new admissions, naming properties he had bought with Brinks–Mat money, and talking about the millions he had moved. He then decided to

co-operate fully and turn supergrass; he was charged and
made a full confession. On 23 October he was remanded
on bail on condition that he reside at a police station.
After supervising this breakthrough, Lundy had to fly
to America again. When he came back, he found out
that Relton had made an about-turn and was denying
everything.

While I'm away I find out that he's twisting the officers round
his little finger. They're taking him home, where he sees his wife,
and meantime he's ducking and diving, admitting a lot of things
but not naming people fully like he should be. Brian Boyce
found out and told Relton, 'Either you co-operate fully or
you'll be remanded to prison', which is what happened. Instead
of being used as a supergrass against the others, Relton ends up
contesting everything and gets convicted. Yet he would *never*
have been nicked if I hadn't decided to act as soon as I heard
of that bribery approach. He was ready to run and he would
have disappeared abroad that night if we hadn't arrested him.
Later we found out that during those very weeks when we
were looking for Relton but could not find him, Bill Front had
flown to Paris with two former detectives [who had been tried
for corruption but acquitted] and met bloody Relton! When he's
questioned about all this during Relton's trial, Front says that
he was conned into meeting Relton – that he didn't know he
was going to meet him until he got to Paris. And still he didn't
report the meeting, to Brian Boyce or me!

In July 1988 at the Old Bailey Relton was jailed for
twelve years. Convicted with him was Micky McAvoy's
second wife, Kathy Meacock, who received an eighteen-
month suspended sentence. Despite all the earlier shenani-
gans, Michael Relton found himself the victim of the legal
system he had exploited so profitably for so many years.
Nothing bad happened to the officer Bill Front, despite
the fact that he had met both Relton and Handy without
prior authority from Task Force chiefs or reporting to
them afterwards. On the contrary, he was promoted soon

after so it seems he had done nothing wrong. Even so, his treatment perplexes Tony Lundy.

What I still can't work out is how I was made to suffer all my hassle and aggravation over nothing, yet Front can go off and meet a wanted suspect in Paris, and never report it until it comes to light later, while at the same time he's led us to believe Relton's in Florida where I'm waiting to meet him.

Lundy was not the only senior officer outraged at Front's conduct. So were Lundy's immediate boss, Chief Superintendent Brian Boyce, and Commander Phil Corbett. 'Here was the biggest inquiry we were conducting,' says Corbett (now retired), 'which had reached a very delicate stage, yet here was a flagrant breach of police protocols and still nothing was done. This illogicality was one of my reasons for leaving the force.'

The illogicality could be explained, of course, if Handy and Relton were police informers and Front was their registered handler; and if – for whatever reason – Front had prior authorization from the top of Scotland Yard to by-pass the entire Task Force command.

Have we been here before?

The Friends of Patrick Diamond

When police had first looked into the Brinks–Mat robbery, in 1983, they had soon come to suspect that a criminal named John Fleming was involved. This heavily built, 5 foot 11 inch, South London resident was a crony of Brian Robinson who, years before, had introduced him to his brother-in-law, Tony Black. He was 'a mean-looking person', felt Black, whose sister Jennifer described Fleming as 'a nasty type who flew off the handle easily'. He would have been arrested along with Robinson, McAvoy and White in December 1983 but he could not be found. Later one of Tony Lundy's Task Force sergeants, Rupert Reid, reported on why this career criminal, convicted in ten trials since 1960, was in the frame:

> Examination of Fleming's financial status showed that immediately prior to the robbery he had no real income and only modest property assets. Shortly after the robbery he purchased a luxury villa in Spain [cost £130,000], a large cabin cruiser [cost £50,000] and invested thousands of pounds in cash. Had he been within the jurisdiction of the English courts, he would have been arrested for the Brinks–Mat Gold Bullion Robbery.

By May 1985 the Task Force had come up with an address for Fleming on Spain's Costa Blanca, so Lundy decided to catch him unawares. With his boss Phil Corbett's approval, Lundy put together a scheme for a major surveillance operation, using the Spanish connections he had made when pursuing Micky Morris in 1978. His friend in the Comisaria de Policia, Jesus de Felipe, had already spied out Fleming's property, a luxurious villa in Mascarat, a new marina complex near Altea, just north of Benidorm. Felipe was keen to lay on local help, provided that a formal request was made to his chiefs in Madrid. They seemed certain to agree as Fleming was suspected of continuing crimes in Spain. A bigger problem was Scotland Yard which at first refused to let Lundy and Corbett go. Behind-the-scenes lobbying overturned this decision, and when the pair arrived in Madrid and told the head of the International Squad of Fleming's alleged role in Brinks–Mat, drugs and money-laundering, he agreed to supply whatever manpower and facilities were required.

The Comisaria already knew a lot about Fleming. In 1970 a Spanish court had sentenced him to twelve years in jail for trafficking in forged currency. He served five, and while inside learned fluent Spanish, developed high-level connections with Spain's underworld and came to know several members of Marseille's Corsican Mafia. Fleming's apparently high criminal status so impressed the Comisaria's chiefs that they accompanied Corbett and Lundy to Benidorm to make sure the local hierarchy, from Valencia to Alicante, knew how important this job was. Even so, as local manpower and expertise were lacking, the Spaniards agreed to let the Yard men import their own surveillance teams, probably the first time that a major national police force had given the Yard such a free hand. The need for this move became overwhelming as soon as a warrant was granted to tap Fleming's telephone, for no Spaniard could comprehend the kind of English spoken between Fleming and his confederates. Now Lundy was able to rotate teams of officers in and out of Spain every month to monitor these calls full-time.

Other warrants targeted a dozen more East End villains who were using Benidorm as a criminal home-from-home, just as some better-known London gangsters used the Costa del Sol 500 miles away. One Benidorm hotel was permanently in the hands of English criminals: owned at one point by a London crook later convicted of distributing amphetamines, then by another hoodlum unexpectedly acquitted of a gangland murder. In the resort's relaxed atmosphere such characters frequently indulged in loose talk about their criminal plans, not only on the telephone but within earshot of bugs planted on their premises. At times Lundy had eight surveillance detectives at work in and around Benidorm, monitoring recorded conversations in an improvised operations room above a butcher's shop. One night a bug was even inserted in Fleming's home: some achievement since the high-walled villa was perched on a cliff, and the owner might have come home at any minute. Other hazards included Fleming's neighbours, who had a mutual interest in watching out for burglars, and regular patrols by the Guardia Civil, who for security reasons had not been informed of the operation. The Yard 'plumbers' had only one safeguard: a poor telecommunications link with their Spanish counterparts who were watching Fleming as he boozed away in a Benidorm nightspot.

The effort paid off, for when Lundy and his team monitored these bugs and phone-taps they found they were eavesdropping on a multi-national conspiracy, linking Fleming with an Isle of Man-based company formation agent named Patrick Diamond and, beyond Diamond, with a worldwide chain of drug racketeers, money-launderers and crooked 'drug-defender' lawyers. A few days after the phone-tap started, the Yard men heard Fleming talking to Diamond in Douglas, capital of the Isle of Man.

Diamond had first come to Lundy's notice through the efforts of an informer. It may have been this fact which led *World in Action* in 1986 to convey the mis-taken belief that Roy Garner had 'grassed' the 'secret money-laundering route' used for the proceeds of the £26 million Brinks–Mat robbery, for a reward. At ten per cent the notional reward was £2.6 million, but neither Lundy nor any other Scotland Yard officer has ever nominated Roy Garner for any such reward or any part of it.

However, Scotland Yard records confirm that, as early as September 1982, Garner had informed on the cocaine-smuggling activities of a convicted armed robber named Bobby Dixey, with connections in Florida. Lundy passed this information to the central Drugs Squad. As a result Dixey was arrested in February 1984 and jailed three months later. He received four years, while two of his US-based confederates were given eight. Patrick Diamond had been arrested with Dixey. In May 1985 he was convicted of possessing cocaine, given an eight-month sentence (six months suspended) and fined £4,000. At the time he protested he had been 'fitted up' but it later emerged that he was addicted to cocaine at that time, and was spending £70,000 a year on his habit. In March 1985 the imprisoned informant reminded Lundy of the connections between Dixey and the 6 foot 4 inches 'Irish solicitor' who had just visited Dixey in jail.

In fact, Diamond was not a solicitor. He had a law degree from Queens University, Belfast, but had never practised. Instead he went to the Isle of Man where in 1976 he set up a firm called Comprehensive Company Management, servicing anyone willing to pay a fat fee for advice on how to exploit the island's highly protective company law. He first met Bobby Dixey in July 1983 in a London drinking club. A couple of months later Dixey introduced him to John Fleming at the legendary 'A&R' club, in Charing Cross Road, which Dixey and Fleming then co-owned. In early December the pair flew to see Diamond on the Isle of Man. They discussed the formation of offshore companies with nominee directors, thus concealing the identity of the true 'beneficial' owners.

In 1985 Lundy knew nothing of this until the informant's reminder about Dixey's 'Irish solicitor' nudged him into taking a routine look at Diamond. He found that Scotland Yard's Special Intelligence Section (SIS) had accumulated a mass of intelligence on Diamond. Lundy was staggered by what he read, and told Commander Corbett that the Irishman should be targeted for drug dealing and money-laundering. However, SIS had recently prepared a report to stop him getting an American visa. If the US Embassy had acted on it, Diamond would have been alerted to the fact that the Yard – in some department or other – was on to him. Through Lundy's intervention, the move to block the visa was stopped. By coincidence, a few days later Diamond came up on the phone-taps talking to John Fleming, 'so all of a sudden we realize here is a man that could be the link into the laundering of Brinks–Mat loot'.

Further research revealed not only that on 1 December 1983 – just five days after the Brinks–Mat robbery – Fleming and Dixey flew from London to see Diamond, but that on 7 December Fleming and Diamond flew to Miami. When stopped by Customs, Diamond was found to be in possession of a bank draft for $185,000. He could give no reasonable explanation, just that he was visiting America on business and pleasure. To Lundy and his Task Force, the implication was that he had been carrying an early instalment of Brinks–Mat money. Two months later Diamond sold Fleming a ready-made, 'shelf' company named Marblemay. Fleming baptized it by handing Diamond a cash wad totalling £100,000, which Diamond later transferred to an account in Kissimee, Florida. In June 1984 Fleming bought another Diamond company named Seapath Investments. Soon Seapath too was receiving large amounts of cash for transfer to Spain where Fleming had another company called Seapath. Task Force officers later heard that, through this Seapath, Fleming bought six apartments in Barcelona and two more villas near Benidorm. Whenever Fleming wanted to move money, Patrick Diamond did the moving. In all he received £370,000 in cash from Fleming between February and July 1984. Lundy recalls:

Diamond is a big individual, very posh-spoken and very intelligent. He really thinks he's God's gift to the underworld, that he's brilliant and way above us mortal plods. He's also a head-case. He was always getting barred from the Palace Casino for being drunk or drugged and shouting his mouth off. Later when we had him under observation, he was in this casino in Douglas one day with three or four dolly birds. They'd all been out on the piss, champagning it, when suddenly he goes to the airport, gets on a plane with these girls and ends up in Blackpool. We then ask the local Regional Crime Squad to tail him. From the airport they all get in a taxi and go to a bank where he's seen using a cash till. Then they go to some hotel where he's either shacked up with the birds or having a cocaine party. The next thing, they're seen driving along in this taxi and he's throwing handfuls of bank notes out of the window!

With Diamond coming up on the Spanish phone-taps, Lundy decided it was time to expand the Task Force's operations into the Isle of Man. This had to be done with extreme delicacy, for the island's political establishment is extremely sensitive about anything likely to undermine confidence in its off-shore banking industry. When he asked there about Diamond, however, Lundy found he was knocking at an open door. The chief constable and his head of CID Operations, Chief Inspector John Platt, were keen to help. So was a Fraud Squad sergeant with a vast store of material which he had piled up over the years as forces from all over the world repeatedly requested information on Diamond's firm, Comprehensive Company Management. For years Diamond had blocked all inquiries by claiming 'confidentiality' over anything to do with hundreds of shady companies he had formed for people who had come to him precisely because of the Isle of Man's much-vaunted financial secrecy.

Almost the first thing Lundy did was request an intercept on Diamond's telephone, the first such request ever made on the island, at least in relation to financial matters. Lundy was able to get it only by first asking the Home Office to authorize an application in London, then taking it directly to the Governor of the Isle of Man for signing.

We feared that the island was so small and Diamond was friendly with so many big fish there, all desperate to avoid financial scandal, that he would learn of any move against him before it happened. That's why we wanted to involve as few people as possible, but the Governor told us that under the island's constitution he could not sign the document without first speaking to the Prime Minister. We were desperately worried but had no need to be. There was no leak and soon we were allowed to draft two of our officers to help the island's Fraud Squad on our own investigations.

Lundy soon found that Diamond talked as freely on the phone in Douglas as Fleming in Spain. Then, out of the blue, a man named Stephen Marzovilla rang up from one European country after another – Holland, Portugal, Spain – asking Diamond to send him thousands of pounds at a time. The Brinks–Mat team had no idea who Marzovilla was, only that he had an American accent. They checked but found there were no criminal files on anyone of that name in America. Then at the end of August 1985 Marzovilla called Diamond to say he was coming to London. On 30 August he checked into the

Westbury Hotel, booking another room for Diamond who had arranged to meet him.

This is the moment we've been longing for, so we can work on him properly and find out who this is who keeps having money sent to him all over the world. Sure enough, Diamond comes to town and for a couple of days they go on the piss. They're up at all the clubs, meeting all the main London villains like the Frasers – long, tall Diamond and this little American – out everywhere for a couple of days until the early hours, crumpet, whatever, then Diamond goes off back to his Chelsea flat, and the American flops out in the hotel. During the day when he wasn't with Diamond, Marzovilla visits three safety-deposit centres. In the meantime we'd got his passport details and checked with the FBI man at the US Embassy, Lowell Strong. They came back with no trace. They didn't know who he was and yet it was obvious, as he was running with Diamond, that he had to be a villain. Then Diamond goes back to the Isle of Man and calls John Fleming to say that the 'Pizza Kid' – their name for Marzovilla – will be flying over to Spain next day to visit him.

So now we know that he knows John Fleming! So I'm thinking, 'Christ, who is this bloke? And what do we do? We still can't identify the bastard, and now [9 September] he's going to Spain to join Fleming. Do we let him run or what?' I said, 'Right! Bugger it! Decision time! When he gets to Heathrow Airport and checks in, search him and see what he's got.' And at Heathrow they found two flick-knives secreted in a vanity-case, which enabled them to arrest him for trying to take offensive weapons on a plane.

We didn't know what we were really nicking him *for*, we'd just got to identify him. Who the hell is he? He tells the arresting officers he's a businessman going to Spain. He had $18,000 on him, and says he's from a rich family and travels the world. At this point we weren't getting very far, but as soon as we'd arrested him, I said, 'Get round to those deposit box centres and find out anything you can.' We had obtained magistrate's search warrants in the name Marzovilla, so we were able to look into his boxes. Two of them contained a total of $80,000 in $100 bills. The third was empty except for a plastic bag and a complete new identity: passport, driving licence, birth certificate, everything –

all under the name Craig Jacobs. With his photograph. Right!
Now we're getting somewhere: we've got a man with a complete
different identity.

Now we ring up Lowell Strong at the Embassy, again, and ask
him to check on Craig Jacobs. It was late at night and we stayed
at the office with a drink, waiting for his call. All of a sudden
Lowell rings up and says, 'You're having a drink? I think I'd
better come and join you.'

When he arrived, Strong revealed that Craig Jacobs
was an alias for a man named Scott Errico who was
wanted by America's Drug Enforcement Administration.
The DEA had put a stop on him under 'Jacobs' so Strong's
request had instantly revealed that, on FBI/DEA com-
puters, Jacobs/Errico was wanted for three first-degree
murders, and for involvement in a massive marijuana-
smuggling operation. Back in May 1981 he was given
five years' jail for possessing marijuana with intent to
distribute. Free on bail, he failed to surrender when
his appeal was dismissed in 1982, and disappeared. Still
nowhere to be found, in 1985 he was re-indicted on
more drug-smuggling charges and on three particularly
unpleasant murders.

The murders had been committed on behalf of the Ray
Thompson organization. 'Little Ray' Thompson – a short,
fat, bespectacled Chicagoan in his fifties – owned a large
yacht harbour in Fort Lauderdale, Florida, called the
Amity Yacht Center. He also owned many large yachts
which sailed to the Bahamas where they were loaded
with marijuana from freighters that had steamed in from
Colombia. Thompson's yachts then sailed back to Amity
from where the drugs were distributed in vans and trucks.
Scott Errico joined Thompson's 100-strong organization
in 1979, toting marijuana and providing security services.
It was in this 'hit-man' role that in August 1980, acting on Thompson's orders, Errico kidnapped two other

members of the organization, Robert Vogt and William Timothy Harris. They were taken in one of Thompson's yachts seven miles out to sea, where Errico shot Vogt and another gang member shot Harris. Both bodies were then weighed down with anchors, pushed overboard and never seen again.

In May 1981 these two murders had not yet come to light so Errico's conviction then was solely for drug smuggling and distribution. Even so, out on bail, he might have been expected to curb his behaviour. Not a bit of it. The twenty-three-year-old continued to smuggle marijuana for Ray Thompson, including fifteen tons confiscated in June 1981, along with three of Thompson's yachts. Soon after these seizures, Ray Thompson entrusted $500,000 to an old friend named James Savoy for safe keeping. The foolish Savoy ran off with the money but in March 1982 he was sighted back in Florida, and kidnapped by Errico. He no longer had the money – he claimed it had been stolen from him by a prostitute in North Carolina – so next day Errico and Thompson took him out on one of Thompson's Scarab racing boats. A mile out at sea Thompson shot him. His corpse was then weighed down with chains and pushed overboard.

Killing Savoy turned out to be a bad mistake because, not long before, Savoy had told federal agents he was likely to be kidnapped and killed. He even named his likely killers. This foresight did not save him but, after his death, it helped police crack two accomplices who later testified against Thompson and Errico. By 1985 Thompson had already been convicted but Errico had become one of America's most wanted fugitives. A later Scotland Yard report described him as 'a member of an international gang who peddle drugs and death on a scale never before encountered in the history of the Metropolitan Police'. His capture in London, after three years on the run, was therefore a major achievement. Lundy and his squad were overjoyed, not least because Errico's shockingly high criminal status cast a long dark shadow on Patrick Diamond and on the sultan of Altea, John Fleming.

As soon as we knew we had a hit-man and hood of this calibre we moved Errico to the high-security cells in Cannon Row police station. Then I start interrogating him, a very cool customer, still only twenty-seven, a typical all-American boy, fair hair, bronzed, living the good life, travelling the world, enjoying himself as best he could under different aliases, and spending the millions he'd accumulated in different places avoiding arrest. I interviewed him at length but under the new PACE rules he soon had to have a solicitor. He just picked one out of the telephone book, saw him alone and gave him instructions. The next thing we hear is the solicitor coming up on the phone-tap to Patrick Diamond on the Isle of Man. We still had Diamond hooked up! He was telling Diamond that Errico had been arrested, that he was to cover his tracks and to make sure everything was properly locked up.

I was fuming because we'd already told the solicitor that this man was a murderer, a baddie, a Mafioso. He said that his father was a jockey arrested in New York State during the race-fixing scandals of the early 1980s and had been jailed for years. We interviewed Errico for days but we didn't get far. He virtually admitted who he was but we still had not formally identified him and he refused to be fingerprinted. After he was charged we did get his fingerprints, which enabled us to formally identify him as Errico. He then admitted to us that he had been involved in the murders and the drug-smuggling, but he thought such confessions would never be admitted as evidence in an American court.

Facing ten years' jail on his 1981 conviction (in America a sentence is doubled if the offender absconds) and the electric chair over the murders, Errico was certain to fight the US extradition warrant tooth and nail. He lost the battle but in July 1986 his lawyers made a last bid for *habeas corpus*. Their main arguments were that two of the murders were committed outside US territorial waters (seven miles offshore) while no jury could be certain that the third murder (one mile offshore) was intended to be committed within the three-mile limit. The sheer nerve of this application astounded the judges who stated that the first two murders were clearly planned on US territory, the victims were kidnapped on US territory and the ship on which they were shot was also American. Nor was the possibility that the third victim, Jimmy Savoy, was meant to be killed further out in the ocean of any relevance. Intention had nothing to do with it.[1]

So now we've got a top-class hit-man, who's in with Fleming and Diamond, my objective is how to use this breakthrough to break Diamond. We've got to find a way to hit him. When we'd arrested Errico, we'd discovered that Diamond had not only sent money to him in various countries, he had supplied him with the company, Castleward Investments, through which the money had been sent. On paper this looked like one of Diamond's own companies but it belonged to Errico.

We knew that if we were to go to Diamond and formally ask him to hand over his files on Castleward, all we would get would be the usual thing about client privilege – it was always privilege, privilege, privilege. So one night an ace Fraud Squad inspector named Ron Smith (who'd been with the Brinks–Mat squad from the time of John Fordham's killing) and I talked into the early hours with Phil Corbett about how to crack the Castleward bank account in the Isle of Man and get hold of the company documents. So Ron came up with a piece of law which enabled us to get an order, from the London magistrate dealing with Errico, demanding that Diamond produce these papers. We then went to the Isle of Man where a High Court judge authorized it with his signature. This meant that when Diamond turned up at court thinking he would get away with the usual privilege argument, he was knocked back instead. The judge slapped on the order and forced him to produce all documentation relevant to Castleward, and we got 'em. We then found that Castleward was linked to eight or ten other companies, all of whose records we forced Diamond to produce. So by now he's buzzing away on the phone. He's getting worried, Errico has been nicked and now his papers had been seized: it wasn't good news time.

When Lundy and his team examined the papers they gasped as they saw that millions of pounds had been moved through Errico's Isle of Man accounts. On 4 July 1983 Diamond had opened an account at the Midland Bank branch in Castleward's name. On 6 July 1983 he deposited $250,000 in cash at the Midland's headquarters in the City of London. Two days later he slapped a further $275,000 in cash down on the same counter.

So he'd paid in $525,000 in just two hits! I was fuming. Diamond had simply walked into Midland Bank head office, with piles of cash for transfer to the Isle of Man. He literally walked in with suitcases full of dollar bills! The second time Errico was with him. They met in London, flew to America, flew straight back next day and unloaded another $275,000 in the same bank: Bump! Horrendous! And the Midland charged a fee for counting the notes!

In October 1985, Tony Lundy and Commander Phil Corbett went to Florida to pursue these discoveries. A trip to the FBI Academy near Washington had been arranged months before, so the pair could learn how to mount US-style 'sting' operations. Now they tacked on a trip to Fort Lauderdale to meet the Strike Force team pursuing Scott Errico and the Ray Thompson mob. It consisted of US attorneys, FBI and DEA agents and local police and had been going for six years. Corbett and Lundy also went to Miami to meet other Strike Force attorneys and regional FBI chiefs to try to interest them in the mass of money-laundering and other criminal intelligence coming up on Diamond's tapped telephone. The offer seemed fitting, as Diamond was doing not just Errico's dirty washing but bent business for some of Miami's leading drug-defender attorneys. Even so, it was rejected. 'They were very nice people, they looked after us no end, but they didn't want to know. In all fairness they have horrendous problems there, endless work, so it was a waste of time.' Corbett flew to New York to further other aspects of the inquiry, Lundy did the same in Los Angeles but nowhere did the FBI seem interested in the jewels unknowingly yielded up by Patrick Diamond.

When Lundy returned to England, Errico's extradition proceedings were under way, and so Diamond was flying back and forth, 'busy as hell on Errico's behalf, visiting him in prison, really putting himself about'. Lundy decided it was time to make Diamond 'roll over', not least because the Task Force was under immense strain concerning its manpower and its finances.

We were getting fantastic intelligence everywhere, but there's so many blinkered people up above you who are all the time saying, 'That's how much you've spent on these operations, but what have we got? A hit-man from America involved in massive drugs operations there, fine, but what's in it for us?' So we're under pressure. The Spanish were being fantastic, we were getting masses of intelligence on drugs there too, but all Phil Corbett and I are getting is hassle. They're telling us, 'All right! You're showing us all these charts, fantastic, but where are the results? It's not our job to police the world!', so in the end I said, 'Right, I'm going to take Diamond apart.'

As Diamond already had a drugs conviction and there was proof he was dealing in drugs monies, Lundy felt he now had enough evidence to justify seizing dozens of Diamond company files to further the Task Force's drug-related inquiries. Co-ordinating with the Isle of Man's Chief Inspector John Platt, he applied for a search warrant under the local Misuse of Drugs Act. He then assembled a specialist twelve-man squad in London, took them to the Isle of Man and had the Governor swear them in as special constables. At 8 a.m. on Wednesday 12 March 1986 Inspector Tony Brightwell served the warrant on Diamond and cautioned him before the squad searched his offices and seized a mass of correspondence.

At first Lundy could get nothing out of him. Eventually he made a gesture of co-operation, volunteering the names of all Errico's companies but refusing to reveal the full spread of his own activities, so Lundy told him there could be no half measures. He was then taken to Douglas police headquarters where Lundy began a formal interview.

He was giving a bit but holding stacks back. This went on for three days, but fortunately PACE hadn't yet come in on the island so they couldn't have cared less if I had kept him for a week. To cut a long story short, I crack him. He was absolutely gutted but he tells us about Fleming taking cash up there to him, giving him hundreds of thousands of pounds, and how he also collected money directly from Fleming's house. So we charge him with the Fleming monies: dishonestly handling some £200,000, part of the proceeds of the Brinks–Mat bullion robbery.

Now Lundy seized Diamond's entire office, reconstituting it in a special incident room in police headquarters and installing a computer to record and cross-reference every company. The local force were overjoyed that Diamond had at last been put out of business, but some members of the island's financial establishment were not happy, as Diamond had many connections and was by no means the only professional adviser there with nefarious links.

Diamond later pleaded guilty to a token charge of handling stolen goods, namely £100,000 cash. He was sentenced to eighteen months' imprisonment (nine months suspended) and fined £10,000. In an uncharacteristically sentimental way, Lundy feels he struck up a rapport with Diamond because they had both run the London Marathon in May 1984, although he completed the course two hours quicker than Diamond. 'Imagine, a coke addict running the Marathon!' Yet by doing so Diamond raised a lot of money for the Manx Hospice. That weekend he stayed with John Fleming at his house in Denmark Hill, South London. Fleming even sponsored his run at £4 a mile and thus contributed over £100 to the Manx Hospice. He also handed Diamond £200,000 in cash for less charitable purposes. Diamond promptly paid £145,000 of it into the City branch of the Bank of Ireland, held in the mocking name of 'G. Reedy', a company registered in the Turks and Caicos Islands. Later Diamond used the entire £200,000 to buy two working oil wells in Kansas on Fleming's behalf. Later still, the wells were capped and Fleming could not get his money back.

All this detail emerged in September 1985 when, like Lundy's earlier supergrasses, Diamond was remanded on bail on condition that he reside at a police station, in this case Douglas police HQ. Even so, Lundy was worried that Diamond might be the victim of a professional hit-man like Errico, for he knew enough to put dozens of Florida gangsters and their lawyer front-men in jail for decades. Among his records, for example, was material linking him with a leading Miami attorney named Michael Levine, including proof of wire transfers totalling hundreds of thousands of dollars to Levine accounts in Florida. Through Diamond, and his ilk in other off-shore tax-havens, Levine had set up dozens of companies to launder the wealth of drug-dealer clients. He had met Diamond years before when the Irishman had travelled to America to expand his contacts. Levine then acquired a stack of Diamond's Manx companies which he used to move millions of dollars of drug revenues all over the world. That was how Scott Errico had come by Castleward Investments.

By the early 1980s, however, the US authorities were finally aware of the most blatant forms of drug money laundering and made it a federal offence to move more than $10,000 out of the country at a time without declaring it. The ever-resourceful Diamond soon found a way round this restriction. Whenever he flew into America he would bring a banker's draft enabling him to draw, say, half a million dollars in cash. He would ostentatiously declare this on entry but, instead of using it, he would pick up half a million in cash from the drug treasurers and take it out of the USA covered by his original declaration. Thus he frequently crossed the Atlantic, depositing millions in London and transferring them to the Isle of Man. Then, whenever the racketeers wanted money, he would transfer it to wherever they asked. Michael Levine also used Isle of Man companies of which Diamond was the nominee director to buy thousands of acres of land in Florida, grand houses, even shopping malls – all on behalf of drug runners such as Errico whose names would never appear on company documents. Lundy says:

> On paper Diamond owned half of Florida, but in reality it belonged to the drug dealers. For providing this service Diamond got more than his fees. Being a coke addict himself at the time, he'd go on sprees with the hoods – bingeing on crumpet and drugs for days on end, but all the time planning further money-laundering wheezes.

Diamond's breath-taking revelations about his work for Errico, Levine and other shady Floridians eventually forced US law enforcement to take notice. The agency taking the initiative was not the FBI but the DEA, which sent two agents, 'Big Bob' McCracken and Dirk Lamagno, to the Isle of Man to assist Lundy's Task Force. (Big Bob – at 6 feet 6 inches even taller than Diamond – would later marry a Manx woman police constable whom he met during the assignment.) Big Bob had been working on Errico for years in the Strike Force investigation into Ray Thompson. That probe had been reinvigorated when

Lundy and his team – henceforth known as Operation Cougar – captured Errico and turned Diamond. In March 1986, on Big Bob's behalf, Lundy persuaded Diamond to make a monitored phone call to Michael Levine in Miami. During that call Levine carelessly made remarks that placed him at the heart of the Errico money-laundering conspiracy.

Lundy then talked Diamond into travelling to America under cover to get better material. He assured him that such co-operation would go a long way to persuade England's DPP not to prosecute him, and to leave him to the Isle of Man's judicial system. There was no question of him getting any written guarantee of immunity in England, but certainly his co-operation would win him immunity in America where he could otherwise face severe charges. This is the deal he eventually secured, but in the meantime he had the nerve-racking task of chatting face-to-face with these racketeers as if he was still one of them. If the truth came out during this exercise he might be killed instantly. In any case he would be an assassination target for the rest of his life. In a bizarre way, says Lundy, the idea appealed to Diamond: 'He was an egotistical bastard, so I was able to manipulate him into doing something that was a first: he was going to do what no one else from Britain had ever done. He was scared for his life, but he agreed to do it.'

Back in London Lundy was retaining the enthusiastic support of Commander Corbett but higher up he was still getting the 'What are *we* getting out of it?' line of objection. 'Ah well,' he would respond, 'we'll get Fleming one day.' He now had additional ammunition: 'Every way I turned was a fight, but they daren't be seen not to agree to Diamond going to America now the DEA wants it. So we take him off to Miami.' Lundy and McCracken went first to prepare the sting, then Diamond was brought over in the custody of the Isle of Man's John Platt. 'We put him in a luxury hotel, we fed him all the stuff, we got him taped, and in he went. He kept a couple of meets with Levine, who still hadn't sussed him and it worked out well.'

Using the Diamond–Errico material as its starting point, Operation Man – which was what the DEA confusingly called Operation Cougar – would turn into a massive long-term success (see Chapter 21). Back in London, however, it did not greatly impress the Yard hierarchy which was becoming increasingly restless at 'Cougar's' cost and the relatively few British criminals it had nailed. 'We were getting superb intelligence from Spain, but financial pressures were mounting and the time was coming when our operation there would have to be wound up. But we knew where Fleming's monies were and we could prove he'd had a couple of million which he could not legitimately account for.' The Spanish police had narrowly missed catching Fleming in connection with several loads of drugs they believed he was financing. In December 1985 they decided to arrest him anyway because, all the while, he was living there on someone else's stolen passport. At first he was kept in custody but he later got bail and lay low at home, awaiting a decision from the Ministry of the Interior. It came in July 1986: he would be expelled in two weeks unless he left the country beforehand. He would not be extradited to Britain, where he was certain to be charged over Brinks–Mat, because there was still no extradition treaty between the countries. That, of course, was why so many leading British criminals had moved to Spain in the 1960s and 1970s.

Suddenly in August 1986 Lundy heard from Jesus de Felipe, his Spanish police friend, that Fleming had booked a multiple-destination air ticket from Madrid to a cluster of countries that also had no extradition treaty with Britain: states like Costa Rica, Cuba, Brazil, Panama. It turned out that he had already arrived in Costa Rica so Lundy, freshly returned to London, immediately called Inspector Tony Brightwell in Florida and told him to fly straight to Costa Rica, locate Fleming and get him expelled. Fleming had made all his travel arrangements on his American Express card, so Brightwell rapidly tracked him and a young Spanish woman down to a San José hotel where he was arrested on 15 August. The Costa Rican authorities were only too willing to expel him and let Brightwell take him straight to England, but there were no direct flights. Then DEA colleagues in Florida had the idea that if he were put on a flight into Miami, they could bundle him straight on a plane to London.

It all went wrong. After a Costa Rican policeman had escorted Fleming on a flight to Miami on 20 August, he sought and gained admittance to the USA. That meant the DEA could not put him straight on a plane to England. Instead US Immigration officials seized his passport from his Costa Rican escort, detained him as an undesirable alien and withdrew his US visa. Now the affair exploded in a mass of publicity with a pack of London reporters sent out to Miami. At the time anything to do with the Brinks–Mat job was front-page news because Kenny Noye and his co-defendants had just been convicted of handling half the stolen gold. Fleming was suspected of being on the robbery but there was no direct evidence so no arrest warrant had been issued. As the press pack checked into luxurious Miami hotels, a replay of the tragi-comical 1974 Rio de Janeiro battle between Ronnie Biggs and Chief Superintendent Jack Slipper appeared to be under way.

A similar element of farce started creeping in at the end of August when big-name Miami attorneys hired to represent Fleming convinced a judge there were no grounds for deporting him to London. After all, no extradition demand had been made by London. The judge decided that although Fleming was not welcome in America he could have a week to find some other country to admit him. He tried Panama but was told he would not be allowed in. He had better luck with the Dominican Republic and was already on board a plane going there, only to be removed minutes before take-off. He might have guessed that Lundy had approached the Republic's consul-general in Miami and persuaded him to ban the fugitive from entering his country. Between such excursions, Fleming was locked up in Krome detention centre, hard by the Everglades, while his lawyers tried to find any country that would let him in. After nearly three months behind barbed wire, a deeply depressed Fleming chose the *Sunday Express* to make an 'amazing appeal to the Yard'.[2] He told the newspaper,

> If the Yard takes Detective Superintendent Tony Lundy off my case I will come straight back home. I have nothing to hide and will answer all questions put to me. I hate being in here – it's full of criminals – but I'd rather be here than having a noose put round my neck in Britain. I'm sure I can last longer than Mr Lundy. I have had Lundy on my back for eleven months. He's driving me crazy. I will never go back while he's in charge of the case, but I've got nothing to hide. I've got absolutely nothing to do with the Brinks–Mat job. The real robbers must be laughing at the way I'm being persecuted. I'm terrified of being stitched up if I go back on British soil. That's why I will continue to fight.

This interview was published on 9 November, a mere six days after *World in Action* broadcast 'The Untouchable', so Fleming's alleged fear of a Lundy stitch-up might have struck a sympathetic chord in some areas of British law enforcement. He even had the tactical nerve to offer to talk to Peter Wright, the South Yorkshire chief constable in charge of the inquiry into 'The Untouchable' allegations. Lundy himself reacted with predictable scorn: 'It's not a question of him dictating who is dealing with his case.

That's a matter for my bosses. I am carrying on with my duties.'³ Today he is happy to admit he was hounding Fleming:

Of course I was, yeh. He was petrified of me because he knew I had rolled Diamond over. I'd nicked Errico, and I'd been working against him in Spain. So all of a sudden, it's splashed all over the papers, 'Take Lundy off my case!' And I was taken off it! The stupid powers-that-be turned round and ordered me off it!

The consequence of that stampeded decision was one of the biggest fiascos in recent Yard history. After getting visas for Peru and Venezuela, then finding them revoked, then being blocked from Colombia, Mexico and Argentina, Fleming ran out of options. In March 1987 he was deported to the only country that would have him, Britain. On arrival he was charged with dishonestly handling £480,000 of proceeds from the Brinks–Mat robbery. Yet three months later he walked free from Horseferry Road Court after committal magistrate Norma Negus said there was insufficient evidence for him to stand trial. Diamond was not the only witness. A commodity broker testified that in May and June 1984 Fleming had given him £50,000 in cash, including £30,000 in a Mothercare bag. The broker had made disastrous investments so Fleming lost the lot. Indeed he ended up owing a further £1,320.36 to the broking firm. Yet despite all the evidence that Fleming had a fortune in illegally acquired cash, no connection with the Brinks–Mat job was ever established, so the case against him collapsed. (Patrick Diamond had pleaded guilty to receiving Brinks–Mat proceeds from Fleming but would not testify against him.) One man who could not be blamed for this hugely expensive cock-up was Tony Lundy, whom Scotland Yard had removed from the case seven months earlier, following Fleming's outburst.

There was no accounting whatsoever for one million pounds which Fleming had suddenly acquired. One minute he was skint, the next he was paying off debts and living in the lap of luxury. There was plenty to go ahead. If it hadn't been for all the publicity, the DPP would probably have applied for a voluntary bill of indictment and still convicted Fleming. Instead he went back to Spain! He was officially barred – expelled, never to return – but then there was a car accident near Benidorm, right next to some Guardia Civil officers who see one bloke suddenly jump out and start running. They chase him, catch him and find it was Fleming! Captured again in Benidorm after he'd been released from court here in London! So they kicked him out again.

Lundy's Operation Cougar colleagues had far fewer problems tracking down several more million pounds' worth of probable Brinks–Mat money. That investigation led to the charging of half a dozen more leading London gangsters, but because they are still awaiting trial as this book is published, the details of their case cannot now be discussed.

However, an even more extraordinary outcrop of Operation Cougar developed from a remark which Patrick Diamond dropped one day to Tony Lundy: 'If you think I've been busy, you wait till you get into a bloke called Shaun Murphy, down in the British Virgin Isles.'

Treasure Islands

The only time Tony Lundy heard Patrick Diamond express modesty was when he talked of the awesome money-laundering activities of Shaun Murphy, his brother company formation agent in the British Virgin Islands (BVI). Born in 1953 in West Kirby, Cheshire, Murphy went to school on the Isle of Man and later married a local girl. He qualified as a chartered accountant and worked for Price, Waterhouse, on the Isle before getting a job in the BVI with Peat Marwick in 1977. Three years later he set up his own firm, Financial Management and Trust (FM&T) Limited, on the main island, Tortola, a far hotter tax-haven than the Isle of Man in more senses than one.

In March 1986 when he first mentioned Murphy, Diamond handed Lundy a PR brochure which Murphy had recently sent him. It stressed the virtues of doing business through this British Crown Colony with 'a very stable government', 'no desire for independence', no exchange controls, low tax rates and – most important – a very high degree of banking secrecy. 'So if you would like a secure home for your money, administered by responsible people in a stable community,' waxed Murphy, 'you may have no better choice than the British Virgin Islands.' Murphy's brochure listed the BVI's Chief Minister and Minister of Finance, Cyril Romney, as FM&T's chairman. On paper the politician was a 99 per cent shareholder. This connection boosted Murphy's image of power and respectability and helped him build a substantial business. In contrast hundreds of his clients were not respectable. They were big-time crooks seeking a safe place to hide bent money.

Alarmed by what he had heard, Lundy convinced DAC Brian Worth that the Task Force inquiry, now called Operation Cougar, should not stop at Florida but should advance to the BVI. Working closely with DEA agents who (confusingly) were calling the same inquiry Operation Man, 'Cougar' officers were already rushing to complete the case against Miami lawyer Michael Levine. However, now Diamond had stressed that the BVI man was even more deeply involved with Levine than he was, it was clear that Murphy had to be 'hit' very soon – before he could know that Levine was under investigation. To enable Lundy and his small team to work securely in the BVI, the Foreign and Commonwealth Office asked the BVI's Governor, David Barwick, to allow Lundy to explain his visit in person, rather than in writing in advance, as was normal. This softly-softly approach was seen to be necessary because of Shaun Murphy's strong local connections.

Barwick agreed, so on 7 April 1986 Lundy flew in with Tony Brightwell and Sergeant Geoff Brown to be confronted with what could have been serious problems: the white chief of police was retiring in days and his successor would not arrive for weeks; and the BVI authorities had proved ineffectual against drug racketeers for years. As Lundy reported back to Scotland Yard: 'Large quantities of drugs have been seized on occasions when aeroplanes have crashed, boats have run aground or premises have been searched as a result of information. However, no one has ever been convicted!' As he soon discovered, the problem did not lie with the black deputy police chief or his sergeants who proved highly co-operative, but until he had a feel for local politics he relied on the guidance of Attorney-General Jack Smith-Hughes, 'a lovely old boy, a character'. As on the Isle of Man, the 'Cougar' detectives had to be sworn in as special constables in order to have full powers of inquiry and arrest.

A first discreet check convinced Lundy he had sufficient cause to apply for a warrant to search Murphy's offices under the local Misuse of Drugs law and to seize all documents on companies relating to Michael Levine. However, on 16 April in Miami Levine was served with a subpoena to produce all documents on forty-one companies linked with Patrick Diamond and Scott Errico, and on a mass of properties bought in Diamond's name. Instantly Levine realized that Diamond must be co-operating with police authorities. Before Murphy could be raided, Levine tipped him off that Diamond had 'turned'. He warned Murphy to expect a police visit and asked him to destroy any papers relating to Levine's own activities.

In fact Murphy did not need a call from Levine to know he was in trouble. Earlier that same 16 April *The Times* of London had splashed a story by Stewart Tendler, its energetic and resourceful crime reporter, about the Task Force operation across the Atlantic. A sub-editor had supplied a melodramatically inaccurate headline, 'Scotland Yard mounts big investigation into Mafia currency deals', but Tendler's piece was alarmingly accurate. He revealed that on the Isle of Man ten policemen were sifting through 170 accounts and that two Yard officers had just flown into Miami with a man on bail in Britain for handling stolen money. 'He has been working in Florida, partly under cover' with the DEA. Even though no name was supplied, this obviously referred to Patrick Diamond. There was also a thinly veiled reference to Scott Errico. In Miami the article was instantly brought to Michael Levine's attention. It was to Tendler's credit that his sources were so good but, by gossiping to him too soon, some high-ranking Yard officer almost ruined the entire operation.

Even more dangerous was a paragraph on the Virgin Islands where officers 'are tracking down another section of the network buried within local financial institutions. They are also talking to a financier living in the islands.' The unnamed financier was obviously Murphy but Lundy had not yet had any chance to raid him, let alone 'talk'. Early that same day someone in London faxed the article to a barrister working on Tortola. He gave a copy to Murphy who was now six days ahead of Lundy and took immediate action. That night, as his wife Jennifer later stated in evidence, 'Shaun and I were having a drink at the Treasure Island Hotel. Lots of people were talking about the article . . . Shaun and I decided to remove from the offices of FM&T a file which could do harm to Michael Levine.' The blame for this potentially catastrophic leak again lay with an officer at the top of the Yard whom Lundy views with justifiable contempt: 'He gave the whole game away by pushing the publicity machine into action before I had done the job!'

The day after the *Times* article appeared, Murphy left Tortola for a pre-arranged rugby tour. He returned on 21 April. Early next day he was swooped on by Lundy, his 'Cougar' colleagues, a local sergeant and Bob McCracken of the DEA. Lundy then used the identical routine he had used to crack Diamond. Murphy was petrified but, like Diamond, at first he merely went through the motions of co-operating: handing over some papers but holding far more back. Lundy realized what was going on and told Big Bob 'that a lot was missing'. They knew they had been overtaken by events in Miami and by *The Times*.

It was funny talking to Murphy, because I was trying to kill him with kindness. Throughout my career I never allowed officers to inflict physical violence on suspects or prisoners. All right, you threaten them, but with years in prison not beatings. I don't agree with any heavy-handed stuff because I don't think it wins any wars. I was proved wrong on this occasion.

Murphy had been buggering us around for two or three days, and one afternoon we were in his office: Murphy, me and Bob McCracken – a giant, fit, larger-than-life guy who didn't touch any booze. We're sitting there and I'm saying, 'Shaun! For God's sake! Look, you've told us this, now you've changed to that. You must realize you're getting yourself in a pickle, 'cos at court if you're shown to be lying . . .' I was giving him the usual spiel.

Anyway, he said something else, and all of a sudden Bob McCracken – he frightened *me* to death, never mind Murphy! – he leapt to his feet and he banged the table and he screams at Murphy, 'You asshole! I'm going to eat you up for fucking breakfast! Rahrahraaargh!' And I go, 'Oh God', and he storms out of the room.

Murphy collapsed. He went white! I just sat there, regained my composure and said, 'Shaun. I told you. I'm doing my best for you, but you see what these Americans are like.' And he was never any trouble after that. He told us everything. So it just shows, you can't always be right in the way you do it. Bob just lost his rag! I thought he was going to hit me, not just the suspect! Later he couldn't apologize enough. 'As it happens,' I said, 'it was the best thing you could have done.' Murphy never told another lie.

Lundy had already waved the stick of the local drugs law with which he could surely put Murphy in jail for many years, but (reinforced by Big Bob) he was also dangling the hefty carrot of immunity in America if Murphy agreed to testify there. So he 'buckled and co-operated', and confessed he had removed the fat file on Levine. He would have destroyed it already but he knew he could never resurrect it, and one day some murderous drug dealers might want to know why. He also saw the opposite mess he would be in if Levine 'turned' like Diamond: he could be jailed for destroying crucial evidence. Instead, as Jennifer Murphy later

admitted, she merely hid the file in a cupboard in the
school where she taught.

When Lundy retrieved it he saw how Levine had constructed a vast money-laundering framework of which
Diamond on the Isle of Man was merely one prop. Levine
had personally handed Murphy over $3 million in cash to
smuggle out of America and bank in covert BVI accounts,
through which many more millions passed by wire transfer. Murphy told Lundy how his companies fell into two
types: 'Cash' companies for moving cash round the world;
and 'Toy' companies for buying 'toys' like boats, planes,
cars and lush villas for drug dealers. The purpose of all
these companies was to conceal the felons' identities. The
anonymity was almost impenetrable. Levine too had insu-
lated himself from the force of US law. He made sure he
never left any paper record that he had knowingly handled
drug cash, always telling Murphy and Diamond to give
him written instructions to carry out the nefarious moves
he himself had devised. He even induced the Britons to
sign incomplete documents which he turned to his own
purpose. Thus without Murphy's knowledge he bought an
entire shopping precinct in south Florida worth millions
of dollars in the name of a BVI company wholly 'owned'
by Murphy: Murphy Investments. His cunning was such
that, if Murphy and Diamond had not confessed and
co-operated, neither he nor his clients could have been
caught. It would have been impossible to discover the
true owners of the wealth he was moving around.

When Murphy was sure he would be getting immunity
he revealed how, from the moment he set up his own
business in 1980, he had formed companies for drug
dealers throughout the USA.

First he only wanted to talk about Levine. Now he starts talking
about five other attorneys fronting for rings in Massachusetts,

California and other states: he's manipulating tens of millions of dollars all over the world for people from all over America! The combination of his records and his testimony blew these conspiracies apart.

Within days of Murphy's decision to turn, Lundy and his team had proof that he had moved over $12 million in drug cash and handled another $100 million in wire transfers and asset purchases. Even more gratifying to the detectives, almost everyone he named was a known or convicted trafficker. He identified one ring based in Boston for whom he had moved tens of millions. On their behalf he 'owned' boats, planes and real estate including office blocks, development land and property on Martha's Vineyard, the exclusive holiday isle so loved by the Kennedys and other New England 'aristocrats'. According to FBI intelligence, this ring had been bribing politicians and police in the Boston area for years. Smarting from earlier convictions, the dealers had shrewdly decided it was worth buying protection but sometimes they acted with breath-taking stupidity, as Lundy recalls:

A few years ago there was a big auction of Beatles memorabilia in London, so some of the Boston boys flew over and bought nearly everything! There was even a grand piano. A couple of other gang members went mad because there was so much publicity about the auction in America, and the last thing they wanted was headlines about sidekicks splashing out on expensive Beatles junk. Later it was all seized because it had been bought with drug money.

On 23 April 1986 Lundy formally charged Murphy but there was an immediate security scare. In America a string of 'drug' lawyers feared knock-on arrests following Diamond's testimony against Levine. One New York attorney named Labon Quimby (doubling as a company formation agent in Nassau, Bahamas) had already flown to Tortola as part of a cover-up operation. At a meeting – monitored by Lundy and his team – Quimby told Murphy to keep his mouth shut and everything would be all right.

For Murphy's safety, the BVI's deputy police chief posted two armed guards outside his house while Lundy's two officers slept inside. The house had a beautiful setting, in semi-jungle up a mountain overlooking the Caribbean. The assignment had its funny side. At bedtime on the first night Murphy handed a baseball bat to each of his Yard minders. They ridiculed him, saying the bats would be a fat lot of good when the hit-men arrived with machine-guns. Murphy replied that they were not for hit-men, but for killing the tarantulas in the bedrooms! Tarantulas aside, Lundy felt Murphy's lotus-eating lifestyle – paid for by the ludicrously high profits of international crime – had gone to the accountant's head.

He was like Diamond, into all the crazy drug routines. He's another one who'd have been dead from drug abuse if I hadn't nicked him. He was on coke, marijuana, the good life, birds! Mad! These people all go stark raving mad!

He had a different money-laundering act than Diamond's. He would fly to Florida where the racketeers would give him, say, a million dollars in a suitcase. He would then fly to St Thomas in the American Virgin Isles, where there was no Customs check because he was still on US territory. Then he would get the boat across from St Thomas to Tortola in the *British* Virgin Islands where there should be checks and immigration controls but, because he was so well-known, he knew he'd never get a pull. He used to walk straight through with millions and pay them into the banks.

I then had to get into these banks, especially Barclays through which most of the money went. The managers were as good as gold but they were quaking because they'd been taking tens of millions of drug dollars from Murphy, paying them into company accounts, then transferring huge sums all over the world. To expose the system I had to get orders forcing them to hand over the records.

Jenny Murphy made statements corroborating her husband's story, painting a bizarre picture of the everyday life of drug money-laundering folk, such as this weekend trip with Shaun to Miami in September 1985 to see Michael Levine.

On Saturday we went shopping all day and bought bed linen from Dadeland Shopping Mall. I think we bought it all from JC Penney. We arrived back at the Mutiny Hotel at about 4 in the afternoon. I tipped all the purchases out on the floor and was going through them when Michael called from reception. Very shortly afterwards he knocked at the door. Shaun opened the door and allowed Michael in. He was wearing a T-shirt and jeans and was carrying a leather sports bag. He said hello to me and went and sat on the edge of the bed. He undid the zip on the bag and tipped the bag upside down. A vast amount of money fell out and was in a pile on the bed. It was note money in bundles about one inch thick. I was looking at my purchases on the floor. Michael was saying things to Shaun but he was mumbling so I couldn't hear anything. I remember both Shaun and Michael counted the number of bundles. After this Michael said goodbye and left. Shaun and I put the money in the bottom of his holdall and put towels and clothing over it. As we had been shopping all day we were tired and did not go out that evening. We left the hotel on Sunday morning and returned to Tortola.

Shaun Murphy revealed precise details of dozens of companies he had fronted for Levine. Some of their names jokily hinted at the industry for which they had been formed: Midnight Express, Dragonbait, Trivial Pursuit, Golden Moments. (None of these companies had any connection with legitimate companies of the same name.) 'In all cases,' said Murphy, 'Michael Levine chose the names for his companies and used them for his purposes.' The speed with which Lundy had 'turned' Murphy caught

Levine and his fellow drug-defenders unawares. At the end of April (through the efforts of Bob McCracken and the Miami Strike Force) the US Justice Department formally granted Murphy immunity so he could testify against seven drug lawyers 'and others relating to money-laundering and/or the importation, possession, manufacture or distribution of narcotics and/or any other criminal activities'. A DEA plane flew to Tortola to pick up his entire office contents. He closed his business, 'Cougar' officers entrusted any genuine companies to the care of another local management agency and he was flown to Florida. Murphy could not dally for fear of assassination. His wife did not want to go, but the people who wanted to kill him would have killed her too. Today the couple are happily relocated under a new identity, but in June 1986 Shaun had to make one last trip to Tortola to wind up his affairs. His visit coincided with the mystery arrival of a twice-convicted Californian drug dealer, Gary Schiller, who sailed in from St Thomas and appeared outside Murphy's shut-down office. Using other names, he had earlier invested over a million dollars in Murphy companies. The BVI police were alerted and apprehended him but, finding no weapon on him or his speedboat, they merely escorted him from the island. Even so, as Lundy reported, 'Murphy is a target for criminals and Schiller was obviously there with an ulterior motive.'

There remained Murphy's partner, Chief Minister Cyril Romney. There was no evidence that he knew of Murphy's drug dealing connections. In an interview with Lundy, he said he had not benefited financially as a director of Murphy's company, FM&T, and would henceforth disclaim all interests in it, but the connection caused his political downfall. A public row about FM&T forced him to call an election in September 1986 when the BVI's 5,000 voters cast him out of office.

With Murphy lodged in a safe house in Florida, Lundy attended a meeting in Miami where DEA chiefs applauded the Diamond–Murphy breakthroughs on which the entire US inquiry, dubbed Operation Man, was based. They also requested the continuing assistance of 'Cougar' officers Tony Brightwell and Geoff Brown. Henceforth the DEA would pay all their travel, living and accommodation expenses. Scotland Yard had to pay only their wages. They would work in Fort Lauderdale alongside McCracken and his squad, and maintain links with the Miami probe into Errico and the Ray Thompson mob. There was much optimistic talk of future co-operation, buoyed up by the prospect that up to 50 per cent of drug-runners' assets seized by Cougar–Man could go to Britain. All Britain had to do was pass an asset seizure law complementing America's. As £100 million-worth of assets had already been discovered, the amount coming the Yard's way looked as if it could reach £50 million, which should then have been used to fund future operations against organized crime.

By now Lundy was a frequent traveller between London, Miami and the Virgin Islands. At the end of May he again flew to Tortola to speak for an absent Murphy at a remand hearing. It was agreed that the BVI's Attorney-General would offer no evidence and drop all charges because the money-launderer was assisting a far bigger investigation elsewhere. The Tortola visit had been preceded by an overnight stop in Miami when Lundy met Sergeant Terry Burke and Inspector John Beadle who updated him on the joint Yard–DEA operation so enthusiastically agreed a few weeks earlier. The pair were disconsolate because they felt they were wasting their time. Nothing had happened since Lundy last saw them: they were still working out of a 'broom cupboard', despite the promise of new offices; Bob McCracken and Dirk Lamagno had been kept busy

on other inquiries. The team had been given the services of
an intelligence analyst from Washington but nothing else.
And no one was really working Murphy or debriefing him
because McCracken, through no fault of his own, was now
busy on other duties.

Lundy pondered this sorry news during his whistle-stop
trip to Tortola. Returning immediately to Miami, he spoke
to Shaun Murphy, who was co-operating fully and had
already testified to a Grand Jury but who confirmed he
was unhappy with the DEA. This was not what Lundy
wanted to hear.

Imagine! I've still got the job on in Spain, with all the 'When
are we going to nick Fleming?' hassle, and I'm already fighting
battles in England to keep Cougar running, so I think, 'What do
I do now?' Then I remembered what Bob once said: 'The only
person who can get things going is Al Coward', a high-flyer he
had worked with in the past, and now head of the DEA's assets
seizure section in Washington. I'd met him myself when he'd
flown down to Tortola. So I decide there's only one answer. Next
morning I dig out Al Coward's card and I ring Washington.

I say, 'Look Al, I don't know how to put this but I've got a lot
of pressures on me in England to keep these operations going.
That's OK, I can overcome them to a degree, but I tell you, I
met my lads last night, and they tell me it's an absolute joke in
Fort Lauderdale. Nothing's happening, they're fed up and they
want to go back to England.' Al Coward was shocked. I said,
'Well, I can only tell you, I've still got a few things to sort out,
but if your side hasn't really got its act together, then I'm afraid
that I'm going to have to report to my superiors that we should
call our people home!'

Lundy had lit a fire. Next day he went to the DEA's Fort
Lauderdale offices and asked McCracken what was going
on, or rather, why nothing was going on. Bob said he had
sent reports to his group supervisor, Paul Teresi, about how
big the Murphy affair was, but Teresi was weighed down
by what Lundy calls 'fire brigade policing'.

In Miami and Fort Lauderdale all they were interested in was statistics, figures, so they were nicking dopers off the streets by the dozen. They were up to their eyes in work – Teresi himself had been called away to investigate internal allegations against DEA agents in North Florida – but our massive multi-national, multi-million-dollar probe had fallen by the wayside. Big Bob had been told to get on with other jobs.

Big Bob expressed his frustration to Lundy. So did the attorneys assigned to Operation Man, for they had witnessed the impact of Diamond and Murphy's evidence on the Grand Jury investigating Michael Levine and their revelation of the massive criminal proceeds washing through his networks the pair could expose, if only the DEA were to allocate enough resources. Unknown to the Cougar–Man team, that was about to happen. Straight after Lundy's call, Al Coward had phoned the DEA's Miami office to announce he was flying straight down. Next day the 'Man' squad vanished from Fort Lauderdale and drove the twenty-five miles south to Miami for a bare-knuckle encounter which became known as Black Tuesday. Late that evening Lundy found out what had happened.

Back comes Bob McCracken, *white*! He said, 'They've been asking me what this job's all about and why nothing's happened.' I felt awful. 'Jeez!' I said, 'I'm sorry if I've caused you problems, Bob.' 'No, it's good,' he said, 'it was the only way to get anything done.' That was the irony. Bob had always been keen to expand the investigation, so I'd called Washington and now he was in deep trouble. He said a big meeting had been set for tomorrow. 'There'll be people down from Washington, US attorneys, DEA chiefs, Teresi's being summoned back from Jacksonville, and they want you there as well.'

Despite his remorse over McCracken, Lundy knew the show had to go on and that it was essential to present the best case at the meeting. He pulled in John Beadle and

Terry Burke to draw up charts showing what Diamond and Murphy had admitted, what had been achieved and what was still to come. The Cougar–Man attorneys were also sharpening their weapons. They had been told not to attend the meeting because it was purely a DEA affair, but they decided to gatecrash and express their commitment. And so on 4 June 1986, in a big boardroom in the DEA's Miami office, the top brass from Washington assembled alongside a nervous local hierarchy, all sorts of Strike Force and US attorneys and three men from Scotland Yard. The atmosphere was electric. To begin, ASAC (Assistant Special-Agent-in-Charge) Sam Bilborough made some soothing remarks about the need to overcome a few misunderstandings. He explained the DEA's immense workload in south Florida, he quoted statistics showing how many thousand kilos of cocaine had been seized and how many hundred arrests the agency had made in the past year. He had been speaking for several minutes when Lundy felt he had to chip in. He recalls he said:

'Will you excuse me a minute? Can I just interrupt? I'm very embarrassed sitting here, because I realize it's probably my fault that this meeting has been called, and so much friction caused, so if you wouldn't mind, I think I ought to put my point of view across. And then, if you want, I'll retire with my officers and leave you to it. It's obviously me who's caused any problems, so please let me just state my view of the situation.'

Lundy and Burke went through the Murphy–Diamond charts, and Lundy explained his own battles at home to justify the far-off detachment of so many Yard officers for so long. He even dared to say that, for all its street-level seizures and arrests, the DEA had not stopped or even contained the cocaine explosion and was losing the wider war against the dealers. However, the Diamond–Murphy revelations provided an opportunity to indict the leaders of some of America's biggest drug rings, along with their fat legal defenders, and to recover vast drug profits. 'I would have thought,' said Lundy, 'this must be a better way of hitting the drug industry than picking up addicts on the streets.' To the obvious discomfort of the local DEA, he referred to the failure to deliver back-up support or decent office space. He then continued:

'I've got problems trying to keep any officers here, so all I want to know – and the reason I've brought the subject to a head – is, do you want our co-operation? Do we want to push these things on through to the Nth degree, or do I say to you all, "Thank you very much, it's been a good job, cheerio"? Because that's the position I'm in.'

Attorney Diane Fernandez spoke up in agreement, saying no real progress had been made, despite the potential. Lundy felt the time had now come to withdraw. He and his team retreated for a cup of tea but they stayed in the building. When the meeting broke up Lundy was approached by Ralph Saucedo, an 'Assistant Special Agent in Charge', who spoke fluent Spanish acquired from years of service in South America: in Lundy's terms, 'a real forward thinker'. Lundy recalls a chuckling Saucedo telling him something like this:

'Do you know what you've done? If only you knew! You just don't *ring* Washington! It doesn't *happen*! All hell's broken loose in this building since yesterday: "Washington?! Coming down here because somebody's *criticized* us?!" You cannot believe what it's done. Anyway, all I can tell you is – as from tomorrow – *I* am going to be officially in charge of setting up this operation. And I'm telling you, it will be done right. I assure you, I'll be up at Fort Lauderdale with decisions on how things are going.'

Lundy was relieved to know one person was laughing.

Everybody else was in despair. When he returned to Fort Lauderdale that night, heads were rolling. Local chief Paul Teresi felt that if Bob McCracken had put in his reports on time, he, Teresi, would have realized the job's potential. Knowing McCracken's shattered state, Lundy told Teresi how brilliantly the agent had performed all the way from the Isle of Man to the Virgin Isles. Teresi would not relent, saying that McCracken should have kept his paperwork up-to-date, and another case agent had been appointed. Teresi was probably right about the paperwork but Lundy felt that Big Bob had been kept so busy, he had simply had no time to do it. Anyway, the die was cast: McCracken had to go.

Ralph Saucedo arrived in Fort Lauderdale two days later, when Lundy was amazed to learn that Cougar–Man now had an entire suite of offices in the Justice building and an additional twelve DEA agents on strength. They had been called off jobs all over Miami. Two more intelligence analysts were coming down from Washington, and four US attorneys would prepare the cases for trial. US Customs investigators were being recruited. So were eight IRS (Internal Revenue) agents to chase the money. As the operation was now so vast, it was decided to appoint an additional supervisor, Herb Williams, an ex-professional heavyweight boxer turned Metro-Dade cop, turned DEA agent. In the end his team was bigger than the rest of the Fort Lauderdale office. Some 'Cougar' officers served there for another three years. Together so long, the Brits and Yanks in Cougar–Man designed an exclusive club tie. The operation is still in progress.

Lundy himself had earned a prodigious reputation among the federal agencies in South Florida. He made a presentation about the entire operation to a sixty-strong meeting headed by US Attorney-General Ed Meese and was also put forward to speak to American TV stations. In

November 1986 the DEA awarded him a Certificate of
Commendation. Paul Teresi told the press why:

> It is in recognition of the vital part he played in uncovering
> the money-laundering racket. Operation Cougar would never
> have been a success without him. He is the most dedicated law
> enforcement agent I have ever had the privilege of working with.
> His integrity and honesty are beyond reproach.[1]

Teresi's outstanding tribute came just one week after
World in Action had broadcast 'The Untouchable'. That
programme generated dozens of national newspaper stories
implying Lundy was corrupt; in predictable contrast, Teresi's
eulogy was scarcely reported.

Cougar–Man persuaded Levine (jailed for nine years) to
plead guilty and turn federal witness. This led to the indictment of one of Scott Errico's prime confederates, Teddy
Prior, then world super-heavyweight kick-boxing champion. He too 'rolled over' and turned informant, helping
to knock down another Errico associate, Patrick Bilton.
When Bilton testified he opened up a scandal which led to
the arrest of the head of the Marine Patrol Section of the
Miami Police Department for corruption. Such witnesses
also talked of going on Caribbean drug runs with Errico, of
killings, hostage-taking and the kidnapping of a Jamaican
police chief. One spectacular all-American casualty was
racing driver Randy Lanier, 'Indianapolis 500 Rookie of
the Year' in 1986, who by 1987 had been indicted in
his absence on drug-trafficking charges. Kick-boxer Prior
alleged that hit-man Scott Errico had given him 2,500
pounds of marijuana which he sold to Lanier for $800,000.
Lanier was only one of nine professional race drivers
indicted or jailed on drug-related charges in a few months.

Dozens of defendants were eventually convicted in
Florida alone, while cash totalling tens of millions of
dollars and fleets of cars, boats and planes were recovered

from America, Anguilla and the Bahamas. Many of the dealers named by Murphy had previously eluded the DEA because they had salted away all the profits of their crimes where they could not be found. Now as Murphy and others revealed where all these assets had been hidden, a combination of crack US attorneys and IRS investigators set about confiscating them.

Previously the DEA had intelligence that these were drug dealers but there was no sign of any money. Now, by adding the evidence of the money to the earlier intelligence, it was possible to indict them. So if DEA investigators went to a drug dealer and said, 'Where did you get this five million?', and the bloke didn't co-operate, the IRS just went in and confiscated the money anyway.

Like the Boston boys. They had a stack of money in St Thomas in the US Virgin Islands, so the IRS said, 'You tell us how you got it!' When they couldn't come up with a legitimate answer, the IRS just seized the lot! You can kill 'em in all sorts of ways when you find the money.

That's how they indicted Ben Kramer, world speed-boat champion. One day I opened up a file in Murphy's office, and inside were these glossy brochures all about Kramer's speed-boat company. So I ask Bob McCracken whether he'd ever heard of these people, and he had, so he checks them out on the phone. Sure enough, there's all sorts of intelligence all over America on them for drug dealing.

During powerboat championships off Florida, Kramer's syndicate would enter some boats that hadn't a hope of winning, just to do drug runs. These boats would roar off, meet a mother drug ship miles out at sea, stash loads of cocaine aboard and then get towed in as a broken-down racer. It was a superb cover. They imported tons of coke that way – and the DEA knew it – but they'd never been nicked because they had no traceable assets. Now Murphy's files reveal that they'd bought land in California, and built huge office developments and sports complexes through offshore companies in the BVI. That way their drug money was being washed so clean they were becoming legitimate! Later Kramer tried to escape from prison by helicopter but it crashed when too many other prisoners jumped on.

Back in April 1986, while Lundy was still absorbing Murphy's ever-more astonishing revelations, the accountant suddenly dropped the remark, 'Of course, they're even bigger than me in Anguilla', and began talking of a company formation agent on that island. Murphy had recently had a lot of dealings with him because, four months before Lundy arrived in Tortola, the managers of the BVI's only banks (Barclays, Chase Manhattan, Bank of Nova Scotia and First Pennsylvania) had at last felt compelled to refuse Murphy's huge cash deposits, which were obviously derived from drugs. Instead they imposed a $10,000 cash limit. This interfered with Murphy's habit of dropping by with half a million dollars at a time, so he switched custom to Anguilla where regulations were non-existent. Murphy explained: '*There* you can pay in *anything*! You can walk in and out the island, pay in limitless sums and move them all round the world!'

After this revelation, Cougar–Man moved rapidly on to Anguilla. At first Lundy did not go ('I couldn't cope with everything') so Owen Griffin and Terry Burke went and acted just as he had done when jumping on Diamond and Murphy. However, because the company formation agent held considerable political clout, they had to conduct their inquiries with great sensitivity. Their stealth paid off. When they raided his premises they found evidence that tens of millions of drug dollars had been passing through his companies, some of which were really owned by Colombian cocaine syndicates.

Before Lundy's arrival Burke and Griffin, backed by Attorney-General Richard Whitehead, had frozen some $5 million of drug money lodged in an island bank. This was a modest sum by 'Cougar' standards but huge compared to the annual budget of the impoverished island where it was lodged. Now the Anguillan government had the chance to pocket a large chunk of it, because of the DEA's policy of allowing any state seizing drug money illicitly exported from the USA to keep a share. All the DEA cared for was that the dopers should lose it, and that states like Anguilla should have an incentive to co-operate again.

Not all drug dealers using Anguilla's facilities were in business for personal profit. Some had political goals, as Burke and Griffin realized when they made an astonishing discovery which should have convinced their Yard masters, once and for all, that 'Cougar' was highly relevant to the UK. As part of a joint inquiry with the FBI, they peeked into a set of files in the company formation agent's offices relating to the Patrick Murray organization of Boston. This had no connection with the 'Boston boys' syndicate for which Murphy had acted, but was a fund-raising front for the IRA. FBI agents had long suspected the Irish-born Murray of funnelling drug profits through Anguilla, but they had never been able to penetrate the island's bank secrecy laws and prove it. Now they rushed there to support Cougar's attempts to freeze two lots of monies: several million dollars of 'pure' drug money placed by some Colombians, and some two millions held on behalf of the Boston IRA cell.

The Yard's interest should have been even greater because it was this Murray organization which had tried to smuggle seven tons of arms into Ireland in September 1984. The weapons (163 guns, 71,000 rounds of ammunition, plus rockets, hand-grenades and bullet-proof vests) had been shipped across the Atlantic on the *Valhalla*, then transferred to the *Marita Ann* a few miles off Ireland. When this trawler slipped into the Republic's waters she was intercepted by Irish Customs and police who had been tipped off by the FBI. Her crew were arrested and later jailed in Dublin. The *Valhalla* was intercepted on her return to Boston where in 1987 the captain, Robert

Anderson, was jailed for four years on separate charges of smuggling weapons and marijuana. Ringleader Patrick Murray was sentenced to ten years. All the defendants received relatively light sentences because they had pleaded guilty.

What should also have interested Scotland Yard was that the gang's money had been laundered through an Anguillan company, Global Holdings Ltd, one of several hundred Anguillan-registered corporations, many of them shells really owned by people known to the DEA as narcotics traffickers. Through Global Holdings, Michael Murray (Patrick's brother) bought a $250,000 farm in New England. According to the FBI, Michael was connected not only with the IRA but with the notorious Boston organized crime syndicate, the Winter Hill gang. It was also alleged that $985,000 switched from Global Holdings in Anguilla to a New York bank had been used to buy the arms found on the *Marita Ann*. This was just a fraction of the cash placed in the island's Caribbean Commercial Bank in person by Murray gang members. A Global Holdings account had been opened there in June 1985 by Michael Murray himself, who walked in and coolly deposited $495,000 in notes.

Although the Yard officers had managed to freeze both the Boston and Colombian funds, lawyers representing the 'owners' were contesting the move in court, for instance by claiming the sums were tax avoidance money and so not seizable under Anguillan law. This obliged the Yard men, on behalf of the island's Attorney-General, to prove the monies had truly been derived from drugs. Neither Lundy nor his DEA colleagues nor FBI Special Agent Roderick J. Kennedy from Boston thought this would be difficult, but the plaintiffs were represented by leading St Kitts-Nevis lawyers determined to contest every aspect of the case. Thus a hearing expected to last days lasted weeks. At the end the magistrate decided in favour of the plaintiffs. Attorney-General Whitehead could lodge an appeal but, until that was heard, the funds were unfrozen. At this point the inevitable happened. Within hours the money was transferred out of the bank and off the island.

Lundy suspected the worst. He felt the magistrate had been intimidated by the lawyers' hectoring manner throughout the hearing. One even had a shouting match with Lundy on the street. The detective had made a combative remark such as, 'You must be very proud of your performance this morning but don't think it's all lost from our point of view.' The advocate reacted with fury, roaring outrage that Lundy had dared speak to him in this manner. He wrote a letter of complaint to Attorney-General Whitehead and claimed to send a copy to Scotland Yard's Complaints Bureau. Whitehead fired off a letter to the Yard saying that, as Lundy had been sworn in as a special constable, this was a purely Anguillan matter which he would deal with. In fact, no such complaint ever reached the Yard so CIB had no power to act.

The day after the magistrate's ruling, Lundy and his colleagues were consoling themselves in their hotel bar when they saw the magistrate, together with the lawyer who had rowed with Lundy and several other figures in the case, going into a room. Lundy asked the hotel manager what these men were doing in there and was told that they were attending a masonic lodge function. Lundy was appalled.

They were all together at a lodge meeting the day after the verdict! As it happened, one of our officers was 'on the square' and he confirmed that masonic lodges of instruction took place in this hotel and he'd been invited to one such himself. Of course, he'd not taken it up.

Some of the unfrozen funds were eventually seized,

and later tens of millions of dollars were recovered in
America on the basis of documents found in the files of
the Anguillan-based company formation agency.

The 'Cougar' paperchase led the British cops and
DEA agents on to the Dutch Antilles, the Bahamas,
and Montserrat. Owen Griffin went on to Nassau and,
again, by opening up the entire office of Labon Quimby,
seized material leading to his arrest and a ten-year jail
sentence. Other arrests followed.

Back in London 'Cougar' officers were in great demand
for a while, running courses at the Detective Training
School on the new Drugs Profit Confiscation Act for
officers from all over Britain. At first Tony Lundy gave
lectures because only he had senior operational experience
of how such laws worked abroad, particularly in the USA.
Later Owen Griffin and Tony Brightwell took over. Lundy
also attended Foreign Office meetings to brief diplomatic
staff and new governors on how the financial systems
of tiny island colonies were being exploited by criminal
money-launderers.

All such expertise had been accrued only because Lundy
had applied his drive and initiative to take the original
Brinks–Mat inquiry into fields where more buttoned-down
officers would not have dared tread. Most of 'Cougar's'
work had nothing to do with Brinks–Mat but it exposed
the grotesque scandal of what was going on in a dozen
Commonwealth tax-havens: not just the cleansing of drug-
money but the wholesale corruption of island politics. In
addition, the Boston IRA case had conclusively proved the
connection – long-denied by some British police chiefs –
between drugs and terrorism. Yet even after Cougar–Man
discovered the full story of how the *Valhalla–Marita Ann*
gun-run had been financed, Lundy was shocked to find
the evidence derided.

Lundy's greatest disappointment, however, surrounded

the huge sums which could have come Scotland Yard's way when US authorities seized the assets of convicted or suspected drug dealers located through Cougar–Man. By 1987 the joint operation had located some £160 million. It was calculated that the UK share was £32.5 million, which would have made 'Cougar' not just self-financing but hugely profitable. However, a classic Whitehall fight now broke out between the Home Office and the Treasury which asserted that it should pocket the money. This in turn upset the US Department of Justice which threatened to withdraw the offer. The *Sunday Telegraph* succinctly described the squabble:

> The problem has been that the Americans were able to offer the cash only if it was to be added to the Yard's existing budget. However, money given to the police in Britain is normally paid into the Consolidated Fund, the nation's purse, and is used in all areas of public spending. The Treasury has been reluctant to yield on this point and there was a serious danger that the American offer would be withdrawn.[2]

In the end the offer was frozen, partly because of the Treasury's obstructive attitude, partly because of the UK's failure to negotiate an appropriate treaty with the USA in time, so Cougar's £32.5 million has still not arrived. This ridiculous state of affairs drove the Metropolitan Commissioner, Sir Peter Imbert, to demand a law saying seized criminal assets should go directly back into furthering crime investigations, not into the Treasury which was not prepared to increase police budgets by the equivalent amount.

By spring 1988 Operation Cougar was being closed down. Soon only two officers were left, mopping up unfinished business. Their colleagues were dispersed to posts where their immense knowledge of international drug syndicates and money-laundering would be squandered. The London *Standard* ran a punchy story revealing the shut-down. Despite using the term 'Mafia' in far too broad terms, the article correctly described the stupidity of the decision.

The new breed of Mafia man has been let off the hook by an increasing tendency for Scotland Yard's budget-conscious bosses to devote resources to solving London crime, because of local political pressures, some detectives believe. One high-ranking detective commented: 'It's a bizarre consequence of not having a national police force. Scotland Yard is now all about policing London for Londoners.'

Deputy Assistant Commissioner Simon Crawshaw, in charge of specialist operations at the Yard, maintained that some specialist units had international functions, such as Special Branch or the Serious Crimes Branch. He denied that any known major criminals would be ignored by the Yard but said: 'We can't police the world. Our inquiries must be beneficial to London and Londoners.'[3]

One 'Cougar' stalwart decided to make a last stand. In August 1988 Sergeant Rupert Reid wrote a report for consideration by the Yard's detective chiefs. After detailing 'Cougar's' history and achievements, he reached the heart of his argument:

If one talks to the DEA, the US Customs and the IRS, all of whom contributed to the US flank of Operation Cougar, one is met with disbelief at the demise of such an effective unit with no apparent comparable substitute. There are many individuals and agencies in the field of offshore investment, so carefully cultivated, who are wondering at the sudden withdrawal of police involvement. The respective Channel Island police forces, hitherto so impressed by the competent approach of Cougar officers, have been left in limbo, often half-way through inquiries on our behalf.

Reid argued that, whatever might be said in police

statements, 'the hard facts' were that the squad had been dismantled without proper regard to the quantity and quality of its information; little attempt had been made to ensure that its unfinished inquiries were taken up by other sections of the force; and other agencies 'who had developed a working relationship with Cougar officers and who had come to expect a certain standard of liaison and professional conduct have been disappointed by the sudden withdrawal of service with no apparent explanation from official sources.'

While agreeing with Crawshaw's response to the *Evening Standard* that the Metropolitan Police 'can't police the world', Reid submitted:

Cougar was not policing the world. It was undertaking a very necessary role, largely UK-based, in monitoring the laundering of proceeds of crime committed mainly by London criminals, wholly or partly within the London area. Those inquiries conducted overseas by officers attached to Operation Cougar were funded largely by the US authorities . . . and therefore were not a substantial burden on Metropolitan Police budgets.

I believe that these fundamental points would be apparent had the contents of Secret Green Dockets [concerning top criminals operating in the London area who have still to be given any police attention] on all Operation Cougar inquiries been made available to those ultimately responsible for the investigation of organized crime by this force . . .

Operation Cougar was beginning to make sense of the previously confused picture of the funding of organized crime in London. It has revealed groups of top criminals effectively commuting between London, Europe and the USA, purchasing high value real estate both here and abroad using off-shore companies, and has begun to identify the persons responsible for laundering the huge sums of money on the criminals' behalf. Furthermore the Cougar team has shown that these launderers were not beyond reach and were capable of being turned to our advantage in what hitherto has seemed to be an overwhelming task . . .

I would urge an immediate review of Operation Cougar in

order that the good work which stands in danger of being wasted should be resurrected, properly discussed and processed, and in order that what promised to constitute a major breakthrough in the attack on organized crime should not be squandered.

Rupert Reid left the Metropolitan Police soon after writing this report. Other Cougar veterans also retired rather than stomach being put to work on comparatively trivial areas of policing. Terry Burke did stay in the same field by transferring to the National Drugs Intelligence Unit to work on yet another spectacular inquiry nurtured by Tony Lundy (see Chapter 22) but many other investigations fell by the wayside because no one in the hierarchy felt inclined to back them. Senior officers told former 'Cougar' men to get rid of the operation's correspondence and clear their cupboards of all intelligence material gathered during years of work in the Isle of Man, Florida and the Caribbean.

Ironically, a year or so later the same senior officers were sidling up and asking if there were any 'Cougar' remnants worth following up, but now the cupboards were bare. They had been full of such stuff, including material on British criminals who had nothing to do with the Brinks–Mat robbery but who had laundered millions of pounds through West Indian tax-havens. These men were still in Britain but had never been pursued because of the negative attitude prevailing at senior levels. The main reason for the change of tune in 1989 seemed to be that leading politicians, including Margaret Thatcher and Douglas Hurd (then Home Secretary), had been making highly-publicized speeches about pursuing drug dealers and their buried treasure. Suddenly the notion of combined international organized crime squads which Lundy had been advocating since 1985 had become politically fashionable.

One thing which hastened 'Cougar's' premature end was the cloud of unjustified rumour surrounding Lundy himself. However, as Rupert Reid stated, 'nowhere in any investigation did any Cougar staff conduct themselves in an unprofessional manner'. In the end the operation was killed on grounds of expense, despite the fact it was costing only a dozen men's salaries and could have recouped £32.5 million if the Treasury and Home Office had stopped bickering in time to receive its share of drug assets seized in America, primarily as a result of Lundy's breakthroughs with Diamond and Murphy. 'Cougar was a Thatcherite ideal,' says one veteran of the operation still serving in Scotland Yard. 'It was the only profit-making centre in the Metropolitan Police – and they closed it down!' Yet, at the same time, millions were being spent pursuing corruption allegations against Lundy which turned out to be wholly unjustified.

The Nailing of Howard Marks

One of the dozen DEA agents in Miami drafted on to Cougar–Man after 'Black Tuesday' was Wendy Lovato. She joined Tony Lundy and the other Yard men on inquiries in the Virgin Isles and Anguilla. An outstanding officer, she was married to fellow DEA agent Craig Lovato who had recently completed a two-year assignment in Spain, attached to the US Embassy in Madrid. He then rejoined the DEA office in Miami. Early in 1987 he and Wendy bought a new home and decided to hold a house-warming party, which would also celebrate Cougar–Man's remarkable successes. The local DEA chiefs turned up, and so did the Brits Terry Burke, Owen Griffin and Tony Lundy.

Lundy had never met Craig Lovato but Wendy had previously said he was downcast about the fate of an operation he had been working on in Spain. One of Lundy's officers then saw a book on Wendy's office desk about a notorious British drug smuggler, Howard Marks. Lundy used the occasion of the party to approach Craig head-on. Craig recalls that, even at this first meeting, he noticed 'Tony is nothing but persistent'. Craig explained that he had been working on a very important case in Spain and then asked if Lundy knew anything of Marks.

I said, 'As it happens, yes, I do know something about him', because when I'd chased over to Rome to catch Joe 'the Greek' Vratsides in 1979, the First Secretary at the British Embassy was Hamilton McMillan who gave us a lot of help. Not long after, his name figured prominently in the newspapers because he had allegedly recruited Howard Marks into the secret service,

MI6. In 1981 Marks was tried at the Old Bailey for smuggling 15 tons of cannabis on to a remote island in the Hebrides, and part of his defence was that he had once worked for MI6. Naturally I took an interest because I knew Hamilton McMillan.

Howard Marks was the fabled if bogus working-class lad from the Welsh valleys whose charm and good looks had beguiled many of his aristocratic contemporaries at Balliol College, Oxford, in the mid to late 1960s. So had his capacity to furnish undergraduates of all classes with liberal supplies of pot in that heyday of student rebellion, Vietnam protest and the Beatles record, *Sergeant Pepper*. Hamilton McMillan had been at Balliol with Marks, then joined MI6 (under the cover of the Foreign Office) on graduation. Neither he nor his employers seemed worried by Marks's drug dealing. Indeed it must have seemed a qualification in 1973 when MI6 put Marks on its books to gather intelligence on his Irish friend and fellow drug dealer, IRA terrorist James McCann. At the time McCann, based in Amsterdam, was buying arms for the IRA with profits from the drug trade.

At his 1981 trial the Crown conceded that Marks had indeed once worked for MI6, if only for three months. However, there was no truth in the evidence given by a self-styled Mexican police chief, that Marks had penetrated the cannabis operation on behalf of Mexican intelligence. It was later claimed that Marks had paid the 'Mexican' $150,000 to give false testimony. If so, it was money well spent. He helped get Marks acquitted when he might otherwise have received fifteen years. He remained in custody to face a 1973 charge of smuggling cannabis into America in huge amplifiers shipped round the world as part of the sound systems on rock tours. In the USA 820 pounds of Marks's hashish had been seized in just one set of speakers. Back in 1973 he had been granted bail and disappeared (faking his own kidnap), but in 1982 he smartly pleaded guilty and was given a mere three years. As he had already spent twenty-one months in custody, with remission he had only three more months to serve. On release he went straight back to the only trade he knew: cannabis smuggling on a massive scale.

With a new wife, Judith Lane, he went to live in Majorca where Spanish police began investigating him in January 1986. They linked up with the DEA which had been interested in him since it became clear that his syndicate was again importing tons of hashish into the USA. On 26 December 1984 over 5,000 pounds were seized at the Alameda Naval Air Rework Center, California, hidden in crates marked 'aircraft propellers' shipped from Karachi, Pakistan. Between June and August 1985 Marks's distributors in Los Angeles cashed cheques totalling $615,000, around the time that another six tons of Thai dope were landed in California from a fishing boat. In September 1985 Dutch and British Customs learned that Marks was planning to move a further ten tons from Pakistan to the USA. Further inquiries in seven countries identified many key members of his organization, but this did not prevent 7.5 tons being imported into America during 1986 or Marks's brother-in-law, Patrick Lane, laundering $12.5 million through America and back out to Europe and the Far East.

At the party in 1987 Craig Lovato told Tony Lundy how for six months he had worked in Majorca, analysing the thinly encoded English in which the drug dealer was running a worldwide distribution empire on his tapped telephone. Lovato had been shocked at the scale of the operation – clearly Marks was one of the biggest cannabis smugglers in the world – but he was also dismayed that, after he had returned to America, the Majorca investigation rapidly came to a halt. Even Britain's Customs and Excise, which had been working successfully with Spanish police and the DEA, dropped out after arresting some minor criminals on the fringes of Marks's organization. When Lundy heard of this withdrawal it struck him as odd, especially as it had been Customs who had brought Marks to trial twice before, though not with conspicuous success.

Lovato told Lundy that, although Marks had set himself up as 'Untouchable', the joint inquiry had built a big case against him. Despite this, British Customs had 'turned their attention to other matters'. Back in America Lovato had found it impossible to activate the DEA. The main obstacle seemed to be that he was based in Florida, whereas Marks's only recent American drug-smuggling acts had occurred in California. He had duly forwarded his evidence to the DEA office in Los Angeles but the US Attorney there refused to prosecute. Lovato's own Florida chiefs were not interested, because there was no obvious Florida angle and they already had far more local prosecutions on their hands than they could cope with. Today Lovato recalls these disappointments with serenity. Lundy remembers him in a grimmer mood.

So he's bleating to me that he's getting nowhere and fighting a losing battle, and then he says, 'I wish you could create something for me. Wendy's having a great time. She tells me you're doing a fantastic job. I just wish we could get a similar organization going against Marks.'

Well, this is a red rag to a bull to me, isn't it! Especially when Craig tells me that Marks is still involved in England. Then he asks, 'Have you read David Leigh's book?' '*Whose* book? *David Leigh*?!' He had it there in his house: *High Time*, all about Howard Marks. I'd never seen it before so I said, 'Right, I'll read this with interest!' because, of course, Leigh was one of the *Observer* reporters who'd been writing stories about me for years.

Lundy quickly read *High Time*. It seemed to be nothing less than the arrogant criminal confessions of Marks himself, almost an authorized biography.[1] What most irked Lundy was the dope dealer's acute awareness of the inability of police forces from different countries to work together. Lovato summed up the Marks view this way: 'Enforcement agencies lack the professionalism and expertise to conduct international investigations. There are too many egos and jurisdictions involved to foster the proper climate of co-operation.' Ironically this was Lundy's view too but, whereas Marks gleefully exploited the chaos, Lundy was determined to end it. For a couple of days he listened to Lovato's tales of the 'Marco Polo' of marijuana. On his return to London he wrote a report based largely on the DEA man's knowledge of Marks's worldwide empire, including his continuing activity right under Scotland Yard's nose.

There was stacks of stuff, including evidence that he was running operations through the Hong Kong International Travel Agency in Denman Street, Soho. What a cover! His own travel firm in the West End! In Karachi he'd bought another front for smuggling dope through Pakistan: a language school run by his brother-in-law, George Lane, while in Miami another brother-in-law, Patrick, was laundering the money. Marks had more sidekicks in Canada, Los Angeles, Bangkok and Hong Kong. I started checking all these names, and we located one of them, John Denbigh, in West London. I had a look at him and found he was just as 'Untouchable' as Marks! There was so much evidence against him. So I talked this over with Phil Corbett and I kept saying, 'How come Customs haven't nicked him?' On the intelligence we'd been fed, it didn't seem possible he could not have been arrested.

I then put forward a paper proposing something like this: 'Marks has set himself up as an Untouchable. So many different agencies have looked at him, and they're not doing anything or getting their act together, but now is the time. This could be the best opportunity to show that there are no Untouchables anywhere and agencies worldwide can work properly together. It doesn't matter *where* anybody gets prosecuted. What's needed is an operation in which every prisoner is taken back to one country, even though the various agencies may be based in many countries. In this case America would seem to be the focal point, so police forces in Spain and Australia, together with Customs and ourselves in Britain, should all join the DEA and FBI in trying to put the entire Marks network behind bars there.'

Lundy submitted his paper to Assistant Commissioner John Dellow who, 'good as gold', according to an immodest Lundy, saw its potential. By coincidence the DEA's new Miami chief, Dodge Galanos, was in England to speak to a drugs conference, so Commander Corbett arranged for him to come to a meeting in Dellow's office, at which Lundy's paper and charts of Marks's empire were analysed. By the end of the meeting, Galanos had said that, in view of the continuing success of the Cougar–Man joint operation, he would back a Howard Marks probe based in Miami. Meantime Lundy was keeping Lovato posted, 'because he's dead! He can't do a thing on it over there.' Lovato himself acknowledges Lundy's role.

The Howard Marks investigation would not have gone ahead if Tony Lundy had not given us his support. We were having a very difficult time selling it to our management but Tony – because of his effectiveness on Operation Man – was able to catch the attention of my administrators and so provide us with the leverage we needed. We thought that he walked on water. He's the epitome of a professional police officer, way ahead of his time when it came to international operations, and he was leading an outstanding body of investigators. He's a motivator and an earth-shaker: he will do whatever he has to do to get the job done.

It was only because Britain's Customs had lost interest in the Marks probe that Lundy was able to step in. Up till that point, says Lovato, 'we had not got involved with Scotland Yard because of our historic involvement with Her Majesty's Customs'. Now Lundy and his chief, Phil Corbett, tried to get Customs involved again. 'Of all the agencies we needed on board, Customs were top of our list, so along we go to tell them what we're proposing and to ask if they'd be willing to contribute some input, but they blanked it: they wouldn't co-operate.'

Later Customs did get involved, agreeing to supply 'historic' evidence and intelligence on Marks, gathered over many years, but leaving the investigation of his continuing crimes to Scotland Yard. This agreement was reached at a top-level meeting at the US Embassy in London. It barely concealed the bitterness felt by Customs at the Yard's invasion of its Marks territory.

This was most obvious in the area of 'flagging': the system whereby one law enforcement unit puts a flag or marker against the names of its targets to prevent other units pursuing the same targets. For example, within Scotland Yard if one squad flags a criminal in the records of C11 (Criminal Intelligence), this should ensure that any other squad inquiring about him through C11 is told not to pursue him, and that the first squad is informed of the second's interest. This is to avoid the embarrassment of two squads pursuing the same criminal with possibly disastrous consequences (especially in armed ambushes or undercover 'drug-buy' operations). However, this system is open to abuse if in reality the first squad is not seriously pursuing the target criminal but is protecting him instead. By flagging its man, that squad may not only block other inquiries, it knows exactly who else is after him.

At inter-force level the National Drugs Intelligence Unit (NDIU) operates a similar system. When Lundy first heard Lovato's tale of woe in Miami, he checked through NDIU to see where Customs officially stood over Marks.

Before I did anything about Marks, I found he was flagged to Customs indefinitely. They'd had him flagged as far back as 1973. They'd kept him as a so-called target so nobody else could do anything on him without them hearing. Not that they said they'd flagged him when Phil Corbett and I first went to see them.

Customs had 'flagged' not only Marks but many of his agents, runners and distributors for many years. This should have blocked Scotland Yard from investigating the Marks syndicate, but when Lundy and Corbett made their approach, Customs had no current investigation running on Marks so it could not stop the Yard take-over. Even then, claims Lundy, Customs had not flagged some of Marks's top lieutenants, such as John Denbigh in Canada and Phillip Sparrowhawk in Thailand.

Neither Denbigh nor Sparrowhawk nor two or three other key players were flagged. So now we flagged them because we were putting them into this operation. But a few days after we've seen Customs and they've refused to co-operate, they suddenly tell Phil we've no right to be working on any of these names because they're flagged to Customs. Phil says, 'No, they're not! These people are flagged to us.' So not only did Customs not want to co-operate, they were trying any means to stop us doing anything on these individuals, and block our operation with the DEA that way.

If they really had flagged Denbigh, it's amazing that they hadn't managed to arrest him. When we target him in London, he flees and disappears. Then we locate him in Canada, we work with the RCMP and he gets arrested in September 1987 just as seven tons of Thai marijuana are seized on a ship coming into Vancouver, along with two million dollars. That was a Howard Marks operation. So Denbigh's captured over there committing a serious crime, when not long before Customs had tried to stop us even looking at him! That's going a lot further than possible distrust of me. It was an attempt to stop the Metropolitan Police doing anything.

In contrast to Customs, Australia's Federal Police instantly agreed to co-operate while in Miami the pressure Lundy had applied through Scotland Yard resulted in Lovato at last getting the go-ahead. It was also partly Lundy's stress on worldwide co-operation which caused the DEA to adopt Lovato's choice of codename for the inquiry – Eclectic – defined in his dictionary as 'selecting from various systems, doctrines or sources; composed of material gathered from various sources'. On 23 June 1987 at another London meeting Lovato and his new boss, Charlie Lutz, briefed other agencies on various ways forward, but already Lundy had helped make the breakthrough which would turn Eclectic into one of the DEA's greatest successes.

Such a breakthrough was essential because, even now, Lovato and the DEA had no evidence to put Marks himself behind bars. That was because the Welshman had so constructed his network that he rarely touched the illegal commodity out of which he made his millions: most of the time he was sitting in Majorca, scheming away, while his marijuana was being shipped 15,000 miles on the other side of the world. It was therefore more than likely that, even if all his underlings were arrested and jailed, Marks would walk free. What the DEA needed was a federal witness – in British crime-speak, a supergrass – an insider who could be persuaded to turn and testify against Marks. His key staff consisted either of loyal quartermasters who had served him for years or his wife's brothers, whom Marks seems to have mesmerized into becoming his unthinking tools. None was likely to 'shop' him even if they were facing twenty years in jail. What was needed was someone whom Marks trusted but who was not dependent on him: preferably someone with no principles that might get in the way. As Lundy reviewed Lovato's reports, he focused on the name of one man who fitted the bill perfectly: Anthony Patrick Andrew Cairnes Berkeley, the third Lord Moynihan – and half-brother to Margaret Thatcher's then Minister of Sport, Colin Moynihan.

Tony Moynihan was a shipwrecked survivor of the 'swinging sixties'. Having married three wives – one nude model and two exotic dancers – this louche, young piano-playing roué got himself into deep trouble. In 1968, according to the Metropolitan Police:

> Moynihan and his accomplices used false identities to open accounts in several banks and set up fictitious companies through fraudulently obtaining goods and credits. The sum involved the amount of £20,000. Moynihan likewise obtained credits in various gambling clubs by issuing worthless cheques and subsequently asking his bank not to honour them but to return them to the drawer.[2]

In 1970 a warrant was issued for his arrest, but by then the 'Lord of Fraud' had fled to Spain. In 1974, by which time he was claiming to be the 'director of a theatrical troupe', he moved to the Philippines which had no extradition treaty with Britain and where the appallingly corrupt Marcos regime provided a business climate which suited him down to the ground: he ran a girlie-bar and, some say, brothels. Other countries were not so tolerant. In 1980 an Australian Royal Commission branded him 'a shadowy figure' associated with a syndicate of Australian heroin smugglers. However, in Marcos's Manila where Moynihan seemed to know everyone with any influence, this allegation did him no harm. In 1981 he married a twenty-year-old Filipino – yet another model – and in 1982 his 'temporary visitor' status was upgraded to 'permanent'. Meantime the British Embassy obligingly renewed his passport every five years.

Lord Moynihan did not meet Howard Marks until 1985 when Marks visited Manila in search of corrupt connections and (in 1986) a large remote area in which to grow hashish. He sought Moynihan out as a man with all the necessary local clout. For his part, the third Baron was only too ready to oblige a potential business partner of such immense, if maybe legendary, wealth. He hired an aircraft and took Marks to a distant island but, to the Welshman's highly experienced eye, its terrain was thoroughly unsuitable. Nothing came of the scheme but they remained on good terms and Moynihan became godfather to Marks's latest child.

The more Tony Lundy researched Moynihan, the more convinced he was that here was a supergrass ripe for the turning. He recalled reading a gossip column piece about the runaway peer, now fat and fifty, encountering problems after Ferdinand Marcos's fall in February 1987 and Corazon Aquino's election as president on an anticorruption ticket. If she was going to start kicking out undesirable aliens, Lord M would come near the top of any list.

I realized that he's in trouble in Manila, so where does he go from there? He can't come back to England. I'd checked and found he was still officially circulated as 'wanted' in this country, even though the warrant was eighteen years old. I saw someone very senior at the DPP's office, and I realized it was only because he was such a prominent person that the warrants had been kept in force. If he hadn't been a lord, a man of stature as well as notoriety, they would have been withdrawn years ago.

It then emerged that Moynihan faced a particular difficulty in Manila over the November 1986 murder of a former business partner and fellow alleged whoremonger, Robert Walden, who had married Moynihan's third wife. The peer was not a front-line suspect and no charge had been laid against him, but he was sufficiently close to Walden for a 'stop' to be placed against his name to prevent him leaving the country. He was also suspected of involvement in a series of eight frauds on Philippine banks, and of being a British spy on an intelligence mission. Back in London Lundy gave all the appearance of targeting Moynihan.

I sent a message to the Philippines saying, 'Lord Moynihan is still wanted in this country. Can you please tell us his current situation?' without mentioning why I was asking. I got this funny message back: 'Could you please expand on your interest in Lord Moynihan? What are your current investigations?' So we sent another message back saying, 'There are ongoing investigations, and we just wish to know his current position.' We sent two or three more messages through Interpol, seeking permission to travel, but no reply.

A few days later, on 2 June 1987, a friend of Lord Moynihan's phoned Scotland Yard and left a message for Lundy. He was not available so Sergeant Owen Griffin spoke to the caller, a businessman based in Australia who was visiting relatives in England. Moynihan had asked him to approach Lundy over his re-investigation of the fraud charges against him. He said, 'Moynihan wanted to return to England but wanted to talk to Superintendent Lundy before he did so.' A former North of England policeman, the friend said he would get Moynihan to call Lundy direct. The call came through on 8 June. Again Lundy was busy but the distressed peer gave Griffin an earful which proved Lundy's instincts had been right yet again, as the record shows.

He said he was anxious to talk to Scotland Yard officers who had been chasing him for twenty years over what he considered a small thing. He was anxious to return to England but not to stay. His mother was getting old and he wanted to see her. Above all, he was still an Englishman and wanted to return to his native land. He was anxious to clear up the fraud case and it was not beyond possibility that he would plead guilty. He said, 'I think you will understand that I have confidential information to discuss with you which neither you nor I would want publicized.' This information had nothing to do with charges he could be facing in the UK. He said, 'If you want to tell me to get fucked then do so. It doesn't suit me and it certainly wouldn't suit you.'

He said on a political note that when he sat in the House of Lords he was connected with certain radical leftist tendencies. He said that he had moved slightly to the right and would be prepared to give a written undertaking not to take up his seat in the House of Lords again. He said he wanted to 'wipe the slate clean once and for all'. He concluded by saying, 'Thank you for talking to me, Mr Griffin. If you want to tell me to get fucked, please do so now.' I told him that I would report the matter to my senior officers and I was sure they would be more diplomatic than that if that were their decision.

Soon Lundy was digesting what Moynihan had said. He was clearly agitated (having jumped to the conclusion that Lundy was really out to nail him over those old fraud offences) but Lundy too was perturbed: how did Moynihan know he wanted to see him? Lundy called him back the same day, taping the call (the contents were duly conveyed to America's DEA). Lundy said he presumed Moynihan knew of his request to the Philippine authorities. 'I got a copy of *all* of those things,' replied the disgraced baron in an accent as languidly upper-class as one would expect from a Coldstream Guards officer educated at Stowe. Lundy explained that he wanted to talk to him about certain matters, but he was still waiting for permission to enter the country via the Interpol liaison office in Manila. 'I am quite sure I could arrange that,' said Moynihan who clearly felt the fall of Marcos had in no way diminished his clout with the country's police chiefs. Lundy then suggested that Moynihan tell them he was willing to talk to Scotland Yard. This could speed up the permission and Lundy could be in Manila almost overnight. 'That might take me two or three days to organize,' said Moynihan with modesty, but he wanted a deal: 'No promises either way, but two reasonable-minded people can sit down and see if this bloody stupid matter can be resolved or if it can't.'

Four days later Lundy called Moynihan again to say he had still not received word from Manila to visit but, in the meantime, 'my bosses are saying if you're so-minded why don't you return voluntarily rather than us have to come out and talk to you first'. As he spoke, Lundy knew this was one of the dumbest messages he had ever been asked to convey: there was no chance that Moynihan would have fallen for so ludicrous a scheme. His reply was predictably scornful: 'The answer to that, I would have thought, is very clear. I would basically under no circumstances consider such a thing. I would want to be assured of various things before I did that.' Such as the dropping of all charges, thought Lundy. Moynihan pointed out other obstacles, such as the 'hold order' stopping him from leaving at the airport, 'but I can have it lifted by tomorrow if I want'. Lundy asked if he had any other affiliations that would not be too happy about him leaving. 'Yes – government affiliations with friendly nations which I am assisting in various ways.' Lundy took this to mean Moynihan was some kind of spy or informer (unknown to Lundy, this is what Philippine intelligence police also suspected). Clearly he was not going to budge unless he was expelled. This prospect seemed unlikely for the moment but was helping to make him so desperate for a deal in London that he even offered to pay Lundy's fare to Manila.

I am perfectly prepared to foot the bill . . . and believe me, Mr Lundy, I am not the sort of person who believes that a gentleman of your rank would be in any way influenced in his position on an issue, by accepting such an invitation. I would consider not that I was doing you a favour but that on the contrary you were doing me one.

Lundy replied that there was no question of him paying the fare, which would be met from Scotland Yard funds. Moynihan then admitted, although 'I can normally get what I want here, I might not be able to get that invitation on your behalf. Maybe *you* can get it through your regular channels more easily than I can.' His clout was weakening in Manila, and he knew it. The conversation came to an affable end, with jocular remarks about the result of Britain's general election which had taken place the previous day. Of his half-brother's easy win in Lewisham East, Lord Moynihan remarked: 'I thought he was going to get wiped out. I'm not a Conservative, but anyhow it's nice to have a brother.' It is not clear if Colin Moynihan MP felt the same.

On Monday 22 June a message was at last received from Manila stating that Lundy's trip was welcome. By now it was clear that Moynihan really did have 'affiliations with friendly nations': he had been an informant for Australia's Federal Police and its National Crime Authority concerning a worldwide drug-smuggling ring. That force had also received reports that the drug traffickers in question were trying to find out who had been informing against them in Manila. No doubt Moynihan knew what they would do to him, if they found out he was the informer. This Lundy identified as an even more compelling reason for him to make a deal for a rapid jail-free return to Blighty.

Lundy decided that if he was now going as far as the Philippines he should also visit Australia where a former British Customs man had recently been caught trying to smuggle in five kilos of heroin. Allan Gregory McLean had joined the Australian Customs Service in 1975 and had risen to inspector until his arrest on information supplied by Scotland Yard's Special Intelligence Section (SIS). In 1986 McLean had flown to England and met high-ranking criminals including several South London 'Untouchables'.

He also met some ex-colleagues who were still working for British Customs. When captured in Sydney he co-operated with local police and offered to give evidence against his co-conspirators. This earned him the reduced sentence of five years in jail. He indicated some knowledge about criminal enterprises back in Britain but had not been fully debriefed about his London heroin connections or his continuing associations with UK Customs officers. Lundy felt that if he was going to see Moynihan in Manila, it made sense that he should save Scotland Yard some travel expenses by going to Sydney on the same trip: 'I'd put the whole thing together! Moynihan was desperate to get out of there on a deal. I had him all done – ready, wound up to do it – just on the telephone when, all of a sudden, I was pulled off the trip.'

By pointing out how near Moynihan was geographically to McLean, Lundy himself may have sown the seeds of a decision from above that two inspectors (one from SIS who was familiar with the McLean case, the other from the Serious Crimes Squad) should handle both matters instead of him. Perhaps some people felt he was getting too many foreign trips. Whatever the reason, it was the inspectors who saw Moynihan in Manila. Lundy feels that because they had no personal involvement in the Howard Marks case, they had no real incentive to 'turn' Moynihan, so he encouraged Lovato to try a direct approach. Lovato had already contacted Moynihan through the DEA's resident agent in Manila. Now he met him in person he bluntly told the peer that his earlier involvement with Marks was enough to put him in an American jail for years. At a second meeting Moynihan realized that, to extricate himself from all his problems, he should do what Lovato wanted and go in to Marks as the DEA's undercover man. Lundy would no longer be closely involved, but he followed Operation Eclectic's progress with fatherly pride.

The DEA worked Moynihan very cleverly to begin with. They got him out of the Philippines without anybody knowing, and flew him to Spain before Marks could find out he had turned. Marks had even sent a cable inviting him over. When he arrived, he was taped up and got vital evidence. With Marks he'd met the IRA drug-runner, James McCann, in Barcelona. McCann turns up in a huge Mercedes with bodyguards carrying machine guns. The meeting was under surveillance but McCann wasn't arrested because that would have exposed the operation against Marks. Despite their earlier upsets – including Marks spying on McCann for MI6 – the pair were still doing massive drug runs together. And McCann is *still* at it!

The DEA took Moynihan on to Miami where he was video-taped negotiating with Marks's brother-in-law, Patrick Lane, who incriminated himself by agreeing to launder $5,000 on Moynihan's behalf. The deal was a DEA set-up but it constituted devastating evidence. After performing in other 'Sting' videos, Moynihan was installed in a safe house and placed under constant protection. Now armed with direct evidence and Moynihan's testimony, the DEA moved in on Marks. On 25 July 1988 he and his wife were arrested at home in Majorca, along with an English courier and an American. Simultaneously Patrick Lane was picked up in Florida and four more Marks runners were held in England. In all eighteen people were arrested on the same day right across the world.

Marks stood accused of smuggling thousands of tons of cannabis from Thailand and Pakistan, through Singapore, Hong Kong, Australia, the Philippines, North Africa, into the major markets of Europe and America. He was said to own fleets of trucks, ships and planes. He was locked in a Madrid jail and eventually taken to the USA. In October 1990 he was jailed for twenty-five years on racketeering, conspiracy, drug-importation and money-laundering charges. By then his wife had served eighteen months (judged to be punishment enough for her role in the conspiracy). Marks pleaded guilty partly because in 1989 his brother-in-law, Patrick Lane, had been jailed for three years and his California-based distributor, Ernest Combs, for forty. Both were now ready to testify against him. In all sixteen members of his syndicate have been convicted, including a London solicitor (James Newton), but only $1.5 million worth of assets have been seized. None of Marks's assets have yet been seized. His known properties in Majorca and London are worth some £500,000. No other wealth has been discovered. If he really has been one of the world's biggest marijuana traffickers, he has hidden his profits very well indeed.

Lundy's work on the Marks case (as on all other inquiries) came to a sudden end in July 1987. It is difficult to say how different Operation Eclectic would have been had he remained on it, but Craig Lovato and the DEA had co-ordinated their approach so closely with him early on that his influence remained strong throughout. His torch was kept alight by Terry Burke, whom he had recruited to 'Cougar' during its Isle of Man days and who stayed on 'Eclectic' until its triumphant end.

Craig Lovato says, 'Tony had motivation and he kept pushing "Eclectic". It was his influence here in the USA which got "Eclectic" off the ground.' Indeed, without Lundy there would have been no 'Eclectic', and Marks would probably still be running his worldwide network today, unimpeded by the law enforcement agencies he so delighted in evading. The Marks case is perhaps the finest memorial to Lundy's methods, but what still perplexes him is why Customs had beaten a retreat in 1987.

I'm convinced that Customs blanked it because they knew there was embarrassment to come out of all this. Every way we turned, they didn't want to know. Their reluctance had nothing to do with my involvement, because they had pulled out long before I became involved. Of course, by the time Phil

Corbett and I approached Customs to join in again, they may not have wanted to get involved with me. By then, as I now know, they'd been fed all those lies about me interfering with Operation Redskin, and they were certainly annoyed about the fact we had arrested two of their officers for corruption. [See Chapter 24.] After that they had no love of Phil, let alone me!

Far from acknowledging it had ever withdrawn from the pursuit of Marks, Customs has told me that it 'played an active and continuing role' in the investigation. It was not prepared to release details of this role but 'we are delighted to have been able to assist in bringing a major international drug trafficker to justice.' Lundy is not impressed.

They had a lot of egg on their face when they lost him years ago, when he faked his own kidnap back in 1973. Then he goes on trial in 1981 and plays the MI6 defence and gets acquitted. Then I think he offered to work for them. I'm sure that's been his passport to freedom, because throughout the 1980s he was coming in and out of London to his flat in Chelsea, running his so-called travel agency and hopping back to Majorca. If Customs had really been targeting him in these years, they *had* to nick him. The man's been the most prolific organizer of drugs importation worldwide there could be! All right, only marijuana – not cocaine or heroin – but absolutely non-stop! And the same people he was working with years before, he was still working with! McCann, Combs, Denbigh – *none* of them nicked!

You couldn't help but nick them if you were running an operation on Marks, yet they'd had him flagged for years and done nothing. I think he was supplying them with information *and* I think he'd had some of them in his pocket. The man's so rich, I think in the past he'd had someone in Customs in his pocket – not anyone who'd been working with Craig. Customs were running scared! Bear in mind, they knew I'd already caused two of their officers to be nicked! They may have thought that if I personally got in to Marks, and turned him into a supergrass, quite a few more might go down.

As Marks now tries to bargain his way out of jail before serving twenty-five years, he may at last tell the truth about his connections with British law enforcement. Turning supergrass is his only option if he wants to be free to see his children grow up. Back in 1987 one of the authors of his misfortune, Tony Lundy, wondered if Her Majesty's Customs and Excise was trying to put him in prison rather harder than it was trying to jail Howard Marks.

Fencing to Fit

While Tony Lundy was fighting an outstandingly successful war against some of the world's biggest drug dealers and drug money-launderers – gaining international acclaim for his efforts – back home the South Yorkshire inquiry was looking into all the allegations against him, old and new. Most of them rapidly crumbled into a handful of hearsay and innuendo, but when some South Yorks officers looked into a hoary old allegation about some garden fencing they may have thought they had Lundy nailed.

Back in the autumn of 1977 the Finchley bookmaker, David Spicer, had needed some fencing. So had his friend from Finchley Boxing Club, Tony Lundy. At the time Spicer was friendly with Stevie Salter who owned a farm and garden centre near Cuffley in Hertfordshire. Salter had bought a lot of fencing for his farm and had been able to get it for a cheap overall price. Spicer ordered one consignment and paid Salter for it. The fencing was then delivered direct to the houses of Lundy and Spicer. Lundy then paid Spicer for his share.

Spicer had known Salter for years, meeting him first at Elton's, and then more often at the boxing club. It had been in Salter's house in the late 1970s that Spicer fell victim to a ferocious and unprovoked assault by 'Burglar Bill' Young. As he was dragged away, Young shouted a vow that he would 'fix' Spicer and Lundy. Sure enough, when he was arrested by Number 5 Regional Crime Squad in 1980 and turned supergrass, he 'fixed' both men, accusing Lundy of corruption and framing Spicer by claiming he had provided tips about suitable premises for Young to

burgle (see Chapter 11). In 1982 Spicer was convicted of
conspiracy to burgle and jailed for three years but he was
later cleared on appeal.

In November 1982 the Stagg inquiry interviewed Lundy
over an allegation coming from Young 'that Stephen Salter,
a criminal known to you, supplied you with fencing free
of charge'. At this time Spicer had not yet been cleared.
Lundy believed him innocent but was understandably
reluctant to cite him in his defence when questioned
by Stagg.

> Q: Did you have a fence erected at one of your houses by
> SALTER or someone acting for him?
> A: No.
> Q: Young alleges that fencing was erected at your house and
> paid for by SALTER. Is that true?
> A: No, it's not true.

Both answers were correct. The fencing was neither
paid for by Salter nor erected by him. He and a driver
had delivered it, then Lundy erected it himself with help
from his father-in-law.

In 1987 South Yorkshire investigated this affair again.
They approached Salter who eventually made a statement
claiming that not only had he delivered fencing to Lundy's
home free of charge, but this was in return for Lundy
getting police surveillance called off his premises. On 15
April 1987 Superintendent Malcolm Seller of South Yorks
handed Lundy a Form 163 listing this far more serious
allegation. It was not true, but Lundy was not surprised to
hear something of the sort. That was because, three days
before, records show that Roy Garner had called him after
he had spoken to Salter who was on the run and in deep
trouble. Garner had claimed:

> South Yorks officers have travelled to Belgium and inter-
> viewed Steve SALTER. Salter is wanted, he states, for absconding

from open prison and for VAT evasion. He stated the officers had questioned Salter about allegedly supplying fencing to me and Salter denied the allegation. He said they had offered a 'deal' to Salter to return to assist them. He stated the allegations were untrue and did not wish to return.

Lundy noted this on a contact sheet which he handed to his chief, Commander Corbett, next day. Lundy believed all such sheets were being forwarded to South Yorks. He therefore wondered why, three days later, Seller asked only two questions about the fencing which he denied receiving as a tactic which, he hoped, would force the Yorkshireman to go over the entire affair including the Salter 'deal', giving Lundy the chance to explain the full story. Seller gave him no such chance, abruptly ending the interview saying he had to clarify a lot of additional information. Thus nothing was said of Garner's amazing claim.

In the next few months Seller and his squad ran all over Hertfordshire to prove that fencing from Salter had been delivered to Lundy's house, which Lundy was ready to tell them anyway. He later complained: 'There was absolutely no need to pressurize honest and genuine people such as ex-neighbours and personal friends by telling them they must not telephone me about the fact that they were being interviewed.'

The South Yorks men were also trying to find out if he had arranged to end the surveillance. They proved no such thing. Certainly Salter's premises had been watched for some months until January 1977 when they were raided. Police were looking for stolen property but found nothing. Then, it seems, surveillance was halted, but not because of Lundy who was in no position to interfere; he was an inspector in Willesden Green at the time, and had no connection with anyone interested in Salter. Nor could he have persuaded anyone to call off the surveillance just to please him. In any event, the fencing was not delivered to his house until September 1977.

In April 1987 he had nothing to fear from the truth. What worried him was Garner's claim of a deal between Salter and South Yorks. This smacked of the deal offered to Spicer in 1981. Then Spicer had not been prepared to tell lies against Lundy, even though he himself had just been fitted up by Young, but this time Lundy feared Salter might tell any lie to get a deal. On 23 April Garner called again, offering news of the cocaine job and asking what was happening. On a contact sheet Lundy noted:

I told him that I had reported what he had said about South Yorkshire visiting Stephen Salter in Belgium and offering a deal to him. I said that was the only subject they asked me about – concerning Salter and the supply of fencing. He said that Salter would have eight months' imprisonment to serve still if he returned to England and as they had offered him a deal he might say anything. I told him I had nothing to fear from the truth and had certainly never called off surveillance as had been suggested . . . He said he would contact Salter and I told him not to do so.

On 9 July Superintendent Seller called Lundy in for another session on the fencing. He ran through all the evidence he had gathered but wrongly asserted, 'we know it was erected in the first part of 1977'. Had that been correct it would have coincided with the apparent end of the surveillance which Lundy was supposed to have fixed, but the fencing was not put up until eight months later. Seller wanted answers to a long stream of questions but Lundy played him at his own game: he refused to answer, as he had the right to do. He told Seller, '[previously] you refused to pursue those questions I could have answered and saved you a lot of work'.

The interview was aborted. Lundy immediately told

Seller's boss, Robin Herold, that he had been answering questions for years but refused this time because he was 'fed up with a couple of questions, then more investigation, then more questions. That can go on and on indefinitely.' By way of apology, Herold said it was as if someone kept 'moving the goalposts'. It was not their fault that they were taking so long, but they would remove this 'festering sore' from the Metropolitan Police once and for all. Lundy replied that he was surprised Seller had not kept questioning him on the previous occasion, even though 'you were aware I had submitted a report a few days before stating South Yorks had offered a deal to Salter in Belgium'.

Herold seemed shocked. So did Seller and his chief inspector on the Salter probe, Ronald Brooke. They knew of no such report. Lundy said he assumed Herold had copies of all contact sheets which he had given Commander Corbett. In fact Corbett had not forwarded the last three because (he later stated) he 'never received any requirement' to supply every sheet to South Yorks. As soon as Lundy dropped this bombshell, Herold asked Corbett for the last sheets. When he read them he was perturbed, particularly by the final one which Lundy had written that very morning:

At 7.25 a.m. today I received a telephone call from the informant's wife at my home address. She said that she had been asked to telephone me by her husband who is currently in custody.

She was emotional and insisted that her husband had nothing to do with the charges he is facing. She said he would not get involved in DRUGS and the reason for the call was that he needed help from Scotland Yard in relation to his situation . . . She was visiting her husband later that day.

I told her that I would pass on the message to senior officers but she could tell her husband that certain information had been passed at a very senior level from Scotland

Yard to senior personnel from the agency dealing with the case.

As shown in Chapter 8, in October 1986 Garner had begun telling the Yard of the cocaine conspiracy but in June 1987 Customs arrested him as part of it. Now facing over twenty years in jail, he wanted Customs to know of his informer role, so they might reduce or even drop charges against him. When Mrs Garner said Roy 'needed help from Scotland Yard', that meant help with Customs. Lundy knew about the 26 June meeting when Yard chiefs disclosed Garner's role to Customs. That was why he told her 'information had been passed at a very senior level'.

Herold believed the contact sheet indicated 'a possible criminal offence or breach of discipline' and promptly complained to the Yard. Ironically, if Lundy had not himself penned the sheet no one could have criticized him. His trouble was that he was *too* honest, even naive. By rigorously reporting every contact made by Garner or his family, he had created not just one rod for his own back but an armful. Every impromptu word he spoke and scribbled down during out-of-the-blue calls from Garner or his clan was picked over for years by men whose goal, he now felt, was to bring him down.

Lundy believed this rage over his contact sheets was a smokescreen to obscure the truth about South Yorks and Stevie Salter. On 13 July he counter-attacked with a long written complaint to his commander. He catalogued his own struggle against corruption among detective colleagues, listing a series of criminal acts which he had exposed only to see them ignored, condoned or covered up. He claimed senior officers had sabotaged his career, possibly because he had trodden on the interests of masonic elements in the force (by jailing their criminal friends). Most importantly, he raised allegations that

South Yorks had promised to help Salter if he came back
from Belgium to finish his jail term; that Salter refused to
co-operate until his solicitor was sure Customs were not
going to pursue a VAT fraud claim against him; and that,
still hesitant, he was threatened with extradition if he did
not co-operate. Lundy stressed these were only allegations
but he made a crucial observation: if Salter was offered a
deal 'it seems inevitable that other persons will have been
similarly approached':

> I repeat once again that I have never been involved in corrupt
> practices and I have paid for anything supplied or obtained. I
> have therefore never been afraid to arrest or prosecute anyone
> . . . I would seem to be the classic example that it does not
> pay to work hard and be successful as a CID officer because,
> as a result, I have been subjected to years of pressure, with
> sinister overtones, from within and without the police service
> . . . I seem to have become a 'sitting duck' waiting to be fitted
> up by someone . . .
> I have continued silently through all the years of aggravation
> but believe I am now justified in asking for an independent
> inquiry.

Lundy delivered the letter to Commander Corbett and
then went sick, but the sitting duck's goose was already
being cooked. Later that day Chief Constable Wright of
South Yorkshire wrote a letter to Assistant Commissioner
Colin Sutton at Scotland Yard, saying: 'I am of the view
that Lundy's conduct has seriously prejudiced the integrity
of my inquiry. On these grounds, therefore, I recommend
to you that Superintendent Lundy should be suspended
forthwith.'

Some time later, when Lundy saw Wright's letter he was
infuriated by the claim that he had 'seriously prejudiced'
the inquiry's integrity. He felt that nothing on his sheets
justified that view. All he had done was record information volunteered by Garner and tell him his previous

information had been passed on. What was prejudicing the inquiry, he felt, was the conduct of some of Wright's officers as they investigated the case of Salter's fencing. So was Lundy seriously expected to utter a bureaucratic formula to shut Garner up, at the very moment Garner was revealing a plot to fit up Lundy himself?

On 14 July, the day after his letter of complaint, Lundy was suspended. This move was unusual in itself for an officer who was already certificated sick. He was thus taken off operational duties, ending his brilliant work on the Brinks–Mat inquiry. He spent the next seventeen months mostly at home, landscaping his new house. 'I must be the highest-paid labourer in London,' he used to lament. Being banned from his vocation, even on full pay, was heart-breaking. It might have broken his spirit too but he kept campaigning for an independent inquiry. During the next two years he was given an astonishing run-around.

On 30 July he received a letter about a meeting between Peter Winship, Director of Scotland Yard's Complaints Investigation Bureau, and Sir Cecil Clothier, Chairman of the Police Complaints Authority which was in overall charge of the South Yorks inquiry.[1] They had agreed that Lundy's complaints against South Yorks would be dealt with by the PCA itself, while his allegations against Metropolitan officers would be referred to Peter Wright and his South Yorks team. Lundy replied that he did not see how Wright could 'independently' investigate those allegations when Lundy had also complained about Wright's own team.[2] In these circumstances he was hardly likely to find in favour of Lundy. As for the PCA, how could it investigate South Yorks 'independently' when it was sponsoring that very inquiry?

His protests fell on deaf ears. On 13 October 1987 he found himself being interviewed about his allegations against London police by the very South Yorks officers – Superintendent Seller and Chief Inspector Brooke – against whom he had complained over Salter. Among fifty-seven questions concerning his original letter of complaint, they wanted him to answer this one: 'Are you prepared to name the person who has supplied information concerning Stephen Salter?'

Lundy was outraged. This very pair, whom he had accused of doing a deal with Salter, were now questioning him about one of his sources *against* Salter, a clear invasion of what the PCA was now to investigate. After this, Lundy refused all co-operation because of what he saw as the total conflict of interest which now engulfed South Yorks. They were investigating him, they knew he had made serious complaints against them, so how could they pursue his complaints against others with vigour or objectivity? He was surprised that the Yorkshire men did not themselves feel that their task had become impossible.

He again complained and received a reply from Assistant Commissioner John Smith of the Metropolitan Police. He spoke of the uppermost 'need for impartiality and fairness toward yourself'. Smith hoped that Lundy would 'have confidence in the professional thoroughness that an investigation by Peter Wright and South Yorkshire officers will bring to bear upon those matters you allege'.[3] But how could Lundy trust in the thoroughness of a team which, he had been told, was offering inducements to Salter?

This point eventually penetrated even the PCA. On 25 November 1987 Deputy Chairman Roland Moyle wrote saying the best way forward was for South Yorks to complete its inquiry into Lundy, then an investigator who was not from South Yorks should probe his complaints. More months dragged by. In January 1988 he was told that Wright's *World in Action* report was now with the PCA.[4] 'Great', he thought, now the independent inquiry into South Yorks would begin, but yet another month went by before Moyle said it would be some time before any decision was reached.

Lundy was furious. He sent another letter to Assistant Commissioner Smith contrasting the speed with which massive inquiries had been set up to investigate him with the seven months of inaction since his own complaints: 'When I complain for the very first time, about the conduct of others, I get suspended from duty.' He attacked the Yard's failure to investigate the continuing stream of anti-Lundy leaks from official police sources to press and TV: 'It would seem that the only way that anyone causes action to be taken is to instigate media attention.'[5] Smith urged him to restrain himself 'from any improper and unauthorized ventilation of your frustration through the media'.[6] Lundy felt this advice contrasted ill with Scotland Yard's failure to identify and punish other detectives – past and present – who had talked to the media, and driven a coach and horses through the Official Secrets Act, in order to defame and diminish him.

In the meantime South Yorkshire had taken well over a year to complete their inquiry – at an undisclosed cost which must have exceeded one million pounds – yet they had found no evidence to justify criminal or discipline charges against Lundy over anything in 'The Untouchable'. They had also failed to prove any allegations against other officers: neither Gerry Wiltshire's claim of a police plot to murder him by pushing him under a train nor his story that a senior detective had offered him a bribe.

They also found nothing to support most allegations they had been given about matters not in the film. One highly damaging complaint, asserted by Andrew Jennings, but wholly without substance, was that Lundy had taken a trip to the USA in 1980 with Roy Garner. Such a trip would have been highly irregular, and Lundy's failure to report it would have merited his dismissal from the police, but he had never been on any such trip with Garner. He did visit the USA in 1980 with a friend called Les Jones who had bought Garner's Hertfordshire farm, but Jones is a respectable businessman, a demolition contractor with no criminal record. The Lundy–Jones friendship is equally legitimate. They were on the Finchley Boxing Club committee together for years. Lundy went on the American trip only at the last minute, when a business friend of Jones's fell ill and could not travel. Lundy paid his own way throughout.[7]

Another South Yorks complaint surrounded Lundy and Jones's visit to Cleveland, Ohio, during that trip, allegedly to buy a smelter. Chief Superintendent Herold suggested to Lundy that Jones might have bought it to melt down silver. Lundy dismissed this as 'absolute rubbish'. In fact Jones's Cleveland equipment had been bought and erected a full two years earlier, in 1978. As for Herold's apparent notion that it could have been used to smelt the silver stolen in the Bullion robbery of March 1980, Jones would have explained to him that the machine was not a smelter but a 'hot-briquetting plant'. This £750,000 piece of technology could not smelt silver or convert it to liquid. All it could do was apply heat so that scrap iron could be compacted into smaller blocks or briquettes. It did not even have a container with a liquid-tight base. Thus any smelted metal would simply flow onto the ground. This allegation must have been made by a very ignorant enemy.

Another discarded allegation concerned Garner's time in Ford prison for the VAT fraud. In 1986 'Albany' found out he had paid a corrupt prison officer, Kenneth Colquhoun, £3,000 to bring him hampers of goodies – vodka, champagne, smoked salmon and cigars – into the jail. When detectives interviewed Colquhoun on 23 May

1986, he said he had been tipped off about their visit by Mark Garner (Roy's son) who cited a 'reliable source'. South Yorks presumed the 'reliable source' might be Tony Lundy, but he pointed out that he first knew of Colquhoun only *after* he had been arrested and charged, and had never discussed him with Mark Garner. In September 1988 Garner was convicted of corrupting Colquhoun and given an eighteen-month sentence.

Another string of false allegations came from a man called Edward D'Arcy Jones, who claimed Lundy had corrupt dealings with the notorious but ageing South London gangsters 'Mad' Frankie Fraser and Charlie Richardson. Lundy had never met either.

Eventually South Yorks assembled the allegations into three main categories: unwise association – Lundy kept up friendships with 'professional criminals of the highest calibre'; improper disclosure – he passed confidential police information to such criminals; and procedural breaches – he ignored evidential rules and police regulations with the aim of perverting the course of justice.

Interviewing Lundy in November 1987 Herold went through allegations from each category but Lundy rejected them with such vehemence that most were never raised again. Indeed, he went on the offensive and prolonged the interview to attack what had done him more damage than anything else: Steventon's 1983 minute with the killer jibe, 'it is my belief that Mr Lundy is a corrupt officer'. This had to be seen in the light of his own confidential request to see the commissioner *about Steventon*, which had been intercepted, blocked and disclosed to that very man less than six weeks earlier (see Chapter 14). In contrast it took Lundy three years to find out about Steventon's minute. When he did, he saw it as breathtakingly inaccurate. Lundy told South Yorkshire that this key sentence was 'a blatant error': 'For a number of years stemming from

Lundy's service as a DC or DS with the Wembley Robbery Squad, then headed by ex-Detective Chief Superintendent James MARSHALL, GARNER using an alias of GRANGER had been LUNDY's informant.'

Wembley Robbery Squad had operated in the early 1970s and handled the first of the supergrasses, Bertie Smalls. Its considerable success was tarnished by the row over the informant pay-out to 'William Wise' rather than 'Mary Frazer' and the scandal of how £25,000 was apparently stolen by two detectives from a robbers' safe-deposit box (see Chapter 8). Jim Marshall had played no part in the affair and was untainted. As it happens, Lundy had respect for Marshall but knew him only slightly, socially. That was why Lundy told South Yorkshire:

I never have worked with Jim Marshall and I was never on the Wembley Robbery Squad. There the interpretation is putting me back into an inquiry . . . when I had no dealings and contacts whatsoever. What I've always said about Garner is from boxing club days . . . and any suggestions that I met him through other ways or means is totally wrong. Now [what Steventon said there] horrifies me because it's making me out to be a liar.

Also, the fact that for years Ronald Steventon never took any action to break the Lundy–Garner bond (and even used to meet Garner himself) indicates there was nothing 'bent' about it:

If he believed I was corrupt, why didn't he stop us meeting? He must have been getting 'corrupt' vibrations back from 'Stagg' witnesses as early as 1981, so why didn't he ban me *then* from speaking to the man? That would have been the end of it. He had the power. Instead he lets the meetings go on. If he thinks I'm so bent, this seems all wrong.

Another thing that vexes Lundy about Steventon's minute is a reference to a Sergeant Thomas Miller. This

detective had been directly implicated by Billy Young
in corrupt acts, such as leaking criminal intelligence files
and supplying police uniforms for money. Lundy had never
worked with Miller or spoken to him. Steventon had also
referred to supergrass Fred Sinfield, as if he corroborated
Young's hearsay allegations in some way. Yet Sinfield had
never met Lundy. Whatever claim he may have made
against Lundy – and none has ever been published – it
must have been double or triple hearsay. The only time
Lundy had come across Sinfield on an operation was in
1978 over the Lambeth Town Hall job when he would
have put Sinfield in jail if he had been allowed to ambush
the gang. Instead Sinfield walked free to commit more
robberies until eventually arrested by 5 RCS. He could
know nothing against Lundy except that he was once
within a whisker of twenty years' jail because of Lundy's
efforts. Hardly an objective witness!

In November 1987 Chief Superintendent Herold was
anxious that Lundy did not see South Yorks as bent on
nailing him, irrespective of the truth.

> If evidence is available and forthcoming, whereby you can be
> shown to have acted either in breach of the discipline regulations
> or in any way criminally, so be it. We shall have explored the
> truth, presented the facts and that will be the outcome. If
> the reverse applies, and our in-depth and sometimes possibly
> insensitive inquiry as perceived by you, proves you to be as
> innocent as driven snow, and the victim of scurrilous repetitive
> allegations by the press, nobody will be happier than South
> Yorkshire officers on behalf of the Metropolitan Police.

No doubt Herold meant this expression of impartiality
but he followed it up by telling Lundy that he was the
inquiry's 'target'. Herold instantly corrected himself by
changing the term to 'subject'. This only left Lundy even
more bewildered as to how South Yorkshire really did
view him.

The summer of 1988 passed with still no start on the inquiry into his complaints about 'Salter' or anything else. He finished building his house, pruned his roses, walked the dog and got to know his wife and daughters again after years sacrificing family life to catch criminals. He kept physically fit by running ten miles a day and also completed his sixth London Marathon.

At last, on 2 August 1988, DAC Winship presented him with the fruits of the South Yorks inquiry. No criminal case had been made but he faced six discipline charges. Three related to the case of a police informant. For legal reasons I must give him a pseudonym, 'Gary Gear'. Lundy was accused of 'knowingly or through neglect' making 'false, misleading or inaccurate statements' in 1985 and 1986 concerning information provided by Gear. Taken together, these charges amounted to an allegation that Lundy had wrongly claimed Gear's information had 'led to arrests', and then allowed that error to be perpetuated in a letter submitted to a judge on Gear's behalf, in order to get him a lighter sentence than his crimes deserved.

The true story behind these charges is yet another tale of fear, loathing and lies in the Metropolitan CID. From the start any calm assessment of the Gear affair was confounded by the fact that Gear is a relative of 'Jim Davis,' a Hertfordshire businessman who is Lundy's friend. To be precise, Gear is the son-in-law of Davis's brother. In May 1985 Jim Davis called Lundy to say that Gear's wife had spotted a black London taxi tailing her car round Harlesden, north-west London. Gear was involved with a team of armed robbers at the time, so when his wife told him about the taxi, he instantly suspected it was part of a surveillance operation run by Finchley Robbery Squad. This caused Gear to worry about future police action against him and he decided to turn informer through Lundy. This was not something Lundy wanted to

get involved in – it was five years since his own days on that
squad and he was now wholly occupied on 'Brinks–Mat'.
However, he did offer to find out if indeed it was Finchley
which had targeted Gear, and, if so, to deliver him into
its care. It happened that Lundy knew the only detective
likely to be driving a black cab around North London
pretending to be a genuine taxi. Lundy arranged to meet
him and his inspector in a Finchley pub, and teased him in a
joking way about 'showing out on a tail' in Harlesden. The
driver made an embarrassed admission that this might have
happened, so Lundy said Gear might be willing to help the
investigation. The inspector said he would tell the squad's
chief inspector of the offer.

Next day Lundy spoke to the chief inspector, Jim
Hutchinson. Lundy said he had no idea what Gear had
done or what Finchley were investigating. However,
Gear was prepared to meet someone from Finchley. This
resulted in a meeting in another Finchley pub between
Gear, Davis, Hutchinson and Lundy who had never met
Gear before. Gear now told Hutchinson that he realized
Finchley suspected him of robberies. He was not admitting anything, but he named the team of robbers with
whom he was working, and gave details of some of their
recent crimes. He also revealed where they were storing
their weapons, in a block of flats in Little Venice, West
London, although he did not know in which flat. On
this basis Gear was registered at Scotland Yard as an
informant. Hutchinson and Lundy were both listed as
his 'handlers', but because Lundy was often abroad on
Brinks–Mat inquiries, Hutchinson was likely to do most
of the handling. He had a couple of meetings with Gear
when he gave useful progress reports.

Hutchinson was a very open officer. He soon told his
entire thirty-strong squad that one of their targets, Gary
Gear, was now an informant. He would no longer be

targeted because he was grassing everyone else. Months later when Lundy found out that Gear was thus exposed, a shiver went down his spine, for he had never revealed any informant's identity to anybody except those who needed to know at the very top of the Yard. The consequences of such an indiscretion could be serious, as they proved to be in this case. Hutchinson did not know that on his squad were two detectives who, it was later claimed, had previously been corruptly involved with one of the remaining targets. That criminal had allegedly paid them £7,000 for not charging him during a previous investigation.

Gary Gear knew about this corrupt payment so, as soon as these detectives heard that Gear had turned informer, they might have feared he would shop them as well. In the next three months the atmosphere on the squad turned poisonous. Hutchinson and his two inspectors correctly resisted immense pressure from below to arrest Gear, which – merely on the basis of what he had disclosed as an informer – would have been premature. However, in August events overtook them. In the same block of flats where Gear had originally said the weapons were stored (but where the squad had failed to locate them) a painter came across the weapons by accident in the caretaker's storeroom. When the squad found out, they knew from Gear's previous tip-off that they must belong to their target robbers. They arrested the caretaker, who confirmed the men's identities. One eluded capture for some weeks but two were arrested immediately. So was Gary Gear.

It was always a possibility that Gear would be arrested one day if, for instance, his role went beyond the definition of a participating informant.[8] What stunned Lundy was the arrest of Gear's wife, when the evidence against her (as an accessory to robbery) lay entirely in what Gear had confided to Chief Inspector Hutchinson back in May. He had said that, a year earlier, two of the other suspects had committed a robbery without him. It went wrong, one robber was wounded, so they fled to Gear's home nearby. He was not there but the pair barged in and washed some blood-stained clothing in the washing-machine, then lay low in the house for some hours. By the time Gear came back they had left, but their incriminating clothing was still in the machine. Gear was furious. Three months after telling this to Hutchinson, he was angry again: distressed by the sight of his eight-months-pregnant wife in a police cell and the thought of his infant daughters deprived of both parents. He crumbled and confessed to two robberies and a conspiracy to rob, in the minor role of driver. He made a statement but refused to name anyone else as he did not wish to 'grass' in open court.

At first Mrs Gear also made a statement against the two robbers about the blood-stained clothing. She was released but the existence of her statement quickly became known to the underworld in suspicious circumstances. She was threatened with violence and intimidated into withdrawing it, which severely weakened the case against them.

In October 1986 they went on trial at the Old Bailey with Gary Gear. He pleaded guilty and was kept in the cells, but the other two fought the case. One denied making a statement admitting some twenty robberies. The jury must have believed him for he and his colleague were acquitted. This meant that Gary Gear was now the sole gang member who would go to jail. He had some slight hope of mercy, however. Months earlier his defence had made a routine request to Scotland Yard that it write a formal letter to be shown to the judge in private, stating that he had helped the police.

The obvious person to prepare this was Chief Inspector Hutchinson. He was not only Gear's co-handler; he was also in charge of the entire Finchley squad, and was in the best position to know the precise value of

Gear's information to the overall investigation. He certainly knew far more than Tony Lundy who was now perpetually crossing the Atlantic and had no role in the case. However, Hutchinson had been transferred so it fell to Lundy to gather together some papers, write a report and send the bundle to Superintendent Roy Ramm who had the duty of writing the letter itself. Ramm noted that both Hutchinson and Flying Squad commander, Jeremy Plowman, had seen the papers before they reached him, so he assumed they could have corrected any weaknesses in Lundy's knowledge. In August 1986 he duly wrote an eight-line letter on Gear's behalf, but in compression there was some unwitting distortion. Wading through the papers, Ramm's eyes had alighted on one phrase in a long and balanced report which Lundy had written the previous year when applying for Mrs Gear to be re-housed (a police leak had already exposed her husband as a grass, so she needed protection). Lundy had said, Gear's information 'was extremely accurate and subsequently led to arrests'. Ramm seized on this and wrote that Gear had provided 'valuable information' and 'as a result three of his co-defendants were arrested and charged with robbery'.

As Lundy was not directly involved, he had no idea that some detectives on the squad took this strictly chronological view of events:

1. The painter had found the weapons in the caretaker's flat.
2. The caretaker was arrested and named the three robbers.
3. Two of the three robbers were arrested. So was Gear. Therefore
4. Gear's information had not led to his co-defendants' arrest.

Equally unaware of this view, Ramm drafted his text for

signature by Lundy and DAC Worth, but 'Mr Lundy was travelling the world extensively and was unable to sign the letter'.[9] Ramm read the text to him over the phone, Lundy agreed, and Ramm signed it on his behalf. During the trial's early stages Lundy returned to Britain for other reasons, and was free one day to go to the Old Bailey to present the letter. However, the judge did not wish to consider it until the trial was over, so Lundy went abroad again, leaving the matter in other hands.

When the time finally came for the letter to be presented, one of the case detectives took violent objection to it. He felt Lundy had greatly exaggerated the value of Gear's information just to help his friend Jim Davis. For some mistaken reason the letter had been shown to this detective for him to sign. Strictly, only Gear's handlers, Hutchinson or Lundy, should have done that because only they knew directly what information he had given. Once he saw it, however, the detective refused to sign and complained to the two prosecution barristers. They became greatly upset: it was now early November 1986 and they had both seen 'The Untouchable' on TV that very week, so they jumped to the conclusion that Lundy was up to his alleged old tricks again. Roy Ramm had to rewrite the letter and tone it down before it was shown to the judge, yet even in its amended and undisputed form it earned Gear some relief. As Judge Nina Lowry later explained, she 'would ordinarily have passed a sentence of ten years, but deducted two years for the guilty plea and three years for the assistance given to the police and referred to in the letter'.[10]

Just as this row was at its height, the South Yorkshire inquiry was set up. Two of its officers soon went to see Gary Gear in jail. He denied any suggestions of malpractice by Lundy and also denied paying him any money through Jim Davis. He was understandably bitter about the way things had turned out: only he had been mug enough to plead guilty, now only he was in jail – and he was just the driver! If he had never met Lundy or Hutchinson and never admitted anything, Finchley Robbery Squad might never have got a case together against him. Even if they had, he would have been acquitted with his confederates.

Similarly, from the state's point of view, it was only because Lundy had steered Gear towards Finchley Robbery Squad that even he was convicted. The squad itself had failed to convict their main targets who had walked out of court, and were now free to go robbing again. *They* were the people who had got any favours going, not Gary Gear. Nothing Lundy had done had perverted justice. Any perversion lay elsewhere.

In his long letter of complaint of July 1987, Lundy had raised the specific allegation that two Finchley-based officers had taken £7,000 from one of the robbers during an earlier operation. Lundy had submitted his letter over a year before the 'Gear' discipline papers were slapped on him, yet still nothing had been done about his counter-allegation. It was one of many corruption allegations in his letter, but none has been investigated to this day.

Two other charges related to Lundy's final Garner contact sheets. He was accused of improperly communicating information during the phone call from Mrs Garner on 9 July 1987; and, on 23 April, of failing to adhere to the text which John Dellow had told him to use with Garner himself. In fact Lundy had conveyed the essence of this ponderous mouthful to Garner in various forms on many occasions. Also, as early as December 1986 South Yorks had been receiving contact sheets on which Lundy said nothing about reciting the text to Garner. If Lundy had done anything wrong, South Yorks would have taken action there and then. However, when they saw these final sheets six months later, they also saw that in them Garner had exposed their deal with Salter. This could not have pleased them.

As Lundy read all the charges, he realized that the pair relating to the Garner calls were inextricably bound up with the last charge: 'You accepted a gratuity, namely a quantity of fencing materials, from Stephen Alfred Salter.' This became even clearer as he waded through 1,000 pages of accompanying papers. There were all the documents and interviews on the Salter affair, including proof that what Garner had told him sixteen months before was absolutely true. One document listed as 'not being used in support of the charges' was a letter to Salter's solicitor from South Yorkshire's Chief Constable Wright. It was dated 26 March 1987, nine days *before* Salter's first statement.

Your client, Stephen Salter, has been put forward as one who may be able to offer information pertinent to my investigation. I am aware that he is currently an absconder from Her Majesty's Prison and have to tell you that should he return to the United Kingdom, either voluntarily or by extradition, he will be required to serve the remainder of his prison sentence.

I also understand that he has expressed concern regarding proceedings which may be instituted against him by Her Majesty's Customs and Excise, as a result of their inquiries into the activities of the following companies with which he was involved.

SAS Components (Export) Ltd. In liquidation.
Parallel Trading Corp Ltd. In liquidation.

I can advise you that having consulted with senior staff of HM Customs and Excise, I am informed that no further action is being contemplated against him in respect of those matters.

The letter seemed to prove everything Lundy had long suspected. Wright's 'understanding' must have come from earlier contact between his team and Salter. The dropping of any criminal proceedings against him was made known only after South Yorks approached Customs. Clearly Salter knew he had committed crimes or he would not have feared prosecution. The crimes appear to have been substantial VAT frauds, but Customs has refused to reveal to me the nature of Salter's offences or why Customs took no action against him.

Having got his deal, Salter obliged. He returned to England, gave himself up and made a statement on 4 April. Unfortunately, the first two pages blew Mr Salter's own case away. He said it was during 1980–81 when Lundy arranged for surveillance on his property to be called off, and when he had asked for fencing posts and panels. 'As far as I was concerned the delivery of fencing to Mr Lundy was in payment for his services in stopping the police surveillance.'

Three weeks later South Yorks showed Salter some old company accounts which proved his dates were all wrong. On 26 April he bounced back out by claiming he must have delivered the fencing before March 1978, but he did not change the period when the surveillance was called off. This therefore remained in 1980–81, two to three years *after* he supplied the fencing – hardly a fast return on a bribe! Worse problems lay ahead. Salter claimed Dave Spicer had acted as his go-between in asking Lundy to end the surveillance. In July 1987 the investigators finally went to see Spicer to ask for a statement (on a previous visit they had never mentioned the fencing). Spicer had already denied Salter's surveillance story. Now he screwed up months of their work by saying,

I know that Mr Lundy and myself had a requirement for fencing. I ordered it all as one lot and paid Salter for it. It is so long ago that I cannot remember the details or how much. I remember it was trade price. I don't know how it was delivered. I'm sure Mr Lundy paid me, but I cannot remember any details.

According to Spicer, the South Yorks officers were vexed and accused him of saying this only because Lundy had told him to. Spicer denied the accusation, saying that he and Lundy had met two weeks before, but the subject of the fencing had not come up. South Yorks sources say the investigators would not have accused Spicer as they had no axe to grind against him or Lundy. They merely took statements, without malice. The day after seeing Spicer they went straight back to Salter who claimed Lundy's fencing 'was never part of any payment from Spicer. Neither Lundy nor Spicer paid me for it. The only involvement of Spicer was to introduce me to Tony Lundy.' This was a palpable lie. Salter had known Lundy for years having met the detective frequently at the boxing club and sometimes in the Torrington Arms. They needed no introduction.

Now Salter added a startling new claim. He said that *after* his first statements he had been contacted by Roy Garner asking if he had made a statement about some fencing, was Garner named in it and could he have a copy. If this were true, Garner could only have learned that Salter was co-operating with South Yorks from Tony Lundy. Thus Lundy could have been accused of interfering with justice by causing a witness against him to be approached. Yet Lundy's contact sheet of 12 April showed that Garner had told *him* of Salter's deal three days *before* South Yorks first asked him about the fencing: it was therefore through Garner – not his inquisitors – that he first knew this allegation had been dug up again. This chronology proved that Salter, or a source close to him, must have told Garner about the deal – not Garner who first approached Salter. South Yorks's ace witness was turning out to be dangerously unreliable.

The South Yorks men may have been flummoxed by Spicer, for when they took his statement they omitted to get him to say what he had earlier demonstrated to them in his garden: that his fencing matched Lundy's. They never followed up this point, even though they had gone to immense pains to prove Lundy's fencing matched with Salter's. Yet around part of Spicer's back garden was the identical material. On 21 August 1988 – more than a year after his statement – Superintendent Seller and Chief Inspector Brooke popped up on the Spicers' doorstep. Odder still, this was a Sunday morning in August. What could have brought two family men 200 miles south on a summer Sunday? It seems that at last the mechanism of internal police justice was grinding into action. They tried to explain their visit to Dave Spicer, who tape-recorded their words:

We're down for this weekend. What we are trying to do is get round every possible witness. The Met Police have asked us to find out the holiday commitment of anyone who gave us a statement . . . so that they can come towards a date for a disciplinary tribunal for Mr Lundy . . . Also to see if each witness is still of a mind to, em, to give the evidence that they gave in the statements . . . All we do then is send them a schedule back and say these are the most suitable dates when you would catch the witnesses, or this witness is reluctant and no longer wishes to be involved.

Dave and his wife Laura said when they might be away, then Brooke and Seller asked if they would report any new holiday plans. After some chit-chat about the state of play with the inquiry and the various TV programmes on Lundy, the detectives took their leave. 'We're going. Take it this isn't a warning. It's just an informal visit. If you are required, we'll contact you.' After they left, Dave thought their visit was peculiar. Why did they not do all this over the telephone? After all, they had phoned him earlier in the week to say they were coming, so why couldn't they ask him about his holiday plans during the same call? Why spend the weekend far from home bothering folk with this kind of stuff? And what was all that chat about 'reluctant witnesses' no longer wishing to be 'involved'? They said this wasn't a warning but it felt like one.

When Lundy heard of the visit it confirmed his worst fears. The officers who had dropped in on Spicer were the same pair he had complained about over Salter, and rejected as unfit to investigate his other complaints. And why were they seeing Spicer anyway? In the discipline papers served on Lundy three weeks earlier, Spicer's evidence was in the bundle marked 'not being used in support' of the charges. As Lundy had not yet asked for Spicer to appear *for* him, why were South Yorks paying him personal attention? Were they really so zealous in Lundy's defence? The visit looked even odder to Lundy when he found out that other witnesses in the 'not being used in support' bundle were never asked about their holiday plans. South Yorks says there was 'nothing sinister' in this. Each senior officer had to check when his witnesses would be available. Seller checked first because he had been first to complete his inquiries and had not seen his witnesses for a year.

Lundy meantime complained again about the continuing delay in starting his inquiry. Assistant Commissioner Smith replied that one 'would not be appropriate' now as it 'might pre-empt some of the options open to you'. This seemed to mean that, if such an inquiry found he had no grounds for complaint, Lundy would be unable to attack South Yorks at the hearing. This rebuff floored him. He had been banking on a prior inquiry because he was sure it would condemn South Yorks and invalidate all the charges. There would then be no hearing. Now, if he had to fight them it would cost him a fortune. He clearly needed a top-flight barrister, who would cost at least £30,000 because it would take weeks to refute all the lies, distortion and innuendo which he saw in the discipline papers. The Superintendents' Association could not put up that kind of money, so he was on 'a hiding to nothing'.

Now Roland Moyle of the PCA chipped in complaining he had still not supplied South Yorks with detailed complaints against Yard officers, including Freemasons.[11] Clearly Moyle had still not grasped Lundy's point that South Yorks could not inquire objectively into *anything* he raised because of his accusations against them. He wrote back asking where was the inquiry into South Yorks which Moyle had recommended nine months earlier. Moyle replied ignoring all Lundy's points, and talked only of the need for him to supply information about his masonic allegations. Just before Christmas Moyle wrote again saying:

> You have only one complaint outstanding as far as the PCA are concerned: this is to the effect that certain officers of the Metropolitan Police who were or are Freemasons have adversely affected your police career. May I ask yet again for you to supply me with details in order that the investigation of your complaint may get underway.

Lundy was infuriated by Moyle's words. Surely the main thing outstanding for the PCA was the inquiry into South Yorks. Lundy wrote a furious letter to Moyle's boss, Sir Cecil Clothier. He replied that Lundy's allegations against Metropolitan officers could not proceed as he had not identified them. He thus missed the fact that Lundy was happy to provide such information but not to South Yorks. As for Lundy's complaints against South Yorks: 'these fall to be considered by . . . the South Yorkshire Police Authority. It is for them to consider whether they should record your complaints, or refer them to this Authority, or appoint an investigating officer.'[12]

For the umpteenth time Lundy was 'gob-smacked'. This was the first time anyone had mentioned the South Yorks Police Authority. A full year and a half had thus passed before the PCA now told him it had no power – unless Peter Wright's own employers chose to call it in.

Yet another three months passed before the PCA even bothered to tell the South Yorks Police Authority of Lundy's complaint. After another month, on 7 April 1989, the authority clerk, R.C. Johnston, wrote from his Barnsley HQ saying he had carried out a 'preliminary investigation' into the allegation 'that Mr Wright had offered an inducement to David Salter to give evidence against you', but the authority has 'resolved that no further action is required as the allegation is without any foundation whatsoever'.

Lundy wanted to know what investigation Johnston had really done. Not much, it seemed: he did not even get Salter's first name right. As for the allegation, it certainly had 'foundation'. There was evidence of an inducement from Wright's men to Salter: not just Roy Garner's original claim but Wright's letter to Salter's solicitor. When Salter was on the run in Belgium he feared Customs proceedings were pending, then Wright approached senior Customs staff and was able to tell Salter he was in the clear. Salter never was dealt with over VAT offences – a gesture uncharacteristic of Customs which went to such trouble to jail Garner for a grander version of the same crime. Johnston had never asked Lundy to provide evidence, so what material did he work from?

Eight days after he wrote to Lundy, in Sheffield on 15 April 1989 the Hillsborough stadium disaster occurred. Ninety-five football fans died. Lord Justice Peter Taylor led a public inquiry. In August 1989 he presented his interim report, including these withering conclusions concerning the senior command of the force which Wright had led for six years:

> In all some sixty-five police officers gave oral evidence at the inquiry. Sadly, I must report that for the most part the quality of their evidence was in inverse proportion to their rank . . . the senior officers in command were defensive and evasive witnesses . . . neither their handling of problems on the day nor their account of it in evidence showed the qualities of leadership to be expected of their rank.[13]

That ferocious verdict, with its implications for the very top of the force, merited that heads should roll. Chief Constable Wright offered his resignation, for he rightly saw himself as ultimately responsible for the conduct of every officer on duty that day. The Police Authority refused to accept his offer. Back in July 1987 Wright had shown no magnanimity towards Tony Lundy when he had recommended the detective's suspension, but South Yorks sources insist that Lundy was treated fairly. They were a neutral force investigating serious allegations, only some of which were against him. There were no 'deals' to make people say things. Each team on the inquiry acted impartially, as obliged by law. The Salter affair had to be most thoroughly investigated, beyond any cost effectiveness, because it was so serious. As for what I believe to be the stark contradictions in Salter's statements, I was told these should give me a clue as to the absolute impartiality of the inquiry, for any discrepancies were there for all to read.

Lundy feels unable to agree.

24

Facts in False Colours

Thursday 9 July 1987 started early for Tony Lundy with Mrs Garner's emotional phone call about whether the Yard had told Customs that Roy had long ago informed on the cocaine conspiracy, and ended when he confronted South Yorkshire over their Salter deal (see Chapter 23). The following day he had an angry encounter with CIB chief, Peter Winship. It had been suggested, said Winship in his circuitous way, that during Mrs Garner's call Lundy 'in effect communicated with Garner in a way which may be interpreted as a conspiracy to pervert the course of justice'. Lundy was appalled. How could one phone call in which he had conveyed only information be branded a conspiracy? Winship suggested a second offence: 'the specific information passed itself contravenes Section 2 of the Official Secrets Act.' What double-standards, thought Lundy. For five years he had been telling his Yard masters to apply the OSA to past and present police who had leaked highly confidential documents to the media. Yet nothing had happened. Now, he was being threatened with that very Act for dropping one opaque remark about matters which the Yard would be legally compelled to reveal for Garner's defence long before any trial. Winship then cautioned Lundy.

An eavesdropping psychoanalyst might have noted incipient paranoia in Lundy's counter-blast: 'Every word and everything I do is called into question.' He said he had no intention of doing anything wrong or corrupt, he just wished he had never received that phone call: 'The whole thing is being twisted and turned.'

Coming on top of six years' microscopic examination of his every move and motive, the Winship confrontation had finally broken Lundy. That weekend, facing the threat of conspiracy and secrets charges, he fell into a clinical depression and 'threw in the towel'. He went to see his doctor who diagnosed 'stress-reaction and depression' and certified he was unfit for duty and unable to be interviewed. On the Monday he reported sick. The next day he was suspended.

Lundy's detractors have claimed that his was a 'mystery illness' – in effect, a sham – but consider the stress Lundy was under. Since February 1985 he had been leading a twenty-strong squad on a gruelling and highly demanding inquiry into the whereabouts of the proceeds of the £26 million Brinks–Mat Gold Bullion robbery. As senior intelligence co-ordinator he was constantly travelling to many countries, coping with different legal systems, with international political sensitivities, and the sheer complexity of a money-laundering probe on a scale Scotland Yard had never before attempted. It was pioneering work which he did outstandingly well but it was taking a huge amount out of him mentally.

Lundy could have coped with all that strain and more, had it not been for the relentless pressure of corruption probes running ever since 1981. In most respects these were not objective. In big cases under intense media scrutiny, 'success' is defined as finding the officer guilty, and failure as deciding he is innocent. Lundy is the most investigated copper in Scotland Yard history. 'Stagg' ran for four years before he was merely given 'words of advice' (as was another officer who is now a deputy assistant commissioner). From 1981 and for the rest of the decade, press and TV ran dozens of 'investigative' stories implying Lundy was corrupt, culminating in *World in Action*'s 'The Untouchable' in November 1986. This provoked the instant setting-up of the South Yorks inquiry which took almost two years to yield six flimsy discipline charges. The fact that neither 'Stagg' nor South Yorks found proof of corruption did not diminish the stress. There was no proof to find, says Lundy, because there had been no corruption. What Lundy always feared was the 'fit-up': he might be found guilty of things he had not done. In addition to the Billy Young allegations, time and again Lundy was the victim or the target of mendacious attempts to discredit him. It is worth recapping some of the worst examples:

1981, January – Anonymous allegation of corruption against Lundy and others over Silver Bullion robbery. Discredited by 'Stagg'.

1981, March, April – Dave Spicer offered deal by senior Regional Crime Squad officer if he confirms corruption by Lundy. He refuses.

1981, April – Burglary at Lundy's home by Bryson and McCarthy.

1982, October – Gervaise conspires to make false allegations against Lundy, from within Supergrass Unit at Reading jail.

1983, February – Bryson gives false testimony about finding an attaché case containing over £40,000 worth of currency in Lundy's home during 1981 burglary. Over a year later McCarthy says this was untrue.

1984, October, November – Francis Attard makes false allegation (to TVS and *Observer*) that Lundy through his solicitor had paid him £2,000 to make false allegations against Gervaise.

1985–86 – 'Gary Gear' case leads to false allegation that Lundy was interfering with justice on behalf of his friend, 'Jim Davis'.

1986, July – Attard revives 1984 allegation in complaint to CIB 2.

1986, September, October – Plot by associates of West and O'Loughlin to plant 2 kilos of heroin at Lundy's home.
1986, October – Anonymous allegation by police officer falsely accusing Lundy of building a house beyond his legitimate means.
1986, November, December – False allegation that Lundy was plotting to murder Chris Robinson.
1987, April – Deal procured for Stevie Salter by South Yorks to induce him to testify against Lundy over fencing allegation.

The stress imposed on Lundy as he fought off fit-ups, false evidence and bogus allegations was immense. Indeed, the idea that his 'stress-reaction and depression' condition was a sham seems to fall into the same tradition as the allegations which provoked it. The most astonishing thing is that he did not succumb earlier.

Then how, ask his critics, could he run many miles each day, and complete the 1988 London Marathon, if he was so ill?

The London Sports Medicine Institute, based at St Bartholomew's Hospital, kindly sent me summary details of thirty articles published in the 1980s (many in medical journals) on the value of exercise in relieving stress. Most appear to support the view that exercise helps people psychologically as well as physically, although researchers do not yet know how. Some advocate running in particular to combat depression, and there is scientific evidence that 'acute physical activity helps in venting tensions, which in turn leads to sustained mental health across time'. It is believed that 'physically fit individuals are better able to cope with stress than are sedentary individuals'. There is research backing for the view that moderate running lifts people's ability to tolerate work stress. Dr Kenneth

Cooper, the former US Air Force flight surgeon who invented aerobics, is often credited with causing America's jogging boom of the 1970s and even a national fourteen per cent drop in heart disease deaths. From his Dallas clinic he told me, 'Exercise is nature's best tranquillizer, if used properly. It makes you feel good for the next three or four hours, it makes the rest of the day more productive.' When I described Lundy's situation, Dr Cooper replied:

I can see very easily that the man was overwhelmed by the stress of his work, and he's using exercise as a means of controlling stress instead of valium or some other medication. He wouldn't have been as productive as he was over the years if he hadn't exercised. Other people resort to using drugs or alcohol, but he used exercise as the main modality of therapy. There comes a point when that is not enough, however, and finally you break. That's apparently what happened to him. I've seen this happen before. I've seen people under tremendous stress who, even when using good exercise programmes, have developed severe coronary artery disease. We have helped police departments to develop exercise programmes to aid officers' physical and mental well-being. With the officer you describe, the stress was out of control so he had to resort to something else. He had to get out of the situation that was causing him so much stress.

In any case, three months after going sick he had elected (against doctor's advice) to come off the sick list. This was solely for South Yorks's convenience, otherwise they would not have been allowed to interview him. Thus he was not technically 'sick' when he ran the London Marathon. Months later, however, he was certified sick again. Lundy had used sport as a mental purgative for many years. Recalling his Finchley days and his ban on lunchtime drinking, he says:

I didn't mind any bloke going off for a run or a game of squash, even if they took two hours, because that refreshed you, got your brain going . . . You go for a run, you're at peace with the world, no distractions, no phones ringing. I used to come to some of my best decisions then. All the team would know when I'd been on a run. I'd come back saying, 'Why didn't I ask him this?' or 'Why haven't you done that?' There'd be mayhem after I'd had a game of squash. I must have been a real pain.

In the 1980s when malicious allegations streamed in year after year, running was my way of fighting back. You can't punch pressmen so you pound tarmac. My condition wasn't physical. It was mental. I'd had enough shit thrown at me. There was no point in going on. Besides, what if I'd beaten the discipline tribunal – Star Chamber, Kangaroo Court though that can be – what if I'd been cleared and gone back to making cases and giving evidence? All the garbage thrown at me during the West–O'Loughlin trial would have been thrown again and again. When the defence has no defence, they can always attack a detective on his record. It doesn't matter if the allegations are lies. Just tossing them in front of the jury may get the gangster off. And that Steventon minute would be brought up ever after: 'Oh, so Lundy's a corrupt officer, is he? Well, we'd better acquit.' The assistant commissioners effectively cancelled that minute after Steventon went but, even so, what jury's gonna believe me?

In December 1988 the Yard's chief medical officer sought two physicians' opinions and then granted Lundy medical retirement. As Dr Kenneth Cooper says, 'That was a life-saving thing. In the end he had to resign from the force to keep his sanity.' After twenty-seven years Lundy would leave the force on an enhanced pension. This news was derided by the journalists who had harried him for the best part of seven years. The Police Complaints Authority's members were no happier and issued a press release saying they had no role in the decision and 'regret there will now be no opportunity either to prove or disprove the charges at a disciplinary hearing'. The PCA had recently been attacked for supervising 'soft' inquiries into complaints against police (for instance, over a black woman paralysed by a bullet fired by police raiding her house in search of her son who was not even there).[1] Now it had been deprived of a rare chance to show it was being tough on cops, and really was as 'independent' as its letterhead proclaimed. 'Lundy' would have been an ideal case to restore the PCA's reputation, but he had been spared.

Soon, however, Lundy would be back at the Old Bailey, not as a prosecuting officer but as a witness in Roy Garner's defence. Garner's 'cocaine conspiracy' trial was starting in January 1989, and Lundy had been requested to explain Garner's long service as a police informant, especially on drugs. As it turned out, this part of the case would be heard secretly, in camera, to maintain the public fiction that Garner was not an informer. This was at the defence's request, not Lundy's.

The 'cocaine conspiracy' story is explained in Chapter 18. The jury rejected Garner's 'informer' defence and convicted him as a participant. He was jailed for twenty-two years. His guilt or innocence in no way reflected on Lundy, yet Lundy too was on trial. That was because the prosecution (run directly by Customs, not the DPP) sought through other evidence to impugn him as a co-conspirator. In his opening statement, Derek Spencer QC mentioned Lundy just once. He said that on 21 May 1986 at Ford open prison Roy Garner 'was paid a visit' by 'a man called Lundy . . . a serving officer at New Scotland Yard'. This reference led nowhere. Spencer made no attempt to link it with any other part of his speech. In fact the event never happened. Lundy never visited Garner in Ford.

Mentioning Lundy seemed gratuitous but it was only too deliberate. The main prosecution witness, Roy White-horne – safe in his state of total immunity but still on oath – talked of Lundy several times. He said that in 1984 he had been kept waiting by 'Henry Radley' (Garner's sidekick) in the foyer of the Pompano beach building where Radley and Garner owned a condominium. Radley told him a number of police 'from here' were upstairs: 'Later I was told a name. Lundy was one of them.' When Lundy gave evidence he dealt with this in open court. He said he had never met Radley or Whitehorne or spoken to either. He knew of no flat owned by Radley or Garner in Florida and had not even been in America in 1984 – a fact which the Customs could easily have checked (and probably did) prior to letting Whitehorne utter the lie. In fact, as Lundy says, 'I was flogging my guts out in Ealing' in 1984 and he made his first visit to Florida in 1986. In court Whitehorne also claimed to have met Lundy at a restaurant in Chingford, north-east London, with Garner and Radley. This was another lie. 'I don't think I've ever been in a restaurant in Chingford in my life,' responded Lundy who would also have pointed out – had he been given the chance – that he had never gone anywhere *with* Roy Garner and never ate with him at any restaurant. Even at 'Lady Ratlings' occasions he did not go in Garner's party or sit at the same table.

It was only because Garner's counsel questioned Lundy about Whitehorne's allegations that he was able to deny them. Prosecutor Derek Spencer put none of these points to Lundy in cross-examination. Suddenly he dropped this line of attack and never justified his mistaken claim that Lundy had visited Garner in Ford. Lundy felt he had been the victim of yet another shabby smear. Out of court he was asked if he thought Garner was guilty? Probably not: 'Everything Whitehorne said about me is lies, so why should anything he says be true?'

There may have been more to the attack on Lundy than a fear that his evidence might clear Garner.

First, there was historical animosity stemming back to the 1960s when the Yard Drugs Squad conflicted head-on with Customs and several of its detectives went to jail (see Chapter 8).[2] Then there was the never-ending feud over who should lead the nation's war on drugs. Britain's police forces and Customs now try to co-operate through the joint National Drugs Intelligence Unit, but 'turf battles' still break out. Over Garner's VAT fraud, Customs nursed extra grievances. They felt the Yard's representations were what brought Garner his reduced sentence on appeal. In any event, Customs never recovered the £2 million he stole from them. Finally, some Customs men wrongly held Lundy responsible for Garner's allegedly charmed life before his VAT arrest. They saw Lundy as a reincarnation of the archetypal corrupt Yard cop whom Customs often encountered in the '60s and early '70s. If that had been true, it might have justified the smear on Lundy during Garner's trial.

There might have been a nastier explanation, however, which had nothing to do with police corruption, and everything to do with corruption in Her Majesty's Customs. Records show that in March 1985 Garner was given hospital leave from jail and met Lundy at Woking Police Station. Among the matters alleged were the activities of a corrupt senior Customs officer who was in league with a major London criminal. In recent years the Customs man had regularly assisted drug couriers to pass through Heathrow Airport, or so Garner said. He then disclosed a plan to pull off the biggest single robbery ever attempted in Britain. Indeed, it had already been tried. In 1984 the Customs man had supplied information, passes and a key enabling a gang to rob the Customs' own bonded warehouse at Heathrow. Inside was property worth £100 million, including gold, silver and seized drugs. The first attempt failed because the thieves cut the wrong wires when trying to by-pass the alarms. They knocked out part of the airport's telecommunications system instead.

Undaunted, they were planning to try again in a few months' time. Or so the story went.

Initially Garner named nobody – he was angling for help on his VAT appeal – but records show that a few days later he began talking of a criminal named Roy 'Max' Mathias. Three years earlier Mathias had been arrested over a Kruger-rand fraud just like Garner's, but had not been charged because he had bribed another Customs officer, or so Garner claimed, and that was the start of a profitable friendship. Police records confirmed that Mathias had come a long way since 1964 when he was jailed for possessing forged currency. He was now very wealthy. Indeed he was as 'big' as Garner and had likewise enjoyed a fifteen-year spell without conviction, due partly to corruption. Had any investigative reporters pursued the Mathias story they could have made it as big a *cause célèbre* as the Garner affair.

At Scotland Yard Chief Superintendent Brian Boyce set up an operation to investigate Garner's claims. For obvious reasons Customs was not told. Garner did not know the name of the officer but had given a precise physical description. Six weeks into the investigation, a Yard surveillance squad tailed Mathias to Warren Street and saw him meet a man of that description. He turned out to be Barry Terry, a Customs man with the background Garner had described. Terry was even seen taking £200 from Mathias. Earlier, the Mathias team had been watched one weekend, staking out a bonded warehouse in Cambridgeshire. They seemed about to rob it but at the last minute they dispersed. Boyce's boss, Commander Corbett, was now under heavy pressure because the operation was consuming much money and manpower. The cost of bank holiday overtime alone was immense. Rather than wait for the 'big one', it was decided to bring the job to a head by arresting everyone on 16 September 1985.

Now inter-agency diplomacy was required. Corbett and Assistant Commissioner Dellow went to a senior member of the Customs Board and told him that not just one but two Customs men were to be arrested: Barry Terry (who was still serving) and Graham Branton (who had recently left). When Corbett's counterparts in the Customs investigation division found out, they were furious that he had not told them first. At a later meeting one of them gave Corbett a fierce tirade. Corbett was unrepentant, and the Mathias gang were charged with smuggling Kruger-rands, and corruption.

The case overlapped with a separate Customs probe into VAT fraud by other crooks. At a high-level conference it was decided to join both jobs together in a nominally Customs prosecution. As the trial unfolded at Southwark Crown Court, however, it was clear that the Customs corruption story would not have come out had it not been for Brian Boyce and his Yard team. The Mathias gang must have had protection as they brought more than £4 million-worth of Kruger-rands into Britain from Jersey. They then sold the gold, pocketing £635,000 VAT. In September 1988 Barry Terry was convicted of conspiracy to corrupt and accepting a bribe. He was jailed for three years. His former Customs colleague, Graham Branton, was convicted of conspiracy to cheat and defraud, then jailed for five years. Mathias went down for seven. Compared with the trials of Roy Garner, the Customs corruption case went almost unreported. It was as if the Customs 'good guy' image had some invisible shield. True, a former uniformed policeman was also convicted (Ian Ramage, who used to work for Garner) but this was the only occasion in the entire Lundy–Garner saga when a serving law enforcement officer was jailed for corruption: and *he was a Customs man, not a Scotland Yard detective.*

In 1989 Terry was cleared on appeal. His defence all along had been that Mathias was his informant, and that the money Mathias gave him was part of the profit on the sale of a car which Mathias had bought with a loan from Terry in a joint venture. As Mathias was the subject of Customs observations by Terry himself at the time, Terry concedes the venture was 'absolutely stupid, I don't know what came over me. We got over-friendly, and I overstepped the mark.'

Terry and Branton's capture had further soured Customs–Yard relations. One senior Customs investigator even had the temerity to ask a Yard detective for the informer's name. The detective correctly refused to say, but the Customs man must have guessed. The suspect Customs men had been arrested in 1985. The man who shopped them, Roy Garner, was arrested over the cocaine job in July 1987. Nailing him must have given Customs extra satisfaction. It was sweet revenge in a grudge match against bitter rivals.

On 3 April 1989 *World in Action* screened a second film on the Garner–Lundy affair. By now the investigator Andrew Jennings had been reunited with Vyv Simson, his producer on the original *Brass Tacks* show banned in 1985. Most of this sequel dealt with the crime for which Garner had just been jailed, and opened by claiming the gang had 'secret links to the Metropolitan Police', hence the title: 'Scotland Yard's Cocaine Connection'.

The programme-makers pointed to various signs that the smugglers had a mole in London's police. By the end most viewers must have believed that the mole – the fastest in history – was Tony Lundy who, while running along Hertfordshire country lanes, had been ambushed by a Granada film crew. It was classic TV journalism – not foot-in-the-door so much as mike-in-the-Nike – with Jennings matching Marathon Man pace for pace. Only slightly puffed, he threw out questions such as 'How much did you know about Roy Garner's involvement in cocaine?', 'Why is it that somebody who's so fit as you, can run like this, is not fit enough to turn up for his discipline board?', 'You were named in a Scotland Yard report as corrupt. Are you corrupt?', 'Mr Lundy, don't you have *anything* to say about any of these matters?'

He might have said a lot, if Granada asked him in a more conventional way. Yet since 1984, when Jennings and Simson started investigating him, they had never directly asked him for an interview before accosting him on his run. They had made requests through the Yard hierarchy which were turned down, but they did not ask Lundy himself. They knew where he lived – they filmed his house – but catching him on the trot was too visual to miss. For anyone except the detective, the shot was hilarious and symbolic. Above all, it seemed to say, 'Mr Lundy, why are you running away?'

The claim that Lundy was the cocaine gang's Yard mole stemmed from an approach by Special Agent Mike Breece of the Florida Department of Law Enforcement. By July 1986 Breece had discovered he shared an interest in Radley and Garner with Sergeant Gordon Bain of Operation Albany in Scotland Yard (see also Chapter 18). In August Breece started sending Bain packages of body-mike tape-recordings made by FDLE informer Jimmy Tullevere of conversations with cocaine co-ordinator Roy Whitehorne, who at the time had not yet been arrested or 'turned'.

In mid-September Breece had another package to send. He had previously used British Airways crew to carry the tapes, but on 17 September a BA official told him of 'a couple of Scotland Yard detectives that were already in the US, staying in Fort Lauderdale'. They were flying back to London two days later, so Breece could give them the package. This seemed a fine idea, especially as they were not far from Breece's own office in Fort Lauderdale. He was given one name: Tony Lundy. Breece called and Lundy said 'no problem'. Breece then phoned Bain in London to tell him the arrangements. Bain went wild, and told Breece he must not give Lundy the tapes. Now Breece had to tell Lundy of the change of plans, so the pair constructed this lie for Breece to tell Lundy: he had found out Bain's tapes were nothing to do with official police business, Bain 'had no right to use FDLE resources on private matters and that I would now send the tapes through the regular mail'.[3]

In the programme Jennings asked Breece, 'Nevertheless, Mr Lundy now knew there was an investigation going in Fort Lauderdale and tapes going back from here to Sergeant Bain in Scotland Yard.' Breece answered, 'Yes, he did.'

According to *World in Action*, a few weeks later US special agents 'secretly taping the criminals as they talked . . . were shocked to hear there'd been a leak, and their secret investigation wasn't secret any more.' According to Breece, the Florida end of the gang had been tipped off, 'there was heat in Fort Lauderdale, not to use the phones and to be careful who you associate with'. There was worse to come, said the commentary: 'the tapes revealed . . . a mole inside Scotland Yard.'

Roy Whitehorne was not named in the film, but the tip-off went to him. He then confided to Tullevere his fear that his phone was being tapped. He had no idea Tullevere was wired. In this conversation (quoted on the show) 'Henry' is 'Henry Radley' (Garner's London confederate for whom Henry Radley is a pseudonym required for legal reasons) and 'Charles' is Charles Flynn, the alias used by Nikolaus Chrastny in the USA.

Whitehorne told Tullevere: 'Henry heard from this guy

in Scotland Yard that Charles had got some problems and he was ninety per cent sure . . .'

Tullevere interjected: 'You've got a guy in Scotland Yard?! Come on! That's like getting an FBI agent here. They're tough to get up.'

Whitehorne: 'They have one. They've had him for a long time . . . He got Henry only fourteen months.'

Tullevere: 'You're knocking my whole image of Scotland Yard.'

Whitehorne: 'They've got the guy paid off.'

The programme's heavy implication was that the 'guy in Scotland Yard' was Tony Lundy. Although the commentary did not spell out the chronology, Whitehorne had got his tip-off sixteen days after Mike Breece's conversation with Lundy about carrying stuff to London. *Post hoc propter hoc* was the logic: because Lundy had learned of a relationship between the FDLE and Garner's longstanding pursuer, Gordon Bain, he must have been the source of the later tip-off that Whitehorne's phone was tapped. After all, Breece says that Lundy knew the package for Bain contained tapes, because Breece had told him so.

There are many flaws to this theory. To expose them requires what may seem a pernickety approach. However, Lundy stands accused by journalists of protecting a £100 million cocaine racket. There could scarcely be a worse allegation against a policeman, so precise analysis is called for.

For a start, Lundy says Breece told him nothing about any tapes, only that he had a package for Bain. He asked Breece if he meant Sergeant Fred Bain, who was working with Lundy, or Gordon Bain. Breece replied, 'Gordon Bain. Do you know him?' Lundy said yes, and that was the end of the call. Next morning Breece called back and said the arrangement was off. 'I remember him going on about it not being police business after all, and then I said, "What's happened? Has Gordon Bain told you on no account to give it to me?" And he just laughed and said, "Anyway, thanks very much but there's no need for you to take the package after all." And that was it.'

As for Whitehorne's comments on the Tullevere tapes, they pose severe evidential problems. They are made by a criminal accomplice whose remarks about the 'guy in Scotland Yard' constitute double, if not triple, hearsay. Yet even if he was told what he claimed to have been told, could it have been true? And could it apply to Lundy?

Whitehorne claimed he was told by 'Charles' (Chrastny) in London that his phone was tapped, and seemed to know there were tapes. He also told Tullevere 'it might be a federal tap' and explained why. Yet, if Lundy had been so corrupt as to be Chrastny's source, he would also have revealed that the tapes were not federal but state – because Mike Breece had told Lundy he worked for the FDLE, *Florida*'s detective force. This crucial difference would have been noted, and passed on, by Lundy who at the time was working closely with America's *Federal* Drug Enforcement Administration. (In contrast to Breece, the DEA's Miami chiefs – and all the DEA agents who knew Lundy – considered him a pillar of integrity. Breece knew only what he had been told.)

Also at Garner's trial Whitehorne said, 'Charles, a friend of Garner and Mark Garner all told me' that the phone was tapped: 'They'd been informed by people at Scotland Yard . . . They were all calling at the same time. They'd all got the message at the same time for me to keep off my telephone.' This is self-evident bunkum. Here we have highly skilled criminals, including the mega-gangster Chrastny, in a £100 million cocaine conspiracy, all chatting on a telephone line which they believe is tapped! That is the last thing they would have done. Yet even if they did, where was the proof? Alas! There was none because Whitehorne's phone was not being tapped after all. The only bug was the body-mike on Tullevere, to whom Whitehorne had told the bad news.[4]

According to a later book by the programme-makers, 'around 8 October Whitehorne was called from London and told that "they had a problem with Customs" . . . That was it: the secret investigation was blown.'[5] Maybe, but by whom? All Lundy knew from Mike Breece was that the FDLE was working with Gordon Bain in Scotland Yard. He knew nothing of any Customs involvement. Indeed, had he been corrupt, all he could have told Garner was that Bain was being sent FDLE tapes, presumably to help his continuing search for £2 million in lieu of the VAT money Garner had magicked away in 1982–83. Lundy would have had no reason to think Customs had anything to do with the tapes. Whoever called Whitehorne around 8 October must have had a source other than Lundy.

In the programme the 'guy in Scotland Yard' tape extract was played twice. Each time it contained an unexplained remark from Whitehorne: 'He got Henry only fourteen months.' This referred to Henry Radley, Garner's co-conspirator in the VAT fraud, who was jailed for two years but was inside from only 8 November 1984 until 14 February 1986. Strictly that is fifteen not fourteen months, but Whitehorne cannot have been referring to anything else. Yet Lundy had absolutely nothing to do with that case. It was a Customs job from start to finish, in which he would not have dared interfere. Nor would he have interceded with the judge or the parole board for Radley who was not his informer. So whoever 'got Henry only fourteen months' could not have been Lundy. Indeed, unless Radley was some other detective's informer, it could not have been any Yard officer. The kind of person most likely to have helped Radley get out so soon would have been a Customs officer.

Furthermore, said Whitehorne, 'Henry heard from this guy in Scotland Yard that Charles had got some problems.' Yet, as Lundy told the Garner trial, he had never met Henry Radley. And all he might have deduced from his talk with Breece was that Garner was in trouble, not 'Charles' about whom he knew nothing, either as Charles Flynn or Nikolaus Chrastny. He would therefore not have told Radley, or Garner, anything about Charles's 'problems'. With the obvious exception of Bain's own tiny Scotland Yard unit, the only people with such knowledge worked on Operation Redskin inside Customs, which was the only British agency giving Charles problems – and for sure, Customs was not telling Lundy anything.

There are other problems with the theory that Lundy was the mole. If he was so diabolically 'bent', why did it take sixteen days for the 'tape' leak to reach Whitehorne? Surely Lundy would have passed this on as soon as he flew into London – not just to safeguard the conspiracy but to make sure no one mentioned him on any future tape. The news would have bounced across the Atlantic in sixteen hours, not sixteen days. There is another huge obstacle. As Lundy neither knew nor ever spoke to Chrastny, Radley or Whitehorne, the only alleged conspirator he did know was Roy Garner who was in Wayland Prison in this period. Between 19 September, when Lundy left Miami, and 8 October, when Whitehorne was tipped off, Lundy neither visited Garner in jail nor met him outside. Nor did he speak to any member of Garner's family or anyone else likely to have visited Garner or spoken to him on the phone.

Summing up, there is no evidence – not even circumstantial – that Lundy was the 'mole'. Indeed, a lot of evidence indicates he could not have been. Even the evidence on the 'mole' tapes points not to Scotland Yard but to Customs. The fact that two Customs men had to be

tried for corruption in 1988 shows a Customs 'mole' cannot
be ruled out. And even if the mole was in the Yard, he
could have been one of many officers other than Lundy.
As far back as 1981 there was clear evidence that Roy
Garner had a mole on Operation Albany. Molehills were
being thrown up all over the place but no firm move was
made to wipe out the little beast or beasts (see Chapter 13).
In 1986 only two officers were left on 'Albany', but neither
Gordon Bain nor his colleague could have been moles.
However, not all leaks are deliberate. In October 1985, it
seems, 'Albany' had a security lapse when DAC Worth's
staff officer, Superintendent John Grieve, was shocked
to receive what he felt should have been a confidential
communication on an open teleprinter.

It stated that [Garner] and two others had been charged with
forgery offences. My reaction was one of annoyance. This was
an unsuitable method of communicating the information to me,
let alone the Deputy Assistant Commissioner . . . There was a
man whose name had been bandied about in public, the subject
of a sensitive inquiry, and Detective Superintendent Wiltshire
had only decided to notify me by telegram.[6]

If Operation Albany chose to pass information so openly
in 1985, it is possible that in 1986 a similar lapse could have
revealed the Trans-Atlantic operation on Whitehorne,
Garner, Chrastny and co. – in which case the 'mole' could
be one of hundreds of detectives, or even a member of the
Yard's civilian staff.

If Lundy was not the 'mole', the programme called
'Scotland Yard's Cocaine Connection' rather missed its
point. On it moved to the accusation for which he was
suspended: 'leaking police information about the cocaine
investigation to Roy Garner after his arrest by Customs
officers.' That meant his response to Mrs Garner: 'She
could tell her husband that certain information had been

passed at a very senior level from Scotland Yard to senior
personnel of the agency dealing with his case.' This did not
deserve the 'criminal caution' for possible conspiracy to
pervert the course of justice, which the programme mentioned – and no such charge was ever laid against him.

The other issues raised in the programme were ancient
history. Salter's fencing, for instance, had been looked at
by 'Stagg' in 1982, discarded, then revived by South Yorks.
No mention was made of its deal with Salter, without
which he would not have given his shaky evidence. What
was mentioned was the bogus 1980 Hatton Garden job
over which Lundy backed Garner for an eventual £37,500
reward. The commentary said, 'Steventon found evidence
suggesting that Roy Garner was not the informant and that
he was exploiting information given to him by Lundy', but,
as explained in Chapters 8 and 14, the true story is the
other way round. Not only did Garner supply the key
information leading to the jewels' recovery and the guilty
pleas of Heath and Hogg; the information supplied by the
Sussex police informer (who was paid the other half of the
reward) proved dangerously and expensively inaccurate.

One valid issue in the film stemmed from a Billy Young
claim which 'Stagg' had investigated in 1982–83 but which
resulted in no action against Lundy. As *World in Action*
told it, three men claiming to be police went to the home
of a businessman in Salmon Street, Wembley, and stole
£64,000 at gunpoint. Years later Young admitted he was
one of the robbers and explained how they had hood-
winked Lundy. At first all they knew was their intended
victim's phone number, not his address, so they arranged
to pass the number to Lundy. He then used a Post Office
facility to get the address. The programme did not say
so, but he must then have passed the address back to
the robbers: 'Young made it clear that Tony Lundy had
no idea he was helping set up an armed robbery, but

he was adamant that it was Lundy they'd turned to for help.'

Despite its antiquity – the robbery occurred in 1974 – and the fact that it had nothing to do with Roy Garner, this story must be explored in greater depth, to show why no action was taken. For a start, Young's allegation was far worse than *World in Action* implied. He said Lundy received £1,000 from the robbers as a reward. Lundy denies this and says Young had been out to destroy him ever since 1980, when a mischievous Regional Crime Squad detective told Young it was Lundy who had supplied the information which had forced him to confess his own crimes.

The two basic facts are these: on 11 December 1974 Lundy used official channels to obtain the address of a Mr Ali in Salmon Street, London NW9; nine days later, on 20 December 1974, Young and two confederates stole £81,000 from Mr Ali and his family.

When questioned by 'Stagg', Lundy could not recall obtaining the address but over the years he had made hundreds of legitimate requests for addresses, including (as it happens) that of 'Burglar Bill' Young himself. He knew nothing of the robbery until 'Stagg' told him eight years later. He said the man who, Young claimed, had asked him for the address was a straight businessman. He must have told Lundy a story about a man being involved in some activity which would be of interest to the police and owing him money. At the time Lundy believed he was getting genuine information from a reliable source about an active criminal, and so disclosed the address. It was an error of judgement, but there are very few detectives – and even fewer successful ones – who can honestly say they have not occasionally dropped information to helpful folk whom they believe to be straight. As one of Lundy's South Yorkshire interrogators put it, 'give a bit to get a bit'.

In Lundy's favour is the very fact that he acquired the address openly. Had he been up to no good, he could easily have used a quicker, back-door way of getting an address *without leaving a trace*.

I obviously had reason to check that information in relation to police duties, otherwise it would have been ridiculous to have done so through official channels, knowing that a record would be available for anyone to check at any time. If any officer wanted to check a subscriber without telephoning officially through CO C1 [Scotland Yard's central CID office] it was quite simple to telephone the exchange operator direct for an *urgent* check; then no record need have been kept . . . It would seem I was tricked into obtaining details of a telephone subscriber for apparently genuine duty reasons.

Former Chief Inspector Peter Walsh appeared on the *World in Action* programme. He was originally in charge of the 'Ali' inquiry but said he was stopped: 'The people telling me to stop it either didn't believe it occurred or they didn't want it investigated, and if they didn't want it investigated that's because they didn't want the perpetrators caught.' Viewers may have wanted to hear more from Walsh, but only later in the programme-makers' book (also called *Scotland Yard's Cocaine Connection*) were his remarks expanded. They say, Walsh used to accost senior officers in pubs, 'denouncing them as "bent bastards"'. He found out the robbers had produced a genuine search warrant allegedly supplied by a sergeant unconnected with Lundy. He was then told to drop his inquiry, and a senior officer assaulted him. He was taken off the case but was still determined to catch the robbers. He was then fitted up, he claims, by being entrapped into meeting a man on bail (in breach of police rules), and falsely accused of taking a £2,000 bribe. He was suspended for two years before being cleared, he never returned to duty and was discharged in 1976 as medically unfit for police service. 'He has never been told what those medical grounds were,' say the authors.[7]

If Walsh were fitted up, no colleague would sympathize more than Tony Lundy: the victim of more attempted fit-ups and false allegations than any other detective. Walsh retired on a sick pension after a long suspension – just like Lundy thirteen years later – but whereas *World in Action* extracted much ironic mileage out of a physically fit Lundy getting an ill-health pension after suspension, it said nothing of Walsh's similar departure.

There were two other curious omissions. The programme quoted Ron Steventon as saying in his 1983 minute, 'It is my belief that Mr Lundy is a corrupt officer' without including his immediate prior qualification, 'regrettably there is a dearth of evidence to support it'. This omission converted what was no more than a personal opinion, for which there was no proof, into an apparent statement of fact.

Finally, there was Harry Clement, lamenting that a senior Yard officer had questioned him about his co-operation with Jennings and Simson (when they were working for the BBC in 1985), and that a report was sent to the DPP 'for consideration to take action against me'. Asked what he thought of the Yard wanting to prosecute him for talking about Garner and Lundy, Clement said, 'Ridiculous!'

This was not so ridiculous, as the BBC's own legal opinion of 5 March 1986 reveals: 'We have had access to, and made use of documents in the possession of Harry Clement who, before his retirement, conducted Operation Albany, and we could be said to be acting in breach of confidence.' So, of course, could Clement who may also have been subject to the Official Secrets Act (see Chapter 15).

Earlier in the programme Clement had been asked if

Lundy had arrested many top criminals. 'Apparently so,' said he. 'But not, it seems, ever Roy Garner?' With a laugh on his face Clement replied, 'No, Mr Jennings, no!' An informed viewer might have wanted to ask one more question, 'But, Mr Clement, Lundy never had the task of catching Garner. You did have that task, and for well over a year you had a team of forty-five people to help you do it, with full powers of surveillance. What did *you* achieve?'

World in Action had again spread the word to some eight million viewers that Lundy was a bent cop, but Andrew Jennings and Vyv Simson had not finished with him. In May and June 1989 the Home Affairs Committee of the House of Commons considered the report of the Police Complaints Authority for 1988. Jennings and Simson submitted a memorandum (in the name of Granada Television) listing many matters they considered relevant to the issue of Lundy's integrity and his retirement on medical grounds while facing disciplinary charges.[8] This contained errors and misinterpretations, and it greatly influenced the committee's view of the Lundy affair.

It is unfortunate but at no time were the MPs told that Lundy's illness was mental rather than physical. Instead, Metropolitan Commissioner Sir Peter Imbert (presumably respecting Lundy's privacy) merely said that two medical opinions were sought (in addition to that of Lundy's doctor), and these confirmed he was 'medically unfit for further police service'.[9] Nothing was said of Lundy's 'stress-reaction and depression'. As a result the MPs assumed that his undoubted physical fitness gave the lie to his retirement on grounds of ill-health. They felt he was surely fit enough to attend a discipline hearing, at least. That may be so, but one reason for his depression was that, after almost two years, the PCA had still not set up an inquiry into his own allegations, against South Yorkshire in particular. Had these been sustained, they would have invalidated much of the case against him. Ignorant of such facts, the MPs commented: 'Even greater anxiety than the inability to pursue the disciplinary charges was occasioned when Mr Lundy was filmed in extremely fit physical condition training for long distance running in Metropolitan Police colours.'[10]

In their book (co-authored with Paul Lashmar) Simson and Jennings quoted this sentence. They modestly omitted to say it was based on paragraph 1.13 of their own memorandum. This said that Lundy was filmed completing the London Marathon in April 1988 'in the colours of the Metropolitan Police Athletic Club'. This was untrue. There is no such thing as the Metropolitan Police Athletic Club. There is a Metropolitan Police Athletic *Association* but Lundy had not been running in MPAA colours, which are dark blue, gold and grey. He has never run in those colours. As a Metropolitan officer he was automatically a member of the MPAA but he has never represented the Metropolitan force in any running event.

This was not a great mistake but it becomes important for being laundered through Parliament and then presented as a fact. It seemed a fitting epitaph on the entire Lundy affair: 'facts' running in false colours.

A Conspiracy of Interests?

After ten years of unrelenting police inquiries and media exposés, nothing had been proved against Tony Lundy. True, he was facing six discipline charges when he retired but I believe these would have been thrown out if his own complaints against South Yorkshire had ever been put to the test. The one charge which might have succeeded – giving Mrs Garner information 'without proper authority' – was a technicality, brought entirely on the basis of Lundy's own contact sheet. By seizing on this petty offence, if it was one, his accusers acted like the dustcart trailing the Lord Mayor of London's Show. Nothing in 'The Untouchable' was worth even a discipline charge, but this 'evidence', proffered by the 'target' himself, was a dropping they rushed to scoop up. Lundy's suspension because of it in July 1987 had the incidental effect that the Stevie Salter 'deal' would go almost unnoticed by the media and would never be fully investigated.

If, as I believe, Tony Lundy was not crooked, how did so many of his pursuers get it wrong? As far as press and TV are concerned, a number of 'investigative reporters' came to the conclusion fairly early on that he was bent and then tended to under-estimate any evidence to the contrary. It is always difficult for journalists to admit they could have 'shot the wrong man', but after spending six years in pursuit of a detective they seem convinced is corrupt, it might be impossible. When the book, *Scotland Yard's Cocaine Connection*, was serialized in *The Sun* in 1990, one paragraph betrayed a breath-taking misreading of evidence which augured ill for the book itself: 'Villain Roy Garner, 54, became a multi-millionaire, as a result of his undercover alliance with Detective Superintendent Anthony Lundy, 47.'[1] The truth is that no alliance with Lundy made Garner a multi-millionaire. He was already very wealthy before he earned his first sizeable reward on Lundy's recommendation in 1978. Within the rules of a very nasty and unsavoury game, Garner deserved all his rewards. And if he had not informed through Lundy, he would have informed through some other detective. Lundy never protected any Garner racket or even knew about them, nor did he block anyone else's investigations into the man. If any law enforcement officers made Garner a multi-millionaire they were in Customs under whose nose, in 1982–83, he scooped up £2 million worth of VAT and made it vanish, even though – according to the *Cocaine Connection* – he and his partner Ross 'had been spotted' by Customs 'from the start'.[2]

Authors may not be responsible for a newspaper adaptation, but they are responsible for their books. In the *Cocaine Connection* the authors embrace former Detective Superintendent Gerry Wiltshire's view that Roy Garner was 'the overlord of crime in London'. Yet it is ludicrous to suggest that in so huge, diverse and criminal a city any individual could be the sole overlord of crime. If such a figure did exist in the late 1970s and early 1980s, Scotland Yard had files on a dozen other contenders for the honour. Many have a greater claim on the title 'Untouchable' than Garner, for they remain untouched.

Another touchstone of the authors' judgement is their reading of DAC Steventon's 1983 minute. They say this 'states unequivocally' that 'Mr Lundy is a corrupt officer'. Yet Steventon hedges his words in a way which could be hardly more equivocal. He says:

I am of the opinion that the D of PP will decline to institute criminal proceedings . . . I feel bound to express a personal opinion and regrettably there is a dearth of evidence to support it, but it is my belief that Mr Lundy is a corrupt officer . . . the evidence is insufficient to warrant suspending Mr Lundy from duty.

So, no criminal charges, no suspension, 'a personal opinion', only 'my belief', and 'a dearth of evidence' (meaning scarcity, want, famine, or none at all). This is equivocation of a high order. Clearly the authors had no idea of the events which had occurred just six weeks before Steventon wrote his minute and which may have coloured his thinking (see Chapter 14), yet if this is how they handle evidence on page 7 of their book, readers may wonder what misinterpretations creep in on the remaining 191 pages. For instance, concerning Garner's rewards over the 1980 Hatton Garden and Silver Bullion robberies, they cite this Steventon comment: 'Some evidence has been deduced . . . which suggests that Garner was not the informant he was claimed to be and that he was merely exploiting information which he received from Lundy.' That means, Lundy fed Garner information so he could make fraudulent reward claims. As the authors put it, 'Steventon's thesis was clear: valuable information appeared to be going . . . from the Yard, through Lundy, to the criminal Garner. Steventon made no suggestions about where the reward money paid to Garner might be ending up. [His] verdict should have been enough to end any detective's career overnight.'

The authors appear to be agreeing with 'Steventon's thesis' that Garner did not deserve the Hatton Garden reward (in my view he did), but they take a different view of the Silver Bullion job. On page 60 they write:

An insurance reward of £300,000 had been advertised and

Garner's greed won out. He had to strike first before Gervaise could admit the robbery, surrender the silver and so deny Garner the reward. Having previously turned down the chance to join the team of robbers going after the silver, Garner always knew who had done it.

The authors produce no evidence that Garner had been offered the chance of going on the robbery, nor do they explain why, if he always knew who had done it, he waited ten weeks before telling Lundy, or even two weeks after Gervaise was arrested. Yet they clearly believe Garner was the true informant, for they show him earning the reward by passing high-grade intelligence to Lundy, not the other way round. Forty-two pages later, however, as they embrace Steventon's devastating character assault on Lundy, they fail to point out that they themselves reckon that on this, the most disputed aspect of the entire Lundy–Garner saga, 'Steventon's thesis' is wrong.

Another logical chasm emerges in their treatment of Nikolaus Chrastny's escape from the secure police station in Dewsbury, West Yorkshire, on 5 October 1987. At that time, they say, 'the British press speculated whether he had been helped to escape by corrupt detectives at Scotland Yard'. Later Mrs Charlotte Chrastny went on trial for helping her husband escape. She was acquitted of this offence, but she was jailed for seven years for her part in the cocaine conspiracy. The authors make much of her counsel's line that 'a number of people had a motive for helping Chrastny escape'. 'Top of his list' was New Scotland Yard.[3]

Readers might feel that these authors' own insights into Chrastny's escape would be more valuable than mere press speculation and the remarks of a barrister trying to get his client off. Yet in their account they offer no evidence that Scotland Yard was involved. The facts appear to be these. Having made a confession, Chrastny was entrusted by Customs to detectives on the South Yorkshire inquiry who interviewed him for some days. They lodged him in Rotherham police station, but when it became clear that he was becoming too friendly with officers there, he was put in the hands of another force, West Yorkshire, and stuck in the women's block at Dewsbury. There too he used politeness and an easy manner to put officers off their guard. Over several nights he sawed through the bars of his cell gate, using hacksaw blades which had been secreted in the binding of a book. Early on 5 October he climbed through the cell gate, out through the unbarred window of a nearby doctor's room and into the station yard. Presumably, he then walked off police property, was driven away by car and was very soon flown out of Britain.

Northumbria's chief constable, Sir Stanley Bailey, was appointed to conduct an inquiry. In his report he blamed West Yorks officers for giving Chrastny the model-making materials (plasticine, paint, glue) which he used in his escape, but Bailey said there was no trace of collusion by the officers. Also, according to written instructions handed to Dewsbury police when Chrastny was put in their care, Customs men were to be in constant attendance. Yet it was several hours before his escape was detected. According to a West Yorkshire Police Authority official, 'Chrastny was visited consistently by Customs officers. He was their prisoner and he remained effectively under the control of Customs men even though he was housed in a West Yorkshire police cell.' In its own report the Authority expressed concern that 'confusion was caused by the officers of Customs and Excise' over Chrastny's status and the manner in which he should have been detained. As one Dewsbury officer puts it, 'they told us to give him anything he wanted.'

Given this background, it is worse than perverse to

blame Scotland Yard for Chrastny's escape. He had been
bailed into Customs custody, entrusted to South Yorks,
then lost in West Yorks. All three forces had kept his
whereabouts a strict secret. Indeed, they had moved him
partly to ensure no Yard folk could know where he was.
One possible leaker was Chrastny's wife who was lodged
at a safe house but visited Dewsbury every week. Yet if she
had been in league with any Yard men, she would surely
have betrayed them to get a lower sentence than seven
years over the cocaine. If corrupt officers were involved,
they presumably worked for an organization which knew
where he was, not Scotland Yard. Journalists who wrote of
a Yard connection failed to state it would have been almost
impossible for any Yard man to know where Chrastny was
– least of all Tony Lundy who was suspended at home,
almost certainly with his phone tapped. They might have
made more of the fact that, earlier in the year, Customs
had waited six weeks before arresting Chrastny, a delay
which gave him and his lieutenants time to release another
£15 million worth of cocaine on to the streets of London.

Even so, the view persists that the Yard wanted to
'disappear' Chrastny because of the statement he began
making on 20 June 1987, soon after his arrest. In this, say
the *Cocaine Connection* authors, he named 'the alleged
gang member inside Scotland Yard who was going to tip
them off if investigations into the drug plot began'. In fact
he said nothing so specific. In his convoluted English, he
merely claimed that, back in 1984, he had asked Garner
about his London intelligence connections: 'Because I
was not interested in vague statements and because I
impressed on him that I had to be conscientious of the
security of all the people involved, he gave me the name
of Mr Lundy.'[4]

Even if Chrastny meant to stick to this statement, it
is only hearsay. At no point does he claim to have met

Lundy, which he did not. And even if Garner really did mention Lundy in that role, he may well have been bluffing or lying. The anti-corruption inquirers may now have hoped to use Chrastny against Garner, to force Garner to plead guilty; then, to earn a far lower sentence than twenty-two years, he might turn supergrass and expose Lundy. According to Lundy, any such scheme would have been doomed to fail because he had never done anything for Garner or the cocaine conspirators. Neither Garner nor Chrastny could say anything truthful which could harm him. Having fought in vain to persuade past Yard bosses that drug-racketeering should be targeted as a top priority, Lundy wanted Chrastny to face trial. He certainly had nothing to gain from Chrastny's escape and yet, between the lines, he was being blamed for it.

But was Chrastny even likely to be telling the truth? The *Cocaine Connection* authors say 'he was more than happy to reveal' Garner's offer of protection from his Yard friend, Lundy. Sure, he was 'happy' because he already knew this was just what some Customs men were longing to hear. The authors say that in November 1986 one member of the cocaine gang had given him a video of 'The Untouchable'. He told Customs interrogators that when he watched it and discovered Garner's true role, 'it made me sick to my stomach'.[5] This mega-gangster was sickened by the image of an informer who indulged in robbery and arson. Who would have thought a death-dealing drug peddler could be so squeamish?

The authors unconsciously indicate what Chrastny was really up to. They say that during his later stay in Dewsbury, 'he manipulated the police brilliantly. [He] exploited his captors' desire to keep him in a co-operative frame of mind.'[6] Even if so, this was a mere extension of the manipulation which, it seems, he had already applied to HM Customs. By claiming Lundy was the 'inside man' –

and not just for betraying the main conspirators – he had won the equivalent of a holiday in Dewsbury, complete with TV and stereo. As Keith Wilson, Chairman of the West Yorks Police Authority, put it: 'Chrastny was treated as a guest, he wasn't a prisoner in the normal sense.'[7] This lax regime must have been witnessed by the Customs men who regularly popped in to see him, but they too had been lulled into complacency by the way his evidence suited their case. He did not need to be told to name Lundy. Having seen 'The Untouchable', he knew that any remarks against the detective would go down well. By then some Customs officers had long been convinced that Lundy was the 'inside man' in the conspiracy. Perhaps some of the South Yorks officers who had been working with them (ever since Sergeant Gordon Bain told them of the Florida tapes allegations) felt the same way. Chrastny must have known that a bit of hearsay evidence to Lundy's discredit would be readily believed and earn him additional goodwill. He duly made statements directly to South Yorkshire against Lundy. Thus he was offering his captors an unspoken arrangement with mutual benefits, a silent deal.

This interpretation might sound far-fetched if South Yorkshire had not previously reached its own deft accommodation with Stevie Salter. As explained in Chapter 23, in March 1987 Chief Constable Wright – courtesy of Customs – had told Salter that no action was contemplated on VAT matters over which he clearly feared prosecution. This freed his tongue to make a statement against Lundy. Three months later South Yorks did Customs the favour of looking after Chrastny, in whom their only interest was his anti-Lundy remarks. With the advancing summer, the Customs–South Yorks alliance became even closer as is evident from a third incident involving a Staffordshire woman who approached Customs for help with her problems.

Carol Cartlidge runs children's educational charities. In 1984 she had been approached by people offering to deposit huge sums of money from overseas in bank accounts especially set up to receive them. In return the charities would keep all the interest earned but the capital sum would later be moved elsewhere. It took time for Mrs Cartlidge to realize this might have been part of an international money-laundering scheme, possibly involving drug money. During the spring of 1987 she read newspaper stories saying that Scotland Yard, searching for the Brinks–Mat Gold proceeds, had arrested a man named Patrick Diamond. Mrs Cartlidge knew Diamond personally because she had been introduced to him in his capacity as a company formation agent. At one point she was taken to his offices on the Isle of Man to set up a company to handle the huge charity deposits.

The newspaper accounts stated that the Yard squad investigating Diamond was led by Superintendent Tony Lundy, a name she remembered from previous articles and TV programmes implying he was corruptly involved with Garner. Months later, when she read of Garner's cocaine arrest, she wondered if there was any connection between Garner, Diamond and her 'funny money' contacts. Media dirt had made her wary of Lundy, so she rang Customs to ask if they might be interested in her mystery investors. She was put through to Bob Gray, who was running Operation Redskin which had arrested Garner and Chrastny. In the course of the call she mentioned Tony Lundy. Gray arranged to visit her at home on 11 August 1987 but he turned up with surprise company. Without forewarning he had brought two senior oficers from the South Yorkshire inquiry. They explained their interest in Lundy but Mrs Cartlidge was very annoyed. She said she knew nothing about Lundy, had never met him and had never had any dealings with him. She said she had contacted Customs in

case there was a link between Garner and Diamond, and
was upset that Customs had breached her confidence by
telling South Yorkshire.

Undaunted, the South Yorks men asked her to come to
their London offices the next week to make a statement.
On 19 August a puzzled Mrs Cartlidge turned up with her
husband at Wellington House where, she says, she was
told her matter had nothing to do with Garner but a lot
to do with Lundy. She repeated that she knew absolutely
nothing about Lundy except what was in the newspapers.
At this, she says, the South Yorks men became angry and
offensive. They accused her of claiming to have information about Lundy when she first rang Customs. When she
said she had done no such thing, they told her she could
be in serious trouble: 'I came out feeling they had treated
me like a criminal. They were trying to use me against
Lundy, when I had never had anything to do with him.
I only knew about Diamond. I never told anybody I had
information about Lundy.'

By doing little more than mention Lundy's name, Mrs
Cartlidge found herself catapulted by Customs into the
role of a front-line anti-Lundy witness for South Yorkshire.
It seems, therefore, that by summer 1987 staff from these
two agencies were bound up in an alliance. Customs,
in turn, was very close to Operation Albany and to a
journalist or two. It also seems that some South Yorkshire
officers' view of Lundy was largely dictated by what they
had inherited. Over the years so much innuendo, abuse
and obloquy had been heaped on him that it would have
taken remarkable political courage for any inquiry to pro-
nounce him 'clean', though strictly Scotland Yard would
have to decide. The truth is that the case against Lundy
had been tainted years earlier, right from the start, and
had never recovered.

The original sponsor of the view that Lundy was corrupt

was Number 5 Regional Crime Squad, composed largely of officers from Hertfordshire and Thames Valley Police. In 1980 5 RCS embarked on Operation Carter, a huge investigation into organized crime founded on the allegations of a career criminal and armed robber named Roger Dennhardt. In February 1980 Dennhardt turned supergrass in the middle of a trial. He then named Fred Sinfield who in turn named Billy Young. Dennhardt said he knew nothing much about police corruption but in 1986 – after Dennhardt had completed a short jail sentence – one of his long-time minders, Sergeant Graham Sayer, was jailed for nine years for taking part in a £307,000 robbery with Dennhardt himself in 1985. In court Sayer's defence portrayed him as crippled with a back injury, and mentally disturbed: a loyal, devoted and trustworthy detective who had been subverted by the 'powerful, persuasive and devious' Dennhardt. In reality, however, Sayer was not this weak-willed. Indeed, he was a more than willing party to the conspiracy. Nor, it seems, was he the only 5 RCS officer with a criminal tendency. To this day Roger Dennhardt has never been charged with the robbery for which Sayer was jailed.

It was another 5 RCS officer (of far higher rank) who told Dave Spicer in March 1981 that he would be treated favourably if he were to make statements alleging corruption by Tony Lundy. The offer of such an inducement is almost certainly unlawful; it would be criminal if the officer made the offer knowing that Spicer was innocent of the crimes for which he had been arrested, or if he was blackmailing him into making false statements against Lundy. But this was not the only offer made by 5 RCS at this time. Another had catastrophic consequences for Operation Carter and destroyed its most important case by far. That same month, March 1981, Sergeant Rodney Pook visited Reading jail to see George Copley, who had been arrested for the notorious £225,000 Williams and Glyn's robbery of May 1978. This was the crime for which the robbers had soon paid £80,000 in bribes to City of London detectives in order to get bail, watered-down evidence and all charges dropped (see Chapter 6). One of those robbers was Fred Sinfield who, on turning supergrass, named all his Williams and Glyn's accomplices. One was George Copley. George knew his law. When Pook came to visit him, Copley secretly tape-recorded their conversation in which Pook confirmed an earlier unlawful offer: if Copley made a statement admitting guilt and gave evidence of corruption against London detectives he would get a mere five-year sentence.

In June 1981 Copley and his colleague Frank Fraser junior came up for trial at Oxford on other robbery charges. When Copley's defence produced his tape the prosecution collapsed and the charges were dropped. In July the Williams and Glyn's trial began and ended on the same day as Stephen Wooler, for the Director of Public Prosecutions, conceded that the case against Copley, Fraser and six other men was hopelessly compromised. Two prosecution officers, Sergeant Pook and Constable Martin Reeve, had been suspended because the Copley tape seemed 'to indicate unlawful inducement'. Indeed, said the DPP man, the implication of all the Copley and Fraser material was that 'two sets of officers had been acting together' in making the offer 'and hardly without the knowledge of a supervisor'. The consequences were severe: 'If the credibility of a senior officer is called into question, the prosecution has to think long and hard.' Not only was the inducement out of order: Copley and Fraser's statements had been backdated by several days in order to ease the deal through. This indicated a far more serious offence by the interviewing officers, and by any of their bosses who knew about it. Such a proverbial 'can of worms' forced the trial to be adjourned. In November 1981 all charges were finally dropped.

This was the biggest single disaster in the battle against organized crime and corruption in Britain in the last thirty years. First it allowed a total of ten of the country's highest-ranking gangsters to walk out of twenty-five-year prison sentences for a crime that every informed London criminal and detective is sure they committed. Several of the men have gone on to lead major drug-smuggling syndicates based on Spain's Costa del Sol. Secondly, it prevented the revelation of the full truth behind the corruption allegations which had inspired Operation Countryman. This Williams and Glyn's robbery was only one of a series involving corruption by senior detectives in the City of London Police and the Metropolitan Flying Squad. Countryman pieced together part of the story and eventually convicted two City officers, but by the time Sinfield 'turned' it had lost its independence and was effectively under Metropolitan Police control. The only hope left was that 5 RCS could complete Countryman's original task. Instead it screwed it up.

An outside police inquiry was conducted into this second Williams and Glyn's fiasco but it got nowhere because the prime witness, George Copley, never made a complaint. After all, he had 'got a result' and did not wish to make more trouble for detectives who might come in handy in future. Yet the unlawful conduct in his case, combined with what happened in the case of Dave Spicer, and the downright criminality of Graham Sayer, make the 5 RCS set-up appear not an ideal conduit for allegations against other detectives. Yet this was the outfit which raised Billy Young to supergrass status and thereby launched the ten-year war on Tony Lundy. Astonishingly, the authors of *Scotland Yard's Cocaine Connection* state that the detectives on 5 RCS 'were totally incorruptible'![8]

Of course, Young was not the only criminal to make allegations against Lundy. Soon others emerged to stir up journalists and detectives against him. Most wanted to get out of jail quick or avoid going back there. They believed that discrediting Lundy was the best way to achieve either goal, especially if it was he who had got them jailed in the first place. Lundy spoke from experience when, after the 1986 *World in Action*, he launched a tirade against 'numerous criminals' determined to discredit him 'and thus open the floodgates from prison'. Exploiting anti-Lundy publicity was certainly how Alf Berkeley tried to wipe out the twenty-year sentence Lundy had inflicted on him. In 1983, having failed to convince the Court of Appeal, he petitioned the Home Office for his case to be reopened, or a free pardon, on the grounds that Lundy was corrupt. His evidence consisted mainly of newspaper cuttings and correspondence with press and TV reporters. He thought general press comment against Lundy should over-rule the belief of both a jury and the Court of Appeal that he himself had committed extremely violent robberies. The Home Office did not agree, perhaps because the 'floodgates' really would burst if pardon by press cuttings became the norm.

That same year burglar Keith Bryson made his bizarre 'briefcase stuffed with currency' allegation. On the *Private Spy* video Bryson said that in jail he had met dozens of prisoners fitted up by Lundy. Nothing could have suited them better than for a 'sublimely self-confident'[9] Bryson to stand before a packed press box and claim Lundy's home was stashed with money which obviously he should not have had. Had such a story been true and proved, busloads of villains would have been back on the streets in no time. The fact that it was a total lie has only come out with the publication of this book more than eight years later.

Some criminals who defamed Lundy had not been

arrested by him, but they too had personal motives. Billy Young was avenging himself on Dave Spicer and simultaneously pleasing some officers hungry for bad news of Lundy. His reward was a supergrass sentence of just six years. John Goodwin, who made so much of the early running with the press against Lundy, wanted to scupper a case against himself based on the word of Micky Gervaise. Lundy had caused the arrest of Gervaise, but he very soon realized he was a liar unworthy of supergrass status. Lundy would not have used him to give evidence against Goodwin, but it suited Goodwin when Gervaise backfired on the prosecution by falsely testifying that he had been promised the Silver Bullion reward. It also suited him to spread false tales that Spicer had made statements against Lundy. Through such manoeuvres Goodwin not only helped himself; by trafficking in underworld gossip, he helped shape some journalists' misconceptions for years to come.

Folk like Francis Attard fall into an even worse category of professional informers ready to lie – in court or out – against total strangers, to get a good deal from the courts. It is appalling that for years such men can beguile press and police into wasting time, money and manpower pursuing their bogus allegations. Unfortunately the Attards of this world are beguiling people; con-men by vocation, they find cops and reporters as easy to hoodwink as the mug-punters and shopkeepers they defraud in the normal practice of their vocation.

And so it happened that in the 1980s – for various separate and coincidental reasons – some criminals, some cops and some reporters all felt driven to discredit or expose Tony Lundy. They were not parts of one big conspiracy. But was there a wider conspiracy?

During the 1980s Lundy became concerned that Freemasonry may have been playing a role in the unrelenting attacks on him. I believe that no journalist who campaigned against him was a mason, and no member of the South Yorks team either, or so Lundy was assured. His own concern was rooted in the events of 1980 surrounding the Silver Bullion job. When Len Gibson was arrested for that crime, he was not only a Freemason; he was also Worshipful Master of Waterways Lodge No. 7913, which meets at Southgate Masonic Centre, only a mile from the garage where he had hidden ten tons of stolen silver! For the full story of Worshipful Bro. Gibson's masonic activities, readers should read an earlier book of mine, *Inside the Brotherhood*,[10] but it is worth repeating here that his confederates Rudolpho and Renalto Aguda were also 'on the square'. A bitter but significant twist to the story is that the informer, Roy Garner, was yet another mason, in Bishop Ridley Lodge No. 6196.

When Gibson was arrested his home was raided. Among a mass of documents taken to Enfield Police Station were many masonic papers: summonses to lodge meetings and souvenir invitations to socials such as ladies' nights. Junior officers going through these papers were astonished to see the names of many detectives far senior to themselves. Len Gibson – number 42 in the top hundred *Handbook of Violent Thieves* and now known to be on the Silver Bullion job – had clearly attended masonic functions at which many high-ranking CID men were also present. At least eight members of his own lodge were policemen, including a former Flying Squad superintendent.

To the junior detectives' dismay, a uniformed officer told them to take all the masonic papers straight back because they could have no bearing on the robbery and would not be accepted as prisoner's property. Since at least three of the robbers were masons, and the 'inside man' at the firm which carried the silver had been their guest at masonic functions, the papers may have had a great bearing on the robbery. The junior detectives suspected that they had been ordered to return them because of Freemasonry's strength in the ranks above them. One protested strongly and soon found himself transferred from criminal intelligence work to routine divisional duties. His protest was in vain. Only one day after all Gibson's papers had been seized, with many other items, two police vans came to his house and returned everything. No one was more astonished than Gibson. Normally it takes months for criminals to get their property back, and only then after a battle to find out where it has been stored. Not even Gibson knew the clout of the fraternity in which he had risen so high so fast.

One of the biggest mysteries in the entire 'Lundy affair' is why the first leaks about Garner's informer role occurred only after the Silver Bullion job and not before. One explanation is that, this time, Garner had informed not only on brother criminals but on brother masons: a far worse sin in many masons' reckoning. Their 'antient charges' tell them to 'cheerfully conform to the laws of the country'. In the Third Degree ritual each mason swears his 'breast shall be the sacred repository' of his brother masons' secrets but there are exceptions: 'murder, treason, felony and all other offences contrary to the laws of God and the ordinances of the realm'. That sounds like an informer's charter, but masons are also sworn to 'form a column of mutual defence and support' and in recent years court cases have proved that some masonic lodges are cells of crime and corruption. In North London crimino-masonic circles, Garner's betrayal of brother masons for huge rewards went down badly. It did not go down any better among the many detectives whom he also knew through Freemasonry. There is, therefore, the possibility that masonic criminals and police decided to expose Garner because he had committed the ultimate masonic crime. If not, why was Garner not exposed years before for informing on other criminals? The answer may be that, until the Silver Bullion job, he had informed only against non-masons who had no fraternal allies in the underworld or the CID to avenge them.

In 1981 when Gibson and the Agudas were jailed, they might have been expected to resign from their lodge or be thrown out. Neither event happened. All three stayed in as country members, and when they were freed in 1986 Gibson and Renalto Aguda resumed active membership. Renalto even joined a second lodge, Olympus No. 5488, which meets at England's masonic headquarters, Free-masons Hall. In the late 1980s this scandal became public, and was attacked in the press and on television. Even so, in March 1989 a Grand Lodge committee decided the robbers should not be expelled from the fraternity because they 'had played a full part in the affairs of their lodge for two and a half years' since leaving jail, and it was not right to apply retrospective punishment. (The committee may not have been aware that all three men had convictions before they were initiated into the fraternity and must have lied to join.) The following month my book *Inside the Brotherhood* appeared, so at last all Freemasons could study a detailed account of the affair. Yet another committee was set up to consider if their membership 'was conducive to the welfare of the Craft'. This decided that all three robbers should at last be expelled, a full nine years after they had committed Britain's biggest robbery.

This was not the end of the affair, because Len and Renalto appealed to Grand Lodge. On 13 September 1989 they put their case before several hundred of England's grandest Freemasons – viscounts, barons, MPs and the odd general among them. Gibson explained: 'I know what I did was wrong, but surely this is in the past and should be forgiven. Even Jesus forgave his disciples who did wrong.

Hiram Abiff forgave his Brethren. Why can we not be forgiven? I do not sit speaking to policemen discussing and asking them to do anything naughty.'[11]

Renalto Aguda pleaded:

> Having been to prison I am a better Freemason for it, because I have been at the other end of the Nine O'Clock Toast. I have been a poor and distressed Freemason . . . When I joined Freemasonry I thought that my Brothers would support me in times of trouble, as I would support them. This I do not feel has been the case . . . I am now holding out my hand to you for some brotherly love and relief on this matter, and for your vote not to expel me.

In fact the assembly did expel the pair, partly out of fear of more hostile publicity if they were allowed to remain, partly because it was felt that an avowedly moral society should not tolerate gangsters in its midst. The vote was no surprise. What was extraordinary was the support they received, even from a serving judge, Alan Garfitt, who said that to expel them now would be 'kicking them in the teeth'. It also emerged that in 1980 Grand Lodge officers had knowingly supported the robbers' continuing membership, so some masons felt it wrong to expel them nearly a decade later. Perhaps the most fascinating speech came from a recently retired policeman, A.J. Englefield, who insisted on expulsion:

> . . . any police officer who either knowingly, or even unwittingly, shared a Lodge room with a Brother so convicted would seriously jeopardize his police career . . . [He] would run the almost certain risk of having his judgement branded suspect, which frankly would be the kiss of death for his career and future promotion prospects.

What Englefield said in 1989 applied equally to 1979–80 when Scotland Yard regarded Worshipful Master Gibson as one of London's most violent thieves. Yet at that time so many senior London detectives rubbed shoulders with crooks at masonic functions that it seems as if promotion, Freemasonry and fraternizing with the underworld were indivisible. For example, in early 1980 the Royal Lancaster Hotel welcomed hundreds of members of the Metropolitan Phoenix Masonic Association for their annual dinner. The Phoenix is composed of past and present police who are all Freemasons. On this occasion, as always, members were allowed to bring guests. On one table surrounded by detective friends sat Worshipful Master Len Gibson, who at that very period was planning the Silver Bullion robbery. There was a prize raffle. Who should win a television set but Len Gibson! As he went to the rostrum with his winning ticket, one detective at his table muttered, 'That's the first TV Len's ever got without stealing it.' Len never heard that remark, but he immediately shamed his detractor by refusing to accept the prize and putting it back in the draw.

At that time professional criminals were accepted by many lodges as a regular component of Freemasonry, so a detective like Tony Lundy, who made a virtue of sending such men to prison, was bound to upset the fraternity. The upset would be all the greater because Lundy was a known Catholic, and likely to excite the hate of more bigoted masons because of 250 years of papal hostility towards the brotherhood. Whether or not Freemasonry played any role in Lundy's downfall, its brotherly bonds are certainly far stronger than any existing between members of Finchley Boxing Club or the drinkers at the Torrington Arms, as Lundy proved when he arrested Gibson.

If Lundy feels he was threatening the masonic axis that exists between criminals and detectives, so does Harry Clement. Responding to a letter from me, Clement said that he felt my book, *Inside the Brotherhood*, contained 'a series of disclosures that perhaps opened many doors into the mystery of why there were no prosecutions in the "Albany" affair.' After saying that he did not know Lundy and had never worked with him (which coincides with Lundy's recollection), Clement told me:

I am certain that in your research into Freemasonry, characters appeared that certainly played a vital role in 'squashing' Albany. I am surprised that an obviously astute person as yourself has not seen the connection between the two. I am only sorry that I was not privy to your research knowledge some years earlier.

Mr Clement may well be correct. Some of Albany's targets were the same Freemasons whom Lundy had sent to jail over the Silver Bullion job. Other masons were named in the statements of Billy Young, who was a mason himself but clearly had little compunction about shopping his brethren. Among them was Roy Garner, Clement's 'number one suspect'. So was his partner, Kenny Ross. I have been unable to discover if Garner received any special protection because of his masonic contacts in the police. If anything, the evidence is to the contrary. Certainly one ardent Freemason, DAC Ronald Steventon, queried Garner's right to rewards and did his best to put Garner in prison. Indeed, as the officer in overall charge of Operation Albany, Steventon appears to have been Garner's fiercest enemy in the Scotland Yard hierarchy. It is also possible that, if Steventon knew Garner was a mason at that time, he would have considered him a disgrace to the fraternity. Back in the 1970s Steventon had played a leading role in getting many Freemason detectives jailed for corruption.[12]

Freemasonry's role, for or against 'Albany', is unclear. What is clear is that Tony Lundy never consorted with any of the leading criminals who are masons at any function of London's 1,600 lodges, whereas hundreds of his fellow police officers did just that. If, for example, any photos were ever to emerge of the Phoenix dinner attended by Len Gibson, or of cops-and-robber shindigs held at various masonic temples, then they would put the photos of Lundy's non-masonic socializing in perspective.

Like so much else in his story, those photos have been blown up out of all proportion – not just literally. His problems stemmed from the fact that he was too successful. He became a weapon, a 'useful tool' in the war against violent crime in what is now one of the world's more violent capitals. He was swept on and up in the embrace of a hierarchy obsessed with statistics and the public relations requirement to bring them down, and by the media's ravenous demand for spectacular coups: big-time robbers caught 'on the pavement' and, if necessary, shot dead. No one was ever killed in a 'Lundy' ambush, but his extraordinary successes propelled him into the front line of Scotland Yard's publicity war, as much as its war on crime.

Then came the down-side: Lundy's very success became a liability. Criminals were getting upset. The cosy partition of spoils between truly crooked cops and the robbers they licensed was being disturbed. He was treading on too many toes – some in masonic footwear, some in hobnail boots, some in Gucci shoes. When a cop turns into a truly prolific thief-taker, then he rapidly acquires many powerful enemies. The astonishing thing about Lundy was not his final downfall on a few flimsy discipline charges, but that he managed to avoid all the traps and fit-ups laid for him during the previous eight years.

Lundy went wrong from the moment he believed that a detective's job is to catch criminals. He did not realize it is really about office politics: ducking action, dodging decisions and spotting the shit before it hits the fan. If a detective really wants to get to the top, he should leave the CID around thirty, go back into uniform, then return to the CID at a very high rank when he is forty or more. The dangerous years for any active detective are the years when his thief-taking skills are at their finest. The more honest he is, the more dangerous it is. Shrewd officers, aspiring to be an assistant commissioner or chief constable somewhere, should do a spell in the Complaints Investigation Bureau. Catching a bent cop can be a lot easier than catching a career criminal whose life can never be under surveillance in the draconian way a detective's entire existence can be scrutinized and picked over. A spell in CIB has the additional advantage of making officers look whiter than white. And if they fail to put a man like Lundy in jail, they can always say, 'He was just too clever – he was so brilliantly bent, we couldn't catch him.' That kind of epitaph on Lundy has been whispered by several top officers in recent years.

The truth is that Lundy was brought down not through any corruption on his part. He was destroyed by a combination of criminals seeking revenge and other detectives who were themselves corrupt or who felt demeaned by his success or slighted by his manner. His last boss in the force, former commander Phil Corbett, sums him up this way:

His energy, enthusiasm and general acumen were infectious and inspirational but at the same time he could be seen as irascible (particularly to seniors whom he found difficult to move), pugnacious and extremely ambitious for personal advancement – but then why shouldn't he have been?

An extremely high-ranking detective, still in Scotland Yard, feels Lundy has had a very raw deal:

I found Tony Lundy to be an uncomfortable, abrasive character who was not easy to cope with, but my experience of *corrupt* policemen was that they generally didn't want to stir people up the wrong way because they didn't want to make enemies. Tony Lundy didn't care who he made enemies of. He just wanted to get on with the job and nick people. My position with 'TL' was always that people should 'put up or shut up', and I never heard anybody who adequately 'put up' about him, despite enormous resources being deployed to investigate his career at different times. I feel that justice was not served in his case.

I could include many more testimonials to this effect from past and present Metropolitan officers of the highest ranks. It might be argued that many of these never worked day by day with Lundy when he was at the height of his thief-taking career, so they cannot know for sure that he was incorruptible. However, in this book as a whole I have included material from many officers who did work very closely with him during those years and who are just as adamant he was never 'bent'. If he was bent, therefore, it follows that all those people are fools or knaves: too stupid to see the corruption going on under their noses, or part of the problem themselves. If Lundy really was as crooked as his critics imply, then many of his juniors, peers and bosses must have been crooked too. It would have been impossible for him to have got away with it so long without having corrupt protectors all the way up.

Even after investigating genuine cases of corruption in Scotland Yard for eighteen years, I find that proposition incredible. I have spoken to many Lundy detractors (formally and informally, both before and after taking a close interest in his career) but none has ever come up with anything worthy of the term 'evidence'. Underworld figures often volunteer phrases such as, 'I'm telling you, Lundy is not whiter than white', or, 'He definitely had part of the reward', or, 'He had to be bent', or, 'Believe me, I *know*,' but, when pressed to provide chapter and verse, either they admit they heard the story from somebody else, or they say, 'Only if the price is right', 'How much is it worth?' or, 'There's got to be something in this for me'. Then they refuse to say anything unless they get the money 'up front'. Any evidence gathered on those terms would not be worth the price of a reporter's notebook, let alone the thousands of pounds such people seem to expect.

Lundy's detractors from the police side have never asked me for money but they tend to be as vague as the villains when it comes to providing details of his crimes. They throw out a remark such as 'Lundy was So-and-so's bag-carrier' (So-and-so being a character of legendary corruption), when Lundy never worked with So-and-so, never 'carried his bag' or never even knew him. Another detective in the anti-Lundy camp may brand him as belonging to the 'S Division Mafia' (the Metropolitan force's old S Division included Finchley and Barnet police stations where Lundy served for some five years in all). Then it turns out that the crooked cops with whom he allegedly associated (but never did) never served on S Division while he was there.

In these circumstances I sympathize with Lundy's critics in the media who have spent so long on his tale but never published any evidence coming within a mile of proving him corrupt. They must have had the same problem as I, when trying to extract real evidence from people who claim the man is a crook. However, when I informed one of Lundy's media detractors that I had reached the view that he was not corrupt, I received a letter back saying, 'You have not seen various key people whom we are sure might cause you to rethink' that view. When I asked this journalist to put me in touch with the 'key people', he refused, so I am none the wiser. But if *I* had convincing evidence that Lundy was corrupt, I would publish it – not sit on it while warning other journalists off publishing a book expressing a contrary view.

I have talked to many 'key witnesses' that other journalists have not: above all Lundy himself. I have always told him that if I were to come across any genuine evidence that he was corrupt, I would publish it in this book. I have found none. If it exists anywhere, no doubt other journalists will dig it up and display it for public scrutiny when it suits them. If anyone reading this book has such evidence, I ask him or her to contact me directly (through the publishers). If it is possible to substantiate that evidence, I shall publish it or – with the agreement of the witness – hand it to an appropriate anti-corruption body.

There may be no 'smoking gun' evidence against Lundy but could there be a smoking Swiss bank account? I think that is unlikely. What I have done is examine all published allegations against Lundy, and a mass of unpublished ones. I have talked to a large number of witnesses on both sides of the issue, and at the end I find the case against Lundy insubstantial and unconvincing.

One detective who knew Lundy well sums him up this way:

Lundy was one of the all-time great detectives. His results were brilliant, his drive and determination were unequalled and his capacity to upset idle or untalented colleagues of whatever rank was second-to-none. You can put a lot of their animosity down to 'penis envy'. Every triumph he scored put more pressure on them. They couldn't admit that he did it all by hard work and the careful cultivation of informants. In pubs, canteens and behind closed doors they used to comfort each other by saying, 'How does he put so many people away? He *must* be bent. He's too good to be true.' That's not what I think. I think he was just too good for anyone else's comfort.

Lundy himself has few regrets: 'I hugely enjoyed my career and worked with great people from Finchley to Fort Lauderdale. My bother stemmed mostly from a few influential folk whose actions only benefited the criminals

I was doing my best to put in jail.' In March 1991 the Court
of Appeal cut Roy Garner's cocaine sentence to sixteen
years but upheld his conviction. Lundy still doubts Garner's guilt. That typifies the ex-cop: refusing to bend, keep
his head down or adopt a politic silence. At his retirement
'do' loyal colleagues reworded a popular song and sang,
'You did it your way'. It was corny but, oh, so apt.

Notes

PROLOGUE

1. John Grieve, in a statement to the South Yorkshire inquiry, 11 March 1987.
2. Remark attributed to DAC David Powis by Montague FitzMaurice when interviewed by Operation Countryman, 17 April 1980.
3. Daniel Defoe, in *A True & Genuine Account of the Life and Actions of the late Jonathan Wild*, 1725.

CHAPTER 1

1. On 28 September 1975 three gunmen attempted to rob The Spaghetti House restaurant in Knightsbridge. The police were alerted while the robbery was still in progress. A long and tense siege occurred in which the gunmen held eight staff members hostage. On the sixth day they released the hostages and surrendered.
2. On links between criminals and police officers within Freemasonry, see *Inside the Brotherhood* by Martin Short, Grafton Books, 1989.

CHAPTER 2

1. 'Supergrass' is obviously derived from 'grass', meaning informer. Not so obviously, 'grass' seems to have been derived from the 1940 hit song, 'Whispering Grass', with its refrain, 'Whispering grass don't tell the trees, 'cause the trees don't need to know.' I owe this information to former Detective Chief Superintendent Bob Robinson and his 1976 Bramshill Command Course thesis on supergrasses.
2. *The Fall of Scotland Yard*, by Barry Cox, John Shirley and Martin Short, Penguin, 1977.

CHAPTER 3

1. 'Rule 43' is the term applied to segregated prison accommodation set aside for inmates such as known informers, sex offenders and former police officers, who are likely to be in danger from other prisoners.
2. In 1979, Lundy's chief,

Philip Corbett, did a formal check on Lundy's thief-taking statistics while on Finchley robbery squad. He found that, of over 200 prisoners committed for trial on the squad's efforts in one twelve-month period, ninety-two per cent pleaded guilty. 'To my mind,' he says, 'these figures spoke much of Lundy's meticulous preparation and thoroughness of investigation. I believe them to be unsurpassed.'

CHAPTER 4

1. The term 'bridewell' is often used outside London to mean a police station with cells attached. It is derived from the name of a house of correction which existed in London by the late 1500s. It soon came to mean any prison.

CHAPTER 5

1. This convicted robber cannot be named here because he is currently awaiting trial on other matters. He made this attack on Amies in a statement from the dock on 12 June 1979. Amies always denied

sexually molesting robbery victims.

CHAPTER 6

1. Headlines from *Daily Mirror*, *Daily Mail*, *Sun* and *Daily Express*, all between 31 January and 2 February 1979.
2. The tape-recording of interviews was introduced on an experimental basis by the Metropolitan Police in 1986, prior to its general application in response to the Police and Criminal Evidence Act 1984.
3. For Frank Cater's own account of the Harry MacKenney investigation, see *The Sharp End*, by Cater and Tom Tullett, The Bodley Head, 1988.
4. Quotation from *Identification Evidence*, a JAIL report by Martin Walker and Bernadette Brittain, 1978.
5. Quotation from Chapter 10 of *Scotland Yard's Cocaine Connection* (hereafter referred to as *SYCC*) by Andrew Jennings, Paul Lashmar and Vyv Simson, Jonathan Cape, 1990.
6. Gilbert Kelland, *Crime in London*, The Bodley Head, 1986. Chapter 13.
7. On 24 July 1978 Leroy Davies pleaded guilty to

fifteen robbery and firearms charges and was jailed for ten years (later reduced to seven). He admitted seventy-one crimes in all, mostly armed robberies.

8. The row between Scotland Yard and Countryman over Warne was written up in the *Observer* on 8 August 1982. Lundy was not named but was referred to as a 'protesting chief inspector' who was also the subject of a secret internal inquiry into the 1980 Silver Bullion robbery. Warne's allegations were against two officers, one of whom Lundy himself had caused to be investigated.

9. Stephen Raymond perpetrated his most spectacular crime in 1976 when, posing as a courier for a security firm, he stole £2,000,000 in currency from British Airways strong-rooms at Heathrow Airport. In 1978 he was jailed for ten years for this offence.

CHAPTER 8

1. On Lansky and Luciano as police informers, see *Crime Inc.* by Martin Short, Methuen, 1984 (now a Mandarin paperback).

2. Grieve to South Yorkshire inquiry, 11 March 1987.

3. In *SYCC*, Chapter 2, the authors state that two 'ex-Flying Squad men. . . retired early from the Met. to work for Garner.' My information is that Garner's ex-police employees had been uniformed officers.

4. The 'overlord' remark was originally made by former Detective Superintendent Gerald Wiltshire on *World in Action*, 3 November 1986. The phrase 'London's top gangster' appeared on the cover of *SYCC*.

5. For more on Bernie Silver see *The Fall of Scotland Yard*, Chapter 4.

6. On Charlie Taylor see article by Steve Haywood in *Time Out*, 14–20 July 1978.

7. On Moody and Davey see *Inside the Brotherhood*.

8. Roy Garner's evidence at Wood Green gun licence hearing, May 1983.

9. In the late 1970s and early 1980s rules governing 'Informants, use of' were laid down in Consolidated Instructions issued by the Assistant Commissioner (Crime). These still apply today (as part of General Orders) but since 1984 all detectives ranked chief inspector and above are given additional 'Informant Handling Guidelines'.

10. See *The Fall of Scotland Yard*, Chapter 2.

11. See *The Fall of Scotland Yard*, Chapter 4.

12. *Sunday People* 27 February 1972. Drury's version appeared in the *News of the World* on the same day, but was rapidly denied by Humphreys, who did not wish to be branded a police informer.

13. *The London Programme* (London Weekend TV), May 1976. Also see *Cops and Robbers* (by John Ball, Lewis Chester & Roy Perrott), André Deutsch, 1978.

14. John Grieve to South Yorkshire inquiry, 11 March 1987.

15. *The Signs of Crime*, McGraw-Hill, 1977.

16. In *SYCC*, Chapter 2, it is claimed that Garner had been the informant of Detective Chief Inspector Alec Eist, now deceased. This does not accord with my information.

CHAPTER 9

1. In *SYCC*, Chapter 7, the authors state that, 'When arrested both Gibson and Aguda had keys in their possession.' Yet no garage key was ever found in Gibson's possession; neither when he was arrested nor when his properties were raided was a key discovered.

CHAPTER 10

1. It seems Lundy's report was among confidential Scotland Yard documents disclosed by Metropolitan Police solicitors acting on behalf of DAC David Powis when he sued the *Observer* newspaper for libel (see Chapter 13). As early as June 1980 the name 'Granger' had appeared on letters to loss adjusters Robert Bishop Ltd from Scotland Yard justifying reward payments. However, Yard documents effectively confirming that Garner and Granger were the same person emerged only as a result of the Powis–*Observer* action.

2. According to a statement made by Colin Holdom of Douglas Jackson & Co. on 4 July 1980, the silver was valued on the basis that it weighed ten tonnes and the 'spot price' was £10.566 per troy ounce on the day it was stolen.

3. Anthony Hart, loss adjuster, speaking on *Panorama*, BBC TV, 8 November 1982.

CHAPTER 11

1. For Spicer on Gibson and

Freemasonry, see *Inside the Brotherhood*.

CHAPTER 12

1. McLagan reporting for BBC Radio Four's *PM* programme, January 1982.
2. Campbell in *City Limits*, 5–11 February 1982.
3. *City Limits*, 4–10 December 1981.
4. *City Limits*, 23–29 April 1982.
5. While most outsiders would share Mrs Price's view that there must have been a connection between the attack on Mr Price and his death, it is very unlikely that this could have been established 'beyond reasonable doubt' and thus persuade a jury to convict Williams and Smith of murder.

CHAPTER 13

1. *Observer*, 25 July 1982.
2. *Private Eye*, 17 May 1985.
3. *Private Eye*, 31 May 1985.
4. 'Hand-picked' is the term used to describe Albany's forty-five detectives in *SYCC*, Chapter 8.
5. In *SYCC*, Chapter 8, the authors state that Garner was kept well-informed of Albany's activities. This is true, in that 'Albany' was leaky, but the fiasco of 7 October 1981 was caused not by leaks but by the surveillance team itself 'showing out' and being spotted by Ross.
6. In *SYCC*, Chapter 8, the authors state: 'The DPP ruled that any offence [alleged by Young] over five years old had to be ignored.' This seems to conflict with the DPP's willingness to consider scores of offences stretching back far more than five years on which Tony Lundy secured convictions. Had 'Albany' managed to 'turn' Gibson and Aguda, the DPP would have been very keen to accept their confessions, no matter how old the crimes.
7. Grieve to South Yorkshire inquiry, 11 March 1987.
8. As quoted in the *Sunday Times*, 22 May 1983.
9. *Observer*, 22 May 1983.
10. *Sunday Times*, 22 May 1983.
11. Account based on Customs case summary, made available to the press.
12. Grieve to South Yorkshire inquiry.
13. Grieve to South Yorkshire inquiry.
14. Powis interview statement, 2 May 1985.
15. Grieve to South Yorkshire inquiry.

CHAPTER 14

1. Grieve to South Yorkshire inquiry.
2. *Observer*, 25 July 1982.
3. *Observer*, 6 February 1982. *City Limits*, 4–10 February 1983.
4. Gervaise's allegation, as defined on a Form 163 issued to Lundy.
5. Whatever Gervaise or Fiori may have told Attard, the *Observer* did not contract to pay for their stories and was never likely to do so.
6. Taken from statement to solicitors for Sean O'Neill, who was tried at the Old Bailey for murder in 1985 (see next paragraph of chapter).
7. *Observer* 8 January 1984.

CHAPTER 15

1. *Private Eye*, 17 May 1985.
2. Jennings's letter to Home Secretary Douglas Hurd was published in *Journalist* (the newspaper of the National Union of Journalists) in February 1988.

CHAPTER 16

1. Powis interview statement, 2 May 1985.
2. See *Hansard*, 3 November 1986, for Soley's motion for an inquiry into the allegations raised in *World in Action*, and *Hansard*, 4 November 1986, for his speech.

CHAPTER 17

1. The brief is as Chief Superintendent Herold defined it to Lundy during their first interview on 25 November 1986.
2. *News of the World*, 19 July 1987.
3. *Time Out*, 4–11 January 1989.

CHAPTER 18

1. In April 1990 Freddie Foreman was convicted of handling proceeds from the 1983 Security Express robbery and jailed for nine years.
2. On 'flagging', see Chapter 22.
3. *SYCC*, Chapter 15.

CHAPTER 19

1. This account of the Brinks–Mat raid and later investigation owes much to *Bullion* (by Andrew Hogg, Jim McDougall and Robin Morgan), Penguin, 1988.
2. The law has since been changed. Now banks must disclose all large movements of cash which, they suspect, may be derived from crime. Various obligations and penalties (including up to

fourteen years in prison)
are defined in the Police
and Criminal Evidence Act
(1984), the Drug Trafficking
Offences Act (1986),
the Criminal Justice Act
(1988) and the Prevention
of Terrorism (Temporary
Provisions Act) Act (1989).

CHAPTER 20

1. In February 1991 in Florida,
   Errico was convicted of
   murdering Vogt and Harris.
   He had not yet been tried
   for the Savoy murder.
2. From an article by John
   Chapman in the *Sunday
   Express*, 9 November 1986.
3. *Sunday Express*, 9 November
   1986.

CHAPTER 21

1. Teresi, as quoted in
   London *Standard*, 10
   November 1986.
2. *Sunday Telegraph*, 27
   December 1987. On 8
   November 1990 the *Daily
   Telegraph* reported that
   Scotland Yard was still
   hoping to receive a sum of
   £26 million as a result of
   Operation Cougar.
3. By Peter Wilson, 4
   April 1988.

CHAPTER 22

1. *High Time* by David

Leigh, William Heinemann
Ltd, 1984.
2. This account is taken from
   information passed to
   the Philippines Criminal
   Investigation Service
   through Interpol.

CHAPTER 23

1. The letter was from
   Colin Sutton, Assistant
   Commissioner, Management
   Support Department, New
   Scotland Yard.
2. Lundy's report to
   Commander Corbett, 6
   September 1987.
3. Smith's letter of 28 October
   1987 (Smith had succeeded
   Colin Sutton as Assistant
   Commissioner, Management
   Support).
4. Letter from Assistant
   Commissioner Smith, 5
   January 1988.
5. Lundy's letter to Smith, 29
   February 1988.
6. Smith to Lundy, 22
   March 1988.
7. In his original submissions
   to South Yorkshire,
   Jennings stated that
   Les Jones 'was on USA
   trip with Garner and
   Lundy'. This claim had no
   foundation but the inquiry
   was still exploring it almost
   one year later, in November
   1987, when Lundy was
   served with a form 163
   allegation that 'you visited

the USA together with
Roy Garner and Leslie
Jones, for the purpose of
a holiday, and that as such
you improperly associated
with suspected criminals'.

8. As laid down in Assistant
Commissioner's Consolidated
Instructions (see note 9 for
chapter 8).

9. Ramm's evidence to South
Yorkshire inquiry, 10
December 1986.

10. Judge Nina Lowry's
evidence to South Yorkshire
inquiry, 5 December 1986.

11. Letters from Moyle to
Lundy: 22 August, 8 and 22
September 1988.

12. Clothier to Lundy, 23
January 1989.

13. 'The Hillsborough Stadium
Disaster' Interim Report by
Lord Justice Taylor, HMSO,
August 1989.

CHAPTER 24

1. This refers to Mrs Cherry
Groce of Brixton, who
was shot by Detective
Inspector Douglas Lovelock
in September 1985. In
January 1987 Lovelock was
acquitted of unlawfully and
maliciously wounding Mrs
Groce. The next month
an inquiry set up by the
PCA cleared him of any
discipline offence.

2. See *The Fall of Scotland
Yard*, Chapter 2.

3. Breece, quoted in *SYCC*,
Chapter 17.

4. Whitehorne's phone had
been tapped earlier in 1986
(over a stolen car racket)
but all US wire-taps have to
be court-approved, 30 days
at a time, and FDLE made
no further application over
Whitehorne and drugs.

5. *SYCC*, Chapter 17.

6. Grieve to South Yorkshire
inquiry.

7. This information comes
from Chapter 11 of *SYCC*.

8. Home Affairs Committee
review of PCA Annual
Report, volume II,
July 1989.

9. Imbert's evidence to Home
Affairs Committee (volume
II, as above).

10. Home Affairs Committee
review of PCA Annual
Report, volume I, para 60.

CHAPTER 25

1. *The Sun*, 15 May 1990. The
serialization ran from 14 to
16 May.

2. *SYCC*, Chapter 11.

3. *SYCC*, Chapter 20.

4. *SYCC*, Chapter 13.

5. *SYCC*, Chapter 19.

6. *SYCC*, Chapter 19. The
authors did not quote the
remarks of Mrs Chrastny's
counsel, Tim Cassel, that
Chrastny exerted 'the most
amazing influence' over not

only the police but Customs officers too.

7. *The Digger*, 23 October 1987.

8. *SYCC*, Chapter 10.

9. 'Sublimely self-confident' was how Duncan Campbell described Bryson in *City Limits*, 4–10 February 1983. Campbell also quoted a lawyer who said Bryson was 'too clever by half'.

10. *Inside the Brotherhood*, Chapter 18.

11. As quoted in the Quarterly Communication of the United Grand Lodge of England. All subsequent quotations from the proceedings come from the same source.

12. See *The Fall of Scotland Yard*, Chapter 4.

Index